BIRDS
of
ILLINOIS

KELLY

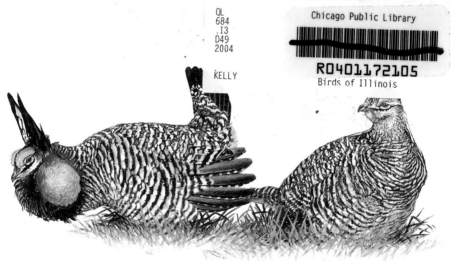

Sheryl DeVore
Steven D. Bailey
Gregory Kennedy

with contributions from
Chris Fisher & Andy Bezener

LONE
PINE

Lone Pine Publishing

Distributed by Lone Pine Publishing
1808 B Street NW, Suite 140
Auburn, WA, USA 98001

Website: www.lonepinepublishing.com

National Library of Canada Cataloguing in Publication Data

DeVore, Sheryl
    Birds of Illinois / Sheryl DeVore, Steven D. Bailey and Gregory Kennedy.

    Includes bibliographical references and index.
    ISBN 1-55105-379-9

    1. Birds—Illinois. 2. Birds—Illinois—Identification. I. Baily, Steven D., 1959–
II. Kennedy, Gregory, 1956–   III. Title.
QL684.I3D49 2004   598'.09773   C2003-907437-4

Editorial Director: Nancy Foulds
Project Editor: Carmen Adams
Editorial: Gary Whyte, Nicholle Carriere, Genevieve Boyer, Carmen Adams
Illustrations Coordinator: Carol Woo
Production Manager: Gene Longson
Layout & Production: Elliot Engley
Cover Design: Gerry Dotto
Cover Illustration: Hairy Woodpecker, by Gary Ross
Illustrations: Gary Ross, Ted Nordhagen
Maps: Curtis Pillipow, Elliot Engley, Chia-Jung Chang
Range Maps: Steven D. Bailey
Scanning & Digital Film: Elite Lithographers Co.

We acknowledge the financial support of the Government of Canada through the Book Publishing Industry Development Program (BPIDP) for our publishing activities.

PC: P1

CONTENTS

ACKNOWLEDGMENTS

We would like to thank the Illinois Ornithological Society and one of its standing committees, the Illinois Ornithological Records Committee, for providing the state checklist in this book. Many skilled Illinois birders worked hard to create this useful and detailed list. We also would like to thank Liane Cordle and the Illinois Natural History Survey for providing the detailed map of Illinois geographic regions. Special thanks to Stephen Bailey for preparing the range maps. Finally, we thank our editor, Carmen Adams, for her patience, diligence and attention to detail.

Thanks are also extended to the growing family of ornithologists and dedicated birders who have offered their inspiration and expertise to help build Lone Pine's expanding library of field guides. Thanks also go to John Acorn, Chris Fisher, Andy Bezener and Eloise Pulos for their contributions to previous books in the series. In addition, thank you to Gary Ross, Ted Nordhagen and Ewa Pluciennik, whose skilled illustrations have brought each page to life.

Greater White-fronted Goose
size 30 in • p. 34

Snow Goose
size 31 in • p. 35

Ross's Goose
size 24 in • p. 36

Canada Goose
size 35 in • p. 37

Mute Swan
size 60 in • p. 38

Trumpeter Swan
size 66 in • p. 39

Tundra Swan
size 54 in • p. 40

Wood Duck
size 17 in • p. 41

Gadwall
size 20 in • p. 42

American Wigeon
size 20 in • p. 43

American Black Duck
size 22 in • p. 44

Mallard
size 24 in • p. 45

Blue-winged Teal
size 15 in • p. 46

Cinnamon Teal
size 16 in • p. 47

Northern Shoveler
size 19 in • p. 48

Northern Pintail
size 23 in • p. 49

Green-winged Teal
size 14 in • p. 50

Canvasback
size 20 in • p. 51

Redhead
size 20 in • p. 52

Ring-necked Duck
size 16 in • p. 53

Greater Scaup
size 17 in • p. 54

Lesser Scaup
size 16 in • p. 55

Harlequin Duck
size 16 in • p. 56

Surf Scoter
size 18 in • p. 57

White-winged Scoter
size 21 in • p. 58

Black Scoter
size 18 in • p. 59

5

WATERFOWL

Long-tailed Duck
size 18 in • p. 60

Bufflehead
size 14 in • p. 61

Common Goldeneye
size 18 in • p. 62

Hooded Merganser
size 17 in • p. 63

Common Merganser
size 25 in • p. 64

Red-breasted Merganser
size 23 in • p. 65

Ruddy Duck
size 15 in • p. 66

GROUSE & ALLIES

Gray Partridge
size 12 in • p. 67

Ring-necked Pheasant
size 33 in • p. 68

Greater Prairie-Chicken
size 17 in • p. 69

Wild Turkey
size 3 ft • p. 70

Northern Bobwhite
size 10 in • p. 71

Red-throated Loon
size 25 in • p. 72

Pacific Loon
size 25 in • p. 73

DIVING BIRDS

Common Loon
size 32 in • p. 74

Pied-billed Grebe
size 13 in • p. 75

Horned Grebe
size 13 in • p. 76

Red-necked Grebe
size 19 in • p. 77

Eared Grebe
size 13 in • p. 78

Western Grebe
size 22 in • p. 79

American White Pelican
size 65 in • p. 80

Double-crested Cormorant
size 29 in • p. 81

HERONLIKE BIRDS

American Bittern
size 25 in • p. 82

Least Bittern
size 12 in • p. 83

Great Blue Heron
size 51 in • p. 84

Great Egret
size 39 in • p. 85

HERONLIKE BIRDS

Snowy Egret
size 24 in • p. 86

Little Blue Heron
size 24 in • p. 87

Cattle Egret
size 20 in • p. 88

Green Heron
size 18 in • p. 89

Black-crowned Night-Heron
size 24 in • p. 90

Yellow-crowned Night-Heron
size 24 in • p. 91

Black Vulture
size 25 in • p. 92

BIRDS OF PREY

Turkey Vulture
size 28 in • p. 93

Osprey
size 23 in • p. 94

Mississippi Kite
size 14 in • p. 95

Bald Eagle
size 37 in • p. 96

Northern Harrier
size 20 in • p. 97

Sharp-shinned Hawk
size 11 in • p. 98

Cooper's Hawk
size 16 in • p. 99

Northern Goshawk
size 23 • p. 100

Red-shouldered Hawk
size 19 in • p. 101

Broad-winged Hawk
size 16 in • p. 102

Swainson's Hawk
size 20 in • p. 103

Red-tailed Hawk
size 20 in • p. 104

Rough-legged Hawk
size 21 in • p. 105

Golden Eagle
size 35 in • p. 106

American Kestrel
size 8 in • p. 107

Merlin
size 11 in • p. 108

RAILS, COOTS & CRANES

Peregrine Falcon
size 16 in • p. 109

Prairie Falcon
size 16 in • p. 110

Yellow Rail
size 7 in • p. 111

Black Rail
size 6 in • p. 112

RAILS, COOTS & CRANES

King Rail
size 15 in • p. 113

Virginia Rail
size 10 in • p. 114

Sora
size 9 in • p. 115

Common Moorhen
size 13 in • p. 116

American Coot
size 14 in • p. 117

Sandhill Crane
size 4 ft • p. 118

SHOREBIRDS

Black-bellied Plover
size 12 in • p. 119

American Golden-Plover
size 10 in • p. 120

Semipalmated Plover
size 7 in • p. 121

Piping Plover
size 7 in • p. 122

Killdeer
size 10 in • p. 123

Black-necked Stilt
size 14 in • p. 124

American Avocet
size 17 in • p. 125

Greater Yellowlegs
size 14 in • p. 126

Lesser Yellowlegs
size 10 in • p. 127

Solitary Sandpiper
size 8 in • p. 128

Willet
size 15 in • p. 129

Spotted Sandpiper
size 7 in • p. 130

Upland Sandpiper
size 11 in • p. 131

Whimbrel
size 17 in • p. 132

Hudsonian Godwit
size 14 in • p. 133

Marbled Godwit
size 18 in • p. 134

Ruddy Turnstone
size 9 in • p. 135

Red Knot
size 10 in • p. 136

Sanderling
size 8 in • p. 137

Semipalmated Sandpiper
size 6 in • p. 138

SHOREBIRDS

Western Sandpiper
size 6 in • p. 139

Least Sandpiper
size 6 in • p. 140

White-rumped Sandpiper
size 7 in • p. 141

Baird's Sandpiper
size 7 in • p. 142

Pectoral Sandpiper
size 8 in • p. 143

Purple Sandpiper
size 9 in • p. 144

Dunlin
size 8 in • p. 145

Stilt Sandpiper
size 8 in • p. 146

Buff-breasted Sandpiper
size 8 in • p. 147

Ruff
size 10 in • p. 148

Short-billed Dowitcher
size 11 in • p. 149

Long-billed Dowitcher
size 12 in • p. 150

Wilson's Snipe
size 11 in • p. 151

American Woodcock
size 11 in • p. 152

Wilson's Phalarope
size 9 in • p. 153

Red-necked Phalarope
size 7 in • p. 154

Red Phalarope
size 8 in • p. 155

GULLS & ALLIES

Pomarine Jaeger
size 21 in • p. 156

Parasitic Jaeger
size 18 in • p. 157

Laughing Gull
size 16 in • p. 158

Franklin's Gull
size 14 in • p. 159

Little Gull
size 10 in • p. 160

Bonaparte's Gull
size 13 in • p. 161

Ring-billed Gull
size 19 in • p. 162

California Gull
size 19 in • p. 163

GULLS & ALLIES

Herring Gull
size 24 in • p. 164

Thayer's Gull
size 23 in • p. 165

Iceland Gull
size 22 in • p. 166

Lesser Black-backed Gull
size 20 in • p. 167

Glaucous Gull
size 27 in • p. 168

Great Black-backed Gull
size 30 in • p. 169

Sabine's Gull
size 13 in • p. 170

Black-legged Kittiwake
size 17 in • p. 171

Caspian Tern
size 21 in • p. 172

Common Tern
size 14 in • p. 173

Forster's Tern
size 15 in • p. 174

Least Tern
size 9 in • p. 175

Black Tern
size 9 in • p. 176

Rock Pigeon
size 12 in • p. 177

Eurasian Collared-Dove
size 11 in • p. 178

DOVES, PARROTS & CUCKOOS

Mourning Dove
size 12 in • p. 179

Monk Parakeet
size 11 in • p. 180

Black-billed Cuckoo
size 12 in • p. 181

Yellow-billed Cuckoo
size 12 in • p. 182

OWLS

Barn Owl
size 15 in • p. 183

Eastern Screech-Owl
size 8 in • p. 184

Great Horned Owl
size 22 in • p. 185

Snowy Owl
size 24 in • p. 186

Barred Owl
size 20 in • p. 187

Long-eared Owl
size 14 in • p. 188

Short-eared Owl
size 15 in • p. 189

Northern Saw-whet Owl
size 8 in • p. 190

NIGHTJARS, SWIFTS & HUMMINGBRIDS

Common Nighthawk
size 9 in • p. 191

Chuck-will's-widow
size 12 in • p. 192

Whip-poor-will
size 9 in • p. 193

Chimney Swift
size 5 in • p. 194

Ruby-throated Hummingbird
size 4 in • p. 195

Rufous Hummingbird
size 3 in • p. 196

Belted Kingfisher
size 12 in • p. 197

WOODPECKERS

Red-headed Woodpecker
size 9 in • p. 198

Red-bellied Woodpecker
size 10 in • p. 199

Yellow-bellied Sapsucker
size 8 in • p. 200

Downy Woodpecker
size 6 in • p. 201

Hairy Woodpecker
size 9 in • p. 202

Northern Flicker
size 13 in • p. 203

Pileated Woodpecker
size 17 in • p. 204

FLYCATCHERS

Olive-sided Flycatcher
size 7 in • p. 206

Eastern Wood-Pewee
size 6 in • p. 207

Yellow-bellied Flycatcher
size 5 in • p. 208

Acadian Flycatcher
size 6 in • p. 209

Alder Flycatcher
size 6 in • p. 210

Willow Flycatcher
size 6 in • p. 211

Least Flycatcher
size 5 in • p. 212

Eastern Phoebe
size 7 in • p. 213

Great Crested Flycatcher
size 8 in • p. 214

Western Kingbird
size 8 in • p. 215

Eastern Kingbird
size 8 in • p. 216

Scissor-tailed Flycatcher
size 13 in • p. 217

SHRIKES & VIREOS

Loggerhead Shrike
size 9 in • p. 218

Northern Shrike
size 10 in • p. 219

White-eyed Vireo
size 5 in • p. 220

Bell's Vireo
size 5 in • p. 221

Yellow-throated Vireo
size 5 in • p. 222

Blue-headed Vireo
size 5 in • p. 223

Warbling Vireo
size 5 in • p. 224

Philadelphia Vireo
size 5 in • p. 225

Red-eyed Vireo
size 6 in • p. 226

JAYS & CROWS

Blue Jay
size 12 in • p. 227

American Crow
size 19 in • p. 228

Fish Crow
size 15 in • p. 229

Horned Lark
size 7 in • p. 230

LARKS & SWALLOWS

Purple Martin
size 8 in • p. 231

Tree Swallow
size 5 in • p. 232

Northern Rough-winged Swallow
size 5 in • p. 233

Bank Swallow
size 5 in • p. 234

Cliff Swallow
size 5 in • p. 235

Barn Swallow
size 7 in • p. 236

Carolina Chickadee
size 4 in • p. 237

Black-capped Chickadee
size 5 in • p. 238

CHICKADEES, NUTHATCHES & WRENS

Tufted Titmouse
size 6 in • p. 239

Red-breasted Nuthatch
size 4 in • p. 240

White-breasted Nuthatch
size 6 in • p. 241

Brown Creeper
size 5 in • p. 242

Carolina Wren
size 5 in • p. 243

Bewick's Wren
size 5 in • p. 244

House Wren
size 5 in • p. 245

Winter Wren
size 4 in • p. 246

Sedge Wren
size 4 in • p. 247

Marsh Wren
size 5 in • p. 248

Golden-crowned Kinglet
size 4 in • p. 249

Ruby-crowned Kinglet
size 4 in • p. 250

Blue-gray Gnatcatcher
size 4 in • p. 251

Eastern Bluebird
size 7 in • p. 252

Veery
size 7 in • p. 253

Gray-cheeked Thrush
size 7 in • p. 254

Swainson's Thrush
size 7 in • p. 255

Hermit Thrush
size 7 in • p. 256

Wood Thrush
size 8 in • p. 257

American Robin
size 10 in • p. 258

Varied Thrush
size 9 in • p. 259

Gray Catbird
size 9 in • p. 260

Northern Mockingbird
size 10 in • p. 261

Brown Thrasher
size 11 in • p. 262

European Starling
size 8 in • p. 263

American Pipit
size 6 in • p. 264

Cedar Waxwing
size 7 in • p. 265

Blue-winged Warbler
size 5 in • p. 266

Golden-winged Warbler
size 5 in • p. 267

Tennessee Warbler
size 5 in • p. 268

Orange-crowned Warbler
size 5 in • p. 269

Nashville Warbler
size 5 in • p. 270

Northern Parula
size 4 in • p. 271

13

WOOD-WARBLERS & TANAGERS

Yellow Warbler
size 5 in • p. 272

Chestnut-sided Warbler
size 5 in • p. 273

Magnolia Warbler
size 5 in • p. 274

Cape May Warbler
size 5 in • p. 275

Black-throated Blue Warbler
size 5 in • p. 276

Yellow-rumped Warbler
size 5 in • p. 277

Black-throated Green Warbler
size 5 in • p. 278

Blackburnian Warbler
size 5 in • p. 279

Yellow-throated Warbler
size 5 in • p. 280

Pine Warbler
size 5 in • p. 281

Prairie Warbler
size 5 in • p. 282

Palm Warbler
size 5 in • p. 283

Bay-breasted Warbler
size 5 in • p. 284

Blackpoll Warbler
size 5 in • p. 285

Cerulean Warbler
size 5 in • p. 286

Black-and-white Warbler
size 5 in • p. 287

American Redstart
size 5 in • p. 288

Prothonotary Warbler
size 5 in • p. 289

Worm-eating Warbler
size 5 in • p. 290

Ovenbird
size 6 in • p. 291

Northern Waterthrush
size 5 in • p. 292

Louisiana Waterthrush
size 6 in • p. 293

Kentucky Warbler
size 5 in • p. 294

Connecticut Warbler
size 5 in • p. 295

Mourning Warbler
size 5 in • p. 296

Common Yellowthroat
size 5 in • p. 297

Hooded Warbler
size 5 in • p. 298

WOOD-WARBLERS & TANAGERS

Wilson's Warbler	Canada Warbler	Yellow-breasted Chat	Summer Tanager	Scarlet Tanager
size 5 in • p. 299	size 5 in • p. 300	size 7 in • p. 301	size 7 in • p. 302	size 7 in • p. 303

SPARROWS, GROSBEAKS & BUNTINGS

Spotted Towhee	Eastern Towhee	American Tree Sparrow	Chipping Sparrow
size 8 in • p. 304	size 8 in • p. 305	size 6 in • p. 306	size 5 in • p. 307

Clay-colored Sparrow	Field Sparrow	Vesper Sparrow	Lark Sparrow
size 5 in • p. 308	size 5 in • p. 309	size 6 in • p. 310	size 6 in • p. 311

Savannah Sparrow	Grasshopper Sparrow	Henslow's Sparrow	Le Conte's Sparrow
size 5 in • p. 312	size 5 in • p. 313	size 5 in • p. 314	size 5 in • p. 315

Nelson's Sharp-tailed Sparrow	Fox Sparrow	Song Sparrow	Lincoln's Sparrow
size 5 in • p. 316	size 7 in • p. 317	size 6 in • p. 318	size 5 in • p. 319

Swamp Sparrow	White-throated Sparrow	Harris's Sparrow	White-crowned Sparrow
size 5 in • p. 320	size 7 in • p. 321	size 7 in • p. 322	size 7 in • p. 323

Dark-eyed Junco	Lapland Longspur	Smith's Longspur	Snow Bunting
size 6 in • p. 324	size 6 in • p. 325	size 6 in • p. 326	size 6 in • p. 327

SPARROWS, GROSBEAKS & BUNTINGS

Northern Cardinal
size 8 in • p. 328

Rose-breasted Grosbeak
size 8 in • p. 329

Blue Grosbeak
size 6 in • p. 330

Indigo Bunting
size 5 in • p. 331

Dickcissel
size 6 in • p. 332

Bobolink
size 7 in • p. 333

Red-winged Blackbird
size 8 in • p. 334

Eastern Meadowlark
size 9 in • p. 335

BLACKBIRDS & ORIOLES

Western Meadowlark
size 9 in • p. 336

Yellow-headed Blackbird
size 9 in • p. 337

Rusty Blackbird
size 9 in • p. 338

Brewer's Blackbird
size 9 in • p. 339

Common Grackle
size 12 in • p. 340

Brown-headed Cowbird
size 7 in • p. 341

Orchard Oriole
size 7 in • p. 342

Baltimore Oriole
size 8 in • p. 343

FINCHLIKE BIRDS

Purple Finch
size 6 in • p. 344

House Finch
size 6 in • p. 345

Red Crossbill
size 6 in • p. 346

White-winged Crossbill
size 6 in • p. 347

Common Redpoll
size 5 in • p. 348

Pine Siskin
size 5 in • p. 349

American Goldfinch
size 5 in • p. 350

Evening Grosbeak
size 8 in • p. 351

House Sparrow
size 6 in • p. 352

Eurasian Tree Sparrow
size 6 in • p. 353

INTRODUCTION

BIRDING IN ILLINOIS

Birding recently has evolved from a pursuit practiced by a few dedicated individuals to a continent-wide activity that includes at least 48 million professional and amateur participants. Birding can offer relaxation as well as outdoor exercise. Opportunities also exist to socialize with like-minded people, to monitor the health of the environment and to connect with nature. Birding can also be an aesthetic, intellectual and a competitive experience. Those who watch birds embark on expeditions to make bird lists, to attempt to separate similar species from one another and to revel in the pure joy of seeing the remarkable colors of such species as the male Blackburnian Warbler with its fiery orange throat or the male Bobolink with its backward black-and-white tuxedo. Birders also learn to distinguish birds by song. Greater Prairie-Chickens give loud booming noises from their throat sacs when courting on their leks, Eastern Towhees sing *drink your tea* from a woodland opening and Wood Thrushes give their flutelike *eeolays* in a deciduous woodland. Birders also get involved with conservation issues, appreciating that to see a bird requires protecting its habitat.

Illinois residents are truly blessed by the geographical and biological diversity of the prairie state. In addition to supporting a wide range of breeding birds and year-round residents, Illinois hosts a large number of spring and fall migrants that travel through the state on the way to their breeding and wintering grounds. In all, 431 bird species have been recorded in Illinois as of November 2003 and upwards of 319 species make annual appearances in the state.

Christmas bird counts, breeding bird surveys, nest box programs, migration monitoring, lectures and workshops all provide a chance for novice, intermediate and expert birders to interact and share their enthusiasm for the splendor of birds. Whatever your level, ample opportunities are available.

BEGINNING TO LEARN THE BIRDS

The Challenge of Birding

Birding can be extremely challenging, and learning to recognize all the birds in Illinois can take time. But guides like this one will help you get started. Although any standard North American field guide will help you identify local birds, such guides can be daunting because they cover the entire continent and present an overwhelming number of species. By focusing specifically on the bird life of Illinois, we hope birding will be a little less overwhelming.

Blackburnian Warbler

Classification: The Order of Things

To an ornithologist (a biologist who studies birds), the species is the fundamental unit of classification because the members of a single species look most alike and they naturally interbreed with one another. Each species has a scientific name (a Latin name, designating genus and species, which is always underlined or italicized) and a single accredited common name, so that the different vernacular names of a species do not cause confusion. A bird has been properly identified only when it has been identified "to species"; most ornithologists use the accredited common name. For example, "American Coot" is an accredited common name, even though some people call it "Mudhen." *Fulica americana* is the American Coot's scientific name. (*Fulica* is the genus, or generic name, and *americana* is the species, or specific name).

To help make sense of the hundreds of bird species, scientifically oriented bird-watchers may lump species into recognizable groups that are closely related. The most commonly used groupings, in order of increasing scope, are genus, family and order. The American Coot and Common Moorhen are different species that do not share a genus (their generic names are different), but they are both members of the family Rallidae (the rail family). The rail and crane families are in turn grouped within the order Gruiformes, which is composed of the grouselike birds.

Ornithologists have arranged all the orders of birds based on the evolutionary ancestors of modern birds as well as their DNA. At first, the evolutionary sequence might not make much sense. Birders, however, know that all books of this sort begin with waterfowl, followed by gallinaceous (grouselike) birds, diving birds, wading birds, shorebirds, birds of prey, and other birds that look more and more like songbirds (known as "passerines"). In practice, the tried-and-true method of grouping birds according to similarities and differences provides the best format for learning.

American Coot

WATCHING BIRD BEHAVIOR

Watching an American Robin build its mud nest or pluck worms from the ground can be just as satisfying as identifying a rare bird, and with still so little known about bird behavior, you can contribute to science by taking notes of what you see birds doing.

Studying birds involves keeping notes and records. The timing of bird migrations is an easy thing to record, as are details of feeding, courtship and nesting behavior if you are willing to be patient. Flocking birds can also provide fascinating opportunities to observe and note social interactions, especially when individual birds can be recognized. Such observations have contributed greatly toward our knowledge of birds. However, casual note-taking should not be equated with more standardized, scientific methods of study.

Birding, for most people, is a peaceful, non-destructive recreational activity. One of the best ways to watch bird behavior is to look for a spot rich with avian life and then sit back and relax. If you become part of the scenery, the birds, at first startled by your approach, will soon resume their activities and allow you into their world.

BIRDING BY HABITAT

Illinois can be separated into 14 biophysical regions or "bioregions" (see p. 30). Each bioregion is composed of a number of different habitats. Each habitat is a community of plants and animals supported by the infrastructure of water and soil and regulated by the constraints of topography, climate and elevation.

Simply put, a bird's habitat is the place in which it normally lives. Some birds prefer the open water, some birds are found in cattail marshes, others like mature coniferous forest, and still others prefer abandoned fields overgrown with tall grass and shrubs. Knowledge of a bird's habitat increases the chances of identifying the bird correctly. If you are birding in wetlands, you will find rails, grebes and Marsh Wrens. If you are wandering through a rich bottomland woods, you may hear the rich and boisterous *who cooks for you? who cooks for you all?* call of the Barred Owl or the repeated, one-pitch song of the Prothonotary Warbler. But head out to the prairies and you won't find those birds—rather you'll see Eastern Meadowlarks, Savanna Sparrows and maybe Dickcissels and Bobolinks.

Habitats are just like neighborhoods: if you associate friends with the suburb in which they live, you can just as easily learn to associate specific birds with their preferred habitats. Only in migration, especially during inclement weather, do some birds leave their usual habitat.

LISTING

Many birders list the species they have seen during excursions or at home. You can keep systematic or casual lists in a field notebook with personalized sketches or observations or you may choose not to make lists at all. However, lists may prove rewarding in unexpected ways, for example, after you visit a new area, your list becomes a souvenir of your experiences there. By reviewing the list, you can recall memories and details that you might otherwise have forgotten. Keeping regular, accurate lists of birds in your neighborhood can also be useful for local researchers. It can be interesting to compare the arrival dates and last sightings of hummingbirds and other seasonal visitors, or to note the first sighting of a new visitor to your area.

Savannah Sparrow

BIRDING ACTIVITIES

Birding Groups

We recommend that you join in on such activities as Christmas bird counts, birding festivals and the meetings of your local birding or natural history club. Meeting other people with the same interests can make birding even more pleasurable, and there is always something to be learned when birders of all levels gather. If you are interested in bird conservation and environmental issues, natural history groups and conscientious birdwatching stores can keep you informed about the situation in your area and what you can do to help. Bird hotlines provide up-to-date information on the sightings of rarities, which are often easier to relocate than you might think. The following is a brief list of contacts that will help you get involved:

Organizations

Illinois Audubon Society
425B North Gilbert St
P.O. Box 2418
Danville, IL 61834
Phone: 217-446-5085
Website: www.illinoisaudubon.org

Chicago Ornithological Society
10th Flr-#C980, 28 East Jackson Building
Chicago, IL 60604
Phone: 312-409-9678
E-mail: cos@chicagobirder.org
Website: www.chicagobirder.org

Illinois Ornithological Society
P.O. Box 931
Lake Forest, IL 60045
E-mail: ios@illinoisbirds.org
Website: www.illinoisbirds.org

Evanston North Shore Bird Club
P.O. Box 1313
Evanston, IL 60204
E-mail: info@ensbc.org
Website: www.ensbc.org

Bird Conservation Network
5225 Old Orchard Road, Suite 37
Skokie, IL 60077
Phone: 847-965-1150
E-mail: bobolnk@ix.netcom.com
Website: www.bcnbirds.org

DuPage Birding Club
Hotline: 630-406-8111
E-mail: president@dupagebirding.org
Website: www.dupagebirding.org

Bird Conservation

Illinois abounds with bird life. You can still find areas of wilderness here, including parks, wildlife reserves and public lands. Nevertheless, agriculture and forestry and development for housing and industry are threatening viable bird habitat throughout the state. We hope that more people will learn to appreciate nature through birding, and that those people will do their best to protect the natural areas that remain. Many bird enthusiasts support groups such as the Bird Conservation Network, among many others, which help birds by either documenting their distribution and numbers in various habitats, or local chapters of the Sierra Club, The Nature Conservancy, the Illinois Audubon Society and other groups that help purchase and protect valuable natural habitat in Illinois.

Landscaping your own property to provide native plant cover and natural foods for birds is an immediate and personal way to ensure the conservation of bird habitat. The cumulative effects of such urban "nature-scaping" can be significant, especially for migrating birds. If your yard is to become a bird sanctuary, you may want to keep the neighborhood cats out; every year, millions of birds are killed by cats. Check with the local Humane Society for methods of protecting both your feline friends and wild birds.

Bird Feeding

Many people attract birds to their yard with a birdfeeder or a native berry- or seed-producing plant in their garden. The kind of food available will determine which birds visit your yard. Staff at birdwatching stores can suggest which plants and food will attract specific birds. Hummingbird feeders are popular in summer to attract the Ruby-throated Hummingbird and are filled with a simple sugar solution made from one part sugar and three to four parts water. Plants such as coral bells, columbine, hosta and impatiens will also attract hummingbirds to your yard.

Contrary to popular opinion, birds do not become dependent on feeders, nor do they subsequently forget to forage naturally. Birds appreciate stocked feeders in winter, but they also visit them in spring, a time when it is difficult to find food before flowers bloom, seeds develop and insects hatch. Birdbaths will also entice birds to your yard at any time of year, and heated bird baths are particularly appreciated in the colder months. Avoid birdbaths that have exposed metal parts because wet birds can accidentally freeze to them in winter. You can find a host of books written about feeding birds and landscaping your yard to provide natural foods and nest sites.

Nest Boxes

Another popular way to attract birds is to set out nest boxes, especially for wrens, bluebirds and swallows. Larger nest boxes can attract kestrels, owls and Wood Ducks. Not all birds will use nest boxes: only species that normally use tree cavities will be comfortable in such confined spaces.

Top Birding Sites

Illinois Beach State Park

Situated along the Lake Michigan shoreline in northern Illinois, this park includes 4100 acres of sandy shoreline, black oak woods and marshes. The South Unit features a nonnative pine woodland, which has attracted rare species such as the state's first Red-cockaded Woodpecker and Brown headed Nuthatch. More than 300 bird species have been documented. In fall, raptors and shorebirds, especially Sanderlings, a few Whimbrels, turnstones and knots, migrate along the lakeshore.

Watching hawks in the North Unit in fall can be particularly rewarding; the Illinois Beach State Park *Hawk Watch* was established in 2000. Hawk numbers are posted with the Hawk Migration Association of North America. Loons, grebes, large rafts of scaup and smaller numbers of scoters and Long-tailed Ducks regularly occur during the colder months. Warblers, tanagers, grosbeaks and flycatchers occur in fall and spring.

Long-tailed Duck

Moraine Hills State Park

This northern, rolling, glaciated region of marshes, lakes and bogs in McHenry County encompasses 1690 acres and attracts some of the state's rarest wetland breeders, including the Pied-billed Grebe, Least Bittern, Yellow-headed Blackbird and Sandhill Crane. To experience a litany of wetland bird song, visit Black Tern Marsh at the McHenry Dam May throughout July. Several pairs of Prothonotary Warblers and American Redstarts breed along the Fox River backwaters. Herons and egrets spend time feeding and loafing. In the main park, Sedge and Marsh wrens, Red-headed Woodpeckers, and Wood Ducks breed. During migration, dabbling ducks such as Northern Shoveler and American Wigeon feast on submerged vegetation. Spring and fall abound with migratory songbirds.

Montrose Harbor and the Magic Hedge

A small spit of land with shrubs, trees and meadows along the Lake Michigan shoreline off Montrose Avenue in Chicago is one of the state's premier birding spots during migration. Spring and fall migration can bring thousands of songbirds if the winds are right. Birders call the shrubs along the lakeshore the "Magic Hedge." Bird species as diverse as ducks, rails, falcons, goatsuckers, warblers, vireos, flycatchers and sparrows, as well as rarities appear here annually. Some past discoveries include Black Rail, Purple Gallinule, Rock Wren, Groove-billed Ani, Tri-colored Heron, Scissor-tailed Flycatcher, Say's Phoebe and Townsend's and Kirtland's warblers—all found in spring. Montrose Harbor (and nearby Meigs Field) is one of the best places in Illinois to search for the Snowy Owl in winter. Most Illinois raptors, including resident Peregrine Falcon, have been seen flying by or hunting the numerous spring and fall migrants.

Morton Arboretum

With its 3600 species of flowering trees, shrubs and conifers, the 1500-acre Morton Arboretum provides great year-round birding. The coniferous areas attract wintering species as well as rarities. Nearly every winter, Northern Saw-whet Owls roost in cedars, and the White-winged Crossbill and Red Crossbill, appear. Rarities include Townsend's Solitaire, Bohemian Waxwing, Evening Grosbeak and Hermit Warbler. Spring and fall migration can be spectacular, especially in the oak-hickory woodlands. Wood Thrushes and Scarlet Tanagers breed in some of the natural oak woodlands.

Barred Owl

The Palos Preserves

About 14,000 acres of woods, sloughs and lakes meander through the Palos Preserves region in Chicago's south suburbs of Palos Park, Palos Hills and Orland Park. The Little Red Schoolhouse Nature Center and nearby sloughs have attracted nearly every migratory songbird and waterfowl species that pass through Illinois. The preserves regularly attract breeding birds, including the Barred Owl, White-eyed Vireo and Hooded, Blue-winged and Kentucky warblers, all of which are more commonly found farther south in Illinois.

Midewin National Tallgrass Prairie and the Des Plaines River Conservation Area

These two adjoining properties encompass 23,000 acres with 21 natural ecosystems including oak woodland, tallgrass prairie and sedge meadow. Midewin was designated in 1996 as the first national tallgrass prairie. Breeding grassland species need large tracts of habitat in which to successfully raise young. The region provides habitat for the endangered Upland Sandpiper and threatened Loggerhead Shrike as well as Bell's Vireo, several rail species and several grassland sparrow species, including the Grasshopper Sparrow and Henslow's Sparrow. Wintering raptors include Short-eared Owls and Rough-legged Hawks. Midewin is evolving, and many factions are working to revitalize this old federal arsenal.

Lost Mound National Wildlife Refuge

Western Kingbird

In 2000, the U.S. Department of Defense released the ownership of the old munitions installation to the U.S. Fish and Wildlife Service. The old depot contains 13,000 acres of sand prairie, savannas and Mississippi River backwater lakes and forests. An impressive list of birds has been obtained here, including 30 species of migratory waterfowl and warblers, and breeding birds such as Blue Grosbeaks, Loggerhead Shrikes, Western Kingbirds, Lark Sparrows and Grasshopper Sparrows. Much of the depot will remain closed until environmental contaminants can be mitigated, but driving the main roads in the region offers excellent birding.

Mississippi Palisades State Park

Nearly 100 species of birds breed, and an additional 100 more species migrate through this 2500-acre park, which includes mature forested bluffs overlooking the Mississippi River and wooded ravines below. Look-out sites are excellent for migrating raptors and wintering Bald Eagles, one of the key species that attracts visitors. The north trail system attracts breeding Carolina Wrens, Yellow-billed Cuckoos, Wood Thrushes, Veeries, Ovenbirds, American Redstarts and Scarlet Tanagers. The pine stands attract crossbills, Pine Siskins and Red-breasted Nuthatches, among others during irruption years. The park offers a satisfying birding experience year-round and tremendous views of this unglaciated or driftless region of the state.

Castle Rock State Park and Lowden-Miller State Forest

More species of warblers breed at these two locations than in all of the Shawnee National Forest in southern Illinois. The breeding warblers to be seen include the Chestnut-sided, Canada and Mourning. Veeries also breed here regularly. Some of the state's rarest breeding records, including Black-throated Green Warbler, occur at the Lowden-Miller State Forest, a former tree farm with extensive white and red pine plantations interspersed among oak-hickory and floodplain forests and secondary growth. Just across the Rock River is the 2000-acre Castle Rock State Park with deep ravines, scenic rock formations and rare plant communities. The ravine system harbors breeding Carolina Wrens, American Redstarts, Acadian Flycatchers, Wood Thrushes and Kentucky Warblers, among many others.

Starved Rock and Matthiessen State Parks

This land of stream-fed canyons, waterfalls, restored grasslands, the Illinois River and St. Peter's forested sandstone bluffs provides habitat for more than 225 bird species within its 5000 acres. Search for wintering Bald Eagles and vagrant gulls at the Army Corps Visitor Center and Lock and Dam. Within and around the parks, creepers, nuthatches, titmice and Carolina Wrens can be found most of the year. Kinglets and Winter Wrens use the parks in fall and winter. Common breeders include Carolina Wrens and Acadian Flycatchers. The Starved Rock Nature Preserve contains a large tract of bottomland woods where Prothonotary Warblers, Louisiana Waterthrush and Pileated Woodpeckers breed. Migratory waterfowl, shorebirds and songbirds use both parks. The Illinois Canyon is particularly fruitful for migrant songbirds in spring. American Woodcocks display at dusk one mile west of the Illinois Canyon parking lot.

Lake Chautauqua National Wildlife Refuge

Nearly 5000 acres of floodplain woods, upland forest, open water and mud flats serve as the gateway to tens of thousands of migratory shorebirds and waterfowl. This refuge has harbored at least 27 species of waterfowl and 30 species of shorebirds. Thousands of American White Pelicans pass through in spring and fall. Tens of thousands of Pectoral Sandpipers and Lesser Yellowlegs migrate through in fall. Large numbers of Great Egrets and small numbers of all of Illinois' other heron species can be found in late summer most years. Other interesting species encountered include Pileated Woodpeckers, Red-headed Woodpeckers and Eurasian Tree Sparrows. The nearby 7500-acre Sand Ridge State Forest contains oak-hickory forest and rare sand prairie, where Lark Sparrows breed. Very rare state breeders, including Northern Saw-whet Owl, Red Crossbill, Pine Warbler, Red-breasted Nuthatch and Blue-headed Vireo have nested in the large stand of mature pines, which also attract the wintering Red Crossbill and White-winged Crossbill.

Northern
Saw-whet Owl

Clinton Lake

Thousands of acres of privately and publicly owned marshlands, grasslands, woods, old fields and pine plantations surround the deep, 10 square-mile Clinton Lake. This is one of the best lakes in central Illinois to find loons, including the Common Loon and the rarer Pacific Loon and Red-throated Loon, all the grebes and large numbers of ducks and gulls. Thousands of Bonaparte's Gulls are common in fall. Rarities have included the Little Gull and Iceland Gull. In spring, open cornfield stubble interspersed with foxtail attracts the migratory Smith's Longspur, a species that is difficult to find. The marshy regions attract the Sora, Virginia Rail and even the rare Yellow Rail (for the extremely patient birder) along with Le Conte's Sparrow and Nelson's Sharp-tailed Sparrow.

Carlyle Lake State Fish and Wildlife Area

This is Illinois' largest human-made lake; some points span one to two miles across. Carlyle Lake, about an hour's drive west of St. Louis, Missouri, contains 80 miles of shoreline, dotted with greenery and mudflats. It's a year-round mecca for birds including migratory shorebirds, songbirds, and waterfowl; winter gulls, owls, and finches; and the state's largest nesting colony of Double-crested Cormorants. Sabine's Gull is a specialty in September, and all three species of jaeger have been found. Eldon Hazlet State Park, within the wildlife area, is especially good in fall for neotropical migrants. In wooded conifers, Northern Saw-whet and Long-eared owls sometimes winter. A flourishing population of Eurasian Collared-Doves and one or two pairs of Monk Parakeets can be found at the Carlyle grain elevator.

Giant City State Park

Deciduous woodlands, impressive sandstone bluffs, streams and some shrubby fields grace this 4000-acre park of winding roads within the Shawnee National Forest. You can hike many scenic trails, varying from easy to strenuous walking, to search for migratory and nesting birds. Regular breeders include Northern Parula, Kentucky Warbler and Yellow-throated Warbler, Louisiana Waterthrush, Scarlet Tanager and Summer Tanager, and Pileated Woodpecker. Nearby successional fields attract breeding Prairie Warbler, White-eyed Vireo, Blue Grosbeak, Orchard Oriole and Field Sparrow. Listen for the occasional call of a Chuck-will's-widow among the more ubiquitous Whip-poor-will in spring and summer. Many Illinoisans consider this one of the state's most scenic parks.

Pine Hills-LaRue Ecological Area

This 4200-acre southern Illinois site with steep, scenic bluffs overlooking the Big Muddy River, the Mississippi River Valley and LaRue Swamp contains more plant diversity than any other place in Illinois.

The many steep ravines jutting through the uplands likely hold one of the state's largest populations of Worm-eating Warbler. Within the ravines and forest areas, you can find numerous breeding Scarlet and Summer tanagers, Kentucky Warbler, Louisiana Waterthrush, Acadian Flycatcher, Wood Thrush, White-eyed Vireo and Yellow-billed Cuckoo.

The Campground regularly hosts breeding Ruby-throated Hummingbird and Yellow-throated Warbler. You may even find nests, especially those built by Acadian Flycatcher, Eastern Wood-Pewee and Red-eyed Vireo placed in a tree alongside or above a road.

In the LaRue Swamp bottomlands, breeding Wood Ducks and Prothonotary Warblers are abundant; rare species such as Fish Crow and Least Bittern also breed. Spring migration can be fantastic especially along the ridge-top roadsides. In spring, park officials close the main road at the base of the bluff for snake migration.

Scarlet Tanager

Union County Conservation Area

More than 6000 acres of bottomland forest, mudflats, ponds, lakes, swamps and sloughs as well as agricultural fields comprise this region designed for waterfowl hunters, but also accessible to birders.

Wintering here are tens-to-hundreds of thousands of Canada Geese, and fewer numbers of Snow Geese, often numbering in the thousands, as well as Greater White-fronted Geese, numbering typically in the hundreds to thousands. The rare Ross's Goose is found regularly.

Numerous Bald Eagles feed on the geese, which feed on the vegetation planted to attract them.

Red-headed Woodpeckers use dying bottomland trees year-round. Barred Owls and Red-shouldered Hawks are also common year-round. The levee road along the east side of the refuge is one of the best places in the state to see the state-endangered Mississippi Kite during breeding season, as well as American Redstart, Prothonotary Warbler and every species of heron and egret known to occur in the state. Yellow-crowned Night-Herons breed in small numbers. Fish Crows and Dickcissels can also be found.

Cypress Creek National Wildlife Refuge

The refuge, in the heart of the Cache River Basin, is adjacent to some of the natural areas mentioned below. Together with the next three sites, this refuge is designated as a national biosphere reserve, one of the most significant designations for any natural area in the nation.

Land is being purchased and restored so that some day 35,000 acres of contiguous oak barrens, buttonbush swamps, cypress-tupelo swamps and bottomland forests will be preserved.

The Cypress Creek refuge is not easily accessed, so wear appropriate footgear and gather good maps and information before going.

The Frank Bellrose Unit harbors migrating shorebirds and marsh birds and large numbers of waterfowl in winter. Rarities have included Marbled and Hudsonian godwits and Glossy Ibis. Bald Eagles also breed here.

The habitat along Cache Chapel Road attracts breeding Northern Mockingbird, Blue Grosbeak, Orchard Oriole and Loggerhead Shrike. Fish Crows breed.

The cypress-tupelo regions harbor small numbers of breeding Yellow-crowned Night-Heron, Red-shouldered Hawk and even the state-threatened Brown Creeper. Prothonotary and Yellow-throated warblers and Northern Parula are common breeders.

Large grasslands in various stages of restoration attract some of the state's most significant wintering populations of Northern Harrier and Short-eared Owl, along with various sparrow species, including Le Conte's. A significant population of the state-endangered Henslow's Sparrow breeds here. Bobolinks occur during migration.

Yellow-throated Warbler

Cache River State Natural Area

The 110-mile long Cache River region in southern Illinois once held more than 250,000 acres of bald cypress-tupelo swamp habitat, and still harbors some of the largest and oldest cypress trees in the state.

Some 5000 of these acres have been preserved. They attract not only many bird species, but also bats, snakes, river otters and bobcats. Breeding Prothonotary and Yellow-throated warblers, Acadian Flycatcher, Pileated Woodpecker, and Wood Duck are common. More uncommon but regular breeders include Fish Crow, Red-shouldered Hawk, Yellow-crowned Night-Heron, and Brown Creeper. Most years, large numbers of Red-headed Woodpecker spend the winter. Rails and bitterns may be found during migration. Rent a canoe nearby for a spectacular birding adventure in spring and summer.

Heron Pond and Little Black Slough State Natural Areas

Heron Pond is the most easily accessed part of the great bald cypress-tupelo swamp in southern Illinois; it serves as a showcase to this region. Breeding birds include Yellow-throated and Prothonotary warblers, Pileated Woodpecker, Red-shouldered Hawk and Brown Creeper.

Black and Turkey vultures roost in the tall cypresses within the natural areas, but can be seen most readily in the open countryside just outside the border.

If you're birding for the first time in southern Illinois, start here for a great introduction to the state's southern region, reminiscent of Louisiana bayous.

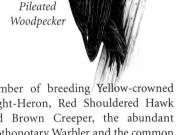

Pileated Woodpecker

Horseshoe Lake Conservation Area

Now probably extinct, the Ivory-billed Woodpecker and Bachman's Warbler once bred in this 9500-acre southern Illinois region of bald cypress and tupelo trees and an oxbow lake next to the Mississippi River. Today, many ducks and geese and dozens of Bald Eagles overwinter.

Some of the state's most southerly breeders can be found. These include the rare and state-endangered Mississippi Kite. Fish Crow is a common breeder.

All of the state's herons and egrets, especially Little Blue Heron and Snowy Egret, can be found at Horseshoe Lake and nearby locations during spring and summer. The very rare Least Tern nests on nearby islands along the Mississippi River and occasionally feeds on or near the refuge. Some of the larger tracts of cypress-tupelo forest harbor a small number of breeding Yellow-crowned Night-Heron, Red Shouldered Hawk and Brown Creeper, the abundant Prothonotary Warbler and the common Barred Owl.

Migratory songbirds fly through in spring and fall. Many linger into early winter. On a Christmas Bird Count day, birders often find Eastern Phoebes, American Pipits, Hermit Thrushes, Eastern Bluebirds and various sparrow species, including the striking and rare Le Conte's.

Rarities have included Brant, White Ibis, Anhinga and Magnificent Frigatebird.

ILLINOIS' TOP BIRDING SITES

Choosing a mere 100 birding sites in Illinois is difficult. Indeed the prairie state boasts more than 125 state parks and 300 state-designated nature preserves, as well as nine national wildlife refuges, the 270,000-acre Shawnee National Forest and countless county and town forest preserves, conservation districts and parks. The following areas have been selected—offering you a taste of every habitat within the state and giving you the opportunity to see most of the species on the state checklist. Be aware that hunting is allowed at certain times of the year at some of these sites; call ahead or check online for more detailed information.

Northeast Region – Lake Michigan shoreline, wetlands, prairies, deciduous woods

1. Illinois Beach SP
2. Waukegan Beach
3. Wadsworth Savanna and Wetlands Demonstration Project
4. Rollins Savanna FP
5. Chain O' Lakes SP
6. Volo Bog SNA
7. Moraine Hills SP
8. Glacial Park CA
9. Kinnikinnick Creek CA
10. Garden Prairie Slough
11. Crabtree Nature Center FP and Baker's Lake
12. Paul Douglas FP and Deer Grove FP
13. Ryerson Woods FP, Wright Woods FP and Half Day FP
14. Chicago Botanic Garden and Skokie Lagoons
15. Gillson Park in Wilmette
16. Morton Arboretum
17. Blackwell FP and Springbrook Prairie FP
18. FermiLab National Accelerator Laboratory
19. Pratt's Wayne Woods FP and McKee Marsh
20. Shabbona Lake SRA and Chief Shabbona FP
21. Montrose Harbor and the Magic Hedge
22. Jackson Park in Chicago
23. The Palos Preserves
24. The Orland Tract, Bartel Grasslands and McGinnis Slough
25. Lake Calumet
26. Lake Renwick Heron Rookery Nature Preserve and the Lockport/Joliet region
27. Goose Lake Prairie SNA and Heidecke Lake
28. Midewin National Tallgrass Prairie and the Des Plaines River CA
29. Iroquois County CA
30. Kankakee River SP, Momence Wetlands and Sod Farms

Northwestern region – river bluffs, woodlands, grasslands, wetlands

31. Winnebago County Forest Preserves
32. Rock Cut SP
33. Apple River Canyon SP
34. Tapley Woods SNA
35. Savanna Army Depot/Lost Mound NWR
36. Mississippi Palisades SP
37. Upper Mississippi River NWR/Thomson and Spring Creek units
38. Mississippi River Corridor, including Lock and Dams No. 13 to 16
39. Castle Rock SP and Lowden-Miller SF
40. Nachusa Grasslands and Franklin Creek SNA
41. Green River CA

Central region – river bluffs, woodlands, wetlands, lakes

42. Hennepin Wetlands
43. Starved Rock SP and Matthiessen SP
44. Marshall SFWA
45. Mark Twain NWR/Keithsburg Division
46. Big River SF and Nauvoo region
47. Cedar Glen Eagle Roost and Preserve/Warsaw Lock and Dam No. 19
48. Lake Argyle SP
49. Jubilee College SP
50. Banner Marsh SFWA and Rice Lake CA
51. Emiquon NWR
52. Lake Chautauqua NWR
53. Sand Ridge SF
54. Beardstown Marsh and Sanganois CA
55. Jim Edgar Panther Creek CA
56. Meredosia NWR
57. Siloam Springs SP
58. Pere Marquette SP and Mark Twain NWR/Brussels District
59. Middle Fork SFWA/Kickapoo SP and Kennekuk County Park
60. Forest Glen Preserve and the Harry "Babe" Woodyard SNA
61. Busey Woods and Meadowbrook Park/Champaign County
62. Moraine View SP
63. Lake Bloomington and Evergreen Lake
64. Clinton Lake
65. Lake Decatur
66. Lake Springfield and Carpenter Park
67. Sangchris SP
68. Arcola Marsh
69. Lake Shelbyville
70. Fox Ridge SP
71. Mark Twain NWR/Brussels District
72. Horseshoe Lake SP

Southern Region – Shawnee National Forest, bald cypress/tupelo swamps, sandstone bluffs, grasslands

73. Carlyle Lake SFWA
74. Stephen A. Forbes SRA
75. Prairie Ridge SNA and Newton Lake SFWA
76. Beall Woods SP
77. Rend Lake Wildlife Management Area
78. Pyramid SP
79. Kidd Lake SNA
80. Lake Murphysboro SP
81. Oakwood Bottoms
82. Crab Orchard NWR
83. Ferne Clyffe SP
84. Giant City SP
85. Pomona/Cave Creek region of the Shawnee National Forest
86. Trail of Tears SF
87. Pine Hills/LaRue Ecological Area
88. Union County CA
89. Atwood Ridge and Hamburg Hill
90. Cypress Pond SNA
91. Cypress Creek NWR
92. Cache River SNA
93. Heron Pond SNA and Little Black Slough SNA
94. Bell Smith Springs
95. Lusk Creek Canyon and Wilderness Area
96. Dixon Springs SP, Penant Bar Ranch and Bell Pond
97. War Bluff Sanctuary
98. Horseshoe Lake CA
99. Mermet Lake CA
100. East Cape Girardeau Wetlands

CA =	Conservation Area
FP =	Forest Preserve
NF =	National Forest
NWR =	National Wildlife Refuge
SF =	State Forest
SFWA =	State Fish & Wildlife Area
SNA =	State Natural Area
SP =	State Park
SRA =	State Recreation Area

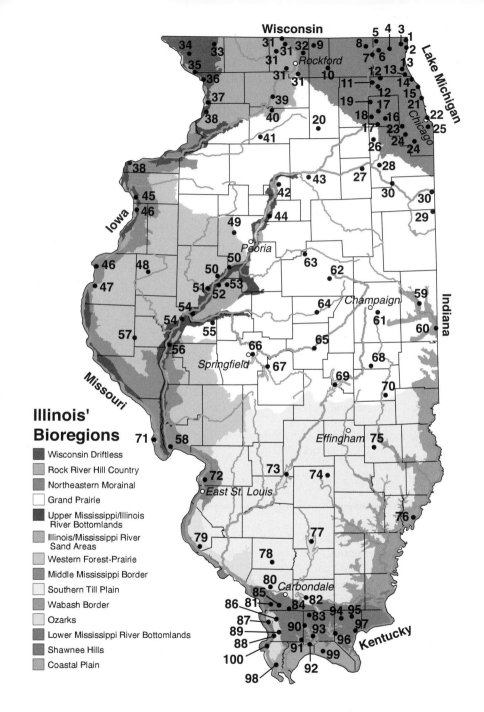

Illinois' Bioregions

- Wisconsin Driftless
- Rock River Hill Country
- Northeastern Morainal
- Grand Prairie
- Upper Mississippi/Illinois River Bottomlands
- Illinois/Mississippi River Sand Areas
- Western Forest-Prairie
- Middle Mississippi Border
- Southern Till Plain
- Wabash Border
- Ozarks
- Lower Mississippi River Bottomlands
- Shawnee Hills
- Coastal Plain

Bioregions map courtesy of the Illinois Natural History Survey

About the Species Accounts

This book gives detailed accounts of the 319 species of birds that can be expected on an annual basis in Illinois. Twenty-two casual species are briefly mentioned in an appendix. These species can be expected to be seen in small numbers every year or every few years because of anticipated range expansion, migration or well-documented wandering tendencies. A state checklist of all 431 birds documented and accepted by the Illinois Ornithological Records Committee is at the back of this book. The order of the birds and their common and scientific names follow the American Ornithologists' Union's *Check-list of North American Birds* (7th edition, published in 1999, and the last one, the 44th supplement, published in 2003).

Personifying a bird helps us to relate to it on a personal level. However, the characterizations presented in this book are based on the human experience and most likely fall short of truly defining the way birds perceive the world. They should not be mistaken for scientific propositions. Nevertheless, we hope that a lively, engaging text will communicate our scientific knowledge as smoothly and effectively as possible.

One of the challenges of birdwatching is that many species look different in spring and summer than they do in fall and winter. Many birds have breeding and nonbreeding plumages, and immature birds often look different from their parents. This book does not try to describe or illustrate all the different plumages of a species; instead, it focuses on the forms that are most likely to be seen in our area.

ID: This section is best used in combination with the illustrations. Where appropriate, the description is subdivided to highlight the differences between male and female birds, breeding and nonbreeding birds and immature and adult birds. The descriptions use as few technical terms as possible. Birds may not have "eye lines" or "chins," but these and other terms are easily understood by all readers, in spite of their scientific inaccuracy. Some of the most common features of birds are pointed out in the Glossary illustration (p. 362).

Size: This section provides an average length, and occasionally a length range, of the birds' body from bill to tail tip. In addition, wingspans are given, although some of the larger birds' wing spreads may be variable. Please note that birds with long tails often have large measurements that do not necessarily reflect "body" size.

Status: A general comment, such as "common," "uncommon" or "rare," is usually sufficient to describe the relative abundance of a species. Situations are bound to vary somewhat since migratory pulses, seasonal changes and centers of activity tend to concentrate or disperse birds.

Habitat: The habitats we have listed describe where each species is most commonly found. In most cases, it is a generalized description, but if a bird is restricted to a specific habitat, the habitat is described precisely. Birds can turn up in almost any type of habitat, but they will usually be found in environments that provide the specific food, water, cover and, in some cases, nesting habitat that they need to survive.

Nesting: The reproductive strategies used by different bird species vary: in each species account, nest location and structure, clutch size, incubation period and parental duties are discussed. Remember that birdwatching ethics discourage the disturbance of active bird nests. If you disturb a nest, you may drive off the parents during a critical period or expose defenseless young to predators. The nesting behavior of birds that do not nest in Illinois is not described.

Feeding: Birds spend a great deal of time foraging for food. If you know what a bird eats and where the food is found, you will have a good chance of finding the bird you are looking for. Birds are frequently encountered while they are foraging; we hope that our description of their feeding styles and diets provides valuable identifying characteristics, as well as interesting dietary facts.

Voice: You will hear many birds, particularly songbirds, which may remain hidden from view. Paraphrases of distinctive sounds may aid you in identifying a species by ear, but some only loosely resemble the call, song or sound produced by the bird. Should one of our paraphrases not work for you, feel free to make up your own—the creative exercise will reinforce your memory of the bird's vocalizations.

Similar Species: Easily confused species are discussed briefly. If you concentrate on the most relevant field marks, the subtle differences between species can be reduced to easily identifiable traits. You might find it useful to consult this section when finalizing your identification; however, even experienced birders can mistake one species for another.

Best Sites: If you are looking for a particular bird, you will have more luck in some places than in others, even within the range shown on the range map. We have listed places that are fairly easy to access.

Range Maps: The range map for each species represents the overall range of the species in an average year. Most birds will confine their annual movements to this range, although each year some birds wander beyond their traditional boundaries. These maps do not show differences in abundance within the range—areas of a range with good habitat will support a denser population than areas with poorer habitat. These maps also do not show how the range may change from year to year.

Unlike most other field guides, we have attempted to show migratory pathways—areas of the region where birds may appear while en route to nesting or winter habitat. Many of these migratory routes are "best guesses," which will no doubt be refined as new discoveries are made. The representations of the pathways do not distinguish high-use migration corridors from areas that are seldom used.

Range Map Symbols

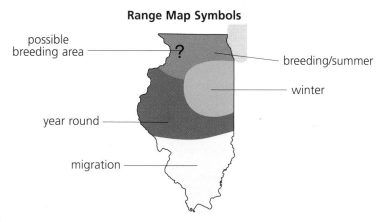

possible breeding area

breeding/summer

winter

year round

migration

Waterfowl

Grouse & Allies

Diving Birds

Heronlike Birds

Birds of Prey

Rails, Coots & Cranes

Shorebirds

Gulls & Terns

Doves, Parrots & Cuckoos

Owls

Nightjars, Swifts & Hummingbirds

Woodpeckers

NONPASSERINES

Nonpasserine birds represent 17 of the 18 orders of birds found in Illinois, about 54 percent of the species in our region. They are grouped together and called "nonpasserines" because, with few exceptions, they are easily distinguished from the "passerines," or "perching birds," which make up the 18th order. Being from 17 different orders, however, means that nonpasserines vary considerably in their appearance and habits—they include everything from the 4-foot-tall Great Blue Heron to the 3-inch-long Rufous Hummingbird.

Generally speaking, nonpasserines do not "sing." Instead, their vocalizations are referred to as "calls." There are also other morphological differences. For example, the muscles and tendons in the legs of passerines are adapted to grip a perch, and the toes of passerines are never webbed. Many nonpasserines are large, so they are among our most notable birds. Waterfowl, raptors, gulls, shorebirds and woodpeckers are easily identified by most people. Some of the smaller nonpasserines, such as doves, swifts and hummingbirds, are frequently thought of as passerines by novice birders, and can cause those beginners some identification problems. With a little practice, however, they will become recognizable as nonpasserines. By learning to separate the nonpasserines from the passerines at a glance, birders effectively reduce by half the number of possible species for an unidentified bird.

GREATER WHITE-FRONTED GOOSE
Anser albifrons

Greater White-fronted Geese breed on the arctic tundra and winter in the southern U.S. and Mexico. In Illinois, their numbers have increased dramatically within the past decade. During spring and fall migration, they stop to refuel on aquatic plants or grains in fields. They often travel among flocks of Canada Geese. The slightly smaller Greater White-fronted Goose can best be distinguished by its bright orange feet and pinky orange bill. In flight, it utters a distinct, laughlike call, unlike the honking of Canada Geese. • With a nearly circumpolar distribution, the Greater White-fronted Goose has the widest range of any species in its genus. It is the only New World representative of the five species of gray geese that can be found in the Old World. Like most geese, White-fronts are long-lived birds that mate for life, with both parents caring for the young. • This goose is probably most familiar to hunters, who know it as "Speckle Belly."

ID: gray brown overall; black speckling on belly; pinkish or orange bill; white around bill and on forehead; white hindquarters; black band on upper tail; orange feet. *Immature:* pale belly without speckles; little or no white on face.

Size: *L* 27–33 in; *W* 4½–5 ft.

Status: fairly common to abundant local migrant; locally common winter resident on southern Illinois reservoirs and waterfowl refuges; generally absent from May to mid-October.

Habitat: croplands, fields, open areas, lakes and ponds.

Nesting: does not nest in Illinois.

Feeding: dabbles in water and gleans the ground for grass shoots, sprouting and waste grain and occasionally aquatic invertebrates.

Voice: high-pitched "laugh"; flock noise is higher-pitched, more rapid and clearer than that of Snow Geese or Canada Geese.

Similar Species: *Canada Goose* (p. 37): white "chin strap"; black neck; lacks speckling on belly.

Best Sites: Union County CA; Horseshoe Lake CA.

SNOW GOOSE
Chen caerulescens

L anding in farmers' fields, these cackling geese feed on waste grain from the previous year's crops. In recent years, Snow Goose populations have increased dramatically in North America, as they take advantage of human-induced changes in the landscape and in the food supply. Watching a flock of Snow Geese rise into the air during winter in Illinois is a spectacular sight. Unlike Canada Geese, which fly in a V-formation, migrating Snow Geese usually form oscillating, wavy lines. • The Snow Goose's strong, serrated bill is well designed for pulling up the root stalks of marsh plants and for gripping slippery grasses. • As with the Sandhill Crane, the plumage of the Snow Goose can be stained rusty red from iron in the water. • This species has two color morphs, a white and a blue, that, until 1983, were considered different species. • At Carlyle Lake, you may see an impressive 20,000 at one time.

ID: white overall; black wing tips; pink feet and bill; dark "grin" on bill; plumage is occasionally stained rusty red. *Blue morph:* white head and upper neck; dark blue gray body. *Immature:* brownish or dusky white plumage; dark bill and feet.
Size: *L* 28–33 in; *W* 4½–5 ft.
Status: fairly common, local migrant and winter resident; occurs from mid-February to mid- to late April and from mid-October to November or December, except at wintering sites on southern Illinois reservoirs and waterfowl refuges.

Habitat: croplands, fields, open areas, lakes and ponds.
Nesting: does not nest in Illinois.
Feeding: grazes on waste grain and new sprouts; also eats aquatic vegetation, grasses, sedges and roots.
Voice: loud, nasal, *houk-houk* in flight, higher pitched and more constant than Canada Goose.
Similar Species: *Ross's Goose* (p. 36): smaller; shorter neck; lacks black "grin." *Tundra* (p. 40), *Trumpeter* (p. 39) and *Mute* (p. 38) *swans:* larger; white wing tips. *American White Pelican* (p. 80): much larger bill, body and wingspan.
Best Sites: Baldwin L.; Carlyle L.; Rend L.; Union County CA.

ROSS'S GOOSE

Chen rossii

Ross's Geese are rare migrants, but, like the Snow Geese, their population is growing in Illinois. During fall migration, a few Ross's Geese may mingle with a migrating flock of Snow Geese. • The Ross's Goose looks similar to the Snow Goose and the inexperienced birder might easily get the two confused. However, upon closer view, the Ross's Goose does not exhibit the "grinning patch" of the Snow Goose and is smaller in size with a shorter, stubbier bill. • Approximately 95 percent of all Ross's Geese nest in the Queen Maud Gulf Migratory Bird Sanctuary in the central Canadian Arctic. • This bird was named after Bernard Rogan Ross, a naturalist and anthropologist who was a fellow of the National Geographic Society and a contributor of specimens to the Smithsonian Institute and the British Museum.

ID: white overall; black wing tips; dark pink feet and bill; lacks "grinning patch"; small bluish or greenish "warts" on base of bill; plumage is occasionally stained rusty by iron in the water. *Blue morph:* very rare; white head; blue gray body plumage. *Immature:* gray plumage; dark bill and feet.

Size: *L* 21–26 in; *W* 4 ft.

Status: rare to uncommon migrant and winter resident; occurs from mid-February through early to mid-April and from mid-October or early November to mid-December, except at favored wintering sites on southern Illinois reservoirs and waterfowl refuges.

Habitat: croplands, fields, open areas, lakes and ponds.

Nesting: does not nest in Illinois.

Feeding: grazes on waste grain and new sprouts; also eats aquatic vegetation, grasses, sedges and roots.

Voice: similar to the Snow Goose, but higher pitched.

Similar Species: *Snow Goose* (p. 35): larger; longer neck; dark "grin" line on bill. *Tundra* (p. 40), *Trumpeter* (p. 39) and *Mute* (p. 38) *swans:* much larger; white wing tips. *American White Pelican* (p. 80): much larger bill, body and wingspan.

Best Sites: Baldwin L.; Carlyle L.; Rend L.; Union County CA; Horseshoe Lake CA.

CANADA GOOSE

Branta canadensis

Canada Geese are among the most recognizable birds in Illinois. At one time, Illinois' resident population of Canada Geese, known as the "Giant" subspecies, was hunted almost to extinction. Populations have been reestablished and, in recent decades, these large, bold birds have inundated urban waterfronts, picnic sites, golf courses and corporate and city parks. Tens to hundreds of thousands of Canada Geese once overwintered in extreme southern Illinois, but with modern agricultural practices and climate changes, they now winter farther north in the state. The Cackling, Richardson's and "Giant" geese subspecies can be observed together in large, wintering flocks. • Fuzzy goslings compel people to get closer, but hissing sounds and low, outstretched necks are warning signs to give these birds some space. Unlike most birds, Canada Goose parents maintain a bond with their young for almost a year, until the beginning of the next year's nesting.

ID: long, black neck with wide, white "chin strap"; white undertail coverts; light brown underparts; dark brown upperparts; short, black tail.
Size: *L* 25–45 in; *W* 3½–5 ft.
Status: common to abundant migrant and winter resident statewide; uncommon to abundant breeder, increasing northward; spring flocks move north in mid-February and are mostly gone by mid- to late March.
Habitat: marshes, lakeshores, riverbanks, corporate and park ponds, cornfields, golf courses and city parks.
Nesting: on an island in a marsh or pond or along a shoreline; usually on the ground, often on a muskrat lodge; female builds a nest of plant material lined with down; female incubates 4–12 white eggs for 25–28 days while the male stands guard.
Feeding: grazes on new sprouts, aquatic vegetation, grass and roots; tips up for aquatic roots and tubers.
Voice: loud, familiar *ah-honk,* often answered by other Canada Geese.
Similar Species: *Greater White-fronted Goose* (p. 34): less common; brown neck and head; orange legs; white around base of bill; dark speckling on belly; lacks white "chin strap." *Brant* (p. 355): much rarer; smaller than most Canada Geese; mainly white tail with black tip; black upper breast; lacks white "chin strap"; sometimes has white "necklace." *Snow Goose* (p. 35): blue morph has white head and upper neck.
Best Sites: *Winter:* Union County CA; Horseshoe Lake CA.

MUTE SWAN

Cygnus olor

Admired for its grace and beauty, this Eurasian native was introduced to eastern North America in the mid-1800s to adorn estates and city parks. Over the years, Mute Swans have adapted well to the North American environment. They have continued to expand their feral populations, and although they are not usually migratory, more northerly nesters have established short migratory routes to milder wintering areas. • Like many nonnative species, Mute Swans are often fierce competitors for nesting areas and food sources. They can be aggressive toward geese and ducks, and may displace native species. In Illinois, their breeding range is mostly restricted to Cook County and Lake County. • A reliable long-distance characteristic for distinguishing a Mute Swan from a native swan is the way a Mute Swan holds its neck in a graceful curve with its orange bill hanging down. When swimming at a distance, the immatures of this species are difficult to separate from the immatures of the Tundra Swan and Trumpeter Swan.

ID: all-white plumage; orange bill with down-turned tip; bulbous, black knob at base of bill; neck usually held in an S-shape; wings often held in an arch over back while swimming. *Immature:* plumage may be white to gray; light bill lacks knob.

Size: *L* 5 ft; *W* 6–6½ ft.

Status: uncommon to locally common year-round resident in northeastern Illinois; rare migrant, breeder and winter resident elsewhere; spring migrants occur mostly from late February to early March; most fall migrants occur in November and early December.

Habitat: marshes, lakes and ponds.

Nesting: on the ground in a marsh, often on an island; female builds a mound of vegetation and incubates 5–10 pale green eggs for about 36 days; male may help to gather nest material; pair tends the young.

Feeding: tips up or dips its head below the water's surface for aquatic plants; grazes on land.

Voice: generally silent; may hiss or issue hoarse barking notes.

Similar Species: *Tundra Swan* (p. 40) and *Trumpeter Swan* (p. 39): lack orange bill with black knob at base; neck tends to be held straight; immatures have subtle differences in bill color and shape.

Best Sites: *Summer:* William Powers CA; Lake Co. wetlands.

TRUMPETER SWAN
Cygnus buccinator

The Trumpeter Swan had been hunted nearly to extinction by the early 20th century. Breeding populations in Alaska and western Canada persisted, but eastern populations were less fortunate and the bird became extirpated as a breeder in Illinois perhaps as early as the 1880s. In 1966, Minnesota pioneered the effort to reestablish this bird. By the 1980s, Trumpeter Swan recovery programs had been initiated in Wisconsin, Michigan and Minnesota by state natural resource agencies. As of yet, this species has not been introduced in Illinois, but small numbers of the populations introduced in the Midwest can be seen during migration. • Both "trumpeter" and *buccinator* refer to this bird's bugling voice, which is produced when air is forced through the long windpipe that runs through the keel of the breastbone. • The neck of a Trumpeter Swan is twice the length of its body, making this bird one of the world's largest species of waterfowl.

ID: all-white plumage; large, solid black bill; black skin extends from bill to eyes; black feet; neck is held with kink at base when standing or swimming. *Immature:* gray brown plumage; gray bill; light-colored feet.

Size: *L* 5–6 ft; *W* 6–7 ft.

Status: rare to casual migrant from mid-October to mid-April; rare and local winter resident.

Habitat: lakes and large wetlands.

Nesting: does not nest in Illinois.

Feeding: tips up, surface gleans and occasionally grazes for vegetation; primarily eats pondweeds, duckweeds, aquatic tubers and roots.

Voice: resonant, bugling *koh-hoh.*

Similar Species: *Tundra Swan* (p. 40): smaller; more common; often shows yellow spot in front of eye; softer, more nasal voice. *Mute Swan* (p. 38): orange bill with black knob on upper base, held down-pointed bill; neck usually held in S-shape; wings often held in arch over back while swimming. *Snow Goose* (p. 35): much smaller; black wing tips.

Best Sites: lakes and wetlands.

TUNDRA SWAN
Cygnus columbianus

The Tundra Swan, which breeds in the Arctic and winters mainly on the Atlantic Coast, migrates in a mostly east-west pattern. Most Tundra Swans found in Illinois migrate through a narrow belt in the northeastern part of the state, especially along Lake Michigan. However, in some years, this species can be found in small numbers along the Illinois and Mississippi Rivers. These hardy birds arrive early in the year for spring migration and return south as late as December in fall migration. • Noting bill color and shape helps to distinguish between the three swan species seen in Illinois. The bright orange bill of the adult Mute Swan is fairly easy to observe, but the subtle difference in slope between the bills of the Tundra, Trumpeter and immature Mute Swan can be more difficult to distinguish. • The Lewis and Clark exploration team collected the first specimen of this bird near the Columbia River, thus its scientific name *columbianus*.

ID: white plumage; large, black bill; black feet; often shows yellow lores; neck is held straight up; neck and head show rounded, slightly curving profile; slightly concave bill. *Immature:* gray brown plumage; pinkish to grayish bill.

Size: *L* 4–5 ft; *W* 6½ ft.

Status: rare to uncommon migrant from February to mid-April and from late October to early December; rare winter resident.

Habitat: shallow areas of lakes, wetlands and agricultural fields.

Nesting: does not nest in Illinois.

Feeding: tips up, dabbles and gleans the water's surface for aquatic vegetation and invertebrates; grazes for tubers, roots and waste grain.

Voice: high-pitched, quivering *oo-oo-whoo* is repeated by migrating flocks.

Similar Species: *Trumpeter Swan* (p. 39): larger; loud, bugling voice; straight line from tip of head to tip of bill; neck and head have more angular profile; lacks yellow lores. *Mute Swan* (p. 38): orange bill with black knob on upper base; neck is usually held in S-shape; downpointed bill; wings often held in arch over back while swimming; immature has subtle differences in bill color and shape. *Snow Goose* (p. 35): smaller; black wing tips; shorter neck; pinkish bill.

Best Sites: L. Michigan shoreline.

WOOD DUCK
Aix sponsa

The male Wood Duck is one of the most colorful birds in North America; books, magazines, postcards and calendars routinely celebrate this duck's beauty. • A bird of forested wetlands, the Wood Duck nests in trees, sometimes a mile or more from the nearest body of water. Although typical clutch size varies from 9 to 14 eggs, some nests contain more than 20 as a result of "dump nesting," in which more than one female lays eggs in the same nest. • Forced into the adventures of life at an early age, newly hatched ducklings often jump 20 feet out of their nest cavities to the ground to follow their mother to the nearest body of water. • Landowners with a tree-lined riverine habitat or other suitable wetland may attract a family of Wood Ducks by building a nest box with a predator guard and lining it with sawdust. The nest box should be erected close to the shoreline at a reasonable height, at least 15 feet from the ground. • Wood Ducks were nearly extirpated as a breeding bird in Illinois. Extensive studies in the Lake Chautauqua region by world-famous ornithologist Dr. Frank Bellrose have helped this species make a comeback.

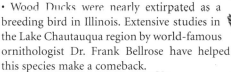

ID: *Male:* glossy, green head with some white streaks; crest is slicked back from crown; white "chin" and throat; purple chestnut breast spotted with white; black-and-white shoulder slash; golden sides; dark back and hindquarters. *Female:* white, teardrop-shaped eye patch; mottled brown breast streaked with white; gray brown upperparts; white belly.
Size: *L* 15–20 in; *W* 30 in.
Status: common migrant and breeder statewide; occurs from mid- to late February through mid-November; rare winter resident.
Habitat: swamps, ponds, river bottomland, forests and lakeshores with wooded edges.
Nesting: in a hollow or tree cavity, typically 30 ft or more above ground; sometimes in an artificial nest box or hollow such as a chimney; usually near water; cavity is lined with down; female incubates 9–14 white to buff eggs for 28–32 days.
Feeding: gleans the water's surface and tips up for duckweeds, aquatic sedges and grasses; eats more fruits and nuts, especially acorns and beech nuts, than other ducks.
Voice: *Male:* diagnostic, resonant, ascending *ter-wee-wee. Female:* loud, squeaky *woo-e-e-k.*
Similar Species: *Hooded Merganser* (p. 63): male has black head with white crest patch, slim, black bill and black-and-white breast. *Harlequin Duck* (p. 56): much rarer; male is blue gray overall, with black-and-white patches and ruddy sides; female has unstreaked breast and white "ear" patch.
Best Sites: Mississippi and Illinois River valleys; L. Chautauqua; Union County CA; Horseshoe Lake CA; Oakwood Bottoms.

GADWALL

Anas strepera

Male Gadwalls lack the striking plumage of most other male ducks, but they nevertheless have a dignified appearance and a subtle beauty. Once you learn their field marks, a black rump and white wing patches, Gadwalls are easy to identify. • Ducks in the genus *Anas,* the dabbling ducks, are most often observed tipping up their hindquarters and submerging their heads to feed, but Gadwalls dive more often than others of this group. These ducks feed equally during the day and night, a strategy that reduces the risk of preda-tion because the birds avoid spending long periods of time sleeping or feeding. • The Gadwall has expanded its range throughout North America, and large numbers can be found in Illinois, especially in fall and winter. Most Gadwalls, however, winter on the Gulf Coast of the United States and Mexico.

ID: white speculum; white belly. *Male:* mostly gray with fine, black-and-white mottling and wavy, irregular lines on sides, breast and head; black hindquarters; dark bill. *Female:* mottled brown overall; black feathers with buffy tips giving arrowlike appearance; brown bill with orange sides.

Size: *L* 18–22 in; *W* 33 in.

Status: common migrant; very rare breeder in the north; occurs from mid-February through early December, or until freeze-up; uncommon to locally common winter resident.

Habitat: *Breeding:* open wetlands with emergent vegetation. *In migration* and *winter:* marshes, lakes, ponds and sewage lagoons.

Nesting: in tall vegetation, sometimes far from water; nest is well concealed in a scraped-out hollow, often with grass arch-ing overhead; nest is made of grass and other dry vegetation and lined with down; female incubates 8–11 white eggs for 24–27 days.

Feeding: dabbles and tips up for water plants; grazes on grass and waste grain during migration; also eats aquatic inverte-brates, tadpoles and small fish; dabbles and dives routinely for food.

Voice: *Male:* simple, singular quack; often whistles harshly. *Female:* high *kaak kaaak kak-kak-kak,* given in series and oscillating in volume.

Similar Species: *American Wigeon* (p. 43): female lacks black hindquarters, has green speculum and is more reddish brown over-all. *Other dabbling ducks* (pp. 41–50): males are much more brightly colored and lack white speculum.

Best Sites: Hennepin Wetlands; L. Chautauqua; Carlyle L.; Horseshoe Lake SP; Union County CA.

AMERICAN WIGEON

Anas americana

The male American Wigeon's characteristic, three-syllable whistle sets it apart from the wetland orchestra of buzzes, quacks and ticks. • Mostly vegetarian, the American Wigeon frequently dabbles for food, and particularly enjoys the succulent stems and leaves of pond-bottom plants. These plants grow far too deep for a dabbling duck, however, so wigeons often pirate from accomplished divers such as American Coots, Canvasbacks, scaups and Redheads. Contrary to most ducks, the American Wigeon can walk well and often grazes on shorelines and in agricultural fields. • This duck nests farther north than any other dabbling duck with the exception of the Northern Pintail. Pair bonds are strong and last well into incubation. • "Wigeon" comes from a French word meaning "whistling duck." Because of the male's bright white crown and forehead, some birders call this bird "Baldpate."

ID: large, white wing patch; cinnamon breast and sides; white belly; black-tipped, gray blue bill; green speculum; reddish brown upperparts; white "wing pits." *Male:* white forehead; green swipe extends back from eye. *Female:* grayish head; brown underparts.
Size: *L* 18–22½ in; *W* 32 in.
Status: common migrant from early to mid-February through mid- to late April and from mid-September to early December; a few summer in northern Illinois; only 1 confirmed breeding record; occasional winter resident.
Habitat: shallow wetlands, lake edges, ponds, marshes, sloughs and flooded agricultural fields.

Nesting: nest is well concealed in tall vegetation on dry ground near a wetland; built with grass, leaves and down; female incubates 8–11 white eggs for 23–25 days.
Feeding: dabbles and tips up for aquatic leaves and the stems of pondweeds; also grazes and uproots young shoots in fields; may eat some invertebrates; occasionally pirates food from other birds.
Voice: *Male:* nasal, frequently repeated whistle: *whee WHEE wheew. Female:* soft, seldom-heard quack.
Similar Species: *Gadwall* (p. 42): white speculum; lacks large, white forewing patch; male lacks green eye swipe; female has orange sides to bill. *Eurasian Wigeon:* very rare; gray "wing pits"; male has rufous head, cream forehead and rosy breast; lacks green eye swipe; female usually has browner head.
Best Sites: Palos Preserves; L. Chautauqua.

43

AMERICAN BLACK DUCK

Anas rubripes

The American Black Duck's population has decreased in recent years as a result of habitat loss and competition with Mallards. A male Mallard will aggressively pursue a female American Black Duck and if she is unable to find a mate of her own kind, she will often accept the offer. Hybrid offspring are less fertile and are usually unable to reproduce. • The American Black Duck usually feeds in shallows where it probes the mud by dabbling below the water's surface with only its rump left exposed. In summer, it eats aquatic insects, salamanders, small frogs and anything else it is able to snatch. • Male and female American Black Ducks are remarkably similar in appearance, which is unusual for waterfowl.

ID: dark brownish black body; light brown head and neck; bright orange feet; violet speculum. *Male:* yellow olive bill. *Female:* dull green bill mottled with gray or black. *In flight:* whitish underwings; dark body.
Size: *L* 20–24½ in; *W* 35 in.

Status: uncommon to fairly common migrant and winter resident from mid-February to mid-April; fall migrants arrive in mid-September, with departure dates obscured by wintering birds; very rare summer resident and breeder, mostly in northern and central Illinois.
Habitat: *Breeding:* open wetlands with emergent vegetation. *In migration* and *winter:* lakes, wetlands, rivers, flooded fields and bottomland forests.

Nesting: usually on the ground among clumps of dense vegetation near water; female fills a shallow depression with plant material and lines it with down; female incubates 7–11 white to greenish buff eggs for 23–33 days; second clutches are common, usually to replace lost broods.
Feeding: tips up and dabbles in shallows for seeds and roots of pondweeds; also eats aquatic invertebrates, larval amphibians and fish eggs.
Voice: *Male:* Mallard-like quack. *Female:* medium loud quack.
Similar Species: *Mallard* (p. 45): male has bright green head, white belly and blue speculum bordered with black and white bars; female is lighter overall and has whitish tail and some orange on bill. *Gadwall* (p. 42): black hindquarters; white speculum.
Best Sites: Hennepin Wetlands; L. Chautauqua; Horseshoe Lake CA.

MALLARD
Anas platyrhynchos

The Mallard is the most numerous duck in Illinois and can be seen almost any day of the year. Often found in flocks near open water, it is the most popular duck with waterfowl hunters. The male is easily recognized by his iridescent green head and chestnut breast. • These ducks have been known to use backyard feeding stations and swimming pools. They also nest atop chimneys, in trees and in suburban backyards. • As well as captivating female American Black Ducks, wild Mallards freely hybridize with domestic ducks. The resulting offspring are a confusing blend of both parents. Mallards establish pair bonds in fall and court all winter. After breeding, male ducks molt, losing much of their extravagant plumage, which helps to camouflage them during the flightless period. They usually molt again into their breeding colors by early fall.

ID: dark blue speculum bordered with white; orange feet. *Male:* glossy, green head; yellow bill; chestnut brown breast; white "necklace"; gray body plumage; black tail feathers curl upward. *Female:* mottled brown overall; orange bill is spattered with black.
Size: *L* 20–27½ in; *W* 35 in.
Status: abundant migrant; common breeder; common to abundant winter resident; spring migrants arrive in February; fall migrants arrive in September, mingling with large breeding and wintering flocks.
Habitat: *Breeding:* open wetlands with emergent vegetation. *In migration* and *winter:* lakes, rivers, flooded fields, bottomland forests and sewage lagoons.

Nesting: in grasslands or dry areas bordering wetlands, occasionally far from water; nest of grass and other plant material is lined with down; female incubates 7–10 light green to white eggs for 26–30 days.
Feeding: tips up and dabbles in shallows for the seeds of sedges, willows and pondweeds; also eats aquatic invertebrates, larval amphibians and fish eggs.
Voice: *Male:* deep, loud quacks. *Female:* deep, loud quacks; very vocal.
Similar Species: *Northern Shoveler* (p. 48): much longer, broader bill; male has white breast. *American Black Duck* (p. 44): darker than female Mallard; purple speculum lacks white borders. *Other female dabblers* (pp. 41–50): lack blue to purple speculum.
Best Sites: La Salle Nuclear Power Plant; L. Chautauqua; Carlyle L.; Crab Orchard NWR; Horseshoe Lake CA; Union County CA.

BLUE-WINGED TEAL

Anas discors

The Blue-winged Teal is one of the last duck species to arrive at breeding sites in spring and the first to depart in the fall. These ducks often wait to establish pair bonds until they are on their breeding grounds. As a result, Bluewings have more nests concentrated in a small area than any other waterfowl. • The small, speedy Blue-winged Teal possesses keen aviation skills. These teals can be identified in flight by their small size, their sharp twists and turns and the powdery blue color of their wings. • Despite the similarity of their names, this bird's closest relative is not the Green-winged Teal. The Blue-winged Teal is more closely related to the Cinnamon Teal and the Northern Shoveler.

ID: *Male:* blue gray head; white crescent on face; black-spotted breast and sides. *Female:* mottled brown overall. *In flight:* blue shoulder patch; green speculum.
Size: *L* 14–16 in; *W* 23 in.
Status: common migrant from early March to mid-May and from early August to early November; most common breeding duck species, decreasing southward; very rare winter resident.
Habitat: *Breeding:* grasslands bordering wetlands with emergent vegetation. *In migration:* shallow lake and pond edges, sloughs and flooded fields.
Nesting: in a grassland or meadow; nest is built with grass and considerable amounts of down; female incubates 8–13 white eggs for 23–27 days.
Feeding: gleans the water's surface for sedges, grass seeds, pondweeds, duckweeds and aquatic invertebrates.
Voice: *Male:* soft *keck-keck-keck*. *Female:* soft quacks.
Similar Species: *Cinnamon Teal* (p. 47): female is virtually identical to female Blue-winged Teal but has plainer face, blackish crown and larger bill. *Green-winged Teal* (p. 50): female has smaller bill, green speculum and buffy area on undertail coverts; also lacks blue shoulder patch. *Northern Shoveler* (p. 48): larger; much longer, broader bill; male has green head, white breast and bright rufous flanks; female has orange on bill.
Best Sites: L. Chautauqua; Carlyle L.

CINNAMON TEAL

Anas cyanoptera

A western species, the Cinnamon Teal is rarely but regularly seen in Illinois each year. If this duck is not in breeding plumage, it can be difficult to identify. However, when the morning sun strikes a spring wetland, a male Cinnamon Teal in breeding plumage glows upon the water with its intense reddish brown coloration accented by ruby red eyes. • In Illinois, a single or, very rarely, a pair of Cinnamon Teals may congregate with other teal species and shovelers. • The scientific name—*cyano*, meaning "blue," and *pteron*, meaning "wing"—reinforces the similarities of this species to the Blue-winged Teal, with which it may occasionally interbreed. • Several hybrids, as well as one Cinnamon Teal–Northern Shoveler hybrid, have been found in Illinois.

VAGRANT

ID: long, broad bill; blue forewing patch; green speculum. *Male:* intense cinnamon red head, neck and underparts; red eyes. *Female:* mottled, warm brown overall; dark eyes. **Size:** *L* 15–17 in; *W* 22 in. **Status:** regular vagrant with most sightings from mid-March to early May; few fall records from August to mid-November. **Habitat:** shallow wetlands with emergent vegetation.

Nesting: does not nest in Illinois. **Feeding:** dabbles in shallow water for grass, sedge seeds, pondweeds, duckweeds and aquatic invertebrates; occasionally tips up. **Voice:** *Male:* whistled *peep. Female:* rough *karr, karr, karr.* **Similar Species:** *Green-winged Teal* (p. 50): smaller, narrower bill; gray body; male has green-and-rust head; female has 2-tone face and is darker overall. *Blue-winged Teal* (p. 46): smaller, narrower bill; male has white crescent in front of eye; female has 2-tone face. **Best Sites:** anywhere statewide, but most records from Carlyle L. and L. Springfield.

47

NORTHERN SHOVELER

Anas clypeata

When meeting this bird for the first time, you may mistake it for a Mallard with an extra-large bill. The Northern Shoveler has a shovel-like bill that allows it to strain small invertebrates from the water and the mud on pond bottoms. The shoveler, with its head and bill constantly moving, draws water into its bill and then pumps it out through the sides with its tongue, filtering minute food particles with long, comblike hairs that line the bill's edge. Shovelers also engage in group feeding: a tightly packed flock spins either clockwise or counterclockwise to create a whirlpool effect, churning up food and bringing it to the flock's center. • During the breeding season, male Northern Shovelers fiercely defend small feeding territories; however, they are remarkably sociable in migration and on their wintering grounds. • The scientific name *clypeata* is Latin for "furnished with a shield," possibly for the reddish patches on the flanks of the male.

ID: large, spatulate bill; powder blue forewing patch; green speculum. *Male:* green head; white breast; chestnut brown flanks. *Female:* mottled brown overall; orange-tinged bill.
Size: *L* 18–20 in; *W* 34 in.
Status: common migrant from mid-February to early March through mid-May and from mid-August to early December; rare breeder in the northern and central parts of the state; casual winter resident.
Habitat: shallow marshes, sloughs, flooded fields, ponds and lakes with muddy bottoms and emergent vegetation.

Nesting: in a shallow hollow on dry ground, near water; female builds a nest with dry grass and down and incubates 10–12 pale greenish buff eggs for 21–28 days.
Feeding: dabbles in shallow and often muddy water; strains out aquatic crustaceans, insect larvae and seeds; occasionally tips up.
Voice: generally quiet; occasionally a raspy quack, often heard during courtship.
Similar Species: *Mallard* (p. 45): deep blue speculum bordered by white; lacks powder blue forewing patch; male has chestnut brown breast and white flanks. *Blue-winged Teal* (p. 46): smaller overall; much shorter, narrower bill; male has spotted breast and sides.
Best Sites: L. Chautauqua; Carlyle L.

NORTHERN PINTAIL
Anas acuta

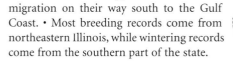

The trademark of the elegant and graceful male Northern Pintail is its long, tapering tail feathers, which are easily seen in flight and point skyward when he dabbles. In Illinois, only the male Long-tailed Duck shares this pintail feature. • Most abundant in the western United States, migrating pintails can still be seen in Illinois in flocks of 20 to 40 birds, rarely numbering to the thousands. Spring-flooded agricultural fields attract pintail flocks, which typically consist of twice as many males as females. • This widespread duck appears to be declining across its main range in central and western North America. At one time, 300,000 pintails used the Mississippi River corridor in Illinois during fall migration on their way south to the Gulf Coast. • Most breeding records come from northeastern Illinois, while wintering records come from the southern part of the state.

ID: long, slender neck; dark, glossy bill. *Male:* chocolate brown head; long, tapering tail feathers; white on breast extends up sides of neck and narrows into white stripe; brown head; dusty gray body plumage; black-and-white hindquarters. *Female:* mottled, light brown overall. *In flight:* slender body; brownish speculum with white trailing edge.
Size: *L* 21–25 in; *W* 34 in.
Status: rare to locally common migrant from early to mid-February through mid-April and from mid- to late August through late November; very rare breeder in the north; fairly common winter resident, decreasing northward.
Habitat: *Breeding:* drier areas of wetlands with emergent vegetation. *In migration:* lakes, ponds, marshes and agricultural fields.

Nesting: in a small depression in vegetation; nest of grass, leaves and moss is lined with down; female incubates 6–12 greenish buff eggs for 22–25 days.
Feeding: tips up and dabbles in shallows for the seeds of sedges, willows and pondweeds; also eats aquatic invertebrates and larval amphibians; eats waste grain in agricultural areas during migration; diet is more varied than that of other dabbling ducks.
Voice: *Male:* soft, whistling call. *Female:* rough quack.
Similar Species: male is distinctive. *Mallard* (p. 45) and *Gadwall* (p. 42): females are chunkier, usually with 2-tone bills; lack tapering tail and long, slender neck. *Blue-winged Teal* (p. 46): green speculum; powder blue forewing patch; female is smaller.
Best Sites: Illinois R. and Mississippi R. corridors, especially at L. Chautauqua; Carlyle L.

49

GREEN-WINGED TEAL

Anas crecca

Green-winged Teals fly swiftly and deftly. When falcons and other hawks cause these small ducks to rocket from wetlands, the birds circle quickly overhead in small, tight-flying flocks, returning to the water only when the threat has disappeared. Female Green-winged Teals carefully conceal their nests among grasses and brush, but some predators still discover their eggs and nestlings. • Weighing less than a pound, the Green-winged Teal is the smallest dabbling duck in North America. This lovely little teal often loiters on ponds and wetlands in Illinois until cold winter weather freezes the water's surface. • The name "teal" possibly originated from the medieval English word *tele* or the old Dutch word *teling*, both of which mean "small" and originally referred to the Green-winged Teal's Eurasian counterpart.

ID: small bill; green-and-black speculum; buffy area on undertail coverts. *Male:* chestnut brown head; green swipe extends back from eye; white shoulder slash; creamy breast is spotted with black; pale gray sides. *Female:* mottled brown overall; light belly.
Size: *L* 12–16 in; *W* 23 in.
Status: fairly common migrant from mid-February to early March through late April to early May and from mid-August through early December; rare breeder in the north; uncommon winter resident, mainly in far southern Illinois.

Habitat: emergent vegetation on mudflats and in shallow ponds and wetlands.
Nesting: well concealed in tall, grassy vegetation; nest is built of grass and leaves and lined with down; female incubates 6–14 cream to pale buff eggs for 20–24 days.
Feeding: dabbles in shallows, particularly on mudflats, for aquatic invertebrates, larval amphibians, marsh plant seeds and pondweeds.
Voice: *Male:* crisp whistle. *Female:* soft quack.
Similar Species: *American Wigeon* (p. 43): larger, cream head patch. *Blue-winged Teal* (p. 46) and *Cinnamon Teal* (p. 47): females have blue forewing patch.
Best Sites: L. Chautauqua; Carlyle L.; Horseshoe Lake SP.

CANVASBACK
Aythya valisineria

While most male ducks sport richly decorated backs, the back of the male Canvasback is bright and clean and looks like it is wrapped in white canvas. In profile, the Canvasback casts a noble image—the long bill meets the forecrown with no apparent break in angle, allowing birds of either sex to be distinguished at long range. • One of the earliest ducks to arrive in Illinois in spring, Canvasbacks seldom stray into wetlands that are too shallow to allow foraging dives. • Along the Illinois and Mississippi rivers in western Illinois, thousands to the tens of thousands of Canvasbacks flock in winter, creating a spectacular sight. Nevertheless, its numbers have declined greatly since the 1940s because of habitat degradation and loss of food sources. • The scientific name *valisineria* refers to one of the Canvasback's favorite foods— wild celery, *Vallisneria americana.*

ID: head slopes upward from bill to forehead. *Male:* canvas white back; chestnut brown head; black breast and hindquarters; red eyes. *Female:* profile is similar to male; dull brown head and neck; grayish back and sides.

Size: *L* 19–22 in; *W* 29 in.

Status: rare to locally common migrant from early to mid-February through early April and from mid-October to mid-December; rare breeder in northeastern Illinois; rare to locally abundant winter resident, mainly on upper Mississippi R.

Habitat: *Breeding:* open wetlands with emergent vegetation. *In migration:* large rivers and deep lakes.

Nesting: basket nest of reeds and grass is lined with down and suspended above shallow water in dense stands of cattails and bulrushes; may also nest on dry ground; female incubates 7–9 olive green eggs for up to 29 days.

Feeding: dives to depths of up to 30 ft (average is 10–15 ft); feeds on duck potato, basal stems of plants, including pondweeds and wild celery, and bulrush seeds; also eats aquatic invertebrates, especially larval midges, mayflies, small clams and snails.

Voice: generally quiet. *Male:* occasional coos and "growls" during courtship. *Female:* low, soft, purring quack or *kuck;* also growls.

Similar Species: *Redhead* (p. 52): rounded rather than sloped forehead; male has gray back and bluish bill.

Best Sites: Illinois R. and Mississippi R., especially in the Nauvoo region and at L. Chautauqua.

REDHEAD

Aythya americana

The best way to distinguish a Canvasback from a Redhead is by the profile. Also, they can be identified by the color of their backs: the Canvasback has a white back whereas the Redhead's is gray. • In the early part of the 20th century, abundant food sources attracted large numbers of ducks including Ring-necked, Canvasback and Redhead species to the Illinois River valley. The Redhead is a diving duck, but also feeds on the surface of a wetland or lake, searching for pondweeds and midge larvae like a dabbler, especially in fall. These ducks dive to the bottom of lakes to gather small snails and fingernail clams, and also freshwater plants and their seeds. In the late 20th century, however, food supplies for diving ducks nearly disappeared in some parts of Illinois and populations of diving ducks, especially Redheads, declined in those regions. This species is in an overall decline throughout North America.

ID: blue gray, black-tipped bill. *Male:* rounded, red head; black breast and hindquarters; gray back and sides. *Female:* dark brown overall; light "chin" and "cheek" patches.
Size: *L* 18–22 in; *W* 29 in.
Status: rare to uncommon migrant from mid-February to early March through early April and from early October to early December; very rare breeder in the north; uncommon to rare winter resident, mainly along upper Mississippi R. and southern Illinois reservoirs.
Habitat: ponds, lakes, open marshes, large rivers.
Nesting: usually in shallow water of marshes, sometimes on dry ground; deep basket nest of reeds and grass is lined with fine, white down and suspended over water at the base of emergent vegetation;

female incubates 9–14 eggs for 23–29 days; female may lay eggs in other ducks' nests.
Feeding: dives to depths of at least 10 ft; primarily eats aquatic vegetation, especially pondweeds, duckweeds and the leaves and stems of plants; occasionally eats aquatic invertebrates, small clams and other mollusks.
Voice: generally quiet. *Male:* catlike *meow* in courtship. *Female:* rolling *kurr-kurr-kurr; squak* when alarmed.
Similar Species: *Canvasback* (p. 51): clean white back; bill extends onto forehead. *Ring-necked Duck* (p. 53): female has more prominent, white eye ring, white ring on bill and peaked head. *Lesser Scaup* (p. 55) and *Greater Scaup* (p. 54): male has dark head and white sides; female has white at base of bill; prominent white wing stripe, not bar.
Best Sites: L. Michigan; Illinois R. and Mississippi R., especially Nauvoo region and L. Chautauqua.

RING-NECKED DUCK

Aythya collaris

After seeing this duck in the wild, birders may wonder why it was not named the "Ring-billed Duck." The scientific name *collaris* originated when an ornithologist observed an indistinct cinnamon "collar" on a museum specimen, but the ring around the bill is much more visible than the one around the collar. • Ring-necked Ducks are generalized feeders, allowing them to capitalize on various resources found in the subarctic and boreal settings where they commonly nest. Although Ring-necks are diving ducks, like scaups, Redheads and Canvasbacks, they behave more like dabbling ducks, occasionally tipping up for food and hiding their young in dense vegetation. • Ring-necked Ducks can spring vertically from the water's surface to become airborne. Also, compared with other diving ducks, they feed in shallower water, typically less than 6 feet deep. They can sometimes be seen in flooded fields in Illinois during migration. • Illinois is a major migration pathway for this species on its way to its Florida, Louisiana and Mississippi wintering grounds.

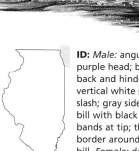

ID: *Male:* angular, dark purple head; black breast, back and hindquarters; vertical white shoulder slash; gray sides; blue gray bill with black and white bands at tip; thin, white border around base of bill. *Female:* dark brown overall; gray head; white eye ring; dark bill with black and white bands at tip; pale crescent on front of face.
Size: *L* 14–18 in; *W* 25 in.
Status: common migrant from mid-February to late April and from mid-October to early December; few breeding records exist; uncommon winter resident, mostly in southern Illinois.
Habitat: *Breeding:* open wetlands with emergent vegetation. *In migration* and *winter:* lakes, wooded ponds, marshes, sloughs and flooded fields.

Nesting: frequently over water; rarely on a shoreline; bulky nest of grass and moss is lined with down; female incubates 8–10 olive tan eggs for 25–29 days.
Feeding: tips up or dives underwater for aquatic vegetation, including seeds, tubers and pondweeds; also eats aquatic invertebrates.
Voice: seldom heard. *Male:* low-pitched, hissing whistle. *Female:* growling *churr.*
Similar Species: *Lesser Scaup* (p. 55) and *Greater Scaup* (p. 54): lacks white ring toward tip of bill; male lack white shoulder slash and black back; female has broad, more clearly defined white border around base of bill. *Redhead* (p. 52): rounded rather than peaked head; less white on front of face; female has paler back and less prominent eye ring.
Best Sites: Rend L.; L. Chautauqua; Carlyle L.

53

GREATER SCAUP
Aythya marila

Substantial flocks of Greater Scaup migrate and winter along and on Lake Michigan, where they can be seen alongside Lesser Scaup. • Look for the rounder, not peaked, more greenish head of the Greater Scaup to distinguish it from its Lesser relative. Greater Scaup and Lesser Scaup often raft far out in the water, making it hard to distinguish between the two species. As a result, many Greater Scaup may go unidentified; however, numbers of this species peak on Lake Michigan after most of the Lesser have left for the season. • Scaups are diving ducks, thus have heavier bones and require a running start across the water's surface to gain takeoff. • Both Greater Scaup and Lesser Scaup are known by the nickname "Bluebill."

ID: rounded head; golden eyes. *Male:* iridescent, dark green head; black breast; white belly and flanks; light gray back; dark hindquarters; blue bill with black tip. *Female:* brown overall; well-defined white patch at base of bill. *In flight:* white stripe through wing extends well into primary feathers.
Size: *L* 16–19 in; *W* 28 in.
Status: common migrant and winter resident along L. Michigan; rare elsewhere; spring migrants occur from mid-February to mid-April; fall migrants arrive in early to mid-October; fall departure dates obscured by wintering birds.
Habitat: large lakes, reservoirs and rivers.

Nesting: does not nest in Illinois.
Feeding: dives underwater, to greater depths than other *Aythya* ducks, for aquatic invertebrates, including clams and mussels, especially in winter; also eats pondweeds and wild celery.
Voice: generally quiet in migration; alarm call is a deep *scaup*. *Male:* may issue a 3-note whistle and a soft *wah-hooo*. *Female:* may give a subtle growl.
Similar Species: *Lesser Scaup* (p. 55): slightly smaller; shorter, white wing stripe in flight; male has peaked, purplish head; female usually has peaked head. *Ring-necked Duck* (p. 53): black back; vertical white shoulder slash; white ring around base and near tip of bill. *Redhead* (p. 52): male has red head and darker sides; female has little or no white at base of bill.
Best Sites: L. Michigan.

LESSER SCAUP

Aythya affinis

In spring and fall migration, this species is most commonly found between Oquawka and Warsaw, Illinois, along the Mississippi River. The Lesser Scaup is one of the most abundant and widespread of the North American ducks and one of the most numerous in Illinois. Early migrant flocks are composed of more males and later flocks consist mostly of females. • Lesser Scaups leap up neatly before diving underwater, where they propel themselves with powerful strokes of their feet. • The scientific name *affinis* is Latin for "adjacent" or "allied"—a reference to this scaup's close association to other diving ducks. "Scaup" might refer to a preferred winter food of this duck—shellfish beds are called "scalps" in Scotland—or it might be a phonetic imitation of one of its calls.

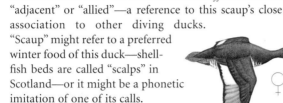

ID: yellow eyes. *Male:* dark, purplish head is peaked; black breast and hindquarters; dusty white sides; grayish back; blue gray, black-tipped bill. *Female:* dark brown overall; well-defined white patch at base of bill.
Size: *L* 15–18 in; *W* 25 in.

Status: common to abundant migrant from mid-February through late April or early May and from early to mid-October through early November; very rare breeder in northeastern and central Illinois; uncommon winter resident.
Habitat: *Breeding:* open wetlands with emergent vegetation. *In migration:* large lakes, ponds and sewage lagoons.
Nesting: in tall, concealing vegetation, generally close to water and occasionally on an island; nest hollow is built of grass

and lined with down; female incubates 8–14 olive buff eggs for 21–27 days; usually nests later than other ducks.
Feeding: dives underwater for fish and aquatic invertebrates, mostly crayfish, shrimp and insect larvae; occasionally takes pondweeds, wigeon grass, wild rice and wild celery.
Voice: alarm call is a deep *scaup. Male:* soft *whee-oooh* in courtship. *Female:* purring *kwah.*
Similar Species: *Greater Scaup* (p. 54): longer white wing stripe in flight; rounded head; male has greenish head. *Ring-necked Duck* (p. 53): white at tip of bill; male has white shoulder slash and black back. *Redhead* (p. 52): male has red head and darker sides; female has less white at base of bill.
Best Sites: L. Michigan; Clinton L.; Carlyle L.; Illinois and Mississippi River valleys.

55

HARLEQUIN DUCK

Histrionicus histrionicus

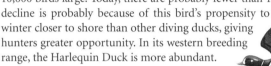

The small, surf-loving Harlequin Duck is a rare migrant and winter visitor to Illinois, where it occupies the rocky shoreline of Lake Michigan. This bird typically occurs singly or in very small groups, and often stays for several days in one place. The male's breeding plumage is spectacular—a slate blue head patterned in white—but most birds seen in Illinois are immatures or females. • Harlequin Ducks breed in two disjunct populations: one group in the mountains of western North America through western Canada and much of Alaska; the other in Atlantic Canada, Greenland and Iceland. The East Coast breeding population was once roughly 5000 to 10,000 birds large. Today, there are probably fewer than 1000. The decline is probably because of this bird's propensity to winter closer to shore than other diving ducks, giving hunters greater opportunity. In its western breeding range, the Harlequin Duck is more abundant.

ID: small, rounded duck; blocky head; short bill; raises and lowers tail while swimming. *Male:* blue gray body; chestnut brown sides; white spots and stripes outlined in black on head, neck and flanks. *Female* and *immature:* dusky brown overall; light-colored underparts; 2–3 pale patches on head.
Size: *L* 14–19 in; *W* 26 in.
Status: rare but regular migrant and winter visitor on L. Michigan; very rare downstate; occurs from mid-October to mid-April, with spring migrants arriving in mid-March

and departing by mid-April and fall migrants arriving from mid-October to mid-November.
Habitat: large lakes and rivers.
Nesting: does not nest in Illinois.
Feeding: tips up or dives for crustaceans, especially crabs, mollusks and aquatic insects.
Voice: generally silent outside the breeding season.
Similar Species: male is distinctive. *Bufflehead* (p. 61): smaller; female lacks white between eye and bill. *Surf Scoter* (p. 57): larger; female has bulbous bill. *White-winged Scoter* (p. 58): larger; female has white wing patch and bulbous bill.
Best Sites: L. Michigan.

SURF SCOTER

Melanitta perspicillata

O f the three scoter species found in Illinois, the Surf Scoter is the most likely to be seen on downstate lakes. With its secretive nesting habits, the Surf Scoter is the least studied of all North American ducks. • These scoters are most often seen in Illinois during spring and fall migration, but more females and immatures are seen than breeding males. Surf Scoters have irregular flock formations and do not fly in a line like White-winged Scoters. • Compared to the White-winged Scoter, the Surf is more abundant on the Pacific Coast than the Atlantic. It is the only one of the three scoter species whose range is confined to North America; the other two can also be found in Eurasia. • This species breeds in northern Canada and Alaska and winters along the eastern and western coasts of North America. It is well adapted to life on rough waters. • The scientific name *Melanitta* means "black duck"; *perspicillata* is Latin for "spectacular," probably referring to this bird's colorful, bulbous bill.

1st winter ♂

ID: large, stocky duck; large bill; sloping forehead. *Breeding male:* black overall; white on forehead and back of neck; orange bill and legs; black spot, outlined in white, at base of bill. *Female* and *immature:* brown overall; dark gray bill; 2 whitish patches on sides of head.
Size: *L* 16–20 in; *W* 30 in.
Status: uncommon migrant and rare winter resident on L. Michigan; uncommon migrant elsewhere; occurs from mid-March to early May and from mid-October to late November.

Habitat: lakes, large rivers and reservoirs.
Nesting: does not nest in Illinois.
Feeding: dives to depths of 30 ft; eats mostly clams and mussels; also takes aquatic insect larvae, crustaceans and some aquatic vegetation as well as fish eggs.
Voice: generally quiet; infrequently utters low, harsh croaks. *Male:* liquid gurgling and explosive *puk-puk. Female:* crowlike *krraak krraak;* wings whistle in flight.
Similar Species: *White-winged Scoter* (p. 58): white wing patches; male lacks white on forehead and nape. *Black Scoter* (p. 59): male is all black; female has well-defined, pale "cheek."
Best Sites: L. Michigan and large downstate reservoirs.

WHITE-WINGED SCOTER
Melanitta fusca

In flight, the wings of the White-winged Scoter reveal a key identifying feature—the white inner-wing patches strike a sharp contrast with the bird's otherwise black plumage. The most likely scoter to be seen in winter, the White-winged Scoter is the largest of the three scoter species found in Illinois and the most common on Lake Michigan. More females and immatures are seen than breeding males. • Because scoters have small wings relative to the weight of their bodies, they require long stretches of water for takeoff. However, once in the air their flight is swift and direct. • Just before diving, scoters have the peculiar habit of flipping out their wings. • The White-winged Scoter often eats hard-shelled clams and shellfishes whole. It relies on its remarkably powerful gizzard to crush shells that would normally require a hammer to open. • The name "scoter" may be derived from the way this bird scoots across the water's surface.

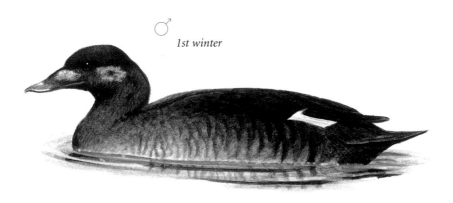

♂ 1st winter

ID: stocky; large; sloping forehead; base of bill is fully feathered. *Male:* black overall; white patch immediately below and behind eye; bill has slight knob and is orangy on adult; white wing patches often seen even when bird is resting on water. *Female* and *immature:* brown overall; grayish bill; 2 whitish patches on sides of head. *In flight:* white wing patches.
Size: *L* 18–24 in; *W* 34 in.
Status: uncommon to locally common migrant and occasional winter resident on L. Michigan; rare migrant and winter resident elsewhere; migrants mostly occur from early February to mid-April and from early October to late November.

Habitat: lakes, large rivers and reservoirs.
Nesting: does not nest in Illinois.
Feeding: underwater dives up to 40 ft deep may last up to 1 minute; eats mostly mollusks; may also take crustaceans, aquatic insects and some small fish.
Voice: courting pair produces harsh, guttural noises, between a *crook* and a quack; wings whistle in flight.
Similar Species: *Surf Scoter* (p. 57): lacks white wing patches; male has white forehead and nape. *Black Scoter* (p. 59): lacks white patches in wings and around eyes. *American Coot* (p. 117): whitish bill and nasal shield; lacks white patches in wings and around red eyes.
Best Sites: L. Michigan and downstate reservoirs.

BLACK SCOTER
Melanitta nigra

These handsome birds are the least common scoter species in Illinois and can be spotted resting on Lake Michigan and other large bodies of water during migration. Most scoters move from the Great Lakes to the coasts, so they are rarer in downstate Illinois. Most Black Scoters breed in Alaska and near the James Bay region in Canada. Most winter in the Aleutian Islands and the northeastern coast of the United States. All three scoter species have been in a steady population decline since the late 1950s. Habitat disturbance, oil spills, lead contamination and heavy metals in prey may be causing their numbers to decrease. • Unlike the other scoters, the Black Scoter throws its head downward while exercising its wings, but floats on the water's surface with its head held high; the other scoters tend to look downward while floating. • Black Scoters are the only uniformly black North American duck and are the most vocal of the scoters, often giving away their presence with their plaintive, mellow, whistling calls from far out on open water.

♂

1st winter

ID: *Male:* black overall; large orange knob on bill. *Female:* light "cheek"; dark "cap"; brown overall; dark gray bill.
Size: *L* 17–20 in; *W* 28 in.
Status: uncommon migrant on L. Michigan; rare migrant elsewhere; occurs from late February to mid-April and from mid-October to late November.
Habitat: large, deep lakes and rivers.
Nesting: does not nest in Illinois.
Feeding: dives underwater; eats mostly mollusks and aquatic insect larvae; occasionally eats aquatic vegetation and small fish.
Voice: generally quiet; occasionally an unusual *cour-loo;* wings whistle in flight.
Similar Species: *White-winged Scoter* (p. 58): white wing patch; male has white patch below eye. *Surf Scoter* (p. 57): male has white patches on forehead and nape; female has 2 whitish patches on sides of head. *Ruddy Duck* (p. 66): female and immature are smaller, have dark line across "cheek" and stiff, cocked tail.
Best Sites: L. Michigan and downstate reservoirs.

LONG-TAILED DUCK

Clangula hyemalis

The Long-tailed Duck often remains in deeper waters, well away from shore, limiting observers to brief glimpses of its long, slender tail feathers. It is not adept at walking on land, but is a skilled diver, often descending to depths of 200 feet. • The breeding and nonbreeding plumages of the Long-tailed Duck are opposites: their spring breeding plumage is mostly dark with white highlights and their winter plumage is mostly white with dark patches. Most birds seen in Illinois are in their winter plumage. • Until recently, this duck, with its circumpolar distribution, was called "Oldsquaw." • Long-tailed Duck numbers have declined drastically on Lake Michigan since the 1950s, possibly because of the same environmental contaminants plaguing other waterfowl species.

nonbreeding

ID: *Breeding male:* dark head; white eye patch; dark neck and upperparts; white belly; pink and black bill; long, dark central tail feathers. *Breeding female:* short tail feathers; gray bill; dark crown, throat patch, wings and back; white underparts. *Nonbreeding male:* pale head with dark patch; pale neck and belly; dark breast; long, white patches on back; pink bill with dark base; long, dark central tail feathers. *Nonbreeding female:* similar to nonbreeding male, but generally lighter, especially on head.
Size: *L* 17–20 in; *W* 28 in.

Status: fairly common migrant and winter resident on L. Michigan; rare migrant and winter resident elsewhere; occurs from late February to early April, with a few early May stragglers, and from late October to early December.
Habitat: lakes, large rivers and reservoirs.
Nesting: does not nest in Illinois.
Feeding: dives for mollusks, crustaceans, fish, fish eggs and aquatic insects; occasionally eats roots and young shoots; most varied diet of sea ducks.
Voice: courtship call is *ow-ow-owlet*, heard less frequently during winter.
Similar Species: *Northern Pintail* (p. 49): male has brown head, all-black bill, black undertail coverts, white line extending up sides of neck, all-white breast and gray sides.
Best Sites: L. Michigan.

BUFFLEHEAD

Bucephala albeola

In their boreal forest summer homes, these ducks usually nest in old flicker holes. Bufflehead males move jerkily and bob their heads frequently to attract the females. They also make short flights over the females, displaying their feet and plumage when landing. • Unlike many diving ducks, Buffleheads migrate in small to moderate-sized flocks and are able to take off from the water without needing a running start along the surface. • A fast flier and one of our smallest ducks, the Bufflehead sometimes feeds in small groups, with some diving and others staying alert for danger. • The Bufflehead is actually a small goldeneye, as similarities in its profile, behavior and scientific name will show. The common name refers to this duck's large head and sloped forehead, which are similar in shape to those of a buffalo. The scientific name *Bucephala*, meaning "ox-headed" in Greek, also refers to the shape of this bird's head; *albeola* is Latin for "white," referring to the male's plumage.

ID: very small, rounded duck; short, gray bill; short neck; white speculum in flight. *Male:* white wedge on back of head; head is otherwise iridescent, dark green or purple, usually appearing black; dark back; white neck and underparts. *Female:* dark brown head; white, oval ear patch; light brown sides.
Size: *L* 13–15 in; *W* 21 in.
Status: common migrant statewide from late February to early May and from mid-October to early December; uncommon winter resident.
Habitat: lakes, ponds, rivers and sewage lagoons.
Nesting: does not nest in Illinois.

Feeding: dives for aquatic invertebrates; takes water boatmen along with mayfly and damselfly larvae in summer; favors mollusks, particularly snails, and crustaceans in winter; also eats some small fish and pondweeds.
Voice: *Male:* growling call. *Female:* harsh quack.
Similar Species: *Hooded Merganser* (p. 63): male's white crest is outlined in black. *Harlequin Duck* (p. 56): female and immature have variable amounts of white between bill and eye. *Common Goldeneye* (p. 62): larger; yellow eyes; male has white patch between eye and bill; female has no white on head. *Other diving ducks* (pp. 51–66): females are much larger.
Best Sites: L. Michigan and large, downstate reservoirs.

61

COMMON GOLDENEYE
Bucephala clangula

The male Common Goldeneye performs an interesting winter courtship, arching his puffy, iridescent head backward until his forehead seems to touch his back. Next, he catapults his neck forward like a coiled spring, while producing a *peent* sound. • Hooded Mergansers, Wood Ducks and other duck species often lay their eggs in Common Goldeneye nests. • *Clangula* comes from the Latin word *clanger* meaning noise, and probably refers to the whistling sound made by their wings while they are in flight. • Along with the Common Merganser, the Common Goldeneye is one of the last ducks to arrive in Illinois in fall.

ID: steep forehead with peaked crown; black wings with large, white patches; golden eyes. *Male:* dark, iridescent, green head; round, white "cheek" patch; dark bill; dark back; white sides and belly. *Female:* chocolate brown head; lighter breast and belly; gray brown body plumage; dark bill, tipped with yellow in spring and summer.
Size: *L* 16–20 in; *W* 26 in.
Status: common migrant; fairly common to common winter resident; spring migration is obscured by the wintering population but influxes occur by late February, with most birds departing by mid-April; fall migrants arrive in late October to early November.

Habitat: lakes, ponds and rivers.
Nesting: does not nest in Illinois.
Feeding: dives for crustaceans, mollusks and aquatic insect larvae; may also eat tubers, leeches, frogs and small fish.
Voice: *Male:* courtship calls are a nasal *peent* and a hoarse *kraaagh. Female:* harsh croak.
Similar Species: *Barrow's Goldeneye* (p. 356): extremely rare; longer, flatter crown; steeper forehead; male has more black on back; black on upper back separates white breast from white of undersides; male also has large, white, crescent-shaped "cheek" patch; female has mostly yellowish bill; some female Common Goldeneyes have similar trait.
Best Sites: L. Michigan and downstate rivers and lakes.

HOODED MERGANSER
Lophodytes cucullatus

Extremely attractive, the Hooded Merganser mostly holds his fan-shaped crest flat. But when aroused or agitated, he quickly unfolds his brilliant black-and-white crest. The drake displays his full range of colors and athletic abilities in elaborate, late-winter courtship displays and chases. He must put on an impressive show because there are usually twice as many males as there are females. • All mergansers have thin bills with small, toothlike serrations to help the birds keep a firm grasp on slippery prey. The smallest of the mergansers, Hoodies have a more diverse diet than their larger relatives. They add crustaceans, insects and even acorns to the usual diet of fish. • Hooded Mergansers are found in fairly small flocks during migration compared with other ducks. • The Hooded Merganser is the only other duck besides the Wood Duck that nests in cavities in Illinois.

ID: slim body; crested head; dark, thin, pointed bill. *Male:* black head and back; bold, white crest outlined in black; white breast with 2 black slashes; rusty sides. *Female:* dusky brown body; shaggy, reddish brown crest. *In flight:* small, white wing patches.

Size: *L* 16–18 in; *W* 24 in.

Status: common migrant from mid-February to mid- to late April; birds seen after early May are likely breeding; fall migrants arrive in late October; uncommon, regular breeder; casual to fairly common winter resident.

Habitat: *Breeding:* forested wetlands, especially swamps and sloughs. *In migration* and *winter:* lakes, ponds, rivers and reservoirs.

Nesting: usually in a tree cavity 15–40 ft above the ground; may also use a nest box;

cavity is lined with leaves, grass and down; female incubates 10–12 spherical, white eggs for 29–33 days; some females may lay their eggs in other birds' nests, including nests of other species and Wood Duck boxes.

Feeding: diverse diet; dives for small fish, caddisfly and dragonfly larvae, snails, amphibians and crayfish.

Voice: low grunts and croaks. *Male:* frog-like *crrrrooo* in courtship display. *Female:* generally quiet; occasionally a harsh *gak* or a croaking *croo-croo-crook*.

Similar Species: *Bufflehead* (p. 61): male has white body with more white on wings and lacks black outline to crest. *Red-breasted Merganser* (p. 65) and *Common Merganser* (p. 64): larger; females have much longer, orange bills and gray backs; Red-breasted has red eyes; Common has dark eyes.

Best Sites: Palos Preserves wetlands; L. Chautauqua.

63

COMMON MERGANSER

Mergus merganser

Like most diving ducks, the Common Merganser runs along the surface of the water beating its wings rapidly to become airborne. This great duck flies arrow-straight, low over the water, making broad sweeping turns to follow meandering rivers and lake shorelines. • The Common Merganser is the most widespread and abundant merganser in North America and one of Illinois' most common winter ducks. It can also be found in Europe and Asia, where it is known as the "Goosander." In January and February, hundreds to thousands of this species are recorded at favored sites. Any source of open water containing whitefish, trout and any small fish can support many of these skilled divers. • Several summer records exist for this species, though it has never bred in Illinois. This cavity-nesting species breeds mostly in Canada's boreal zone and in the mountainous regions of the western United States. • A hardy species, the Common Merganser may not appear in large numbers in Illinois until mid- to late December or after ice-up has occurred farther north. • "Merganser" is derived from the Latin words meaning "diving goose."

ID: large, elongated body. *Male:* glossy, green head without crest; blood red bill and feet; white body plumage; black stripe on back; dark eyes. *Female:* rusty neck and crested head; clean white "chin" and breast; orange bill; gray body; orangy eyes. *In flight:* shallow wingbeats; body is compressed and arrowlike.
Size: L 22–27 in; W 34 in.
Status: common winter resident.
Habitat: lakes, large rivers, reservoirs and power plant cooling lakes.

Nesting: does not nest in Illinois.
Feeding: dives to depths of 30 ft for small fish, including salmon, roe, carp, shad, suckers, perch, shiners and minnows.
Voice: *Male:* harsh *uig-a,* like a guitar twang. *Female:* harsh *karr karr.*
Similar Species: *Red-breasted Merganser* (p. 65): thinner bill; orangish to red eyes; male has shaggy, green crest and spotted, red breast; female lacks cleanly defined white throat.
Best Sites: L. Michigan; Heidecke L.; La Salle L.; Mississippi R. and Illinois R.

RED-BREASTED MERGANSER

Mergus serrator

The glossy, slicked-back crest and red eyes give the Red-breasted Merganser the disheveled look of a punk rocker. This bird was once called "Sawbill" and "Sea-Robin." • Unlike the other two mergansers, which nest in tree cavities, the Red-breasted nests on the ground. After their mates have begun incubating, the males fly off to join large offshore rafts for the duration of the summer. This species has been confirmed breeding only once in Illinois. • Most wintering Red-breasted Mergansers are found on or near Lake Michigan. • Red-breasted Mergansers sometimes feed cooperatively, funneling fish for easier capture. Unlike other ducks, mergansers dive for fish, propelling themselves with both wings and feet underwater. Like loons, they may also sit on the surface, "snorkeling" with their heads underwater to find prey.

ID: large, elongated body; red eyes; thin, serrated, orange bill; shaggy, slicked-back head crest. *Male:* green head; light rusty breast is spotted with black; white "collar"; gray sides; black-and-white shoulders. *Female:* gray brown overall; brownish head; white foreneck and breast. *In flight:* male has large, white wing patch crossed by 2 narrow, black bars; female has 1 dark bar separating white speculum from white upperwing patch.
Size: *L* 19–26 in; *W* 30 in.
Status: common migrant and uncommon to locally common winter resident, mainly on L. Michigan; spring migrants arrive in late February and depart by early May; fall birds return by mid-October; departure dates are obscured by wintering birds.

Habitat: usually near water in a hollow scrape under tall grasses or trees; sometimes among roots or driftwood; nest is lined profusely with down and feathers; female incubates 8–12 olive eggs for 26–28 days.
Nesting: only 1 confirmed record.
Feeding: dives underwater for small fish; also eats aquatic invertebrates and fish eggs.
Voice: generally quiet. *Male:* catlike *yeow* during courtship and feeding. *Female:* harsh *kho-kha.*
Similar Species: *Common Merganser* (p. 64): thicker bill; dark eyes; male has clean, white breast, blood red bill and lacks head crest; female's rusty foreneck contrasts with white "chin" and breast. *Hooded Merganser* (p. 63): smaller; shorter yellow or darkish bill; ashy gray brown overall; yellow eyes.
Best Sites: L. Michigan; downstate lakes; reservoirs and rivers.

65

RUDDY DUCK

Oxyura jamaicensis

Male Ruddy Ducks display energetic courtship behavior with comedic enthusiasm, a show Illinoisans can enjoy during spring migration. The small males vigorously pump their bright blue bills, almost touching their breasts. The *plap, plap, plap-plap-plap* of the display increases in speed to its climax: a spasmodic jerk and sputter • Female Ruddies commonly lay an average of eight eggs at a time—a remarkable feat, considering they are a significantly smaller duck than a Mallard, but their eggs are larger. Female Ruddies often dump eggs in a communal dummy nest, which may finally accumulate as many as 60 eggs that will receive no motherly care. • Migratory Ruddy Duck populations vary considerably, from 300 to as many as 30,000, along the Illinois and Mississippi River flyways.

ID: large bill and head; short neck; long, stiff tail feathers (often held upraised). *Breeding male:* white "cheek"; chestnut red body; deep powder blue bill; black tail and crown. *Female:* brown overall; dark "cheek" stripe; darker crown and back. *Nonbreeding male:* similar to female but with white "cheek."
Size: *L* 15–16 in; *W* 18½ in.
Status: common migrant from late February to early May with some non-breeders remaining until June, and from late September to early December; rare to uncommon breeder, mainly in Lake Co. and Cook Co.; rare nonbreeding summer resident statewide; rare to uncommon winter resident.

Habitat: *Breeding:* shallow marshes with dense emergent vegetation and muddy bottoms. *In migration* and *winter:* lakes, ponds and reservoirs.
Nesting: in marshes among cattails, bulrushes or other emergent vegetation; female suspends a woven platform nest over water; may use an abandoned duck or coot nest, muskrat lodge or exposed log; female incubates 5–10 rough, whitish eggs for 23–26 days; an occasional brood parasite.
Feeding: dives to the bottom of wetlands for the seeds of pondweeds, sedges, bulrushes and the leafy parts of aquatic plants; also eats a few aquatic invertebrates.
Voice: *Male:* courtship display is *chuck-chuck-chuck-chur-r-r-r*. *Female:* generally silent.
Similar Species: *Black Scoter* (p. 59): female and immature are large and lack dark line across "cheek."
Best Sites: L. Chautauqua; Carlyle L.; Rend L.; Arcola Marsh.

GRAY PARTRIDGE

Perdix perdix

The Gray Partridge, native to Eurasia, was introduced in Illinois between 1906 and 1927. It has never grown to substantial numbers in our state in the way that other introduced species, such as the the Ring-necked Pheasant, have. Observations are decreasing, and this species may not persist much longer in Illinois, probably because it doesn't like humid summers. • A systematic trek along country roads in the northern quarter of the state may give you the best chance of glimpsing these birds as they come to roadsides for gravel. The gravel accumulates in the gizzard, a muscular pouch in the digestive system, and crushes the hard grain and other seeds the Gray Partridge eats. • In spring, listen carefully for a distinctive call that sounds like a rusty gate hinge. • When incubating their eggs, females sit motionless on their nests and risk being stepped on rather than being detected.

ID: small, rounded, gray body with chestnut brown barring on flanks; brown-mottled back; bare, yellowish legs; rufous brown tail in flight. *Male:* chestnut brown patch on white belly; orangy face and throat. *Female:* no belly patch; paler face and throat.

Size: *L* 11–14 in; *W* 19 in.

Status: rare year-round in La Salle, DeKalb and Kane counties, as well as westward and northward.

Habitat: grassy and weedy fields and agricultural croplands with scattered brush piles and shrubs; often near wet areas.

Nesting: in a hayfield or pasture, or along a fenceline or field margin; on the ground in a scratched-out depression lined with grass; female incubates 15–17 olive-colored eggs for 23–25 days; male helps care for the brood until the following spring.

Feeding: at dawn and dusk during summer; throughout the day during winter; gleans the ground for waste agricultural grains and seeds; may also eat leaves and large insects.

Voice: at dawn and dusk; sounds like a rusty gate hinge: *kee-uck* or *scirl*; call is *kuta-kut-kut-kut* when excited.

Similar Species: *Northern Bobwhite* (p. 71): white crescents and spots edged in black on chestnut brown sides and upper breast; male has white throat and long eye line; female has buff throat and eye line.

Best Sites: Lee, Ogle and DeKalb counties.

RING-NECKED PHEASANT

Phasianus colchicus

The colorful Ring-necked Pheasant, native to Eurasia, was introduced to Illinois in the early 20th century as a game bird for hunters, and it continues to be introduced today to maintain that supply. Roughly 90,000 hand-raised pheasants are released in Illinois annually. Grain and corn crops have helped this species survive in the state. • In Illinois, the Ring-necked Pheasant population has decreased, partly because of hard winters, but mainly because of changes in agricultural practices. Most small, diversified farms have disappeared, and large, monoculture farms, which leave little habitat for these birds, are all that remain. As well, overgrazing and early and repeated mowing destroys many pheasant nests. • The male pheasant's loud *ka-squawk* call can be heard for some distance across agricultural lands and grasslands. The female rarely calls and remains secretive most of the year. • Ring-necked Pheasants are not very strong long-distance fliers, but they can run swiftly and fly in explosive bursts over small open areas to escape predators. • This species is most common in central Illinois, where some grassland habitat remains. It is rarely seen south of the 39th degree latitude in Illinois.

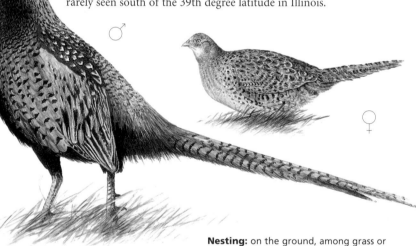

Nesting: on the ground, among grass or sparse vegetation; in a slight depression lined with grass and leaves; female incubates 10–12 olive buff eggs for 23–28 days; male takes no part in parental duties.

Feeding: gleans the ground and vegetation for weed seeds, grains and insects in summer; eats mostly seeds, corn kernels and buds in winter.

Voice: *Male:* loud, raspy, crowing *ka-squawk;* whirring of the wings, usually just before and after sunrise.

Similar Species: much larger and longer-tailed than any other gallinaceous bird in Illinois; brightly colored male is distinctive.

Best Sites: grasslands and agricultural areas in northern two-thirds of state.

ID: large gamebird; long, barred, pointed tail; unfeathered legs. *Male:* green head; white "collar"; bronze underparts; gray rump; naked, red face patch. *Female:* mottled brown overall; light underparts.

Size: *Male: L* 30–36 in; *W* 31 in. *Female: L* 20–26 in; *W* 28 in.

Status: uncommon to fairly common year-round resident; absent in southern Illinois.

Habitat: mainly grasslands; also hayfields and other agricultural fields.

GREATER PRAIRIE-CHICKEN

Tympanuchus cupido

From March through May, male Greater Prairie-Chickens congregate on "leks," or booming grounds, to win the favor of females. With their tails cocked upward and their wings low at their sides, males rhythmically inflate and deflate their golden air sacs, repeatedly producing a hollow "boom." Occasionally, males chase one another with their air sacs inflated and their neck tufts and tails erect. A male may even leap into the air, emitting loud cackles and striking his opponent with feet, wings and beak. • The Greater Prairie-Chicken was one of the most abundant prairie birds statewide until the early 1900s. Today, the state's entire population is restricted to 3000 acres of preserves in two counties in southeastern Illinois. Reasons for the decline include extensive habitat loss and disturbance, as well as nest parasitism by the non-native Ring-necked Pheasant. Active land management and habitat protection is essential if this bird is to remain on the state checklist. Genetic inbreeding has eliminated nearly all of the native population of this species; the remaining population is composed almost entirely of birds introduced from other states.

ID: medium-sized; heavily barred with brown, rufous and buff above and below; long, dark neck feathers (longer on male); short, rounded tail. *Male:* yellow "eyebrow;" yellow neck sacs are inflated when displaying (not visible otherwise) all-dark tail. *Female:* brown-barred tail.
Size: 17–18 in; W 28 in.
Status: state-endangered; rare and local in southeastern Illinois.
Habitat: formerly tall-grass prairie; now found in nonnative cool season grasslands, smaller native prairie patches, agricultural areas and brushy fields.

Nesting: on the ground in a shallow scrape lined with grass, feathers and leaves; female incubates 10–12 olive-colored, speckled eggs for 23–26 days.
Feeding: eats mostly seeds, waste grain, leaves and occasionally acorns; supplements its diet in summer with buds, berries and insects; forages on the ground and occasionally in trees.
Voice: *Male:* during courtship produces a series of 3–4 booming notes that do not accelerate in speed; sometimes emits loud cackles.
Similar Species: *Ring-necked Pheasant* (p. 68): female has longer tail, mostly unmarked underparts, is buffier brown overall and lacks streaking on back.
Best Sites: Prairie Ridge SNA.

WILD TURKEY
Meleagris gallopavo

Reintroduction efforts have reestablished the Wild Turkey as a common, permanent resident in Illinois. Wild Turkeys were common before European settlement; overharvesting and habitat loss rendered these birds nearly extirpated. Wild Turkeys are now established in 101 out of 102 Illinois counties. The largest populations are in extreme southern and extreme northwestern Illinois, where flocks of 50 to 100 gather. • Wild Turkeys prefer to feed on the ground and travel on foot. They can run faster than 19 miles per hour and can fly short distances. They roost high in large trees at night. • In their natural habitat, Wild Turkeys are wary birds with acute senses and a highly developed social system. • After heavy snows in winter, turkeys can often be found following the footsteps of white-tailed deer. • If Congress had taken Benjamin Franklin's advice in 1782, our national emblem would be the Wild Turkey instead of the Bald Eagle.

ID: dark, glossy, iridescent body plumage; barred, copper-colored tail; mostly bare legs. *Male:* naked, red and blue head; long central breast tassel; red wattles. *Female:* smaller; grayish head; less iridescent body; some older females have short breast tassel.
Size: *Male: L* 3–3½ ft; *W* 5½ ft. *Female: L* 3 ft; *W* 4 ft.
Status: uncommon to locally common year-round resident in more heavily wooded areas; rare to uncommon in urbanized and less forested regions.
Habitat: deciduous, mixed and riparian woodlands; cornfields.

Nesting: in woodlands and field and grassland edges; in a depression on the ground under thick cover; nest is lined with grass and leaves; female incubates 10–12 speckled, pale buff eggs for about 28 days; often deserts nest if discovered.
Feeding: in fields near protective woods; forages on the ground for seeds, fruits, especially acorns and beech nuts, bulbs and sedges; also eats insects, especially beetles and grasshoppers; may take small amphibians.
Voice: wide array of sounds; courting male gobbles loudly; alarm call is a loud *pert;* gathering call is a *cluck;* contact call is a loud *keouk-keouk-keouk.*
Similar Species: all other gallinaceous birds are much smaller.
Best Sites: Stephenson Co. and Jo Daviess Co.; southernmost 2 tiers of counties.

NORTHERN BOBWHITE

Colinus virginianus

Throughout fall and winter, Northern Bobwhites travel in large family groups called "coveys," collectively seeking food and huddling together on cold nights. When they huddle, members of the covey face outward, allowing the group to detect danger from any direction. When summer arrives, breeding pairs leave their coveys to perform elaborate courtship rituals. • The male's characteristic, whistled *bob-white* call, usually given in spring, is often the only evidence of this bird's presence among the dense, tangled vegetation of its rural woodland home. Bobwhites benefit from habitat disturbance, utilizing the early successional habitats created by fire, agriculture and forestry. However, as land use has intensified and pesticide use has increased, populations have declined, especially in central and northern Illinois. Severe winters also reduce numbers considerably, with a slow recovery during ensuing years. • The Northern Bobwhite is the only native quail in eastern North America.

ID: mottled brown, buff and black upperparts; short, gray tail; white crescents and spots on flanks and belly. *Male:* white throat; broad, white "eyebrow." *Female:* buff throat and "eyebrow."
Size: *L* 10 in; *W* 13 in.
Status: uncommon to common year-round resident, decreasing northward; very few left in its northern Illinois range.
Habitat: farmlands, open woodlands, woodland edges, grassy fencelines, roadside ditches and brushy, open country.
Nesting: in a shallow depression on the ground; often concealed by surrounding vegetation or a woven, partial dome; nest is lined with grass and leaves; pair incubates 12–16 white to pale buff eggs for 22–24 days.
Feeding: seasonally available seeds, berries, leaves, roots, nuts, insects and other invertebrates.
Voice: whistled *hoy* is given year-round. *Male:* a whistled, rising *bob-white* given in spring and summer.
Similar Species: *Gray Partridge* (p. 67): much rarer; gray breast; chestnut brown outer tail feathers; male has orange brown face and throat and dark belly patch; female is grayer overall.
Best Sites: rural grasslands in southern quarter of state.

71

RED-THROATED LOON

Gavia stellata

The Red-throated Loon typically swims low in the water with its bill held high. In Illinois, we mostly see the Red-throated Loon in nonbreeding plumage during fall migration when it stops on large lakes to rest. Flybys also occur along the Lake Michigan shoreline. • The Red-throated Loon is not closely related to any other living loon species. It is the smallest of the loons and can leap from the water or land directly into flight. Other loons require 30 feet or more of open water to gain flight. This trait allows Red-throated Loons to nest on smaller bodies of water, unlike their larger, less-agile relatives. • Somewhat reliable meteorologists, Red-throats often become noisy before the onset of inclement weather, perhaps sensing changes in barometric pressure. • These loons can live for 20 years or longer, but they encounter many threats, including entanglement in large fishing drift nets, as well as oil spills and slaughter. • The scientific name *stellata* refers to the starlike, white speckles on this bird's back in nonbreeding plumage.

nonbreeding

ID: slim bill is held upward. *Breeding:* red throat; gray face and neck; black and white stripes from nape to back of head; plain, brownish back. *Nonbreeding:* back is speckled with white; white face; dark gray on crown and back of head; often has thin, brownish "chin strap." *In flight:* hunched back; legs trail behind tail; rapid wingbeats.
Size: *L* 23–27 in; *W* 3½ ft.
Status: rare migrant from February to April and from October to December.
Habitat: L. Michigan and large, inland lakes and reservoirs.

Nesting: does not nest in Illinois.
Feeding: dives deeply and captures small fish; occasionally eats aquatic insects and amphibians as well as aquatic vegetation in early spring.
Voice: Mallard-like *kwuk-kwuk-kwuk-kwuk* in flight; mournful wail during courtship; distraction call is a loud *gayorwork.*
Similar Species: *Common Loon* (p. 74): larger; heavier bill; lacks white speckling on back in nonbreeding plumage. *Pacific Loon* (p. 73): larger; purple throat and white patches on back in breeding plumage; all-dark back in nonbreeding plumage.
Best Sites: L. Michigan shoreline; Clinton L. and other large, downstate reservoirs.

PACIFIC LOON
Gavia pacifica

The Pacific Loon may likely be the most abundant loon species in North America, but it takes luck to find this more westerly species in Illinois. This rare Illinois migrant is usually seen singly and in nonbreeding plumage along Lake Michigan and large inland lakes. It remains here for only a short time while flying between its northern Canadian and Alaskan nesting grounds and its southern wintering grounds along the Atlantic and Pacific coasts. • The Pacific Loon swims with its head underwater before diving beneath the surface to pursue fish or invertebrates. • Loons' legs are placed far back on the body, making the birds somewhat awkward on land, but giving them the power and agility they need in water. Unlike other waterbirds, loons rely solely on their feet for propulsion when diving, using their wings only for balance and turning. Loons find their prey visually; their eyes are well adapted for seeing both in the air and under water.

nonbreeding

ID: *Breeding:* silver gray crown and nape; dark throat is framed by white stripes; white breast; dark back with large, bold, white spots. *Nonbreeding:* well-defined, light "cheek" and throat; dark upperparts; dark "chin" stripe. *In flight:* hunched back; legs trail behind tail; rapid wingbeats.
Size: *L* 23–28½ in; *W* 3½–4 ft.
Status: rare to casual migrant most often seen from mid-October to early December.
Habitat: large lakes.

Nesting: does not nest in Illinois.
Feeding: dives deeply for fish and occasionally aquatic invertebrates; average dive is 45 seconds; sometimes eats aquatic vegetation.
Voice: calls include a doglike yelp, a catlike meow and a ravenlike croak.
Similar Species: breeding plumage is distinctive. *Common Loon* (p. 74): larger; lacks sharp definition between black and white on face and neck; often has light "collar" in nonbreeding plumage. *Red-throated Loon* (p. 72): tilts bill upward; extensive white spotting on back in nonbreeding plumage.
Best Sites: large, inland reservoirs, especially Clinton L.

73

COMMON LOON

Gavia immer

The quavering wail of the Common Loon pierces the quiet night on its northern breeding grounds. A former breeder in Illinois, this bird's haunting call can be heard on large lakes during spring and fall migration. This loon is most common on large inland reservoirs in central and southern Illinois, in deep glacial lakes in northeastern Illinois and along the Lake Michigan shoreline. • Loons are well adapted to their aquatic lifestyle. Most birds have hollow bones, but these divers have nearly solid bones that make them less buoyant, and their feet are placed well back on their bodies for underwater propulsion. Excellent underwater hunters, Common Loons feast on small bass, perch, sunfish, pike and whitefish. On land, a loon appears awkward; its rear-placed legs make walking difficult, and its heavy body and relatively small wing size require it to make a lengthy sprint across water before taking off. Loons float low on the water, disappearing behind swells only to reappear elsewhere like ethereal guardians of the lakes. When diving for food, they may emerge far away from the point of entry, leaving the observer to wonder where they went.

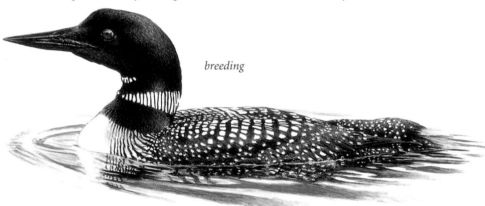

breeding

ID: *Breeding:* green black head; stout, thick, black bill; white "necklace"; white breast and underparts; black-and-white "checkerboard" upperparts; red eyes. *Nonbreeding:* much duller plumage; sandy brown back; light underparts. *In flight:* wings beat constantly; hunchbacked appearance; legs trail behind tail.
Size: *L* 28–35 in; *W* 4–5 ft.
Status: common migrant; former Illinois breeder.
Habitat: deep lakes with open water.
Nesting: no longer breeds in Illinois because of habitat degradation.
Feeding: pursues small fish underwater to depths of 180 ft; occasionally eats large,

aquatic invertebrates and larval and adult amphibians.
Voice: alarm call is a quavering tremolo, often called "loon laughter"; contact call is a long but simple wailing note. *Male:* territorial call is an undulating, complex yodel.
Similar Species: *Red-throated Loon* (p. 72): smaller; slender bill is held upward; red throat in breeding plumage; sharply defined white face and white-spotted back in nonbreeding plumage. *Pacific Loon* (p. 73): smaller; dusty gray head often looks silver; sharp contrast between white and dark areas of neck; nonbreeding has darker back.
Best Sites: glacial lakes of Lake Co.; Clinton L. and other large, downstate reservoirs.

PIED-BILLED GREBE
Podilymbus podiceps

The exuberant, maniacal laughter of the Pied-billed Grebe blends well with the cacophony of Illinois' wetland communities. A state-threatened species, the Pied-billed Grebe breeds mostly in marshes, giving its haunting chuckle or whinny call in spring through summer as it defends territory and raises young. • The Pied-billed Grebe builds a floating nest among sparse vegetation in the shallow waters of quiet lakes and marshes, a strategy that allows it to see predators approaching from far away. When frightened by an intruder, the bird covers its eggs and slides underwater, leaving a nest that looks like a mat of debris.
• A Pied-billed Grebe can swim submarine-style, slowly submerging so that only its nostrils and eyes remain above the water. • The adults carry their newly hatched, striped young on their backs. • The scientific name *podiceps*, which means "rump foot," refers to the way the bird's feet are situated toward the back of its body.

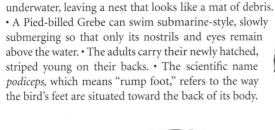

breeding

ID: *Breeding:* all-brown body; black ring on light-colored bill; laterally compressed "chicken bill"; black throat; very short tail; white undertail coverts; pale belly; whitish eye ring. *Nonbreeding:* pale yellowish eye ring; pale yellowish bill lacks black ring; white "chin" and throat; brownish crown.
Size: *L* 12–15 in; *W* 16 in.
Status: common migrant from late February to early March through early May and from late August to early September through early December; largest migrant flocks occur in October; state-threatened, locally common breeder found in marshes spring through summer.
Habitat: *Breeding:* wetlands with emergent vegetation. *In migration:* lakes, ponds and rivers.
Nesting: among emergent vegetation in sheltered ponds and marshes; floating platform nest is made of wet and decaying plants; pair incubates 4–5 white to buff eggs and raises the young together.
Feeding: makes shallow dives and gleans the water's surface for aquatic invertebrates, small fish, adult and larval amphibians and occasionally aquatic plants.
Voice: loud, whooping call that begins quickly, then slows down: *kuk-kuk-kuk cow cow cow cowp cowp cowp.*
Similar Species: *Eared Grebe* (p. 78): red eyes; golden "ear" tufts and chestnut flanks in breeding plumage; black-and-white head in nonbreeding plumage; seen only during migration. *Horned Grebe* (p. 76): red eyes; golden "ear" tufts and red neck in breeding plumage; black-and-white head in nonbreeding plumage; seen only during migration. *American Coot* (p. 117): all-black body; pale bill extends onto forehead; lacks white eye ring.
Best Sites: *Summer:* northeastern Illinois, Moraine Hills SP and Hennepin wetlands. *In migration:* ponds and lakes statewide.

HORNED GREBE
Podiceps auritus

When the glacial lakes of northern Illinois begin to thaw in early spring, the Horned Grebe passes through on its journey to breed in the North. Birds arrive in various plumages, with some still in winter garb and others nearly in breeding plumage showing off golden yellow "ear" tufts on a black head and back with rufous neck and sides. They are often found in the company of migratory Common Loons and other waterfowl. • Horned Grebes also inhabit parts of Europe, Asia and Central Africa. • Unlike the fully webbed front toes of many swimming birds, grebe toes are individually webbed, or "lobed"—the three forward-facing toes have individual flanges that are not connected to the other toes. • This bird's common name and its scientific name, *auritus* (eared), refer to the golden feather tufts or "horns," acquired in breeding plumage.

nonbreeding

ID: *Breeding:* rufous neck and flanks; black head; golden "ear" tufts; black back; white underparts; red eyes; flat crown. *Nonbreeding:* lacks "ear" tufts; dark upperparts; white "cheek," foreneck and underparts. *In flight:* wings beat constantly; legs trail hunchbacked appearance; behind tail.

Size: *L* 12–15 in; *W* 18 in.

Status: fairly common migrant from February to May and from September to December.

Habitat: lakes, ponds and sloughs.

Nesting: does not nest in Illinois.

Feeding: makes shallow dives and gleans the water's surface for aquatic insects, crustaceans, mollusks, small fish and adult and larval amphibians.

Voice: loud series of croaks and shrieking notes and a sharp *keark keark* during courtship; usually quiet outside the breeding season.

Similar Species: *Eared Grebe* (p. 78): golden head plumes on black head and neck in breeding plumage; black "cheek" and darker neck in nonbreeding plumage; more peaked head; thinner, slightly curved bill. *Pied-billed Grebe* (p. 75): thicker, stubbier bill; mostly brown body. *Red-necked Grebe* (p. 77): larger; dark eyes; lacks "ear" tufts; white "cheek" in breeding plumage.

Best Sites: lakes and large reservoirs statewide, including L. Springfield, Carlyle L., Clinton L. and L. Michigan.

RED-NECKED GREBE
Podiceps grisegena

Red-necked Grebes are usually seen singly in winter plumage on large lakes in Illinois during early spring and late fall. This species loses the red color on its neck when not in breeding plumage, but the long neck and bill help identify this second-largest North American grebe, a migratory species in the state. • Like all grebe species, the Red-necked Grebe feeds, sleeps and courts on water. It maneuvers extremely well underwater, diving leisurely in an instant or sinking slowly to capture minnows, small fish and aquatic insects. This grebe will also eat salamanders and plant matter. • The Red-necked Grebe is a rare and welcome sight in Illinois, but its numbers may be declining. In Wisconsin, for example, this species is an endangered breeder. Wetland habitat loss and degradation contribute to the decline. • The scientific name *grisegena* means "gray cheek"—a distinctive field mark of this bird in non-breeding plumage.

nonbreeding

ID: stockier than other grebes. *Breeding:* rusty neck; whitish "cheek"; black crown; straight, long heavy bill is dark above and yellow underneath; black upperparts; light underparts; dark eyes. *Nonbreeding:* grayish white foreneck, "chin" and "cheek."
Size: *L* 17–22 in; *W* 24 in.
Status: rare to casual migrant from mid-February to April and from early September to early December.
Habitat: lakes and reservoirs.
Nesting: does not nest in Illinois.
Feeding: dives and gleans the water's surface for small fish, eels, aquatic invertebrates and amphibians.

Voice: during courtship only, an often-repeated, loonlike, excited *ah-ooo ah-ooo ah-ooo ah-ah-ah-ah-ah;* usually quiet outside the breeding season.
Similar Species: *Horned Grebe* (p. 76): much smaller; dark "cheek" and golden "horns" in breeding plumage; red eyes, all-dark bill and bright white "cheek" in nonbreeding plumage. *Eared Grebe* (p. 78): much smaller; black neck in breeding plumage; black "cheek" in nonbreeding plumage. *Pied-billed Grebe* (p. 75): much smaller; thicker, stubbier bill; mostly brown body. *Western Grebe* (p. 79): red eyes; black-and-white neck in breeding plumage. *Loons* (p. 72–74): larger bodies; heavier, darker bills; lack large, white wing patch in flight.
Best Sites: L. Michigan; Clinton L.

EARED GREBE
Podiceps nigricollis

These little grebes are typically found farther west, but a few are found in Illinois during migration and in winter. Eared Grebes also inhabit parts of Europe, Asia, Central Africa and South America, making them the most abundant grebes not only in North America, but also around the world. • Eared Grebes undergo cyclical periods of atrophy and hypertrophy throughout the year, meaning that their internal organs and pectoral muscles shrink or swell, depending on whether or not the birds need to migrate. This strategy leaves Eared Grebes flightless for a longer period—nine to ten months per year—than any other bird. • The Eared Grebe eats feathers to protect the stomach lining and intestines from sharp fish bones or parasites. Also, feathers slow the passage of food, allowing more time for complete digestion. • The scientific name *nigricollis* means "black neck"—a characteristic of the bird's breeding plumage.

nonbreeding

ID: *Breeding:* thin, straight bill; red eyes; slightly raised crown; black neck, "cheek," forehead and back; red flanks; fanned-out, golden "ear" tufts; white underparts. *Nonbreeding:* dark "cheek" and upperparts; light underparts; dusky upper foreneck and flanks. *In flight:* wings beat constantly; hunchbacked appearance; legs trail behind tail.
Size: *L* 11½–14 in; *W* 16 in.
Status: rare migrant from March to May and from mid-August to early December.
Habitat: lakes and reservoirs.
Nesting: does not normally nest in Illinois; 1 nesting with 3 broods recorded near Chicago in 1981.

Feeding: makes shallow dives and gleans the water's surface for aquatic insects, crustaceans, mollusks, small fish and larval and adult amphibians.
Voice: mellow *poo-eee-chk* during courtship; quiet outside the breeding season.
Similar Species: *Horned Grebe* (p. 76): rufous neck and solid golden patch of feathers extending back from eye and covering black head in breeding plumage; white "cheek" in nonbreeding plumage; less pointed head; thicker bill. *Pied-billed Grebe* (p. 75): thicker, stubbier bill; mostly brown body. *Red-necked Grebe* (p. 77): larger overall; longer bill; red neck and whitish "cheek" in breeding plumage; dusky white "cheek" in nonbreeding plumage.
Best Sites: lakes, ponds and sewage lagoons; records scattered throughout the state.

WESTERN GREBE

Aechmophorus occidentalis

As its name implies, the Western Grebe breeds mostly in the western half of North America. • This bird performs an elaborate courtship display that is not usually seen in Illinois. A pair runs side by side on the water, virtually airborne. • Though the Western Grebe has not been observed spearing fish, it has a unique, heronlike ability to thrust its head forward like a spear. Western Grebes feed on schooling fish at night, using what is known as bioluminescence (light produced by a chemical reaction within an organism) to see their prey. Grebes forage at night, feeding on fish that remain well below the surface during the day and then migrate to the water's surface after dusk. • The species name *Aechomophorus* is derived from Greek words meaning "spear bearer."

nonbreeding

ID: long, slender neck; blackish upperparts from base of bill to tail; white underparts from "chin" through belly; long, thin, yellow bill; white "cheek"; black on face extends down around red eyes.
Size: *L* 20–24 in; *W* 24 in.
Status: rare to casual migrant from April to early May and from September to early December.
Habitat: large, deep lakes.

Nesting: does not nest in illinois.
Feeding: gleans the water's surface and dives for small fish and aquatic invertebrates.
Voice: high-pitched, froglike *crreeet-crreeet*, not usually heard in Illinois.
Similar Species: *Clark's Grebe:* eyes are surrounded by white; orange yellow bill. *Double-crested Cormorant* (p. 81): all-black body. *Common Loon* (p. 74): shorter, stocky neck. *Eared* (p. 78), *Horned* (p. 76) and *Red-necked* (p. 77) *grebes:* much smaller.
Best Sites: L. Michigan; Clinton L.; Carlyle L.; other large, downstate reservoirs.

AMERICAN WHITE PELICAN

Pelecanus erythrorhynchos

In the past few decades, the American White Pelican has altered its migratory route so that it is now commonly seen in much of western Illinois along rivers and lakes. Before then, this bird was rarely seen in the state. In March, April and September through early November, you may find groups of 4500 or more white pelicans resting, feeding or circling in the air, showing off the black in their impressively large, white wings. • The American White Pelican's porous, bucketlike bill is dramatically adapted for feeding. Groups of foraging pelicans deliberately herd fish into schools, then dip their bills and scoop up the prey. In a single scoop, a pelican can hold over 3 gallons of water and fish, two to three times as much as its stomach can hold. White pelicans eat about 4 pounds of fish per day; preferring nongame fish, they do not pose a threat to a fishermen's catch. • All other large, white birds with black wing tips fly with their necks extended; the American White Pelican is the only one to fly with its neck pulled back toward its wings.

nonbreeding

ID: extremely large; stocky and white with largest wingspan of any Illinois bird; long, orange bill and throat pouch; black primary and secondary wing feathers; short tail; naked orange skin patch around eye. *Breeding:* small, keeled plate develops on upper mandible; pale yellow crest on back of head. *Nonbreeding* and *immature*: white plumage is tinged with brown.
Size: L 4½–6 ft; W 9 ft.
Status: common to abundant migrant during March, April, September and October

along the Illinois R., Mississippi R. and other large lakes and rivers; rare to uncommon migrant elsewhere; may breed in Illinois sometime soon; rare local winter and summer resident.
Habitat: lakes and rivers.
Nesting: does not nest in Illinois.
Feeding: surface dips for small fish and amphibians; often feeds cooperatively by herding fish into large concentrations.
Voice: generally quiet; adults rarely issue piglike grunts.
Similar Species: no other large, white bird has a long bill with pouch and dwarfs all other large waterfowl.
Best Sites: L. Chautauqua; Mark Twain NWR.

DOUBLE-CRESTED CORMORANT

Phalacrocorax auritus

The slick-feathered Double-crested Cormorant is the only North American cormorant that occurs inland in large numbers. Once endangered in Illinois, it now breeds here in good numbers. • The cormorant's long, rudderlike tail, excellent underwater vision and sealed nostrils contribute to the success of its aquatic lifestyle. Like many other birds, this species has no oil glands; this lack of waterproofing decreases the cormorant's buoyancy, allowing it to stay underwater for a long time. After diving, the Double-crested Cormorant often perches on a rock or in a tree with its wings partially spread, a posture thought to aid in drying wet feathers. Though once believed to compete with fishermen, these birds typically take the more undesirable fish such as shad and alewives. • Cormorants usually nest in tall snags, often in colonies interspersed with nesting herons. • "Cormorant" is derived from a Latin word meaning "sea crow."

breeding

ID: all-black body; long, crooked neck; thin bill, hooked at tip; blue eyes. *Breeding:* throat pouch becomes intense orange yellow; fine, black plumes trail from "eyebrows." *Immature:* brown upperparts; buff throat and breast; yellowish throat patch. *In flight:* rapid wingbeats; kinked neck.

Size: *L* 26–32 in; *W* 4¹/₂ ft.

Status: common migrant, locally common breeder and nonbreeding summer resident from late February to early March through late November to early December; locally common winter resident in the south, usually on large reservoirs.

Habitat: lakes, wetlands, rivers, reservoirs.

Nesting: colonial, often with herons and egrets; in a snag; nest platform is made of sticks, aquatic vegetation and guano; pair incubates 3–6 bluish white eggs for 25–33 days; young are fed by regurgitation.

Feeding: long underwater dives to depths of 30 ft or more; eats small, schooling fish; also amphibians and invertebrates; uses bill to grasp prey; brings prey to surface to swallow.

Voice: generally quiet; may issue piglike grunts or croaks, especially near nesting colonies.

Similar Species: *Common Loon* (p. 74): shorter, thicker neck; thinner, less-pointed black bill lacks hooked tip; spotted back in breeding plumage; white underparts in nonbreeding plumage.

Best Sites: Lake Renwick Heron Rookery Nature Preserve; Baker's L.; Rend L.; Carlyle L.; other large, downstate reservoirs.

AMERICAN BITTERN

Botaurus lentiginosus

The lucky birder may hear the American Bittern's mysterious *oonk-a-lunk* call emanating from an Illinois wetland in springtime. Catching a glimpse of an American Bittern can be difficult, and even honed and patient eyes are no match for this elusive bird. • At the approach of an intruder, a bittern reacts immediately by freezing with its bill pointed skyward—its vertically streaked, brown plumage blending perfectly with its marshy surroundings. • An observer often gets very close to this species without knowing it's there until the bittern flushes at the last second, exhibiting an ungainly flight with loose, floppy wings and dangling feet and legs. • The American Bittern is state-endangered and only breeds at a few favored sites. Habitat loss and degradation have greatly reduced the nesting numbers of this species.

ID: brown upperparts; white throat with bold, reddish brown streaking from lower throat to lower breast; straight, stout bill; yellow legs and feet; black outer wings; short tail.
Size: *L* 23–27 in; *W* 3½ ft.
Status: state-endangered; rare to uncommon migrant and breeder from mid-March to mid-December.
Habitat: large wetlands and lake edges with tall, dense grasses, sedges, bulrushes and cattails; grasslands interspersed with wet meadows.
Nesting: singly; above the waterline in dense vegetation; nest platform is made of grass, sedges and dead reeds; nest often has separate entrance and exit paths; female incubates 3–5 pale olive or buff eggs for 24–28 days.

Feeding: patient, stand-and-wait predator; makes quick stabs at frogs and other amphibians, small fish, crayfish, reptiles, insects and small mammals.
Voice: deep, resonant, repetitive *oonk-a-LUNK;* most often heard at dusk or at night.
Similar Species: *Immature Black-crowned Night-Heron* (p. 90) and *Yellow-crowned Night-Heron* (p. 91): white spots and streaks on solid brown backs; red eyes; shorter, thicker necks; lack strongly contrasting flight feathers. *Least Bittern* (p. 83): much smaller; rich buff on wings and neck. *Green Heron* (p. 89): much smaller; rich, reddish brown neck; dark green crown, back, wings and tail.
Best Sites: *Summer* and *in migration:* Illinois Beach SP; Red Wing Slough; Goose Lake Prairie SNA; Arcola Marsh; Prairie Ridge SNA. *In migration:* Arcola Marsh; Oakwood Bottoms.

LEAST BITTERN

Ixobrychus exilis

A reclusive marsh bird, the Least Bittern inhabits marshes where dense stands of cattails conceal most of its movements. An expert climber, it clings to vertical stems and hops around 3 feet or more above the water without getting its feet wet. • State-threatened in Illinois, the Least Bittern may be more common than thought because it is so secretive and does not readily respond to recorded imitations of its call, a muted *coo, coo, coo.* The call resembles that of a Black-billed Cuckoo, a species tied to woodlands rather than wetlands. Birders relish seeing this slender, shy bittern, which is Illinois' smallest heron. • Nestlings adopt a comical erect neck posture, with eyes looking straight ahead.

ID: rich buff flanks and sides; streaking on foreneck; white underparts; mostly pale bill; yellowish legs; short tail; dark primary and secondary feathers. *Male:* black crown and back. *Female* and *immature:* chestnut brown head and back; immature has darker streaking on breast and back. *In flight:* large, buffy shoulder patches.
Size: *L* 11–14½ in; *W* 17 in.
Status: state-threatened; rare to uncommon migrant and breeder from late April to early October.
Habitat: freshwater marshes with cattails and other dense emergent vegetation.
Nesting: mostly the male constructs a platform of dry plant stalks on top of bent marsh vegetation, typically cattail blades; nest site is usually well concealed within dense vegetation; pair incubates 4–5 pale green or blue eggs for 17–20 days; pair feeds the young by regurgitation.
Feeding: stabs prey with its bill; eats mostly small fish; also takes insects, tadpoles, frogs, small snakes, leeches and crayfish; may build a hunting platform.
Voice: *Male:* muted, guttural *coo, coo, coo. Female:* a ticking sound. Both issue a *tut-tut* call or a *koh* alarm call.
Similar Species: *American Bittern* (p. 82): much larger; bold, brown streaking on underparts; in flight shows large, dark contrasting flight feathers. *Black-crowned Night-Heron* (p. 90) and *Yellow-crowned Night-Heron* (p. 91): much larger; immatures have dark brown upperparts with white flecking. *Green Heron* (p. 89): immature is much darker overall.
Best Sites: *Summer:* Glacial Park in McHenry Co.; McHenry Dam; Arcola Marsh; Beardstown Marsh; Kidd L.; Mermet L.

GREAT BLUE HERON
Ardea herodias

When flying over a marsh the Great Blue Heron, with its six-foot wingspan, appears prehistoric, giving you a glimpse of what pterodactyls must have looked like in flight. • The Great Blue Heron nests in small to large colonies, sometimes even singly in Illinois. Its communal treetop nests, known as rookeries, are sensitive to human disturbance. If you are fortunate enough to discover a colony, observing the birds from afar makes good sense. • Great Blue Herons can successfully survive winter in Illinois where there is open water and sufficient food. • Often mistaken for a crane, the Great Blue Heron flies with its neck folded back over its shoulder in an S-shape. A crane holds its neck outstretched in flight. • A stealthy hunter, the Great Blue Heron stands quietly at the edge of a marsh, watching the water intently for prey to swim past. Though mostly a fish eater, this heron also stalks fields and meadows in search of frogs, snakes and rodents.

breeding

ID: large, blue gray bird; long, curving neck; long, dark legs; straight, yellow bill; chestnut brown thighs. *Breeding:* richer colors; black plumes trail from just behind eye several inches down neck. *In flight:* neck folds back over shoulders; legs trail behind body; slow, steady wingbeats.
Size: *L* 4–4½ ft; *W* 6 ft.
Status: common to locally abundant migrant and breeder from mid-February to early March through early to mid-December; uncommon to locally common in winter.
Habitat: forages along the edges of rivers, lakes, sloughs, swamps and marshes; also seen in fields and wet meadows.
Nesting: colonially or singly; usually in a tree but occasionally on the ground; stick-and-twig platform can be up to 4 ft in diameter; pair incubates 3–6 pale blue eggs for approximately 28 days.

Feeding: patient, stand-and-wait predator; strikes at fish, amphibians, small mammals, aquatic invertebrates and reptiles, especially snakes; often swallows prey whole; rarely scavenges.
Voice: usually quiet away from the nest; a deep, harsh *frahnk frahnk frahnk* during takeoff or when alarmed.
Similar Species: *Green Heron* (p. 89), *Black-crowned Night Heron* (p. 90) and *Yellow-crowned Night-Heron* (p. 91): much smaller; shorter legs. *Egrets* (p. 85–88): all are mostly white. *Sandhill Crane* (p. 118): red "cap"; shorter, less dagger-shaped, darker bill; lacks black head plumes; flies with neck outstretched. *Little Blue Heron* (p. 87): much smaller; dark overall; purplish head; lacks yellow on bill. *Tricolored Heron* (p. 354): much rarer; much smaller; darker upperparts; white underparts; smaller size.
Best Sites: Lake Renwick Heron Rookery Nature Preserve; Mark Twain NWR; L. Chautauqua; Carlyle L.; Rend L; Horseshoe Lake SP; Horseshoe Lake CA.

GREAT EGRET
Ardea alba

The Great Egret was once threatened in Illinois, but habitat restoration and other measures have brought this bird back from near extirpation. Breeding Great Egrets are more common farther south in Illinois. After the breeding season, young egrets may move northward in the state where they can be seen in hundreds, foraging in wetlands and along rivers and lakes. • The plumes of the Great Egret and Snowy Egret were widely used to decorate hats in the early 20th century. An ounce of egret feathers cost as much as $32—more than an ounce of gold at that time. As a result, egret populations began to disappear. Some of the first conservation legislation in North America was enacted to outlaw the hunting of Great Egrets. • Egrets are actually herons, but were given their name for their impressive breeding plumes, referred to as "aigrettes." • The Great Egret is the symbol for the National Audubon Society, one of the oldest conservation organizations in the U.S.

breeding

ID: all-white plumage; black legs; yellow bill. *Breeding:* white plumes trail from throat and rump; green skin patch between eyes and base of bill. *In flight:* neck folds back over shoulders; legs extend backward.
Size: *L* 3–3½ ft; *W* 4½ ft.
Status: common to abundant migrant, decreasing northward; common breeder in southern Illinois wetlands, decreasing northward; occurs from mid-March to early April through mid- to late October.
Habitat: marshes, sloughs, open riverbanks, backwater lakes and lake shorelines.
Nesting: colonial, often with Great Blue Herons and Double-crested Cormorants;

may nest in isolated pairs; in a tree or tall shrub; pair builds a platform of sticks and incubates 3–5 pale blue green eggs for 23–26 days.
Feeding: patient, stand-and-wait predator; occasionally stalks slowly, stabbing at frogs, lizards, snakes and small mammals.
Voice: rapid, low-pitched, loud *cuk-cuk-cuk.*
Similar Species: *Snowy Egret* (p. 86): smaller; black bill; yellow feet in breeding plumage. *Cattle Egret* (p. 88): much smaller; stockier; orange bill and legs. *Whooping Crane:* much larger; red crown; black-and-red "mask"; black primaries; extremely rare.
Best Sites: Clear L.; L. Chautauqua; Swan L.; Mark Twain NWR; Horseshoe Lake SP.

85

SNOWY EGRET
Egretta thula

The Snowy Egret wears golden slippers and has spotless white plumage. When it reaches adulthood, its black legs make the bright yellow feet even more prominent. • This state-endangered bird possibly suffered even more from plume hunting than the Great Egret because of its softer and more delicate plumes. After staging a comeback in the 1960s and 1970s, widespread population declines occurred in the late 20th century, likely attributable to the Snowy Egret's sensitivity to a variety of conservation threats. • Herons and egrets, particularly Snowy Egrets, use various feeding techniques. By poking their feet in the muck of shallow wetlands, these birds spook potential prey out of hiding places. In an even more ingenious hunting strategy, Snowy Egrets will create shade by extending their wings over open water to lure a fish into the cooler, shaded spot and then seize and eat it. • After breeding season, the Snowy Egret can sometimes be found foraging in the Illinois wetlands farther north.

breeding

ID: white plumage; black bill and legs; bright yellow feet. *Breeding:* long plumes on nape, lower breast and lower rump; erect crown; yellow to orangish red lores. *Immature:* similar to adult; mostly yellow legs. *In flight:* yellow feet are obvious in adult.
Size: L 22–26 in; W 3½ ft.
Status: state-endangered; rare to casual migrant and breeder in the north; rare to uncommon, local migrant and breeder in the south; occurs from early to mid-April through mid- to late September.
Habitat: marshes, ponds, sloughs, lakes and streams.

Nesting: colonial, often among other herons, especially Little Blue Herons; in a tree or tall shrub; pair builds a platform of sticks and incubates 3–5 pale blue green eggs for 20–24 days.
Feeding: stirs wetland muck with its feet; stands and waits with wings held open; occasionally hovers and stabs; eats small fish, amphibians and invertebrates.
Voice: low croaks; bouncy *wulla-wulla-wulla* on breeding grounds.
Similar Species: *Great Egret* (p. 85): larger; yellow bill; black feet. *Cattle Egret* (p. 88): orange yellow legs and bill. *Little Blue Heron* (p. 87): juvenile has pale bluish gray legs, 2-tone bill and grayish facial skin.
Best Sites: Alorton nesting colony in East St. Louis region; Kidd L.; Stump L.; Mark Twain NWR; East Cape Girardeau wetlands.

LITTLE BLUE HERON

Egretta caerulea

With dark plumage and a lack of aigrette plumes, the Little Blue Heron was only occasionally taken by hunters in the 19th century and did not suffer the same population decimation as many of its close relatives. • Although adults of the species look quite different from Snowy Egrets, the white-plumaged young can be easily confused. It takes two years for Little Blue Herons to reach the completely dark plumage of adult birds. During the change from white to blue, the bird obtains a "calico" phase, with blue splotches interspersed among the white plumage. • Feeding behavior is one way to distinguish herons. The Little Blue Heron does not wade as deeply as other heron species, often hunting ashore, in shallow water or mud. • These birds nest in colonies, sometimes composed of other heron species. • The Little Blue Heron breeds mostly in southwestern Illinois. After the breeding season, the Little Blue Heron occasionally disperses farther north where it forages in wetlands in large numbers.

ID: medium-sized heron; rich slate blue overall. *Breeding:* shaggy, maroon-colored head and neck; black legs and feet. *Nonbreeding:* purplish head and neck; dull green legs and feet. *Immature:* all-white plumage becomes blotched with blue in a calico pattern as bird matures; greenish legs; 2-tone bill.
Size: *L* 24 in; *W* 3½ ft.
Status: state-endangered; rare to uncommon migrant; uncommon, very local breeder in the southwest; rare to uncommon summer wanderer in the rest of the state; present from April to early October.

Habitat: marshes, ponds, sloughs, lakes and streams.
Nesting: nests in a shrub or tree above water; pair builds large nest of sticks; pair incubates 3–5 pale greenish blue eggs for 22–24 days.
Feeding: patient, stand-and-wait predator; may also wade to stalk prey; usually feeds with Snowy Egrets; eats mostly fish; also takes grasshoppers and other insects.
Voice: generally silent.
Similar Species: *Snowy Egret* (p. 86): immature has yellow feet, yellow lores, yellowish legs and uniformly colored bill.
Best Sites: Alorton nesting colony in East St. Louis region; wetlands in Alexander Co. and Union Co.

CATTLE EGRET
Bubulcus ibis

Over the last century, the Cattle Egret has dispersed from Africa to inhabit every continent except Antarctica. Like most herons, the Cattle Egret is a natural wanderer. It probably colonized the New World more than a century ago. The first Illinois record of the Cattle Egret was in 1952 at Saganashkee Slough in the Palos Preserves. Today, it breeds mostly in southwestern Illinois. • The Cattle Egret gets its name from its habit of following grazing animals. Unlike other egrets, its diet consists of terrestrial invertebrates—it feeds mainly on insects found around ungulates and on frogs in wetlands. When foraging, Cattle Egrets sometimes feed by leapfrogging over one another, stirring up insects for the birds that follow. • This bird's scientific name *Bubulcus* means "belonging to or concerning cattle."

ID: mostly white; yellow bill and dark legs. *Breeding:* long plumes on throat and rump; buff orange throat, rump and crown; orange red legs and bill; purple lores. *Immature:* similar to adult, but with black feet and dark bill.

Size: *L* 19–21 in; *W* 3 ft.

Status: rare to uncommon migrant and summer resident; rare to uncommon local breeder in the southwest; generally absent from November to March.

Habitat: agricultural fields and wetlands.

Nesting: colonial; usually among other herons in Illinois, especially Great Egrets, Snowy Egrets, Little Blue Herons and Black-crowned Night-Herons; in a tree or tall shrub; male supplies sticks for the female who builds a platform or shallow bowl; pair incubates 3–4 pale blue eggs for 21–26 days.

Feeding: eats grasshoppers, other insects, worms, small vertebrates, spiders and frogs; often associated with livestock.

Voice: generally silent.

Similar Species: *Great Egret* (p. 85): much larger; black legs and feet. *Snowy Egret* (p. 86): black legs; yellow feet; black bill.

Best Sites: wetlands in East St. Louis region; Union Co. and Alexander Co.

GREEN HERON

Butorides virescens

This crow-sized heron, which breeds throughout Illinois, primarily eats small fish. It hunts in shallow, weedy wetlands, where it often perches just above the water's surface. While hunting, Green Herons sometimes drop or even hold small debris, including twigs, vegetation and feathers, on the water's surface to attract fish within striking range. The usage of such tools is rare among birds, and is most often observed in species considered to be more intelligent such as corvids and parrots. • A harsh *kowp* often alerts you to the Green Heron's presence. • If the light is just right, you may see a glimmer of green on the back and outer wings of this bird. • Unlike most herons, Green Herons generally nest singly rather than communally, although they can sometimes be found in loose colonies. • The scientific name *virescens* is Latin for "growing or becoming green," and refers to this bird's transition from a streaky, brown juvenile to a greenish adult.

ID: small, but stocky; green black crown; chestnut brown face and neck; white foreneck and belly; blue gray back and wings mixed with iridescent green; relatively short, green yellow legs; bill is dark above and greenish below; short tail. *Breeding male:* bright orange legs. *Immature:* heavy streaks along neck and underparts; dark brown upperparts.
Size: *L* 15–22 in; *W* 26 in.
Status: common breeder statewide; generally absent from late September to early April.
Habitat: freshwater marshes, lakes, ponds and streams with dense shoreline or emergent vegetation.
Nesting: nests singly or in small groups; male begins construction of the stick platform in a tree or shrub, usually close to water; pair incubates 3–5 pale blue green to green eggs for 19–21 days; young are fed by regurgitation.
Feeding: stabs prey with its bill after stalking or standing and waiting; eats mostly small fish; also takes frogs, aquatic and terrestrial insects, small rodents, snakes, snails and worms.
Voice: generally silent, except when giving loud alarm and flight call: *kowp, kyow* or *skow;* aggression call is a harsh *raah.*
Similar Species: *Black-crowned Night-Heron* (p. 90): immature is larger, with relatively short, stout bill and red eyes. *Yellow-crowned Night-Heron* (p. 91): immature is larger, with all-dark, thick bill and uniformly dark upperparts. *Least Bittern* (p. 83): extensive yellow shoulder patches, "cheek," neck and flanks; usually found only in cattail marshes.
Best Sites: *Summer:* common in wetlands statewide.

BLACK-CROWNED NIGHT-HERON

Nycticorax nycticorax

When the setting sun has sent most wetland waders to their nightly roosts, Black-crowned Night-Herons arrive to hunt the marshy waters and to utter their hoarse squawks. These herons patrol the shallows for prey, which they can see in the dim light with their large, light-sensitive eyes. They remain alongside water until morning, when they flap off to daytime roosts. • Young night-herons are commonly seen around large cattail marshes in fall. Because of their heavily streaked underparts, they can be confused with other immature herons and American Bitterns. • During the breeding season or in unusual weather, the Black-crowned Night-Heron sometimes forages by day. A popular hunting strategy for day-active birds is to sit motionless atop wetland vegetation. Anything passing below the perch becomes fair game—even ducklings, small shorebirds or young muskrats. • *Nycticorax*, meaning "night raven," refers to this bird's distinctive nighttime calls.

ID: black "cap" and back; white "cheek," foreneck and underparts; gray neck and wings; dull yellow legs; stout black bill; large red eyes. *Breeding:* 2 white plumes trail down from crown. *Immature:* lightly streaked underparts; brown upperparts with white flecking.
Size: *L* 23–26 in; *W* 3½ ft.
Status: state-endangered; rare to uncommon migrant and summer resident; locally common breeder in large communal colonies near E. St. Louis and northeastern Illinois; a few recorded annually in winter.
Habitat: cattails and nonnative *Phragmites;* swamps, sloughs and marshes.
Nesting: colonial, sometimes with Great Blue Herons and Great Egrets; loose nest platform of twigs and sticks is placed in a tree or shrub and lined with finer materials; male gathers the nest material and

female builds the nest; pair incubates 3–4 pale green eggs for 21–26 days.
Feeding: often at dusk; patient, stand-and-wait predator; stabs for small fish, amphibians, aquatic invertebrates, reptiles, young birds and small mammals.
Voice: deep, guttural *quark* or *wok,* often heard as the bird takes flight.
Similar Species: *Great Blue Heron* (p. 84): much larger; longer legs; blue gray back. *Yellow-crowned Night-Heron* (p. 91): white "cheek" patch completely framed in black; buffy white crown; slate blue overall; immature is similar to adult, but has all-black bill, longer legs and neck, and fine, evenly patterned, white speckling. *Green Heron* (p. 89): smaller; chestnut brown face and neck; blue gray back with green iridescence; immature has heavily streaked underparts.
Best Sites: wetlands in the Palos Preserves; L. Calumet region; wetlands in the East St. Louis region.

YELLOW-CROWNED NIGHT-HERON
Nyctanassa violacea

The Yellow-crowned Night-Heron's partiality for crustaceans has earned it the name "Crab Eater" in some parts of its range. In Illinois, this state-endangered bird replaces crabs with crayfish. It also eats frogs, insects and some fish. In fall, when it returns to subtropical and tropical locations, this night-heron feeds primarily on crabs. The Yellow-crowned Night-Heron typically grabs a crayfish by its legs or pinchers and shakes vigorously until they fall off, making the crayfish more edible. Like many other herons, this bird is a patient predator—it stands and waits for prey to glide underneath its still body. Despite its name, the Yellow-crowned Night-Heron feeds by day as well as at night. • During the breeding season, Yellow-crowned Night-Heron pairs greet each other with their crests raised and delicately preen each other's feathers.

ID: blue gray overall; black head; buffy white crown; white "cheek" framed in black. *Breeding:* long, white head plumes. *Immature:* similar to Black-crowned Night-Heron, but fewer and smaller white spots; black bill; longer legs and neck. *In flight:* feet extend well beyond tail.
Size: *L* 24 in; *W* 3½ ft.
Status: state-endangered; rare to uncommon migrant and breeder mainly in extreme southern Illinois; generally absent from mid-October to early April.
Habitat: along rivers and swamps, especially cypress and tupelo swamps in extreme southern Illinois.

Nesting: singly or in very small colonies; often in a tree or shrub over standing water; pair builds a nest of heavy twigs lined with finer twigs, rootlets and sometimes leaves; pair incubates 2–4 pale greenish blue eggs for 21–25 days.
Feeding: stands and waits or wades slowly in shallow water to catch crayfish, other freshwater invertebrates, fish and frogs; forages alone or in small groups.
Voice: a loud *quok* that is less harsh and slightly higher in pitch than the Black-crowned Night-Heron's call.
Similar Species: *Black-crowned Night-Heron* (p. 90): black crown and back; shorter legs; thinner bill; immature is similar.
Best Sites: Stump L. near Pere Marquette SP; Oakwood Bottoms; East St. Louis wetlands.

BLACK VULTURE

Coragyps atratus

This large, black scavenger serves the environment well. Feeding primarily on carrion, it helps convert the nutrients of the dead back into nutrients that support the living. These large birds live only in the extreme southern part of Illinois. There, you can see them soaring high among the clouds, scouring the earth below for signs of their next meal or gathering to roost at dusk. At the southern tip of Illinois, Black Vultures gather with Turkey Vultures in large communal roosts during winter. To distinguish these vulture species in the air, observe their flight patterns. Compared with the flight of the Turkey Vulture, the Black Vulture requires many more wingbeats to become airborne and while soaring. As well, Black Vultures soar on flattened wings; Turkey Vultures hold their wing in a shallow "V." • Both of these bird species, if disturbed, will regurgitate their food and hiss loudly at an intruder. The young also lift their wings to appear larger and more menacing.

ID: all-black plumage; grayish head, legs and feet; base of primaries are whitish.
Size: *L* 25 in; *W* 4½–5 ft.
Status: rare to locally common year-round resident in southern Illinois.
Habitat: forages over open country, but roosts and nests in forested areas near rocky outcroppings close to water.
Nesting: in a large tree cavity, a rocky shelf on a cliff or in an abandoned building; both adults incubate 1–3 gray green or creamy white eggs, with reddish brown or faint purple blotches, for 42–50 days and raise the young together.
Feeding: carrion forms the bulk of the diet; also eats eggs, small reptiles, amphibians, small mammals, food waste and occasionally plant material.
Voice: generally silent; may hiss or grunt at the nest site or around communal food sources.
Similar Species: *Turkey Vulture* (p. 93): red head; 2-tone wings with dark wing linings and pale flight feathers; longer, narrower wings and tail; wings usually held in a shallow "V."
Best Sites: Heron Pond SNA; Fern Clyffe SP; Johnson Co. and Pope Co.

TURKEY VULTURE
Cathartes aura

Turkey Vultures can gain lift from the slightest pocket of rising air and patrol the skies when other soaring birds are grounded. • With a bill and feet that are not powerful enough to kill prey, the Turkey Vulture eats primarily carrion. Its red, featherless head allows it to remain relatively clean while feeding on messy carcasses. • Vultures have mastered the art of regurgitation. This ability allows parents to transport food over long distances and also enables engorged birds to repulse an attacker or "lighten up" for an emergency takeoff. • Recent studies have shown that American vultures are most closely related to storks, not to hawks and falcons as was previously thought. Molecular similarities with storks, and the shared tendency to defecate on their own legs to cool down, strongly support this taxonomic reclassification.

ID: all-black plumage; bare, red head. *Immature:* gray head. *In flight:* head appears small; silver gray flight feathers; black wing linings; wings are held in a shallow "V"; rocks from side to side while soaring. **Size:** *L* 26–32 in; *W* 5½–6 ft. **Status:** common migrant; common breeder in central and southern Illinois; uncommon to fairly common breeder in the north, except for northeastern corner; occurs from mid-February to early March through mid-November, with numbers peaking in October; rare to locally common winter resident in extreme southern Illinois and occasionally elsewhere. **Habitat:** usually seen flying over open country, shorelines or perched along roads. **Nesting:** on a cliff ledge or among boulders, in a hollow stump, log, abandoned barn or building; little to no nest material is used; female lays 2 dull white eggs; pair incubates the eggs for up to 41 days; young are fed by regurgitation. **Feeding:** eats carrion and occasionally small mammals, reptiles and amphibians as well as vegetable matter; commonly seen at roadkills. **Voice:** generally silent; occasionally produces a hiss or grunt if threatened. **Similar Species:** *Golden Eagle* (p. 106): golden brown plumage; immature has white uppertail feathers and white patches in flight feathers; usually holds wings flatter. *Bald Eagle* (p. 96): lacks silvery gray wing linings; wings are held flat in flight; does not rock when soaring; head is more visible in flight. *Black Vulture* (p. 92): seen only in extreme southern part of state; gray head; silvery tips on otherwise black wings; shorter tail; flaps faster when flying and holds wings flatter. **Best Sites:** areas where forest meets open country.

OSPREY
Pandion haliaetus

The state-endangered Osprey is the only species in its family and, unlike other such birds, is found on every continent except Antarctica. These raptors are always found near water and eat fish exclusively. • Most fish-eating birds such as cormorants land on water and dive for their food or enter the water headfirst like gannets. The Osprey takes the middle ground—it hovers above the water then folds its wings and hurls itself in a perilous head-first dive toward a flash of silver or a slowly moving shadow. An instant before striking the water, the Osprey rights itself and thrusts its feet forward to grasp its slippery prey. • Two toes face forward, two face backward, all of them with sharp spines that help the Osprey clamp tightly onto the slipperiest of fish. • The Osprey returned as a breeder in Illinois in 1996 after a long absence of 44 years, but it has never been a common breeder in the state.

ID: dark brown upperparts; white underparts; dark eye line; light crown; yellow eyes; gray feet. *Male:* all-white throat. *Female:* fine, dark "necklace." *In flight:* long wings are held in shallow "M"; dark "wrist" patches; brown and white tail bands.

Size: *L* 22–25 in; *W* 4½–6 ft.

Status: state-endangered; uncommon migrant from late March to early May and from mid- to late August to mid-November; July migrant records increasing; rare breeder with only a few confirmed breeding locations.

Habitat: lakes and slowly flowing rivers and streams.

Nesting: on a treetop, usually near water; also on a platform, utility pole or tower up to 100 ft in height; massive stick nest is reused over many years; pair incubates 2–4 eggs for about 38 days; both adults feed the young, but the male hunts more.

Feeding: feet-first dives into water; small fish make up most of the diet.

Voice: series of melodious ascending whistles: *chewk-chewk-chewk;* also, a frequent *kip-kip-kip.*

Similar Species: *Bald Eagle* (p. 96): larger; holds wings straighter while soaring; larger bill with yellow base; yellow legs; white head and tail on otherwise dark body; lacks white underparts and dark "wrist" patches. *Rough-legged Hawk* (p. 105): smaller; hovers with wings in an open "V"; light morph has whitish wing linings and light tail band.

Best Sites: *Summer:* Bergman Slough at the Palos Preserves; Mermet Lake CA. *In fall migration:* Illinois Beach SP.

MISSISSIPPI KITE
Ictinia mississippiensis

This gregarious inhabitant of riparian woodlands and swamps relies on the protection of tall trees for nesting and social nighttime roosting, but also needs adjacent areas of open country to provide ample hunting opportunities. Constantly fanning and twisting its long tail, using it as a rudder to swiftly adjust its position, the Mississippi Kite deftly pursues flying insects including dragonflies, cicadas, beetles and grasshoppers. Most of these common prey items are caught on the wing or hawked out of the air and eaten from the bird's clutches while it continues to astound observers with its lissome flight. The Mississippi Kite also occasionally catches bats, swallows and swifts during acrobatic aerial pursuits. • Breeding populations of this bird declined in Illinois in the early 1900s and the state-endangered Mississippi Kite is currently confined to the southern part of the state. This bird winters in South America.

ID: long, swept-back wings with obviously shorter first primaries and pale secondaries; dark gray upperparts; dark tail; pale gray head and underparts; chestnut at base of primaries often inconspicuous. *Juvenile:* dark brownish upperparts; streaky brown underparts; pale, translucent bands in dark tail.
Size: *L* 14½ in; *W* 35 in.
Status: state-endangered; uncommon migrant and local breeder in southern Illinois; rarely seen elsewhere; occurs from late April or early May to late August or early September.
Habitat: mature bottomland forests near open grassy fields; upland river bluffs mainly along Cache, Mississippi and Ohio River floodplains; prefers large, mature cottonwood trees for nesting.

Nesting: nests in small, loose colonies or singly; both adults construct a flimsy stick platform lined with leaves in a relatively tall tree or shrub near the edge of a wooded area; pair incubates 1–3 bluish white eggs and raises the young together.
Feeding: large flying insects form bulk of diet, typically caught on the wing; small mammals, small birds, frogs, toads, lizards, turtles, snakes and bats are also caught on the wing; may scavenge roadkill.
Voice: generally silent; alarm call is *kee kew, kee kew.*
Similar Species: *Northern Harrier* (p. 97): larger; facial disc; white rump patch; male has dark wing tips and gray-banded tail; female has brown tail with black bands. *Sharp-shinned Hawk* (p. 98): immature has broader, rounder, lighter-colored wings; white tail with black stripes, opposite to kite, extends well beyond folded wing when bird is perched.
Best Sites: Union County CA; Fort Kaskaskia State Historic Site; Shawnee NF near Thebes; Pomona.

95

BALD EAGLE

Haliaeetus leucocephalus

Once nearly extirpated from Illinois as a breeding bird, the Bald Eagle is making a comeback with the banning of certain pesticides and the restoration and preservation of appropriate habitat. Except for Alaska, more Bald Eagles winter in Illinois than in any other state. Birders and non-birders alike make winter trips to locks and dams along the Mississippi and Illinois Rivers to search for wintering Bald Eagles. Hundreds can sometimes be found in one place. • Bald Eagles, which remain on the state-threatened list, feed mostly on fish and scavenged carrion. • Bald Eagles generally mate for life. They renew their pair bonds each year by adding new sticks and branches to their massive nests, the largest of any North American bird. The number of breeding Bald Eagles in Illinois continues to increase annually.

immature

ID: white head and tail; dark brown body; yellow bill and feet; broad wings are held flat in flight. *1st-year:* dark overall; dark beak; some white in underwings. *2nd-year:* dark "bib"; white in underwings. *3rd-year:* mostly white plumage; yellow at base of bill; yellow eyes. *4th-year:* light head with dark facial streak; variable pale and dark plumage; yellow bill; paler eyes.
Size: *L* 30–43 in; *W* 5½–8 ft.
Status: state-threatened; uncommon migrant from late February to early March; fall migrants arrive in September with largest numbers in October and November; rare breeder, but increasing; fairly common to locally abundant winter resident.
Habitat: large lakes and rivers, locks and dams with open water in winter.
Nesting: usually in a large, dead tree bordering a lake or large river, but may be far from water; huge stick nest, up to 15 ft across, is often reused for many years, typically until nest or tree falls down; pair incubates 1–3 white eggs for 34–36 days; pair feeds the young; young remain in the nest until they can fly.
Feeding: injured waterfowl and small mammals, also fish and carrion.
Voice: thin, weak squeal or gull-like cackle: *kleek-kik-kik-kik* or *kah-kah-kah.*
Similar Species: adult is distinctive. *Golden Eagle* (p. 106): dark overall, except for golden nape; tail may appear faintly banded with white; immature has prominent white patch on wing and at base of tail; holds wings in a slight "V." *Osprey* (p. 94): similar to 4th-year Bald Eagle, but has crooked wing appearance and dark "wrist" patches; banded tail; solid, white belly.
Best Sites: locks and dams along the Mississippi R. and Illinois R., especially in winter; Union County CA and Horseshoe Lake CA year-round, but especially in winter.

NORTHERN HARRIER

Circus cyaneus

The Northern Harrier may be the easiest raptor to identify in flight, because no other midsized hawk routinely flies with its wings slightly angled upward. This bird cruises low over fields and marshes, relying on sudden surprise attacks to capture its prey. Although the harrier has excellent vision, its owl-like, parabolic facial disc allows it to hunt easily by sound as well. • The Northern Harrier is an endangered breeder in Illinois. Habitat destruction and degradation has made it difficult for this species to find appropriate places for nesting. • The Northern Harrier often shares feeding and roosting sites with the Short-eared Owl, its evening counterpart; at dusk you may observe the "changing of the guard" as harriers and short-ears chase one another.

ID: long wings and tail; white rump; owl-like facial disc. *Male:* blue gray to silver gray upperparts; white underparts; black wing tips; indistinct tail bands, except for 1 dark subterminal band. *Female:* dark brown upperparts; streaky, brown-and-buff underparts. *Immature:* rich reddish brown underparts; dark tail bands.
Size: *L* 16–24 in; *W* 3½–4 ft.
Status: state-endangered; fairly common migrant from late February to early May; fall migrants arrive by late August; difficult to discern fall migration departure dates because of wintering population; rare summer resident; uncommon to locally common winter resident.
Habitat: open country including fields, wet meadows, cattail marshes and croplands.
Nesting: on the ground, often on a slightly raised mound, usually in grass, cattails or tall vegetation; shallow depression

or platform nest is lined with grass, sticks and cattails; female incubates 4–6 bluish white eggs for 30–32 days.
Feeding: hunts in low, rising and falling flights, often just above the tops of vegetation; eats small mammals, birds, amphibians, reptiles and some invertebrates.
Voice: most vocal near the nest, during courtship and in shared roosts with Short-eared Owls, but generally quiet; high-pitched *ke-ke-ke-ke-ke-ke*.
Similar Species: *Rough-legged Hawk* (p. 105): broader wings; dark "wrist" patches; black tail with wide, white base; dark belly. *Red-tailed Hawk* (p. 104): larger; lacks white rump and long, narrow tail. *Mississippi Kite* (p. 95): smaller; gray overall; wing tips extend beyond tail; small, black "mask" surrounds bright red eyes; solid black tail; large, white patches on upperwing; lacks white rump; immature has mostly black tail with thin, white bands.
Best Sites: Midewin National Tallgrass Prairie; Prairie Ridge SNA; Cypress Creek NWR; Pyramid Lake SP.

97

SHARP-SHINNED HAWK

Accipiter striatus

After a successful hunt, the Sharp-shinned Hawk usually perches on a favorite "plucking post," grasping its meal in its talons. Sharpies, also called "accipiters" after their genus name, prey almost exclusively on small birds, pursuing them in high-speed chases. • Most Illinois residents never see a Sharpie nest, because the bird is a rare breeder in the state and it remains still and quiet even when approached closely. • The Sharp-shinned Hawk, like other birds of prey, experienced population declines in the 1950s because of pesticide use. Despite the banning of pesticides such as DDT in the United States, the Sharp-shin's population continues to decline. There is speculation that this is linked to pesticide use in their winter homes in South America as well as increased competition with the larger Cooper's Hawk. Nevertheless, Sharp-shins remain a common raptor at Illinois hawk migration sites.

immature

ID: short, rounded wings; long, straight, heavily barred, square-tipped tail; dark barring on pale underwings; blue gray back; red horizontal bars on underparts; red eyes. *Immature:* brown overall; yellow eyes; vertical, brown streaking on breast and belly. *In flight:* flap-and-glide flier; very agile in wooded areas.
Size: *Male: L* 10–12 in; *W* 20–24 in. *Female: L* 12–14 in; *W* 24–28 in.
Status: common migrant from mid-March to early May and from early to mid-September to mid-November; very rare breeder; uncommon winter resident, decreasing northward.
Habitat: *Breeding:* large forests. *In migration* and *winter:* L. Michigan shoreline, most woodlands, including suburban and urban backyards.

Nesting: in a coniferous or deciduous tree; usually builds a new stick nest each year but might remodel an abandoned crow nest; female incubates 4–5 bluish white, brown-blotched eggs for 34–35 days; male feeds the female during incubation.
Feeding: chases small birds; rarely takes small mammals, amphibians and insects.
Voice: silent, except during the breeding season, call is a repeated *kik-kik-kik-kik.*
Similar Species: *Cooper's Hawk* (p. 99): larger, with some size overlap; tail tip is more rounded and has broader terminal band; thicker legs on perched bird; in flight, head protrudes beyond wings. *American Kestrel* (p. 107): long, pointed wings; 1 dark "tear streak"; 1 dark "sideburn"; typically seen in open country. *Merlin* (p. 108): pointed wings; rapid wingbeats; 1 dark "tear streak" on "cheek"; brown streaking on buff underparts; dark eyes.
Best Sites: *In migration:* Illinois Beach SP; Mt. Hoy at Blackwell FP.

COOPER'S HAWK
Accipiter cooperii

Larger and heavier than the Sharp-shinned Hawk, the Cooper's Hawk glides silently along forest clearings, using surprise and speed to catch its prey. This hawk also frequently visits rural and suburban feeders, foraging for songbirds. • Cooper's Hawks began to decline when DDT was used in North America, however, since the banning of DDT in 1972, they are increasing in number and are recolonizing former breeding habitat in Illinois. • Distinguishing the Cooper's Hawk from the Sharp-shinned Hawk can be challenging. In flight, the Sharp-shin's square tail may appear rounded like the Cooper's. Molting also changes the appearance of the Cooper's Hawk. • This forest hawk bears the name of William Cooper, one of the many hunters who supplied English and American ornithologists with bird specimens for museum collections during the early 19th century.

immature

ID: short, rounded wings; long, straight, heavily barred, rounded tail; dark barring on pale undertail and underwings; squarish head; blue gray back; red horizontal barring on underparts; red eyes; white terminal tail band. *Immature:* brown overall; dark eyes; vertical brown streaks on breast and belly. *In flight:* flap-and-glide flyer.
Size: *Male: L* 15–17 in; *W* 27–32 in. *Female: L* 17–19 in; *W* 32–37 in.
Status: fairly common migrant and winter resident; uncommon to common breeder; migration obscured by the increasing breeding population; usually arrive by March and return by mid- to late August.
Habitat: mixed woodlands, riparian woodlands and woodlots, and increasingly urban and suburban yards.
Nesting: nest of sticks and twigs is built 20–65 ft above the ground in the crotch of a deciduous or coniferous tree; often near a stream or pond; might reuse an abandoned crow nest; female incubates 3–5 bluish white eggs for 34–36 days; male feeds the female during incubation.
Feeding: pursues prey in flight; eats mostly songbirds, squirrels and chipmunks; may use a plucking post or nest for eating.
Voice: fast, woodpecker-like *cac-cac-cac-cac.*
Similar Species: *Sharp-shinned Hawk* (p. 98): smaller, with some size overlap; squared tail tip; thinner terminal tail band; slimmer legs; head barely protrudes beyond wing in flight. *Northern Goshawk* (p. 100): immature male is larger, with wavy tail bands, white "eyebrow" stripe and streaked undertail coverts. *American Kestrel* (p. 107): long, pointed wings; 1 dark "mustache" mark; 1 dark "sideburn." *Merlin* (p. 108): smaller; pointed wings; 1 dark "mustache" mark; brown streaking on buff underparts; dark eyes rapid wingbeats.
Best Sites: Illinois Beach SP; Mt. Hoy at Blackwell FP; suburban backyards year-round.

NORTHERN GOSHAWK

Accipiter gentilis

The Northern Goshawk, an agile, powerful predator, can negotiate lightning-fast turns through dense forest cover. This raptor preys on a wide range of animals, including mammals as large as squirrels, and many bird species, including the Ring-necked Pheasant in Illinois. The goshawk may even chase its prey on foot should it disappear into dense thickets. • Northern Goshawks breed in extensive forests north of Illinois. In winter, goshawks may move farther south, sometimes into Illinois. • This species' populations increase and decrease with some regularity in response to fluctuations in prey numbers. Goshawk numbers peak every 10 or 11 years, but overall this species' population has declined because of habitat loss, especially in the western United States. Seeing a Northern Goshawk in Illinois is indeed a rare winter treat.

immature

ID: rounded wings; long, banded tail with white terminal band; white "eyebrow"; dark crown; blue gray back; fine, gray, vertical streaking on pale breast and belly; gray barring on pale undertail and underwings; red eyes. *Immature:* brown overall; brown, vertical streaking on whitish breast and belly; brown barring on pale undertail and underwings; grayish yellow eyes.
Size: *Male: L* 21–23 in; *W* 3–3½ ft. *Female: L* 23–25 in; *W* 3½–4 ft.
Status: rare migrant and winter resident in northern Illinois, decreasing southward.
Habitat: forest and forest edges, occasionally in more open areas.

Nesting: does not nest in Illinois.
Feeding: low foraging flights through forests and more open areas; feeds primarily on songbirds, pheasants, rabbits and squirrels.
Voice: generally silent in winter.
Similar Species: *Cooper's Hawk* (p. 99): smaller, but with some size overlap; reddish breast bars; lacks white "eyebrow" stripe. *Red-tailed Hawk* (p. 104): immature has thinner, more numerous tail bands compared with immature goshawk, white undersides usually with distinct belly band, and lacks white "eyebrow" stripe. *Gyrfalcon* (p. 356): more pointed wings; dark eyes; often has dark "mustache"; underparts usually darker and more boldly streaked; lacks bold, white "eyebrow" stripe.
Best Sites: Illinois Beach SP, but very rare.

RED-SHOULDERED HAWK

Buteo lineatus

The Red-shouldered Hawk prefers wetter habitats compared with the closely related Broad-winged Hawk and Red-tailed Hawk. Heard more often than it is seen, the Red-shouldered Hawk nests in mature forests, in bottomland swamps and river bottoms, hunting in woodlands rather than over open fields. Its loud, shrieking *kee-yar* calls can be heard half a mile away and sometimes farther. • A state-threatened species, the Red-shouldered Hawk once bred throughout most of the state, but is now mostly seen in southern Illinois. Disturbance, habitat loss and pesticide use have led to the decline of this hawk. If left undisturbed, the Red-shouldered Hawk remains faithful to productive nesting sites and, in the far south of Illinois, the bird is likely a permanent resident. Those found in northern and central Illinois in winter may be birds that migrated from the north.• Blue Jays often imitate this hawk's call as well as that of the Red-tailed Hawk.

ID: chestnut red shoulders on otherwise dark brown upperparts; reddish underwing linings; narrow, white bars on dark tail; barred, reddish breast and belly; reddish undertail coverts. *Immature:* large, brown streaks on white underparts. *In flight:* light and dark barring on underside of flight feathers and tail; white crescents or "windows" at base of primaries.
Size: *L* 19 in; *W* 3½ ft.
Status: state-threatened; rare to uncommon year-round resident in northern Illinois; uncommon year-round resident in southern Illinois; uncommon migrant statewide; threatened breeder and rare in central Illinois; rare winter resident in northern and central Illinois.
Habitat: mature deciduous and mixed forests, especially bottomland swamps and along rivers.

Nesting: pair assembles a bulky nest of sticks and twigs, usually 15–80 ft above the ground in the crotch of a deciduous tree; nest is often reused; female incubates 2–4 darkly blotched, bluish white eggs for about 33 days; both adults raise the young.
Feeding: small mammals, birds, reptiles and amphibians often caught from a low perch after a swooping attack; may catch prey flushed by low flight.
Voice: repeated series of high *kee-yar* notes.
Similar Species: *Broad-winged Hawk* (p. 102): broader, brighter white wings; wider, white tail bands; lacks reddish shoulders. *Red-tailed Hawk* (p. 104): lacks barring in tail and light "windows" at base of primaries; immature has little or no streaking on breast and lacks pale wing crescents in flight.
Best Sites: Heron Pond SNA; Union County CA; Oakwood Bottoms.

BROAD-WINGED HAWK

Buteo platypterus

The generally shy and secretive Broad-winged Hawk prefers different habitat than most other buteos. Shunning the open fields and forest clearings favored by the Red-tailed Hawk, it secludes itself in dense, often wet forests. In this habitat, its short, broad wings and highly flexible tail help it to maneuver in the heavy growth. • The Broad-winged Hawk is a rare breeder in Illinois, needing large stands of contiguous forests. One of the more reliable places to find this bird in summer is the Shawnee National Forest in southern Illinois. • At the end of the nesting season, "kettles" of buteos and other hawks spiral up from their forest retreats, testing thermals for the opportunity to head south. Broad-wings are often the most numerous species in these flocks. In good flight years, large concentrations of these birds can be seen. In mid-September, hundreds to thousands may fly over Mount Hoy or other inland locations.

light morph

ID: broad, black and white tail bands; broad wings with pointed tips; heavily barred, rufous brown breast; dark brown upperparts. *Immature:* dark brown streaks on white breast, belly and sides; buff and dark brown tail bands. *In flight:* pale underwings are outlined with dark brown or black.
Size: *L* 14–19 in; *W* 32–39 in.
Status: uncommon to common migrant, seen in fall more than in spring; rare summer resident.

Habitat: *Breeding:* dense mixed and deciduous forests. *In migration:* shorelines, woodlands.
Nesting: usually in a deciduous tree, often near water; bulky stick nest is built in a crotch 20–40 ft above the ground; usually builds a new nest each year; mostly the female incubates 2–4 brown-spotted, whitish eggs for 28–31 days; both adults raise the young.
Feeding: swoops from a perch for small mammals, amphibians, insects and young birds.
Voice: high-pitched, whistled *peh-teeee;* generally silent during migration.
Similar Species: *Red-tailed Hawk* (p. 104) and *Rough-legged* Hawk (p. 105): lack bold, broad banding on tail. *Red-shouldered Hawk* (p. 101): thinner, more numerous white bands on tail. *Accipiters* (p. 98–100): long, narrow tails with less distinct banding.
Best Sites: *In migration:* Illinois Beach SP; Mt. Hoy; Blackwell FP. *Summer:* Trail of Tears SF; Pine Hills–LaRue Ecological Area.

SWAINSON'S HAWK

Buteo swainsoni

The Swainson's Hawk requires extensive open country for breeding. The presence of this state-endangered species is tenuous, with only a few breeding pairs remaining. Much of the savanna-like habitat they prefer has been replaced by subdivisions and other suburban sprawl. • Swainson's Hawk is the only breeding hawk in Illinois with a reddish chest. In flight, the bird shows clean white underparts and wing linings combined with darker flight feathers. It also exhibits relatively pointed wing tips and slightly uptilted wings. • Swainson's Hawks undertake long migratory journeys that may lead them as far south as the southern tip of South America. Flying up to 12,500 miles in a single year, the Swainson's Hawk is second only to the arctic-breeding Peregrine Falcon for long-distance travel among birds of prey. Unfortunately, many of these hawks are killed by insecticides in Argentina, reminding us that the conservation of migratory species requires international cooperation.

light morph

light morph

light morph

ID: long wings with pointed tips; narrowly banded tail; dark flight feathers. *Light morph:* more common; rufous "bib"; white belly; white wing linings contrast with dark flight feathers. *Dark morph:* seen only in migration; dark overall; brown wing linings blend with flight feathers. *In flight:* holds wings in a shallow "V."
Size: *L* 20 in; *W* 4½ ft.
Status: state-endangered; very rare migrant; breeds in only a few northern Illinois locations.
Habitat: savanna-like areas, including open fields, grasslands and croplands.
Nesting: in a solitary tree, usually a large oak, or a small grove in an open field; builds a large stick nest; often uses the abandoned nest of another raptor or crow; uses the same nest repeatedly; female incubates 2–3 sparsley marked, whitish eggs for 28–35 days.
Feeding: dives for voles, mice and ground squirrels; also eats snakes, small birds and large insects such as grasshoppers and crickets.
Voice: typical hawk call, *keeeaar,* is higher pitched than a Red-tail's.
Similar Species: *Red-tailed Hawk* (p. 104): more rounded wing tips; wings held flat in flight; lacks dark "bib." *Other buteos* (pp. 101–05): flight feathers are lighter than wing linings. *Golden Eagle* (p. 106): much larger; massive bill; golden nape; immature has white wing patches and white base to tail.
Best Sites: *Summer:* Kane Co. and McHenry Co.

RED-TAILED HAWK

Buteo jamaicensis

The Red-tail, one of the most common buteos in Illinois, can be found year-round, especially in open fields near woodlands. An afternoon drive through the country often reveals resident Red-tailed Hawks perching on exposed tree limbs, fence posts or utility poles overlooking open fields and roadsides. • During spring courtship, Red-tailed Hawks dive at each other, sometimes locking talons and tumbling through the air together. • The tail of this hawk does not obtain its brick red coloration until the bird matures into a breeding adult. During migration and winter, the dark and very light morphs from other parts of North America can be found in Illinois. Most eastern birds are pale morphs. • The Red-tailed Hawk has an impressive, piercing call that television commercials and movies often misrepresent by pairing it with the image of an eagle.

ID: red tail; dark upperparts with some white highlights; dark brown band of streaks across belly. *Immature:* variable; lacks red tail; generally darker; band of streaks on belly. *In flight:* fan-shaped tail; faint barring on underwing.
Size: *Male: L* 18–23 in; *W* 4–5 ft. *Female: L* 20–25 in; *W* 4–5 ft.
Status: common year-round.
Habitat: open country with some trees; roadsides, fields, woodlots, hedgerows, mixed forests and woodlands.
Nesting: in woodlands adjacent to open habitat; usually in a deciduous tree; materials usually added to bulky stick nest each year; pair incubates 2–4 brown-blotched, whitish eggs for 28–35 days.
Feeding: scans for food while perched or soaring; drops to capture prey; rarely stalks

prey on foot; eats voles, mice, rabbits, chipmunks, birds, amphibians and reptiles, especially snakes; rarely takes large insects.
Voice: powerful, descending, drawn-out scream: *keeearrrr.*
Similar Species: *Rough-legged Hawk* (p. 105): white tail base; dark "wrist" patches on underwings, except for dark morph; broad, dark terminal tail band. *Broad-winged Hawk* (p. 102): smaller; broadly banded, black-and-white tail; lacks dark belly band. *Red-shouldered Hawk* (p. 101): slightly smaller and slimmer; reddish wing linings and underparts; reddish shoulders; black and white tail bands. *Swainson's Hawk* (p. 103): all-dark back; more pointed wing tips; dark flight feathers and pale wing linings while soaring; holds wings in shallow "V."
Best Sites: *In migration:* open country, agricultural fields statewide; L. Michigan shoreline.

ROUGH-LEGGED HAWK

Buteo lagopus

While hunting, the Rough-legged Hawk is one of few buteos that regularly hovers—a technique that serves as an excellent long-distance identification tool for birders. This habit of hovering is necessary because its open-country tundra breeding habitat often lacks high perches. • The Rough-legged Hawk winters in Illinois. Its white tail base and dark "wrist" patches can be striking against a clear winter sky. • Rough-legged Hawks show great variety in coloration, ranging from a whitish light morph with dark patterning to dark morph birds, which are virtually solid black. The light morph is the most common in Illinois. • The name *lagopus*, meaning "hare's foot," refers to this bird's distinctive feathered legs, an adaptation for cold climate survival.

light morph ♀

♂ *light morph*

ID: white tail base with 1 wide, dark subterminal band; dark brown upper-parts; pale flight feathers; legs are feathered to toes. *Light morph:* wide, dark abdominal "belt"; dark streaks on breast and head; dark "wrist" patches; light underwing linings. *Dark morph:* dark wing linings, head and underparts. *Immature:* lighter streaking on breast; bold belly band; buff leg feathers. *In flight:* frequently hovers; most birds show dark "wrist" patches.
Size: *L* 19–24 in; *W* 4–4½ ft.
Status: uncommon to locally common migrant and winter resident, decreasing southward.
Habitat: fields, meadows and croplands.
Nesting: does not nest in Illinois.

Feeding: soars and hovers while searching for prey; eats small rodents, especially voles; occasionally eats birds, amphibians and large insects.
Voice: alarm call is a catlike *kee-eer*, usually dropping at the end.
Similar Species: *Other buteos* (pp. 101–05): rarely hover; lack dark "wrist" patches and white tail base. *Northern Harrier* (p. 97): facial disc; lacks dark "wrist" patches and dark belly band; longer, thinner tail lacks broad, dark subterminal band. *Golden Eagle* (p. 106): compared to dark-morph Rough-legged Hawk, immature is much larger, with solid white, unbanded uppertail feathers, 2 roundish white patches at base of primaries on dark wings, more massive bill and feet and never hovers.
Best Sites: Illinois Beach SP; Goose Lake Prairie SNA; Midewin National Tallgrass Prairie; Sand Ridge SF.

105

GOLDEN EAGLE

Aquila chrysaetos

With the advent of widespread human development and intensive agricultural practices, the Golden Eagle became a victim of a lengthy persecution. Perceived as a threat to livestock, bounties were offered, encouraging the shooting and poisoning of this species. • The Golden Eagle is more closely related to the buteo hawks than it is to the Bald Eagle. The Golden Eagle is an active, impressive predator, taking animals as large as foxes and herons. • It is a rare treat for an Illinoisan to see a Golden Eagle soaring high in the sky during migration over open areas. The best chance to see this rare species is in winter in extreme southern Illinois where large numbers of geese congregate. The lucky birder may spot a single Golden Eagle hunting geese with the more common Bald Eagle. • Although the adult Golden Eagle is uniformly colored, except for its tawny head, the immature is readily distinguished by the white patch in the center of each wing and at the base of the tail.

immature

ID: very large; all brown with golden tint to neck and head; brown eyes; dark bill; brown tail has grayish white bands; yellow feet; legs are fully feathered. *Immature:* white tail base; white patch at base of underwing primary feathers. *In flight:* relatively short neck; long tail; long, large, rectangular wings often held at slight angle while soaring.
Size: *L* 30–40 in; *W* 6½–7½ ft.
Status: rare migrant and winter resident.
Habitat: along lake shorelines and over open fields.
Nesting: does not nest in Illinois.

Feeding: swoops down on prey from soaring flight; eats rodents and other mammals; occasionally takes herons and other large birds, often injured waterfowl in Illinois, and sometimes carrion.
Voice: generally quiet; rarely a short bark.
Similar Species: *Bald Eagle* (p. 96): longer neck; shorter tail; immature lacks distinct, white underwing patches and tail base. *Turkey Vulture* (p. 93): naked, pink head; pale flight feathers; dark wing linings. *Rough-legged Hawk* (p. 105): dark morph is much smaller, with pale flight feathers edged in black, white tail base, smaller bill and feet and frequently hovers while feeding.
Best Sites: Horseshoe Lake CA; Union County CA.

AMERICAN KESTREL
Falco sparverius

The American Kestrel, the smallest and most common of Illinois' breeding hawks, hunts small rodents, birds, bats and insects in open areas. In summer it dines on grasshoppers, crickets and dragonflies. • A kestrel perched on a telephone wire or fence post along an open field is a familiar sight throughout Illinois year-round. This bird is attracted to habitats that have been modified by humans, including pastures, parklands and even urban areas. • The kestrel often hovers in the wind, then dives to the ground to snatch its prey. • The American Kestrel's small size allows it to nest in small tree cavities, often those excavated by woodpeckers, especially flickers. Kestrels will even use nest boxes. • Birders often recognize the bird's presence by its loud *klee klee klee* call. Old field guides refer to this bird as "Sparrow Hawk"; its scientific name *sparverius* means "pertaining to a sparrow."

ID: 2 distinctive facial stripes. *Male:* rusty back; blue gray wings; blue gray crown with rusty "cap"; lightly spotted underparts. *Female:* rusty back, wings and breast streaking. *In flight:* frequently hovers; long, rusty tail; buoyant, indirect flight style.
Size: *L* 7½–8 in; *W* 20–24 in.
Status: fairly common to common year-round.
Habitat: grasslands, croplands and forest edges.
Nesting: in a tree cavity, usually an abandoned flicker or woodpecker cavity or nest box; mostly the female incubates 4–6 finely speckled, white to pale brown eggs for 29–30 days; both adults raise the young.
Feeding: swoops from a hovering position or a perch in a tree, on a fenceline, post, road sign or power line; eats insects and some small rodents, birds, reptiles and amphibians.
Voice: loud, often repeated, shrill *killy-killy-killy* or *klee-klee-klee* when excited; female's voice is lower pitched.
Similar Species: *Merlin* (p. 108): only 1 facial stripe; gray to brown overall; lacks rufous tones; does not hover; flight is more powerful and direct. *Sharp-shinned Hawk* (p. 98): short, rounded wings; reddish barring on underparts; lacks facial stripes; flap-and-glide flight.
Best Sites: *In migration:* Illinois Beach SP; grasslands and agricultural areas statewide year-round.

MERLIN
Falco columbarius

Most Merlins migrate to Central and South America each fall, but a few may winter in Illinois. Birders find more Merlins during fall migration than they do during spring, and will more often see them in flight rather than perched. Compared with the American Kestrel, the Merlin flies more directly and rarely hovers. • The main weapons of this small falcon, like all its falcon relatives, are speed, surprise and sharp, daggerlike talons. Merlins migrate on the heels of some of their later migrating prey, including the White-throated Sparrow, juncos and the Yellow-rumped Warbler. This bird, with its sleek body, long, narrow tail and pointed, aerodynamic wings, can also be seen chasing shorebirds. • Medieval falconers named the Merlin "the lady's hawk," and Catherine the Great and Mary Queen of Scots were among the enthusiasts who would pitch Merlin and Sky Lark *(Alauda arvensis)* into matches of aerial prowess. • The Merlin was formerly known as "Pigeon Hawk," and the scientific name *columbarius* comes from the Latin for "pigeon."

Taiga form

Nesting: does not nest in Illinois.
Feeding: overtakes smaller birds in flight; also eats rodents and large insects such as grasshoppers and dragonflies; may also take bats.
Voice: loud, noisy, cackling cry: *kek-kek-kek-kek-kek* or *ki-ki-ki-ki;* calls in flight or while perched, often around the nest.
Similar Species: *American Kestrel* (p. 107): 2 facial stripes; more colorful; less direct flight style; often hovers. *Peregrine Falcon* (p. 109): larger; well-marked, dark "helmet"; pale, unmarked upper breast; black flecking on light underparts. *Sharp-shinned Hawk* (p. 98) and *Cooper's Hawk* (p. 99): short, rounded wings; reddish barring on breast and belly.
Best Sites: *In migration:* Illinois Beach SP.

ID: banded tail; heavily streaked underparts; 1 indistinct facial stripe; long, narrow wings and tail. *Male:* blue gray back and crown; rufous leg feathers. *Female:* brown back and crown. *In flight:* very rapid, shallow wing-beats.
Size: *L* 10–12 in; *W* 23–26 in.
Status: rare to locally common migrant; rare winter resident.
Habitat: open areas and lakeshores.

PEREGRINE FALCON

Falco peregrinus

No bird elicits more admiration than a hunting Peregrine Falcon in full flight, and nothing causes more panic in a tightly packed flock of ducks or shorebirds. Every twist and turn the flock makes is matched by the falcon until it finds a weak or inexperienced bird. Diving at speeds of up to 200 miles per hour, the Peregrine clenches its feet and then strikes its prey with a lethal blow that often sends both falcon and prey tumbling. • The Peregrine Falcon is one of the most widely distributed bird species in the world. • Despite its amazing speed and hunting skills, this bird was defenseless against the pesticide DDT, which caused contaminated birds to lay eggs with thin shells that broke before hatching. As a result, the Peregrine Falcon was extirpated in Illinois by the early 1960s. DDT was banned in North America in 1972 and, in the 1980s, the Peregrine Falcon was successfully reintroduced in cities throughout the Midwest. Several pairs nest in downtown Chicago; a few other pairs nest in Springfield and Alton. In cities, their favorite food is the Rock Pigeon.

ID: blue gray back; prominent, dark "helmet"; light underparts with fine, dark spotting and flecking. *Immature:* brown back; heavier breast streaks; gray feet and cere. *In flight:* pointed wings; long, narrow, darkly banded tail.

Size: *Male:* L 15–17 in; W 3–3½ ft. *Female:* L 17–19 in; W 3½–4 ft.

Status: state-endangered; uncommon migrant; very rare breeder and year-round resident.

Habitat: lakeshores, mudflats, river valleys, urban areas and open fields.

Nesting: building ledges and bridges; no material is added, but the nest is littered with prey remains, leaves and grass; nest sites are often reused; mostly the female incubates 3–4 eggs for 28–29 days.

Feeding: high-speed, diving stoops; strikes birds with clenched feet in midair; prey is consumed on a nearby perch; pigeons, waterfowl, shorebirds, flickers and larger songbirds are the primary prey; rarely takes small mammals or carrion.

Voice: loud, harsh, continuous *cack-cack-cack-cack-cack* near the nest site.

Similar Species: *Gyrfalcon* (p. 356): extremely rare; larger; lacks dark "helmet" and prominent "mustache" mark; wing tips do not reach tail tip. *Prairie Falcon* (p. 110): very rare; sandy brown overall, especially compared with immature; black "wing pits" in flight; wing tips do not reach tail tip. *Merlin* (p. 108): much smaller; lacks prominent dark "helmet" and prominent "mustache" mark.

Best Sites: Illinois Beach SP and L. Chautauqua in fall; downtown Chicago year-round.

PRAIRIE FALCON

Falco mexicanus

The Prairie Falcon prefers the dry regions of western North America. Along with the Golden Eagle and Common Raven, the Prairie Falcon breeds on cliffs or bluffs interrupted by open plains and deserts. In late fall and winter, however, to the delight of birders, this falcon occasionally comes to Illinois. Places where there are expansive agricultural fields, often near large reservoirs, attract this bird to hunt. • Although Prairie Falcons are about the same size as Peregrines, they are more closely related to Gyrfalcons and hunt in the same manner, initiating high-speed chases close to the ground. The Prairie Falcon alternates quick, powerful wing-beats with gliding. • In Illinois, this bird is mostly seen singly, but up to four birds spent six consecutive winters at Lawrenceville Airport in southeastern Illinois. The species was observed in 1991 and 2003 in LaSalle County, in both instances with Gyrfalcons. Prairie Falcons enter and exit the state in east-to-west movements.

ID: sandy to brown upperparts; light face with dark, narrow "mustache" stripe; light underparts with brown spotting. *In flight:* black "wing pits"; pointed wings; long, narrow, banded tail; rapid wingbeats.
Size: *Male: L* 14–15 in; *W* 3 ft. *Female: L* 16½–18 in; *W* 3½ ft.
Status: rare migrant and winter resident from November to March.
Habitat: open country, such as fields and grasslands.
Nesting: does not nest in Illinois.

Feeding: high-speed aerial pursuits, often overtaking songbirds and shorebirds in midair; also surprises ground squirrels in low, fast attacks.
Voice: alarm call is a rapid, shrill *kik-kik-kik-kik*.
Similar Species: no other falcon has dark "wing pits." *Peregrine Falcon* (p. 109): dark "helmet" or prominent dark, as opposed to sandy or brown, "mustache"; in perched bird, wing tip reaches tail tip. *Gyrfalcon* (p. 356): larger; generally lighter-colored "mustache"; lacks black "wing pits."
Best Sites: possible in open agricultural lands statewide; many records come from open areas near Clinton L.

YELLOW RAIL
Coturnicops noveboracensis

The Yellow Rail is one of the most challenging birds to find in Illinois, although it's likely this elusive species is more common than records show. A few historical breeding records exist in Illinois and this bird may still nest in a few locations where its specialized habitat remains. • The Yellow Rail slips quietly through sedges, grasses and cattails, more like a small mammal than a bird, picking food from the ground and searching for snails. • If this bird feels threatened, it will freeze until you are almost on top of it or run ahead of a pursuer through the dense vegetation without flushing. • Finding this bird in Illinois usually requires a lengthy, sustained effort. For a few weeks in April and early May and again in September and October, Illinois birders willing to wade through this bird's habitat may be lucky enough to come upon a Yellow Rail. But, in most cases, it remains the mythical unicorn figure of the birding world. • In spring, you would be very fortunate to hear the call of the Yellow Rail, which sounds like two stones being tapped together in a short, percussive rhythm. In fall, these birds are rarely found because they tend to use drier upland habitats, making them harder to flush.

ID: short, pale bill; black and tawny stripes on upperparts; black stripes have fine, white barring; broad, dark line through eye. *In flight:* very noticeable white patches on inner wing.
Size: *L* 6 ½–7 ½ in; *W* 11 in.
Status: rare migrant; typically occurs from late March to early May and from late September to late October; reported less often in fall than in spring.
Habitat: wet sedge meadows and marshes.
Nesting: does not nest in Illinois.
Feeding: picks food from the ground and aquatic vegetation; eats mostly snails,

aquatic insects and larvae, spiders and earthworms; also eats seeds.
Voice: like 2 small stones clicking together: *tik, tik, tik-tik-tik.*
Similar Species: *Sora* (p. 115): lacks stripes on back and white wing patches; breeding bird has black face and throat and bright yellow bill; distinctly different call. *Virginia Rail* (p. 114): long, reddish bill; rusty breast; gray face; lacks stripes on back and white wing patches. *Black Rail* (p. 112): dark gray and black overall; red eyes; rufous nape; white speckling on back; lacks white wing patches.
Best Sites: Clinton L.

BLACK RAIL

Laterallus jamaicensis

The sparrow-sized Black Rail is one of North America's most elusive and seldom-seen marshland birds. Its small size and secretive, partly nocturnal habits leave most birders wondering if this bird really exists. Its voice—a repeated *ki-kee-der* from the male—is often the only clue that it is present. • Because the Black Rail is rarely seen and is nearly impossible to observe for any extended period of time, much remains to be learned about its natural history and population dynamics. Most records indicate that this bird occurs in Illinois in May. • Likely once a common breeder in the formerly extensive Kankakee wetlands and Lake Calumet marshes, the Black Rail is now a state-endangered species in Illinois. Protection of marshland and reevaluation of the consequences of draining fragile marshes will help ensure the survival of this enigmatic creature. • Like the Yellow Rail, the Black Rail uses upland grasslands in fall and prefers running from danger rather than taking flight. • The Black Rail is likely more common during migration and possibly during the breeding season than Illinois records indicate.

ID: short, black bill; small, roundish body; large feet; blackish upperparts with white flecking; chestnut nape; dark grayish black underparts with white barring on flanks; red eyes.
Size: *L* 6 in; *W* 9 in.
Status: state-endangered; rare migrant and very rare breeder; migrants occur between late April and late May; fewer migrants occur from early September to late October.
Habitat: sedge meadows and cattail marshes.
Nesting: a cup-shaped nest of vegetation with a woven, domed canopy is located among dense vegetation above the water or the ground; nest entrance is connected to the ground or to the water's surface by a ramp of dead vegetation; pair incubates 6–10 finely speckled, white to buff eggs for 17–20 days.
Feeding: foraging behavior and diet are poorly understood; eats mostly insects, small crustaceans and seeds.
Voice: male call note is a repeated *ki-kee-der;* also a harsh, growling *krr, krrr, krr;* female call note is a deeper *who-whoo.*
Similar Species: *Virginia Rail* (p. 114): larger; longer, reddish bill; rusty breast; gray "cheek." *Sora* (p. 115): browner upperparts; yellow bill; black "mask" in breeding plumage. *Yellow Rail* (p. 111): golden yellow underparts; white wing patches in flight.
Best Sites: none.

KING RAIL

Rallus elegans

The King Rail is the largest rail in North America. Unlike some of the more secretive rails, this bird will wade through shallow water along the edge of a marsh, sometimes stalking its prey in full view of eager onlookers. Its varied diet includes crustaceans, small fish, spiders, beetles, snails, frogs and a wide variety of aquatic insects. Prey caught away from the water is usually brought to the water and submerged before eating; larger prey is usually beaten against debris. The King Rail regurgitates indigestible parts of its food in pellets similar to those of an owl. • This bird's populations have declined significantly throughout large portions of its range, mostly as a result of habitat destruction. This species is an endangered breeder in Illinois. Although its breeding range stronghold is in northern Illinois, the King Rail still nests locally statewide in suitable habitat. • The black young of this and other rail species can sometimes be confused with the much rarer Black Rail.

ID: very large; long, slightly downcurved bill; black back feathers have buffy or tawny edges; cinnamon shoulders and underparts; strongly barred, black-and-white flanks; grayish brown "cheeks." *Immature:* similar plumage patterning with lighter, washed-out colors.
Size: *L* 15 in; *W* 20 in.
Status: state-endangered; rare migrant and rare, local breeder; migrants occur from mid-April to late May; fewer fall records occur from late August to early October.
Habitat: marshes, upland fields and wet meadows.

Nesting: among clumps of grass or sedge just above the water or ground; often includes a protective dome of woven vegetation and an entrance ramp built by the male; pair incubates 10–12 pale buff eggs, lightly spotted with brown, for 21–24 days.
Feeding: aquatic insects, crustaceans and occasionally seeds; forages in shallow water for small fish and amphibians, often in or near dense plant cover.
Voice: chattering call is 10 or fewer evenly spaced *kek* notes; also a series of grunts steadily falling in pitch.
Similar Species: *Virginia Rail* (p. 114): much smaller; brown back feathers; gray face; red bill; white undertail coverts. *Black Rail* (p. 112): downy King Rail chick lacks rufous nape and white speckling on back.
Best Sites: Illinois Beach SP; Goose Lake Prairie SNA; Beardstown Marsh; Prairie Ridge SNA.

113

VIRGINIA RAIL

Rallus limicola

One way to find a Virginia Rail is to sit alongside a wetland marsh in spring, clap your hands three or four times and wait for the bird to respond. You may even glimpse it peering out from the vegetation. Farmers mowing hayfields often encounter rails in spring and fall. • When pursued, a rail will almost always attempt to scurry away through dense, concealing vegetation, rather than risk exposure in a fluttering getaway flight. Rails are very narrow birds that have modified feather tips and flexible vertebrae, which allow them to squeeze through the narrow confines of their marshy homes. • The Virginia Rail and its relative, the Sora, often live in the same marshes. They can successfully coexist because of their microhabitat preferences and distinct diets. The Virginia Rail favors the dry shoresides of marshes and feeds on invertebrates, but the Sora prefers deeper water and eats plants and seeds.

ID: long, downcurved, reddish bill; deep gray face; rusty breast; barred flanks; chestnut brown wing patch; pinkish to orangish legs; very short tail. *Immature:* much darker overall; pale bill.
Size: *L* 9–11 in; *W* 13 in.
Status: fairly common migrant from late March to early May with fewer numbers from late August to mid-November; fairly common breeder in northeastern Illinois; rare to uncommon breeder elsewhere; rare winter resident.
Habitat: wetlands, especially cattail and bulrush marshes.
Nesting: concealed in emergent vegetation, suspended over water; loose basket nest is made of coarse grass, cattail stems or sedges; pair incubates 5–13 spotted, pale buff eggs for up to 20 days.

Feeding: probes into soft substrates and gleans vegetation for invertebrates; also eats some pondweeds and seeds.
Voice: call is an often-repeated, telegraph-like *kidick, kidick;* series of grunts descending in pitch and volume; also utters a single *kek* when near nest.
Similar Species: *King Rail* (p. 113): much larger; dark legs; bold, black stripes on undertail coverts; lacks reddish bill and deep gray face; louder series of grunts descending in pitch and volume; juvenile is mostly pale gray. *Sora* (p. 115): short, yellow bill; black face and throat; gray breast; yellow to greenish yellow legs. *Yellow Rail* (p. 111): short, pale yellowish bill; buff yellow overall; black and tawny stripes on back; white trailing edges of wings in flight. *Black Rail* (p. 112): downy Virginia Rail chick lacks rufous nape and white speckling on back.
Best Sites: Illinois Beach SP; Chain O'Lakes; Moraine Hills SP; Goose Lake Prairie SNA; Arcola Marsh; Beardstown Marsh.

SORA

Porzana carolina

The Sora is the most common and widespread rail in North America, as well as the most common breeding rail in Illinois. However, you'll need some patience to observe this bird because, like other rail species, it spends most of its time concealed in marshy vegetation. On occasion it parades around in more open areas searching the shallows for food, giving birders a chance to observe. • The Sora calls a clear, whistled *coo-wee* or sings a descending whinny. It responds readily to human imitation of the whinny. • Even though its feet are not webbed or lobed, the Sora swims quite well over short distances. Though it appears to be a weak and reluctant flyer, the Sora migrates hundreds to thousands of miles each year between its breeding and wintering wetlands. • Habitat destruction has reduced the rail population in Illinois. Also, hunting season takes place throughout much of the Sora range, contributing to their decline. Perhaps it is time to end this practice, considering that important information on the life history of these secretive birds is still lacking.

ID: short, yellow bill; black face, throat and foreneck; gray neck and breast; long, greenish legs. *Immature:* no black on face; more buff with paler underparts; bill is greener. **Size:** *L* 8–10 in; *W* 14 in. **Status:** common to locally abundant migrant from mid-March to early May, with fewer numbers from mid-August to early November; common breeder in northeastern Illinois; rare to uncommon breeder elsewhere; rare winter resident. **Habitat:** wetlands with abundant emergent cattails, bulrushes, sedges and grasses. **Nesting:** usually over water, but occasionally in a wet meadow under concealing vegetation; well-built basket nest is made of grass and aquatic vegetation; pair incubates 10–12 darkly speckled, buff or olive buff eggs for 18–20 days. **Feeding:** gleans and probes for seeds, plants, aquatic insects and mollusks. **Voice:** usual call is a clear, 2-note *coo-wee;* alarm call is a sharp *keek;* courtship song begins *or-Ah or-Ah,* descending quickly in a series of maniacal *weee-weee-weee* notes. **Similar Species:** *Virginia Rail* (p. 114): much longer, orangy bill; rusty breast; orangy legs; lacks black face and throat. *King Rail* (p. 113): much larger; long, down-curved bill; chestnut brown wing patch; rufous breast. *Yellow Rail* (p. 111): streaked back; tawny upperparts; white throat; white trailing edges of wings in flight. *Black Rail* (p. 112): juvenile Sora lacks rufous nape and white speckling on back. **Best Sites:** Chain O'Lakes SP; Moraine Hills SP; Arcola Marsh.

COMMON MOORHEN

Gallinula chloropus

The Common Moorhen has the bill of a chicken, the body of a duck and the long legs and large feet of a small heron. • Once rather abundant statewide, this species is now state-endangered and restricted to northeastern Illinois. The Common Moorhen, as well as other rare breeding wetland species, requires what is known as "hemi-marsh," which contains areas of open water interspersed with dense vegetation, especially cattails. Most of the state's hemi-marsh habitat has been destroyed or degraded. • Common Moorhens associate with coots, grebes and ducks during the breeding season, when they respond quite readily to an imitation of their creaking calls. They also produce a variety of clucks and squeaks. • This somewhat secretive bird is more difficult to see than its cousin, the American Coot, but its bright red frontal shield alerts the birder to the moorhen's presence. • The scientific name *chloropus* is Greek for "green foot."

ID: reddish forehead shield; yellow-tipped bill; gray black body; rich brown back; white streak on sides and flanks; long, greenish yellow legs. *Breeding:* brighter bill and forehead shield. *Juvenile:* paler plumage; dull-colored legs and bill; white throat.

Size: *L* 12–15 in; *W* 21 in.

Status: state-threatened; uncommon to rare migrant from mid-April to mid-May and from mid-August to mid-November; locally common breeder in northeastern Illinois; very rare and local breeder elsewhere.

Habitat: marshes and ponds with marshy borders.

Nesting: pair builds a platform nest or a wide, shallow cup of bulrushes, cattails and reeds in shallow water or along a shoreline; often built with a ramp leading to the water; pair incubates 6–17 buff-colored, spotted or blotched eggs for 19–22 days.

Feeding: eats mostly aquatic vegetation, berries, fruits, tadpoles, insects, snails, worms and spiders; may take carrion and eggs.

Voice: noisy in summer; various sounds include chickenlike clucks, screams, squeaks and a loud *cup;* courting males give a harsh *ticket-ticket-ticket.*

Similar Species: *American Coot* (p. 117): white bill and forehead shield; lacks white streak on flanks and rich, brown back.

Best Sites: Almond Marsh; Black Tern Marsh; Broberg Marsh; Nelson Lake Marsh; L. Calumet; Arcola Marsh; Kidd Lake SNA; Horseshoe Lake SP.

AMERICAN COOT
Fulica americana

L ike a duck, the American Coot dabbles in the water and also grazes confi-
dently on land. Like the most accomplished grebe, the American Coot dives
and swims skillfully with its lobed feet. This species, however, is most closely
related to the rails. • American Coots squabble constantly during the breeding season, not just among themselves, but also with any waterbird that enters their territory. These birds can often be seen scooting across the surface of the water, charging
rivals with flailing, splashing wings in an attempt to intimidate. Outside the breeding season, coots gather amicably in large groups. • A male American Coot often
swims with his head down and his bill thrust forward to show off his white forehead
shield to females. • The American Coot is one of the most abundant migratory
waterfowl in Illinois, but it is a relatively uncommon breeder. • Unlike its cousin, the
Common Moorhen, the American Coot doesn't
respond readily to imitations of its grunting call.

ID: gray black body;
white, chickenlike bill
with dark ring around tip;
reddish spot on white
forehead shield; long,
green yellow legs; lobed
toes; red eyes. *Immature:*
lighter body color; darker
bill and legs; lacks prominent forehead shield.
Size: *L* 13–16 in; *W* 24 in.
Status: common to abundant migrant
from mid-February to mid-May and from
mid-August to late November; uncommon
to locally common breeder in northeastern
Illinois; rare breeder elsewhere; rare to
uncommon winter resident.
Habitat: shallow marshes, ponds, lakes
and wetlands with open water and emergent vegetation.
Nesting: in emergent vegetation; pair
builds a floating nest from cattails and

grass; pair incubates 6–11 buff white,
brown-spotted eggs for 21–25 days; regularly produces 2 broods in a season.
Feeding: gleans the water's surface; sometimes dives, tips up or grazes on land; eats
aquatic vegetation, especially pondweeds
and wild celery; also insects, snails, crayfish,
worms, tadpoles and fish; may steal food
from ducks.
Voice: calls frequently in summer, day and
night: *kuk-kuk-kuk-kuk-kuk;* also grunts.
Similar Species: *Ducks* (pp. 41–66): all lack
white, chickenlike bill and uniformly black
body. *Pied-billed Grebe* (p. 75): light
brownish gray overall; white eye ring; lacks
red spot on upper base of bill. *Common
Moorhen* (p. 116): reddish forehead shield;
yellow-tipped bill; white streak on flanks.
Best Sites: *Breeding:* northeastern Illinois
marshes. *In migration:* ponds and lakes
statewide.

SANDHILL CRANE

Grus canadensis

Each March, Illinois birders listen for the deep, resonant, rattling calls overhead that signal the arrival of migrating Sandhill Cranes. Most of the 20,000 or more migrating Sandhills pass over northeastern Illinois on their way between staging grounds in northwestern Indiana and breeding grounds farther north. Like hawks, Sandhill Cranes circle upward on thermals, then slowly soar downward until they find another rise. • Several decades ago, the Sandhill Crane was extirpated as a breeder in Illinois because of a reduction in the species' Upper Midwest population. Habitat loss as well as overhunting contributed to its decline. Today, the Sandhill Crane once again breeds in Illinois. Its stronghold is in McHenry and Lake Counties, where its required marsh and upland woodland habitats remain. During migration, small numbers may occur throughout Illinois. • Cranes mate for life, reinforcing pair bonds each spring with an elaborate courtship dance. • Sandhill Cranes are sensitive nesters, preferring to raise their young in areas that are isolated from human disturbance.

ID: very large, gray bird; long neck and legs; naked, red crown; long, straight bill; plumage is often stained rusty color from iron oxides in water. *Immature:* lacks red crown; reddish brown plumage may appear patchy. *In flight:* extends neck and legs; often glides, soars and circles.
Size: *L* 3 ½–4 ft; *W* 6–7 ft.
Status: state-threatened; locally common to abundant migrant in northeastern Illinois from mid-February to mid-April and from mid-September to mid-November; uncommon migrant in eastern Illinois; very rare to rare migrant elsewhere; uncommon breeder in northeastern Illinois; rare, local breeder in northwestern Illinois.

Habitat: *Breeding:* large, open marshes, often near upland woods. *In migration:* agricultural fields and wetlands.
Nesting: on a large mound of aquatic vegetation in the water or along a shoreline; pair incubates 2 olive-splotched eggs for 29–32 days; egg hatching is staggered.
Feeding: probes and gleans the ground for insects, soft-bodied invertebrates, waste grain, shoots and tubers; frequently eats small vertebrates.
Voice: loud, resonant rattling *gu-rrroo gu-rrroo gurrroo.*
Similar Species: *Great Blue Heron* (p. 84): lacks red forehead patch; longer, yellow, daggerlike bill; black plumes on head; neck folds back over shoulders in flight. *Whooping Crane:* extremely rare; all-white plumage; black flight feathers.
Best Sites: *Breeding:* Chain O'Lakes SP; Moraine Hills SP. *In migration:* Cook Co. and Lake Co. suburbs away from L. Michigan shoreline.

BLACK-BELLIED PLOVER

Pluvialis squatarola

The Black-bellied Plover shows off its stunning black-and-white breeding plumage briefly in spring and, for some birds, again in early fall. Most fall birds show a much more subtle silver gray color overall. • Black-bellies choose a variety of wet habitats in migration, such as beaches, mudflats and flooded agricultural fields. Birders typically find them singly or in small flocks. This plover is more of a "beachcomber" than its cousin, the American Golden-Plover, which is found more often in agricultural fields in Illinois. • Black-bellied Plovers forage for small invertebrates with a robinlike run-and-stop technique, frequently pausing to lift their heads for a reassuring scan of their surroundings. • Most plovers have three toes, but the Black-bellied Plover has a fourth toe higher on its leg, like most sandpipers. Black-bellies are the most widespread of the larger plovers and are found in the greatest variety of habitats.

breeding

nonbreeding

ID: short, black bill; long, black legs. *Breeding:* black face, breast, belly and flanks; white under-tail coverts; white stripe from crown down to "col-lar," neck and sides of breast; mottled black-and-white back. *Nonbreeding:* mottled gray brown upperparts; lightly streaked, pale under-parts. *In flight:* black "wing pits"; whitish rump; white wing linings.
Size: *L* 11–13 in; *W* 29 in.
Status: common migrant along L. Michigan; rare to uncommon spring migrant and relatively common fall migrant downstate; occurs from late April

to early June and from late July to late November.
Habitat: L. Michigan beaches, plowed fields, mudflats and sewage lagoons.
Nesting: does not nest in Illinois.
Feeding: run-and-stop foraging technique; eats insects, mollusks and crustaceans.
Voice: rich, melancholy, 3-syllable whistle: *pee-oo-ee.*
Similar Species: *American Golden-Plover* (p. 120): upperparts are mottled with gold; black undertail coverts in breeding plumage; lacks black "wing pits." *Red Knot* (p. 136): nonbreeding birds have longer bills, shorter legs and lack black "wing pits."
Best Sites: L. Michigan beaches; Carlyle L.; Rend L.; L. Chautauqua.

119

AMERICAN GOLDEN-PLOVER
Pluvialis dominica

Like several other shorebird species, numbers of the attractive American Golden-Plover were drastically reduced by merciless harvesting in the late 1800s—a single day's shooting often yielded tens of thousands of birds. Populations have recovered somewhat, but they will likely never return to their former numbers. Still, each spring, birders often see flocks of 500 to 5000 golden-plovers in wet agricultural fields in central Illinois. Hundreds to thousands of plover wings knifing through the April wind, low overhead, is a sound not to be missed. • In late summer and early fall, American Golden-Plovers with much more subdued colors migrate through Illinois in substantially smaller flocks than in spring. Migrating fall flocks typically vary in size from 50 to 100 birds. Interestingly, most fall golden-plovers choose mudflats and sod farms rather than agricultural fields. • The cryptic coloration of speckles on the top of the body blends well with the golden, mottled earth of its arctic tundra breeding grounds.

breeding

nonbreeding

ID: straight, black bill; long, black legs. *Breeding:* black face and underparts; S-shaped, white stripe from forehead to shoulders; dark upperparts speckled with gold and white. *Nonbreeding:* broad, pale "eyebrow"; dark streaking on pale neck and underparts; much less gold on upperparts. *Juvenile:* somewhat brighter colored than adult; white forehead. *In flight:* gray underwings.
Size: *L* 10–11 in; *W* 26 in.
Status: abundant spring migrant in central Illinois; less common elsewhere; fairly common, local fall migrant; occurs from

mid-March to early June and from mid-July to mid-November.
Habitat: *Spring:* mostly wet agricultural fields. *Fall:* sod farms, lakeshores, mudflats and sewage lagoons.
Nesting: does not nest in Illinois.
Feeding: run-and-stop foraging technique; snatches insects, mollusks and crustaceans; also takes seeds and berries.
Voice: soft, plaintive whistle: *quee, quee-dle.*
Similar Species: *Black-bellied Plover* (p. 119): white undertail coverts; whitish crown; conspicuous black "wing pits"; lacks gold speckling on upperparts.
Best Sites: *Spring:* wet agricultural fields in central Illinois. *Fall:* H&E Sod Farms in McHenry Co.; Momence Sod Farms in Kankakee Co.; L. Chautauqua.

SEMIPALMATED PLOVER

Charadrius semipalmatus

On their way to northern breeding grounds between late April and early June, small flocks of Semipalmated Plovers commonly touch down on our shorelines and flooded fields. Spring migration is a brief, hurried affair because there is tremendous pressure for these long-distance migrants to begin breeding before the end of the short arctic summer. After nesting, adults leave the breeding grounds as early as July to enjoy a prolonged migration to the coastlines of the southern U.S. and Central and South America. Like most shorebirds, the young begin their journey as soon as they are strong enough to fly. • Semipalmated Plovers are usually encountered in small, loosely associated groups, but flocks of 50 to 100 are occasionally seen in Illinois. • The scientific name *semipalmatus* means "half-webbed" and refers to the slight webbing between the toes of this plover. The partial webbing is thought to give the bird's feet more surface area when it is walking on soft substrates.

breeding

ID: *Breeding:* dark brown back; white breast with 1 wide, black, horizontal band; orange legs; stubby, orange, black-tipped bill; white patch above bill; white throat and "collar"; black band across forehead; small, white "eyebrow"; brown uppertail coverts. *Nonbreeding:* duller; mostly dark bill. *Immature:* dark legs and bill; brown banding.
Size: *L* 7 in; *W* 19 in.
Status: common migrant from mid-April to early June and from early July to mid-October.

Habitat: sand beaches, lakeshores, mudflats and sewage lagoons.
Nesting: does not nest in Illinois.
Feeding: run-and-stop feeding, usually on shorelines and beaches; eats crustaceans, worms and insects.
Voice: crisp, high-pitched, 2-part, rising whistle: *tu-wee*.
Similar Species: *Killdeer* (p. 123): larger; 2 black bands across breast; longer, black bill; pinkish to dull yellow legs. *Piping Plover* (p. 122): much rarer; much lighter upperparts; narrower breast band, incomplete in females and most males; white uppertail coverts; lacks dark band through eyes.
Best Sites: L. Michigan shoreline; L. Chautauqua; Carlyle L.; Rend L.

121

PIPING PLOVER

Charadrius melodus

The Piping Plover's pale, sand-colored plumage blends in well with its preferred sandy beach habitat. • This plover's cryptic plumage has done little to protect it from increased predation and disturbance by humans. The recreational use of beaches during summer and an increase in human-tolerant predators, such as gulls, raccoons, dogs and skunks, has impeded its ability to reproduce successfully. Consequently, this species has been extirpated as a breeder in Illinois from a historic breeding population of more than 100 pairs. Without public interest and concern enough to set aside some beach habitat, this species will not likely return as a breeder to the state. • On beaches with wave action, Piping Plovers often employ a foot-trembling strategy to entice invertebrates to the surface of the sand.

breeding

♂ *breeding*

ID: pale gray upperparts; white underparts; bright yellow legs. *Breeding:* black-tipped, orangy bill; black forehead band; black "necklace," usually incomplete, especially on females. *Nonbreeding* and *juvenile:* pale breast band; no forehead band; all-black bill. *In flight:* white uppertail coverts.
Size: *L* 7 in; *W* 19 in.
Status: state and federally endangered; very rare but regular migrant; occurs from mid-April to late May and from mid-July to mid-October; 3 November records; most records from July and August.
Habitat: sandy beaches, mudflats and lakeshores.
Nesting: does not nest in Illinois.
Feeding: run-and-stop feeding; eats crustaceans, mollusks, worms, insects and their eggs and larvae.
Voice: clear, whistled, melodic: *peep peep peep-lo*.
Similar Species: *Semipalmated Plover* (p. 121): more common; dark band through eyes; wider breast band; much darker upperparts; brown uppertail coverts in flight.
Best Sites: Waukegan Beach; Illinois Beach SP; L. Chautauqua; Carlyle L.; Rend L.

KILLDEER

Charadrius vociferus

The widespread Killdeer is often the first shorebird a birder learns to identify. Its boisterous *kill-deer* calls rarely fail to catch the attention of people passing through its various nesting environments. The Killdeer's preference for open fields, gravel driveways, beach edges, golf courses and abandoned industrial areas has allowed it to thrive throughout our rural and urban landscapes. • Many sitting birds remain tight on the nest at the approach of an intruder, confident that their disruptive coloration will render them virtually invisible. However, if an intruder happens to wander too close to a Killdeer nest, the parent will try to lure it away, issuing loud alarm calls, feigning a broken wing and exposing its rufous rump. • Along with waterfowl, the Killdeer is one of the first migrants to return in spring, often arriving with the first warm front in February.

ID: long, dark yellow legs; white underparts with 2 black breast bands; brown back; brown head; white "eyebrow"; white face patch above bill; black forehead band; rufous rump. *Immature:* downy; only 1 breast band.

Size: *L* 9–11 in; *W* 24 in.

Status: abundant migrant and breeder; often recorded on Christmas bird counts, but few overwinter; migrants occur from early February to early April and from August to early December.

Habitat: open ground, short grass, fields, lakeshores, sandy beaches, mudflats, gravel stream edges, agricultural fields, sod farms and wet meadows; also urban areas and parks, railroad beds, edges of rural gravel roads and even gravel driveways; often some distance from water.

Nesting: on open ground; in a shallow, usually unlined depression; pair incubates 4 buffy eggs with heavy black markings for 24–28 days; occasionally raises 2 broods.

Feeding: run-and-stop feeder; eats mostly insects; also takes spiders, snails, earthworms and other invertebrates.

Voice: loud and distinctive *kill-deer kill-deer kill-deer* and variations, including *deer-deer*.

Similar Species: *Semipalmated Plover* (p. 121): smaller; only 1 breast band; shorter, bicolored bill; brighter orange yellow legs; lacks rufous tones on back.

Best Sites: L. Chautauqua; sewage lagoons, sod farms and mud-lined lakeshores, especially in fall.

BLACK-NECKED STILT

Himantopus mexicanus

The Black-necked Stilt strides daintily around wetlands on long, gangly, bubble-gum pink legs. Proportionately, this bird has the longest legs of any North American bird and is truly deserving of the name "stilt." • While incubating, adults wet their belly feathers to cool their encased young. • Before the 1990s, only a few records of the migrant Black-necked Stilt existed in Illinois. Then, after the extensive floods of 1993 along the Mississippi River, it began breeding in Illinois with some regularity. Most breeding records come from Jackson, Union, Alexander and a few other counties in far southern Illinois. • This species often shares its habitat with American Avocets.

VAGRANT

ID: very long, bubblegum pink legs; dark upperparts; clean white underparts; long, straight, needlelike bill; small, white "eyebrow"; female has brown on back.
Size: *L* 14–15 in; *W* 29 in.
Status: very rare migrant and breeder in extreme southern Illinois; very rare migrant and breeder elsewhere; occurs from mid-April to late May with breeders departing by late August.
Habitat: flooded agricultural fields; mudflats.
Nesting: in a shallow depression on slightly raised ground near water; nest is lined with pebbles or vegetative debris;

pair incubates 4 darkly blotched, buff eggs for about 25 days; both adults tend the precocial young.
Feeding: picks prey from the water's surface or from the bottom substrate; primarily eats insects, fish, crustaceans and other aquatic invertebrates; rarely eats seeds of aquatic plants.
Voice: not vocal during migration; loud, sharp *yip-yip-yip-yip* in summer; *kek-kek-kek-kek* in flight.
Similar Species: *American Avocet* (p. 125): upturned bill; large, white patches on otherwise black wing; blue gray legs; lacks black on head.
Best Sites: flooded agricultural fields just west of East Cape Girardeau in Alexander Co. and along Illinois Rt. 3 in Union Co. and Jackson Co.

AMERICAN AVOCET

Recurvirostra americana

An American Avocet in full breeding plumage is strikingly elegant, with its long, peachy neck, black-and-white back and bluish, stiltlike legs. Usually by August, the peach-colored hood has been replaced by more subdued winter grays. This is the only avocet in the world that undergoes a yearly color change. • The American Avocet's long, upturned bill is ideal for efficiently skimming aquatic vegetation and invertebrates off the surface of shallow water. The female's bill is more strongly upturned than the male's, possibly an adaptation for their slightly different diets. • During courtship, the female extends her bill forward and lowers her "chin" until it just clears the water's surface. Following mating, the pair crosses their bills and walks away in unison. • This species is much more common in the western part of the United States than it is in eastern regions.

breeding ♂

ID: long, upturned, black bill; long, pale blue legs; black wings with wide, white patches; white underparts; female's bill is more upturned and shorter than male's. *Breeding:* peach head, neck and breast. *Nonbreeding:* gray head, neck and breast. *In flight:* long, skinny legs and neck; black-and-white wings.
Size: *L* 17–18 in; *W* 31 in.
Status: rare to uncommon migrant from mid-April to early June and from early July to early November.

Habitat: beaches, lakeshores, wetlands and exposed mudflats.
Nesting: does not nest in Illinois.
Feeding: sweeps its bill from side to side along the water's surface, picking up aquatic invertebrates, insects and occasionally seeds; male sweeps lower in the water than the female; occasionally swims and tips up like a duck.
Voice: harsh, shrill *plee-eek plee-eek*.
Similar Species: *Black-necked Stilt* (p. 124): straight bill; mostly black head; red legs.
Best Sites: L. Michigan shoreline; L. Chautauqua; Rend L.; Carlyle L.

GREATER YELLOWLEGS

Tringa melanoleuca

The Greater Yellowlegs' far-carrying, three-note, descending whistle alerts a mixed flock of shorebirds to the presence of danger, often sending them aloft. When alarmed, this large sandpiper bobs its head and calls incessantly. • Many shorebirds, including the Greater Yellowlegs, often stand on one leg. This stance conserves body heat. • The Greater Yellowlegs is typically found in smaller flocks than its counterpart, the Lesser Yellowlegs. This boreal forest muskeg breeder is one of the more familiar and earlier spring migrant shorebirds to be seen on Illinois mudflats and wetlands. Its breeding range is less extensive than the much more common Lesser Yellowlegs. • A high flier, the Greater Yellowlegs circles several times over a wetland or other potential feeding site, then flies in a zigzag pattern until it lands, reminiscent of its courtship behavior.

nonbreeding

breeding

ID: long, bright yellow legs; dark bill (paler toward forehead) is slightly upturned and noticeably longer than head length; white upper-tail evident in flight. *Breeding:* brown black back and upperwing with white spotting; fine, dense, dark streaking on head and neck; dark barring on breast extends along flanks. *Nonbreeding:* gray overall; fine streaks on breast; clear belly. *Juvenile:* warmer brown upperparts; back and wing feathers edged more extensively with white; clear, brown streaks on breast.
Size: *L* 13–15 in; *W* 28 in.

Status: common migrant from mid-March to early June and late June to late November.
Habitat: lakeshores, beaches, flooded fields, mudflats, sewage lagoons and wetlands.
Nesting: does not nest in Illinois.
Feeding: usually wades in water "knee" deep; sometimes sweeps its bill from side to side; primarily eats aquatic inverte-brates, but will also eat minnows.
Voice: loud, quick, whistled series of *tew-tew-tew*, usually 3 notes.
Similar Species: *Lesser Yellowlegs* (p. 127): noticeably smaller and has less extensive barring on flanks in breeding plumage; straight, all-dark bill is roughly the same length as head; thinner "knees"; call is generally a pair of higher notes: *tew-tew. Willet* (p. 129): bold, white wing bars; heavier, straighter bill; relatively shorter, blue gray legs in all plumages; distinctive, clear *will-will-willet* call.
Best Sites: widespread in appropriate habitat.

LESSER YELLOWLEGS

Tringa flavipes

Less solitary than its larger relative, the Greater Yellowlegs, the Lesser typically occurs in small flocks of 5 to 25 birds, but flocks in the tens of thousands occur at Lake Chautauqua, an important Midwestern staging area for this species in the fall. • Some birders find it a challenge to distinguish between the two Yellowlegs species. However, with practice, you will notice that the Lesser's bill is straighter and about the same length as its head. The Greater Yellowlegs often strays into deeper water and may even swim at times. The birds' calls are also different. • Both yellowlegs species were popular game birds in the late 1800s. The birds were easy targets because of their tendency to return and hover above wounded flockmates. • The scientific name *flavipes* is derived from Latin words meaning "yellow foot."

breeding

nonbreeding

ID: bright yellow legs; all-dark bill about same length as head; mottled brown-and-black back and upperwing; fine, dense, dark streaking on head and neck; slight barring on belly; frequently bobs head; white upper-tail in flight. *Nonbreeding:* much plainer and grayer overall; more evident white speckling on lower back and wings.

Size: *L* 10–11 in; *W* 24 in.

Status: common to abundant migrant from mid-March to early June and from late June to mid-November.

Habitat: lakeshores, beaches, flooded fields, mudflats, sewage lagoons and wetlands.

Nesting: does not nest in Illinois.

Feeding: picks prey from the water's surface; eats primarily aquatic invertebrates; also takes small fish and tadpoles.

Voice: typically a high-pitched, rapid *tew tew* call.

Similar Species: *Greater Yellowlegs* (p. 126): noticeably larger and bulkier; bill is slightly upturned; thicker "knees"; *tew* call is usually given in a series of 3 notes. *Solitary Sandpiper* (p. 128): smaller; white eye ring; darker upperparts; paler bill; yellow green legs. *Willet* (p. 129): much larger and bulkier; black-and-white wings; blue gray legs; heavier bill. *Wilson's Phalarope* (p. 153): nonbreeding is plumper, has lighter breast and plain, grayish tail.

Best Sites: widespread in appropriate habitat; L. Chautauqua.

SOLITARY SANDPIPER

Tringa solitaria

True to its name, the Solitary Sandpiper is often seen alone, bobbing its head as it forages for insects along streams, wooded swamps, marshes, rivers, shorelines and mudflats. • Like the yellowlegs, the Solitary Sandpiper breeds in boreal forest muskeg and often perches and nests in trees found there. Its nesting strategy of laying its eggs in other birds' abandoned nests remained a mystery until 1903, when a homesteader in western Canada peered into what he thought was a robin's nest, but found a sandpiper instead. This sandpiper has also been recorded laying its eggs in the abandoned nests of the Rusty Blackbird, Gray Jay and Cedar Waxwing. Most other sandpipers lay their eggs on the ground. Because of this shorebird's propensity to migrate singly or in small flocks and its often remote, inaccessible nesting locations, knowledge of its breeding habits remains scant. • Any sandpiper encountered in wet Illinois woodlands during migration is most likely the Solitary. It's one of the earliest shorebird species to pass through Illinois in spring on the way to its breeding grounds.

breeding

breeding

Habitat: wet meadows, sewage lagoons, muddy ponds, open wetlands, wet woodlands, wooded streams and rivers.
Nesting: does not nest in Illinois.
Feeding: stalks shorelines and wetlands, picking up aquatic invertebrates such as water boatmen and damselfly nymphs; also gleans for terrestrial invertebrates; occasionally stirs the water with its foot to stir up prey.
Voice: high, thin *peet-wheet* or *wheat wheat wheat* when alarmed.
Similar Species: *Lesser Yellowlegs* (p. 127): larger; no eye ring; longer, bright yellow legs. *Spotted Sandpiper* (p. 130): incomplete eye ring; pinkish or yellow legs; black-tipped, brown tail; spotted breast and orange, black-tipped bill in breeding plumage; plain brown upperparts in non-breeding plumage.
Best Sites: widespread in appropriate habitat.

ID: white eye ring; short, yellow green legs; dark yellowish bill with black tip; brown gray back with white spots; fine, white streaks on brown gray head, neck and breast in breeding plumage; dark rump and central tail feathers with black-and-white barring on sides. *In flight:* dark underwings.
Size: *L* 7–9 in; *W* 22 in.
Status: common migrant; occurs from late March to late May and from late June to late October.

WILLET

Catoptrophorus semipalmatus

The moment a Willet takes flight, its black-and-white wing pattern alerts other shorebirds to danger. This distinctive wing pattern may also distract predators. • The Willet uses various feeding strategies including pecking at the water's surface and "mowing," a feeding strategy in which the bird walks across the ground, rapidly opening and shutting its bill while quickly moving its head up and down. Willets also "mow" while wading, sometimes belly deep. • Two distinct eastern and western subspecies exist. The eastern subspecies mainly nests in coastal salt marshes; the western subspecies found in Illinois breeds along prairie marshes, ponds and lakes.

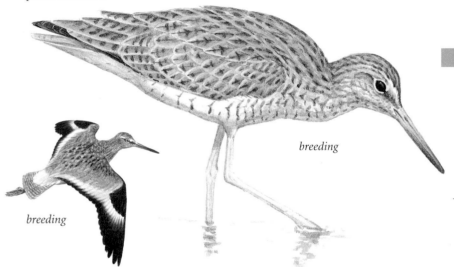

breeding

breeding

ID: large, stocky wader; heavy, straight, 2-tone bill; blue gray legs. *Breeding:* dark streaking on somewhat buff breast and sides; gray brown upperparts with some black barring and splotches. *Nonbreeding:* gray breast on otherwise light underparts; plain gray upperparts. *In flight:* black-and-white wing pattern.
Size: *L* 14–16 in; *W* 26 in.
Status: rare to uncommon migrant from early April to early June and from late June to late September.
Habitat: wet fields, mudflats, beaches and shorelines along marshes, lakes and ponds.
Nesting: does not nest in Illinois.

Feeding: probes for small mollusks, fish fry and aquatic insects; also gleans the ground for insects; occasionally eats shoots and seeds.
Voice: loud, rolling *will-will-willet, will-will-willet.*
Similar Species: *Hudsonian Godwit* (p. 133): nonbreeding has much longer, pink-and-black, upturned bill; white on wing is much less extensive in flight; distinctive white-and-black tail. *Marbled Godwit* (p. 134): much longer, pink-and-black, upturned bill; black legs; warm buff overall with bright cinnamon underwings in flight. *Greater Yellowlegs* (p. 126) and *Lesser Yellowlegs* (p. 127): long, yellow legs; slightly upturned bills; lack black-and-white wing pattern.
Best Sites: L. Michigan shoreline; L. Chautauqua; Rend L.; Carlyle L.

SPOTTED SANDPIPER

Actitis macularia

This small shorebird breeds throughout Illinois in small numbers and is the most frequently encountered sandpiper in June. The Spotted Sandpiper is typically seen individually or in a pair. • In 1972 , researchers discovered this bird's unusual breeding habits. The female defends a territory and mates with more than one male, leaving the males to tend the nests and eggs. This unusual nesting behavior, known as polyandry, is found in about one percent of all bird species on Earth. • The Spotted Sandpiper's stiff-winged, quivering flight pattern can help to identify it from a distance. Even more so than the Solitary Sandpiper, the Spottie teeters almost continuously as it forages. • Like many shorebirds, the Spotted Sandpiper lays very large eggs relative to its size, which are incubated for comparatively long periods. The moment sandpiper chicks break out of their eggs, they are ready to run, hide and feed on their own.

breeding

breeding

ID: teeters almost continuously. *Breeding:* white underparts heavily spotted with black; yellow orange legs; yellow orange, black-tipped bill; white "eyebrow." *Nonbreeding* and *juvenile:* pure white breast, foreneck and throat; brown bill; dull yellow legs. *In flight:* flies close to the water's surface with very rapid, shallow wingbeats; white upperwing stripe.
Size: *L* 7–8 in; *W* 15 in.
Status: fairly common to common migrant and breeder; migrants occur from early April to late May and from mid-July to mid-October.
Habitat: shorelines, gravel pits, beaches, ponds, marshes, rivers, streams, swamps

and sewage lagoons; occasionally seen during migration in flooded fields.
Nesting: usually near water; often under overhanging vegetation among logs or under bushes; in a shallow depression lined with grass; male almost exclusively incubates 4 creamy buff, heavily blotched and spotted eggs for 19–22 days and raises the young.
Feeding: picks and gleans along shorelines for terrestrial and aquatic invertebrates; also snatches flying insects from the air.
Voice: sharp, crisp *eat-wheat, eat-wheat, wheat-wheat-wheat-wheat*.
Similar Species: *Solitary Sandpiper* (p. 128): complete eye ring; on breast; dark yellowish bill with black tip; yellowish green legs; dark rump and central tail feathers; lacks spotting on breast.
Best Sites: widespread in appropriate habitat.

UPLAND SANDPIPER
Bartramia longicauda

In summer, Upland Sandpipers often perch atop tall fence posts belting out airy, "wolf-whistle" courtship tunes. Excited males will even launch into the air to perform courtship flight displays, combining song with shallow, fluttering wing-beats. At the height of the breeding season, however, these large-eyed, inland shorebirds are rarely seen, remaining hidden in the tall grass of abandoned fields and lightly grazed pastures. • Twice each year, the wide-ranging Upland Sandpiper makes the incredible journey between Canada and the pampas of Argentina in southern South America. • In Illinois, loss of habitat has led to a significant decrease in breeding populations of this state-endangered species. There are few grasslands left in Illlinois that are large enough to sustain this bird. Also, land management practices, such as overgrazing and overharvesting in hayfields, may further inhibit the Upland Sandpiper's success in Illinois.

ID: small head; long, skinny neck; dark eyes are large relative to head and body; bright yellow legs; mottled brownish upperparts; lightly streaked breast, sides and flanks; white belly and undertail coverts; 2-tone bill is about same length as head.

Size: *L* 11–12½ in; *W* 26 in.

Status: state-endangered; rare to uncommon migrant statewide from early April to late May and from mid-July to mid-September; very rare and local breeder in the northern two-thirds of the state.

Habitat: hayfields, moderately grazed pastures, grassy meadows, abandoned fields, natural grasslands, airports and agricultural areas; prefers areas where it can see above the grass.

Nesting: in dense, medium-height grass; sometimes near a wetland; in a depression; pair incubates 4 lightly spotted pale to pinkish buff eggs, for 22–27 days; both adults tend the young.

Feeding: gleans vegetation and soil for insects, especially grasshoppers and beetles.

Voice: courtship song is a mournful rising and falling whistle, often given high in the sky; also gives a rolling trill in flight; alarm call is *quip-ip-ip.*

Similar Species: *Buff-breasted Sandpiper* (p. 147): smaller; warm buff overall; shorter neck; larger head; shorter, daintier, all-dark bill; clear buff breast; lacks streaking on "cheek" and foreneck. *Pectoral Sandpiper* (p. 143): more robust; shorter, thicker neck; streaking on breast ends abruptly; smaller eyes; shorter tail; dark bill; usually seen in larger numbers.

Best Sites: Midewin National Tallgrass Prairie; sod farms in fall.

131

WHIMBREL

Numenius phaeopus

The Whimbrel enjoys a widespread distribution, nesting across northern North America and Eurasia and spending its winters on the shores of six continents. In migration, this bird is primarily coastal and oceanic, though some fly overland and find their way into our region. • In Illinois, Whimbrels are usually seen singly or in small groups in spring along Lake Michigan, and often as singles along Lake Michigan and on the mudflats of large downstate reservoirs in fall. A sighting of this large, impressive shorebird with its long, downcurved bill in our prairie state is truly a special treat. In Illinois, recent observations have shown that a small number of Whimbrels also migrate through the interior of the United States to the Gulf Coast. Some may undertake nonstop, 2500-mile flights from the Atlantic Coast to South America. • Both the Whimbrel and the Eskimo Curlew *(N. borealis)* suffered devastating losses to their populations during the commercial hunts of the late 1800s. The Whimbrel population slowly recovered, but the Eskimo Curlew vanished—the last confirmed sighting of this bird was in 1963.

ID: long, 2-tone, down-curved bill; striped crown; dark eye line; mottled brown body; pale underparts; long, blue gray legs. *In flight:* dark primaries.
Size: *L* 17½ in; *W* 32 in.
Status: rare migrant from late April to early June and from mid-July to early September.
Habitat: mudflats, sandy beaches, lakeshores and rarely in flooded agricultural fields.

Nesting: does not nest in Illinois.
Feeding: probes and pecks for invertebrates, especially crabs, in mud or vegetation; farther north during fall migration, eats enormous amounts of berries including cloudberries and crowberries.
Voice: a rippling *bibibibibibibi*.
Similar Species: *Marbled Godwit* (p. 134): buffy overall; upturned bill; cinnamon underwings in flight.
Best Sites: Illinois Beach SP; Waukegan Beach.

HUDSONIAN GODWIT

Limosa haemastica

S mall numbers of these large, handsome shorebirds migrate through Illinois, with small flocks sometimes seen in spring and often singles in fall. Hudsonian Godwits are attaining their colorful breeding plumage when they pass through Illinois in spring. • Of the world's four godwit species, the Hudsonian is the least known. It was considered to be one of the rarest birds in North America until the 1940s, when biologists discovered large flocks along the coastlines of James Bay and Hudson Bay in northern Canada. • The Hudsonian Godwit probes sandy and muddy depths for worms, mollusks and crustaceans, sometimes with its bill buried to its eyes. • The Hudsonian Godwit is smaller than its cousin, the Marbled Godwit, and has distinctive, black underwings that are easily seen in flight.

nonbreeding

breeding

ID: long, yellow orange bill with dark, slightly upturned tip; white rump; black tail; long, blue black legs. *Breeding:* heavily barred, chestnut red underparts; dark grayish upperparts; male is more brightly colored. *Nonbreeding:* grayish upperparts; whitish underparts may show a few short, black bars. *Juvenile:* dark gray brown upperparts fringed pale buff; well-marked scapulars and tertials; underparts washed with brownish buff. *In flight:* white rump; black "wing pits" and wing linings.
Size: *L* 14–15½ in; *W* 29 in.
Status: rare but regular migrant; occurs from mid-April to early June and from late August to mid-October.
Habitat: flooded fields, mudflats and lakeshores.

Nesting: does not nest in Illinois.
Feeding: probes deeply into water or mud; walks into deeper water than most shore-birds but rarely swims; eats mollusks, crus-taceans, insects and other invertebrates; also picks earthworms from plowed fields.
Voice: usually quiet in migration; some-times a sharp, rising *god-WIT!*
Similar Species: *Marbled Godwit* (p. 134): larger; mottled brown overall; lacks white rump; cinnamon underwings in flight. *Short-billed Dowitcher* (p. 149) and *Long-billed Dowitcher* (p. 150): smaller; straight, all-dark bills; yellow green legs; white rump extends halfway up back; feed with repeated up-down bill motion; mottled, rusty brown upperparts and rusty "cheek" in breeding plumage; back and wings have black centers to feathers in nonbreeding plumage.
Best Sites: downstate reservoirs especially in fall; L. Michigan shoreline and mudflats in spring.

133

MARBLED GODWIT

Limosa fedoa

A rare but regular Illinois migrant, the Marbled Godwit is usually seen in small flocks in spring and often singly in fall. The Marbled Godwit often submerges its head beneath the water or presses its face into a mudflat while feeding. It usually stands with its bill pointed down, compared with Whimbrels and Willets, which hold their bills horizontally. • Besides the Long-billed Curlew and oystercatchers, the Marbled Godwit is the largest North American shorebird, with a bill that can be as long as 5½ inches. • Unlike the Hudsonian Godwit, which undertakes long migrations from the Arctic to South America, Marbled Godwits breed on the Canadian Prairies and the American Great Plains and migrate relatively short distances to coastal wintering areas in the southern U.S. and Central America. • One of the most relentlessly persecuted of North American shorebirds, the Marbled Godwit was extirpated from much of its former eastern range by the middle of the 19th century.

breeding

nonbreeding

ID: long, yellow orange bill with dark, slightly upturned tip; long neck and legs; mottled buff brown plumage, darkest on upperparts; long, blue black legs. *In flight:* cinnamon wing linings.
Size: *L* 16–20 in; *W* 30 in.
Status: rare but regular migrant; occurs from early April to early June and from late July to early October.
Habitat: flooded fields, wet meadows, mudflats and lakeshores.
Nesting: does not nest in Illinois.
Feeding: probes deeply in soft substrates for worms, insect larvae, crustaceans and mollusks; picks insects from grass; may also eat the tubers and seeds of aquatic vegetation.

Voice: loud, 2-syllable squawks: *god-wit god-wit.*
Similar Species: *Hudsonian Godwit* (p. 133): smaller; chestnut red neck and underparts; white rump; nonbreeding plumage mostly gray. *Whimbrel* (p. 132): downcurved bill; dark gray brown overall; dark underwing. *Short-billed Dowitcher* (p. 149) and *Long-billed Dowitcher* (p. 150): smaller; straight, all-dark bills; yellow green legs; white rumps; feed with repeated updown bill motion.
Best Sites: L. Chautauqua; Carlyle L.; Rend L. in fall; Chicago lakefront in spring.

RUDDY TURNSTONE
Arenaria interpres

From mid-May to mid-June, boldly patterned Ruddy Turnstones forage along the shores of Lake Michigan singly or in small flocks. These birds' painted faces and eye-catching, rusty black backs set them apart from the multitudes of little brown-and-white sandpipers. • Ruddy Turnstones are truly long-distance migrants. Individuals that nest along the shores of islands in Canada's High Arctic routinely fly to wintering grounds in South America. • The name "turnstone" is appropriate for this bird, which uses its bill to flip over pebbles, shells and washed-up vegetation to expose hidden invertebrates. Its short, stubby, slightly upturned bill is ideal for its unusual foraging style. The Ruddy Turnstone has a varied diet that may occasionally include the eggs of other birds or even bread crumbs from picnic tables. • The flickering calico wing pattern of this bird while it is in flight sets it apart from other shorebirds.

♂

breeding

ID: white belly; black "bib" curves up to shoulder; stout, black, slightly upturned bill; orangy red legs; white tail with black terminal band; calico wing pattern in flight. *Breeding:* ruddy upperparts; female is slightly paler; black-and-white face; black "collar"; streaky crown. *Nonbreeding:* brownish upperparts and face.
Size: *L* 9½ in; *W* 21 in.
Status: uncommon to locally common migrant on L. Michigan; rare to uncommon migrant downstate; occurs from mid-April to early June and from mid-July to mid-November.
Habitat: beaches and rocky shorelines and jetties along L. Michigan, mudflats at downstate reservoirs and wet, cultivated fields.

Nesting: does not nest in Illinois.
Feeding: probes under and flips rocks, weeds and shells for food items; picks, digs and probes for invertebrates from the soil or mud; also eats bivalves, barnacles, zebra mussels, crabs, berries, seeds, spiders and carrion.
Voice: clear, staccato, rattling *cut-a-cut* alarm call and lower, repeated contact notes.
Similar Species: *Other sandpipers* (pp. 126–55): all lack Ruddy Turnstone's bold patterning and flashy wing markings in flight. *Plovers* (pp. 119–22): equally bold plumage, but in significantly different patterns; more inconspicuous wing bars.
Best Sites: L. Michigan shoreline, especially Illinois Beach SP; Waukegan Beach; downstate reservoirs.

RED KNOT

Calidris canutus

Small flocks of Red Knots appear for a brief period between mid-May and early June in Illinois, when their bright rufous plumage easily distinguishes them from migrating plovers and sandpipers. These plump shorebirds are usually encountered as individuals in the fall when they are more difficult to identify because of their duller plumage. • At one time, the Red Knot was one of the most abundant North American shorebirds, but market hunting in the late 19th century contributed to its decline. Today, overharvesting of horseshoe crabs on the Atlantic Coast, whose eggs are a key food source during migration, continues to make survival difficult for the Red Knot. • The Red Knot is another migratory champion, flying up to 19,000 miles in one year.

nonbreeding

breeding

ID: round, chunky body; pale gray rump; greenish legs. *Breeding:* rusty face, breast and underparts; brown, black and buff upperparts. *Nonbreeding:* pale gray upperparts; white underparts with some faint streaking on upper breast; faint barring on rump and flanks. *Immature:* scaly-looking back. *In flight:* white wing stripe.
Size: *L* 10½ in; *W* 23 in.
Status: rare to locally uncommon migrant from mid-May to early June and from late July to early October; most common on L. Michigan beaches.
Habitat: L. Michigan shoreline and mudflats.

Nesting: does not nest in Illinois.
Feeding: gleans shorelines for insects, crustaceans and mollusks; probes soft substrates, creating lines of small holes.
Voice: usually silent; low, monosyllabic *knut,* reminiscent of its name.
Similar Species: *Sanderling* (p. 137): smaller; much more common; less chunky; brick red head and chest; black legs; whitish in fall. *Dunlin* (p. 145): nonbreeding has brownish tone on upperparts, proportionately longer, thinner bill, drooping at tip, black legs, more prominent white wing stripe and unmarked flanks. *Purple Sandpiper* (p. 144): much rarer; nonbreeding is darker overall, has orangy legs, bicolored bill, spotted flanks and wing tips do not extend to tail.
Best Sites: L. Michigan shoreline.

SANDERLING

Calidris alba

A spring or fall stroll along the Lake Michigan shoreline often produces close views of Sanderlings running in and out of the waves. Their well-known habit of chasing waves has a simple purpose: to snatch washed-up aquatic invertebrates before the next wave rolls onto shore. Sanderlings can also expertly tweak marine worms and other soft-bodied creatures from just below the surface of mudflats. • In spring, the Sanderling sports a bright, rufous neck, but in non-breeding plumage, it becomes so white in color that it can be identified at great distances. Illinois birders typically see the Sanderling in its light-colored plumage. • This sandpiper is one of the world's most widespread birds and also has one of the longest migration routes. It breeds across the Arctic in Alaska, Canada and Russia, and spends the winter along sandy shorelines in North America, South America, Asia, Africa and Australia. • The Sanderling population along the East Coast has greatly declined over the last decade, but because of its widespread distribution, it may have a better chance for long-term survival than other declining shorebirds.

nonbreeding

nonbreeding

ID: straight, black bill; black legs; white underparts; white wing bar and pale rump. *Breeding:* dark spotting or mottling on rusty head, back and breast. *Nonbreeding:* pale gray upperparts; black shoulder patch (often concealed).

Size: *L* 7–8½ in; *W* 17 in.

Status: locally common migrant; occurs from early May to early June and from late June to mid-November.

Habitat: lakeshores; mudflats, especially near reservoirs.

Nesting: does not nest in Illinois.

Feeding: gleans shorelines for insects, crustaceans and mollusks; probes repeatedly, creating a line of small holes in the sand or mud.

Voice: flight call is a sharp *kip*.

Similar Species: *Dunlin* (p. 145): breeding adult has black belly patch; nonbreeding is plumper, darker, has longer, slightly down-curved bill, feeds in deeper water. *Red Knot* (p. 136): larger; gray-barred, light rump; paler legs; breeding adult has unstreaked, reddish belly. *Semipalmated Sandpiper* (p. 138) and *Western Sandpiper* (p. 139): nonbreeding birds are smaller, slightly darker, less noticeable wing stripe in flight; much less active when feeding.

Best Sites: L. Michigan shoreline.

137

SEMIPALMATED SANDPIPER
Calidris pusilla

The small, plain Semipalmated Sandpiper can be difficult to identify among the flocks of similar-looking *Calidris* sandpipers that appear each spring and fall. Known collectively as "peeps," because of the similarity of their high-pitched calls, these strikingly similar miniatures, which include the Semipalmated, Least, Western, White-rumped and Baird's sandpipers, can make shorebird identification very challenging. • Semipalmated Sandpipers prefer wetter areas along mudflats and shorelines compared with Least Sandpipers and Pectoral Sandpipers, which feed in grassy areas. • Pecking and probing soft substrates, the Semipalmated Sandpiper, like most shorebirds, must feed constantly to replenish its body fat for the remainder of its long migratory journey. Semipalmated Sandpipers arrive later in spring than the other common peeps, usually in May. Possibly the most abundant North American shorebird, the Semipalmated flies almost the entire length of the Americas during migration.

breeding

nonbreeding

ID: short, straight, black bill; black legs. *Breeding:* mottled upperparts; slight brownish tinge on ear patch, crown and scapulars; faint streaks on upper breast and flanks. *Nonbreeding:* white "eyebrow"; gray brown upperparts; white underparts with light brown wash on sides of upper breast. *Juvenile:* similar to breeding but with more pronounced, smudged markings on upper breast; white line above eye. *In flight:* narrow, white wing stripe; white rump is split by black line.
Size: *L* 5½–7 in; *W* 14 in.
Status: common to locally abundant migrant from late April to mid-June and from early July to mid-October.

Habitat: mudflats, shores of ponds, lakes and reservoirs, sewage lagoons and flooded agricultural fields.
Nesting: does not nest in Illinois.
Feeding: probes soft substrates and gleans for aquatic insects and crustaceans.
Voice: flight call is a harsh *cherk;* sometimes a longer *chirrup* or chittering alarm call.
Similar Species: *Least Sandpiper* (p. 140): slightly smaller; yellowish legs; darker upperparts; browner breast. *Western Sandpiper* (p. 139): slightly downcurved bill; bright rufous wash on shoulder, crown and ear patch in breeding plumage. *Sanderling* (p. 137): paler gray upperparts and blackish trailing edge on flight feathers in nonbreeding plumage; much more active feeder.
Best Sites: statewide in appropriate habitat; L. Chautauqua.

WESTERN SANDPIPER

Calidris mauri

The bulk of Western Sandpipers winter along the Pacific Coast, but some fly through Illinois on their way to the Atlantic and Gulf Coasts for the winter. In Illinois, larger numbers of Westerns are observed in fall rather than spring. The Western is probably not as rare as was thought in Illinois—it just takes some work to find it among the many other more common "peeps." It often feeds in deeper water than the other sandpipers. • The Western Sandpiper is often confused with the more common Semipalmated Sandpiper. A few clues to separate the two species include bill length, size and call notes. The bill of the Western is slightly longer, downcurved at the tip and wider at the base. The call notes of the Semipalmated are lower in pitch and include "r" sounds; the Western utters more of an "e" sound. The best way to distinguish these birds is to find both in one spot and make careful comparisons of all three characteristics mentioned above.

nonbreeding

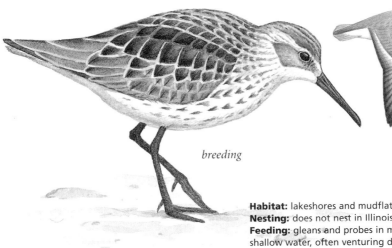

breeding

ID: black bill slightly downcurved at tip; black legs. *Breeding:* rufous patches on crown, ear and scapulars; V-shaped streaking on upper breast and flanks; light underparts. *Nonbreeding:* white "eyebrow"; gray brown upperparts; white underparts. *Juvenile:* streaky, light brown wash on upper breast; rufous scapulars. *In flight:* narrow, white wing stripe; white rump is split by black line.
Size: *L* 6–7 in; *W* 14 in.
Status: uncommon, regular migrant; occurs from late April to early June and from early July to mid-October.

Habitat: lakeshores and mudflats.
Nesting: does not nest in Illinois.
Feeding: gleans and probes in mud and shallow water, often venturing deeper than other small peeps; occasionally submerges its head; primarily eats aquatic insects, worms and crustaceans.
Voice: flight call is a high-pitched *cheep*.
Similar Species: *Semipalmated Sandpiper* (p. 138): typically shorter, straight bill; light brownish rather than rufous on crown, ear patch and scapulars. *Least Sandpiper* (p. 140): smaller; yellowish legs; darker brownish breast wash in all plumages; lacks rufous patches. *Sanderling* (p. 137): lighter; fewer markings; nonbreeding is larger; back of juvenile is spangled with black and white; more active feeder.
Best Sites: L. Calumet; L. Chautauqua; Carlyle L. and Rend L. in fall; sporadically found in spring where suitable habitat exists.

139

LEAST SANDPIPER

Calidris minutilla

The Least Sandpiper, the smallest North American shorebird, migrates almost the entire length of the globe twice each year. • Arctic summers are incredibly short, so shorebirds must maximize their breeding efforts. Least Sandpipers lay large eggs relative to their body size, and the entire clutch may weigh over half the weight of the female. • These shorebirds begin moving south as early as late June. They are one of the first fall shorebirds to arrive in Illinois as well as one of the last to leave, occasionally being recorded on Christmas bird counts. They are also one of the earliest to arrive in spring, sometimes appearing here in late March. • Least Sandpipers are usually encountered in small flocks, but can occur in large concentrations of hundreds to thousands of birds. • Although light-colored legs are a good field mark for this species, bad lighting or mud can confuse matters. The Least Sandpiper is browner than other peeps.

breeding

ID: *Breeding:* black bill; yellowish legs; dark, mottled back; brown breast, head and nape; dense breast streaking. *Nonbreeding:* much duller; often lacks back stripes; prominent, streaked breast band. *Immature:* similar to breeding, but with faintly streaked breast.
Size: *L* 5–6½ in; *W* 13 in.
Status: common to abundant migrant from late March to early June and from late June to early November; occasionally recorded on Christmas bird counts.
Habitat: sandy beaches, lakeshores, sewage lagoons, mudflats, wet grassy areas and flooded agricultural fields.

Nesting: does not nest in Illinois.
Feeding: probes or pecks for insects, crustaceans, small mollusks and occasionally seeds.
Voice: high-pitched *kreee;* in flight, a prolonged *screee-ee-ee;* often maintains an almost constant twittering while foraging.
Similar Species: *Semipalmated Sandpiper* (p. 138): slightly larger; black legs; lighter upperparts; brownish tinge on crown, ear patch and scapulars. *Western Sandpiper* (p. 139): slightly larger; black legs; lighter breast wash in all plumages; rufous patches on crown, ear and scapulars in breeding plumage. *Other peeps* (pp. 138–42): larger; dark legs.
Best Sites: L. Chautauqua; common in suitable habitat statewide.

WHITE-RUMPED SANDPIPER
Calidris fuscicollis

The White-rumped Sandpiper's prominent white rump gives away its identity when the bird is in flight. This bird is one of the more uncommon shorebirds to be found in Illinois. • Because of its elliptical migration pattern, the White-rump is more common in Illinois in spring than in fall. Fall migrants make a nonstop flight across the Atlantic Ocean from eastern Canada to northeastern South America, sometimes flying 60 hours at a time. After wintering in South America, they return to their nesting grounds via a spring migration route through central North America, including Illinois. The very similar Baird's Sandpiper is more common in fall. Often, the white rump is all that distinguishes the two species. The White-rump also utters a squeaky *tzeet*, higher pitched than other peeps. • This sandpiper's white rump may serve as a visual signal to alert other birds to danger or it may be used to attract mates during courtship.

breeding

breeding

ID: black legs; black bill; streaked upperparts; wings extend well beyond tail when perched; body is held more horizontally than most peeps. *Breeding:* mottled brown and rufous upperparts; streaked breast, sides and flanks. *Nonbreeding:* mottled gray upperparts; white "eyebrow." *Immature:* black upperparts edged with white, chestnut and buff. *In flight:* white rump; dark tail; wing bar.
Size: *L* 7–8 in; *W* 17 in.
Status: uncommon spring migrant and rare fall migrant; occurs from late April to mid-June and from late July to late October.

Habitat: lakeshores, sewage lagoons, reservoirs, mudflats and flooded fields.
Nesting: does not nest in Illinois.
Feeding: often forages in water up to its belly, submerging entire head; gleans the ground and shorelines for insects, crustaceans and mollusks.
Voice: flight call is a characteristic, high pitched *tzeet*, higher than any other peep.
Similar Species: *Other peeps* (pp. 138–42): smaller; all have dark line through rump; all have wings either even with or shorter than tail when perched. *Baird's Sandpiper* (p. 142): lacks clean, white rump; buff breast has fine streaking; fall juvenile has more "scaly" than streaked upperparts.
Best Sites: L. Chautauqua; Rend L.; Carlyle L.

141

BAIRD'S SANDPIPER
Calidris bairdii

Like the White-rump, the Baird's Sandpiper can be separated from other peeps by its larger size and wings that extend beyond the tail when perched. In Illinois, these birds are usually encountered individually or in small flocks. • Like its *Calidris* relatives, this shorebird flies twice annually between South America and the Arctic. The female Baird's performs a remarkable feat: just after arriving in the Arctic, with little or no stored body fat, she lays a clutch of eggs that is up to 120 percent of her body mass. As with many other shorebird species, soon after the chicks hatch and are able to fend for themselves, the adults migrate south, arriving in Illinois before the young. Juveniles arrive in a second wave of southbound migrants. • Elliot Coues named this bird in recognition of his mentor, Spencer Fullerton Baird, director of the Smithsonian Institution in the 1800s.

nonbreeding

nonbreeding

ID: black legs and bill; faint, streaky, gray buff breast speckling; folded wings extend beyond tail; body held more horizontally than most peeps. *Breeding:* black, diamond-like pattern on back and wing coverts; lacks streaked flanks. *Juvenile:* brighter and browner; distinctive "scaly" appearance to back.
Size: *L* 7–7½ in; *W* 17 in.
Status: rare spring migrant and uncommon fall migrant; occurs from late April to early June and from mid-July to mid-November.
Habitat: sandy beaches and sandbars; short grassy areas such as golf courses, airports and sod farms; mudflats, meadows and drier edges of short vegetation along wetlands.
Nesting: does not nest in Illinois.
Feeding: gleans aquatic invertebrates, especially larval flies; also eats beetles and grasshoppers; rarely probes.
Voice: soft, rolling *kreep kreep*.
Similar Species: "scaly" back of juvenile is distinctive. *White-rumped Sandpiper* (p. 141): clean white rump; head and back are more streaked; usually frequents wetter habitats. *Pectoral Sandpiper* (p. 143): dark breast ends abruptly at edge of white belly. *Least Sandpiper* (p. 140): smaller; yellowish legs. *Western Sandpiper* (p. 139) and *Sanderling* (p. 137): lack streaked, gray buff breast. *Semipalmated Sandpiper* (p. 138): smaller; shorter bill.
Best Sites: L. Chautauqua; H&E Sod Farms, McHenry Co.; Momence Sod Farms in fall.

PECTORAL SANDPIPER
Calidris melanotos

This widespread traveler may be found in Siberia as well as the Canadian Arctic and its epic annual migrations include destinations such as South America, Australia and New Zealand. The most common Illinois shorebird, the Pectoral Sandpiper gathers in small flocks of 25 to 50 birds. However, at Lake Chautauqua, one of the most important interior U.S. shorebird stopovers east of the Mississippi River, groups number in the tens of thousands. First arrivals in Illinois occur in mid-March; peak numbers occur in April and May and from late August to early September. Fall migrants arrive not long after the latest spring migrants have departed. • Unlike most sandpipers, the Pectoral exhibits sexual dimorphism—the females are only two-thirds the size of the males. • The name "pectoral" refers to the location of the male's prominent, blackish air sacs. When courting the female, the male inflates these air sacs, creating a hooting noise, one of the most unusual sounds heard on the tundra. • The Pectoral Sandpiper has been called "Grass Snipe" because of its preference for wet fields and grassy meadows.

nonbreeding

breeding

ID: brown breast streaks end abruptly at edge of white belly; dark bill; relatively long, yellow legs; mottled upperparts; may have faintly rusty, dark crown and back; folded wings extend to tail. *Juvenile:* similar to adult. **Size:** *L* 8½ in; *W* 18 in. (female is noticeably smaller).
Status: common to abundant migrant from mid-March to early June and from late June to mid-November.
Habitat: lakeshores, mudflats, flooded fields; wet pastures; sewage lagoons; sod farms and other wet, grassy areas.

Nesting: does not nest in Illinois.
Feeding: probes and pecks for small insects, primarily flies, but also beetles and some grasshoppers; may also take small mollusks, crustaceans, berries, seeds, moss, algae and other vegetation.
Voice: sharp, short, low *krrick krrick*.
Similar Species: *Peeps* (pp. 138–42): lack well-defined, dark "bib" contrasting with white belly; all have dark legs, except for *Least Sandpiper* (p. 140), which is much smaller. *Ruff* (p. 148): very rare; larger; white patch at base of bill; orange yellow legs; distinct, humpbacked appearance.
Best Sites: L. Chautauqua; Meredosia NWR; backwater areas of Illinois R. and Mississippi R.; large, downstate reservoirs.

PURPLE SANDPIPER
Calidris maritima

Unlike most shorebirds, which prefer shallow wetland edges, beaches or mudflats, the hardy Purple Sandpiper forages perilously close to crashing waves along rocky breakwaters and piers in Illinois. These birds expertly navigate their way across rugged, slippery, algae-covered rocks while foraging for crustaceans, mollusks and insect larvae. • Rarely seen on beaches that are not near rocky areas, the Purple Sandpiper winters along the Atlantic Coast and breeds in high arctic coastal regions. A few individuals also visit the Lake Michigan shoreline in Illinois annually, especially in late fall and early winter. No other shorebird winters as far north in the Midwest. The Thanksgiving holiday weekend is a good time to search for this bird in Illinois; it is almost always seen here in nonbreeding plumage. • The Purple Sandpiper can swim and often lands on floating vegetation on the water's surface. • The name "purple" was given to this sandpiper for the purplish iridescence that is occasionally observed on its shoulders.

nonbreeding

ID: *Nonbreeding:* dull gray to blue gray overall; long, slightly drooping, black bill with orange yellow base; orange yellow legs; dull streaking on breast and flanks; unstreaked, gray head, neck and upper breast form "hood"; gray spots on white belly.
Size: *L* 9 in; *W* 17 in.
Status: rare but regular migrant from mid-November to mid-December; very few spring records.
Habitat: sand and gravel beaches, rocky shorelines, piers and breakwaters.
Nesting: does not nest in Illinois.
Feeding: food is found visually and is snatched while moving over rocks and sand; eats mostly mollusks, small fish, insects, crustaceans and other inverte-brates; also eats a variety of plant material; pecks rather than probes.
Voice: call is a soft *prrt-prrt*.
Similar Species: *Dunlin* (p. 145): much more common; nonbreeding has plain, dull brown back, clean, white flanks and belly, long, black bill, black legs, lighter tail; wings even or just short of tail on standing bird. *Red Knot* (p. 136): more common; juvenile and nonbreeding are lighter overall, with greenish yellow legs, relatively short, straight, black bills, barring on flanks, wing tips extending to tail, pale gray rumps and tails and less prominent white wing stripes in flight.
Best Sites: Waukegan Beach; Winthrop Harbor; L. Michigan shoreline, especially in rocky areas or jetties.

DUNLIN

Calidris alpina

Outside the breeding season, Dunlins form dynamic, synchronous flocks and rarely mingle with other species. Sometimes hundreds of these birds fly wing tip to wing tip. Cosmopolitan, with nine subspecies identified, this is among the most well-studied of sandpipers. • Unlike many of their shorebird relatives, Dunlins overwinter in North America, mostly in coastal areas where they number in the tens of thousands, providing fodder for Peregrine Falcons and Merlins. • In Illinois, Dunlins are usually among the last shorebirds to arrive in fall along with Long-billed Dowitchers. • Similar shorebird species foraging in the same area can coexist because they have different diets: migrant Dunlins often eat large numbers of worms, Red Knots feed on mollusks and Sanderlings concentrate on insects.

breeding

nonbreeding

ID: plump; relatively short, black legs; black bill droops at tip and is heavy at base. *Breeding:* prominent, diagnostic black belly; streaked white neck and underparts; rufous scapulars, back and crown. *Nonbreeding:* gray tinged with brown overall. *In flight:* white wing stripe.
Size: *L* 7½–9 in; *W* 17 in.
Status: common to abundant migrant; larger flocks in fall; occurs from mid-April to mid-June and from late August to late November.
Habitat: mudflats and shores of ponds and lakes; occasionally seen in pastures, flooded fields and sewage lagoons.
Nesting: does not nest in Illinois.

Feeding: gleans and probes for aquatic crustaceans, worms, mollusks and insects.
Voice: flight call is a grating *cheezp* or *treezp.*
Similar Species: black belly in breeding plumage is distinctive. *Sanderling* (p. 137): nonbreeding is less plump, paler, has straight bill, usually seen running in surf. *Stilt Sandpiper* (p. 146): longer neck; longer, yellow green legs; white "eyebrow"; feeds with repeated up-down bill motion. *Purple Sandpiper* (p. 144): much rarer; nonbreeding is darker overall with bicolored bill and orangy legs; tail extends beyond wings in standing bird. *Red Knot* (p. 136): nonbreeding is larger and has proportionally shorter, stouter bill, barred flanks, olive legs and less prominent white wing stripe.
Best Sites: L. Michigan shoreline; L. Chautauqua and other large, downstate reservoirs.

145

STILT SANDPIPER

Calidris himantopus

With the silhouette of a Lesser Yellowlegs and the foraging behavior of a dowitcher—two species with which this bird often associates—the Stilt Sandpiper can easily be overlooked in a mixed flock of these species. Named for its relatively long legs, this shorebird feeds in shallow water, often dunking its head, probing for prey. Because its bill is shorter than a dowitcher's, the Stilt Sandpiper has to lean farther forward to feed, a characteristic that can help in identification. This sandpiper may also wade into deep water up to its breast in search of a meal that consists of everything from insects to vegetation and seeds. • Spring migrants usually arrive in May. After the nesting season, adult Stilt Sandpipers arrive in Illinois in late June or July along with some of the other early shorebirds. Immatures appear in early to mid-August. In fall, the adults are often still in breeding plumage and can look very much like yellowlegs, although their drooping bills and distinctive feeding manner can help to distinguish the two species.

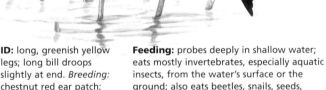

breeding

nonbreeding

ID: long, greenish yellow legs; long bill droops slightly at end. *Breeding:* chestnut red ear patch; white "eyebrow"; striped crown; streaked neck; barred underparts. *Nonbreeding:* less obvious white "eyebrow"; white belly; dark brownish gray upperparts. *In flight:* white rump; legs trail behind tail; no wing stripe.

Size: *L* 8–9 in; *W* 18 in.

Status: uncommon spring migrant; common to locally abundant fall migrant; occurs from late April to early June and from early July to mid-October.

Habitat: edges of lakeshores and reservoirs; flooded fields, mudflats and sewage lagoons.

Nesting: does not nest in Illinois.

Feeding: probes deeply in shallow water; eats mostly invertebrates, especially aquatic insects, from the water's surface or the ground; also eats beetles, snails, seeds, roots and leaves.

Voice: soft, rattling *querp* or *kirr* in flight; clearer *whu*.

Similar Species: *Greater Yellowlegs* (p. 126) and *Lesser Yellowlegs* (p. 127): speckled backs and wings; barred tails; straight bills; lemon yellow legs; lack chestnut ear patch and crown. *Dunlin* (p. 145): nonbreeding has shorter neck, shorter, black legs, lacks distinct white "eyebrow" and feeds by probing. *Nonbreeding Long-billed Dowitcher* (p. 150) and *Short-billed Dowitcher* (p. 149): larger and plumper; longer, straighter bills; white rump patch extends to back in flight.

Best Sites: L. Calumet; L. Chautauqua; Carlyle L.; Rend L.

BUFF-BREASTED SANDPIPER
Tryngites subruficollis

The Buff-breasted Sandpiper frequents drier habitats more than most other sandpipers. The peak time to look for this bird in Illinois is from mid-August to mid-September, especially on sod farms. The Buffie is rarely seen in our region in spring. • During migration in Illinois, they occasionally perform part of their fascinating courtship display, raising their wings to expose the brilliant white undersurfaces. On the breeding grounds, males gather on large leks to display for females or any moving object, including humans. • The Buff-breasted Sandpiper winters in Paraguay, Uruguay and northern Argentina. The world population of this species of special concern is only about 15,000. • Most Buff-breasts migrate through the center of the continent, so the individuals seen in Illinois are mainly dispersing juveniles heading south for the first time.

breeding

nonbreeding

ID: dark crown; buff, unpatterned face and foreneck; large, dark eyes; very thin, straight, black bill; buff underparts; small spots on crown, nape, breast, sides and flanks; yellow legs. *Juvenile:* "scaly" back and upperwings; different scapular and wing covert pattern than adult. *In flight:* pure white underwings, except small black comma at base of primaries; no wing stripe.
Size: *L* 7½–8 in; *W* 18 in. (male noticeably larger than female).
Status: very rare spring migrant and uncommon fall migrant; occurs from late April to late May and from early August to late September.

Habitat: sod farms, flooded grassy fields, mudflats and dry grassy edges of lakes and reservoirs.
Nesting: does not nest in Illinois.
Feeding: gleans the soil and shorelines for insects, spiders and small crustaceans; may eat seeds.
Voice: low *pr-r-reet* or series of harsh *tik* notes.
Similar Species: *Upland Sandpiper* (p. 131): larger; darker; bolder breast streaking; longer neck; larger bill; streaking on "cheek" and foreneck; black rump; darker upper primaries and heavily streaked underwing in flight. *Ruff* (p. 148): very rare; juvenile is larger and bulkier, has sloping forehead, less rounded head, humpbacked appearance, "scaly" back edged in buff and greener, longer legs.
Best Sites: H&E Sod Farms in McHenry Co.; Momence Sod Farms; L. Chautauqua.

147

RUFF
Philomachus pugnax

A breeding male Ruff in Illinois is truly a rare sight. • The male of this species is called a "Ruff" and the female is known as a "Reeve." In spring, males are particularly unmistakable with their prominent neck and "ear" ruffs. It is not known whether the male was named for his neck-feather ruffs or if ruffs were named after the bird. "Reeve" also has unknown origins, but it has been suggested that it is linked to the meaning of "observer" or "baliff"—the females oversee the tussling males, which, like the Greater Prairie-Chicken and other grouse species, gather in leks on their breeding grounds. There, they attempt to attract females through courtship displays, which are more elaborate than those of any other shorebird. Males raise their head tufts, wings and ruffs to deter other males and attract females. Males also chase one another in short flights. • The scientific name *pugnax* means "pugnacious," which is an appropriate description of the courting males.

nonbreeding

ID: plump body; brown gray upperparts; variably colored legs from pinkish to orange. *Breeding male:* bare face; black, white or orangy neck ruff, usually flattened, but erected during courtship; dark underparts; white belly; variable rufous-and-black back; yellow legs. *Breeding female:* lacks ruffs, brownish upperparts and breast with black blotching. *Nonbreeding:* grayish upperparts; white underparts; white area at base of bill. *In flight:* U-shaped, white rump divided by dark central stripe.
Size: *L* 9–12 in; *W* 21 in.
Status: very rare migrant; occurs from early April to mid-May and from early July to early November; more fall records than spring.

Habitat: lakeshores, flooded fields, mudflats and wet grassy areas.
Nesting: does not nest in Illinois.
Feeding: probes and picks at the surface of mudflats for earthworms, snails and small crustaceans; also eats terrestrial insects, plant seeds, including cultivated grains, plus weed seeds, grasses and berries.
Voice: rarely vocal; call is a short *tu-whit*.
Similar Species: *Greater Yellowlegs* (p. 126) and *Lesser Yellowlegs* (p. 127): slimmer bodies; longer legs; streaked underparts. *Buff-breasted Sandpiper* (p. 147): smaller; compared with juvenile Ruff, lacks sloping forehead and hump-backed appearance, has rounder head; "scaly" back edged in white.
Best Sites: L. Calumet; L. Chautauqua.

SHORT-BILLED DOWITCHER

Limnodromus griseus

In the midst of summer, Short-billed Dowitchers are already arriving from their northern breeding grounds to feed and rest on mudflats in Illinois. These plump shorebirds are seen in large numbers during spring migration, but the largest concentrations usually occur during the protracted fall migration, which begins as soon as early July. • Dowitchers tend to be stockier than most shorebirds and they generally avoid venturing into deep water. While foraging along shorelines, these birds feed in the mud with a rhythm like a sewing machine. This drilling motion liquifies the mud or sand, allowing dowitchers to reach their hidden prey. Although all shorebirds can swim, dowitchers seems to be especially good at it. • The best way to distinguish between the Short-billed Dowitcher and the very similar Long-billed Dowitcher is by their flight calls. Despite their names, there is considerable overlap in bill length between these two species and, at one time, they were considered a single species.

breeding

ID: straight, long, dark bill, white "eyebrow"; reddish brown "cap"; chunky body; yellow green legs. *Breeding:* white belly; dark spotting on pinkish buff to orangy neck and upper breast; prominent dark barring on white sides and flanks. *Nonbreeding:* dirty gray upperparts; dirty white underparts. *In flight:* white wedge on rump and lower back; numerous thin, black bands on white tail.
Size: *L* 11–12 in; *W* 19 in.
Status: uncommon to locally common migrant; occurs from late April to early June and from late June to late September.
Habitat: edges of lakes and reservoirs, mudflats, sewage lagoons and flooded fields.
Nesting: does not nest in Illinois.
Feeding: wades in shallow water or walks on mud, probing the substrate with a repeated up-down bill motion; eats aquatic invertebrates; may also feed on seeds, aquatic plants, grasses and mosses.
Voice: distinctive flight call is a mellow *tututu, toodulu* or *toodu.*
Similar Species: *Long-billed Dowitcher* (p. 150): brick red underparts with black-and-white barring on flanks in breeding plumage; very little white on belly; dark spotting on neck and upper breast; alarm call is a high-pitched *keek*; nonbreeding very similar, best separated by call. *Stilt Sandpiper* (p. 146): nonbreeding has shorter, slightly drooping bill, much slimmer body, much less extensive white rump patch in flight; call is soft, rattling *querp* or *kirr* in flight.
Best Sites: *In spring migration:* Rend L.; Carlyle L. *In fall migration:* L. Calumet; L. Chautauqua; Meredosia NWR.

149

LONG-BILLED DOWITCHER

Limnodromus scolopaceus

Every spring and especially in late fall, Illinois mudflats host small to fairly large numbers of Long-billed Dowitchers. This species' elliptical migration route takes it west in spring, making it much more common in Illinois during fall. • Long-billed Dowitchers are more apt to use freshwater wetlands; Short-billeds prefer salt water. A diet of insects, freshwater shrimp, mussels, clams and snails provides migrating birds with plenty of fuel for flight and essential calcium for bone and egg development. • Dowitchers have shorter wings than other shorebirds that migrate longer distances. • Various shorebird species are able to coexist because of their different foraging styles and specialized diets. In mixed flocks of shorebirds, some species probe deeply, while others pick at the water's surface or glean the shorelines. • Long-billed Dowitchers tend to arrive later and stay later during fall migration. They also arrive earlier in spring migration compared with the very similar Short-billed Dowitcher.

nonbreeding

nonbreeding

ID: very long, straight, dark bill; white "eyebrow" stripe; chunky body; yellow green legs. *Breeding:* black-and-white barring on orangy to brick red underparts; little or no white on rufous belly; dark, mottled upperparts interspersed with rufous. *Nonbreeding:* gray overall; dirty white underparts. *Juvenile:* grayer overall. *In flight:* white wedge on rump and lower back; numerous thin, black bands on white tail.
Size: *L* 11–12½ in; *W* 19 in.
Status: uncommon spring migrant; uncommon to locally common in fall; occurs from

early April to mid-May and from mid-August to late October.
Habitat: edges of lakes and reservoirs, mudflats, sewage lagoons and flooded fields.
Nesting: does not nest in Illinois.
Feeding: probes shallow water and mudflats with a repeated up-down bill motion; frequently plunges its head underwater; eats aquatic and terrestrial invertebrates; also eats plant material, including seeds of grasses, sedges, smartweeds and bulrushes.
Voice: flight call is a loud, high-pitched *keek*, occasionally given in series.
Similar Species: *Short-billed Dowitcher* (p. 149): white sides, flanks and belly; nonbreeding is very similar, best separated by call. *Stilt Sandpiper* (p. 146): nonbreeding has shorter, slightly drooping bill, slimmer body; white rump patch does not extend onto back.
Best Sites: L. Calumet; L. Chautauqua; Meredosia NWR in fall; Rend L. and Carlyle L. in spring.

WILSON'S SNIPE

Gallinago delicata

In spring, the eerie, hollow winnowing sound of courting Wilson's Snipes resonates over the wetlands of northern Illinois. Specialized outer tail feathers vibrate rapidly as the bird performs daring, headfirst dives high above the marshland. The winnowing sound can carry for half a mile. During the early part of the breeding season, both sexes may perform this courtship ritual. • The well-camouflaged Wilson's Snipe remains concealed in vegetation, flushing only when an intruder approaches too closely. It escapes with aerial zigzags to confuse predators. Because of this habit, hunters that were skilled enough to shoot a snipe came to be known as "snipers," a term later adopted by the military. • This short-distance migrant is recorded yearly on Illinois Christmas bird counts and is one of the earliest shorebirds to arrive in spring, closely following the Killdeer and American Woodcock.

ID: long, sturdy, bicolored bill; relatively short, gray legs; wide, dark crown stripe; boldly striped back; barred flanks contrast with unmarked white belly; orange tail. *In flight:* quick zigzags upon takeoff.

Size: *L* 10½–11½ in; *W* 18 in.

Status: common migrant from early March to early May and from late June to early December; very rare breeder in northeastern Illinois; overwinters in small numbers in southern Illinois.

Habitat: cattail and bulrush marshes, sedge meadows, poorly drained floodplains, wet ditches and agricultural fields, bogs, fens, willow and red-osier dogwood tangles.

Nesting: usually in dry grass near a wetland; often under vegetation; nest is made of grass, moss and leaves; female incubates 4 darkly marked, olive buff to brown eggs for 18–20 days; both parents raise the young.

Feeding: walks with bill slightly downward; plunges pliable bill with a hard tip into soft substrates for aquatic invertebrates, worms, spiders, lizards and small amphibians including frogs and salamanders; also eats seeds; drinks large amounts of water.

Voice: courtship song is produced in flight by air rushing through tail feathers: *woo-woo-woo-woo-woo-woo;* often sings *wheat wheat wheat* from an elevated perch; alarm call is a nasal *scaip.*

Similar Species: *American Woodcock* (p. 152): plumper; shorter legs; unmarked, buff underparts; gray nape extends to breast and back; larger eye and head; black crown with 2–3 pale bars; buff underwing in flight; thick neck.

Best Sites: *Breeding:* Illinois Beach SP; Moraine Hills SP; Goose Lake Prairie SNA. *In migration:* widespread in wetland habitats statewide.

AMERICAN WOODCOCK

Scolopax minor

At twilight, the male American Woodcock struts in an open woodland clearing or a brushy, abandoned field, uttering a series of loud *peeent* notes. He then launches into the air, twittering upward in a circular flight display until, with wings partly folded, he begins chirping and then plummets to the ground in the zigzag pattern of a falling leaf, landing right where he started. • In Illinois, woodcocks arrive with some of the first warm fronts; nests with complete clutches have been found in March. When frightened, young woodcocks will either freeze or raise their wings and run about erratically like windup toys. • Woodcocks have large eyes set high on the head, supposedly to help them see predators while feeding or in the nest. • Other names for woodcocks include "Timberdoodle," "Bog Sucker" and "Labrador Twister."

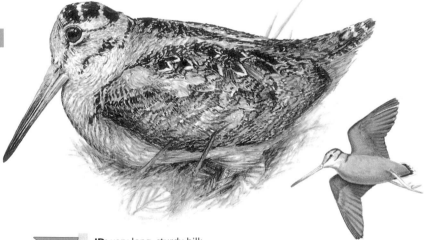

ID: very long, sturdy bill; very short legs; proportionally large head and thick, short neck; chunky body; large, dark eyes; unmarked, buff underparts; gray nape extends to breast and back; black crown with 2–3 buff bars. *In flight:* orange buff underwings contrast with black primaries; makes a twittering sound when flushed from cover.

Size: *L* 11 in; *W* 18 in.

Status: common migrant and breeder statewide from mid-February to mid-December; rare winter resident in southern Illinois and occasionally elsewhere.

Habitat: moist woodlands and brushy thickets adjacent to grassy clearings or abandoned fields; after breeding, often found along edges of marshes, swamps and other wetlands.

Nesting: on the ground in woods or an overgrown field; shallow depression lined with dead leaves and other debris; female incubates 4 pinkish buff eggs, blotched with brown and gray, for 20–22 days; female tends the young.

Feeding: probes soil for earthworms and insect larvae; may eat its weight in earthworms within 24 hours; stamps feet on soil to stimulate worm movement; also takes spiders, snails, millipedes and some plant material, including berries and the seeds of sedges and grasses.

Voice: nasal *peent;* during courtship flight male produces high-pitched, twittering, created by air rushing over outer primaries.

Similar Species: *Wilson's Snipe* (p. 151): slimmer; thin neck; heavily striped head, back, neck and breast; dark barring on sides and flanks; orange tail.

Best Sites: widespread in appropriate habitat throughout state.

WILSON'S PHALAROPE

Phalaropus tricolor

The Wilson's Phalarope is the only phalarope that breeds exclusively in North America and, today, this species has nearly disappeared as a breeder in Illinois. • Phalaropes practice a rather uncommon mating strategy known as polyandry: each female mates with several males. After laying a clutch, the female usually abandons her mate, leaving him to incubate the eggs and tend the precocial young. This reversal of gender roles also includes a reversal of plumage characteristics—females are more brightly colored than males. • The Wilson's Phalarope is often observed creating a whirlpool that brings prey to the surface of the water. It spins at 60 revolutions per minute, spearing the water with its bill at each turn. • Phalaropes have lobed feet for swimming; however, the Wilson's Phalarope is more terrestrial than its relatives and lacks this characteristic.

♂   *breeding*

♀

ID: dark, needlelike bill; white "eyebrow," throat and nape; light underparts; black legs. *Breeding female:* gray "cap"; chestnut brown on sides of neck; wide, broad, black band extends from base of bill through eye, down side of neck and onto back. *Breeding male:* duller overall; dark "cap." *Nonbreeding:* all-gray upperparts; white "eyebrow"; gray eye line; white underparts; dark yellowish or greenish legs. *Juvenile:* dark brown upperparts appear "scaly"; buff sides of breast; pinkish yellow legs.
Size: L 9–9½ in; W 17 in.
Status: state-endangered; rare to uncommon migrant from early April to early June and from early July to mid-October; very rare and sporadic breeder in northern Illinois and occasionally in central Illinois.
Habitat: *Breeding:* marshes and shallow wetlands. *In migration:* lakeshores, ponds, mudflats, marshes and sewage lagoons.

Nesting: often near water; well concealed in a depression lined with vegetation; male incubates 4 brown-blotched, buff eggs for 18–27 days; male rears the young.
Feeding: whirls in tight circles in shallow or deep water to bring prey to the water's surface; eats insects, worms and small crustaceans; on land makes short jabs to pick up invertebrates.
Voice: deep, grunting *work work* or *wu wu wu*.
Similar Species: *Red-necked Phalarope* (p. 154): shorter bill; breeding female has gray breast extending to flanks, chestnut patches on black back and wings; nonbreeding has dark nape and line behind eye and streaked gray back. *Red Phalarope* (p. 155): heavy, thicker bill; breeding has reddish brown neck, breast and underparts, chestnut patches on black back and wings, blackish crown and yellow bill; broad, dark line behind eye in nonbreeding. *Lesser Yellowlegs* (p. 127): slimmer; darker breast and throat; wing tips extend beyond tail in standing bird.
Best Sites: L. Calumet; Arcola Marsh; L. Chautauqua; Carlyle L.

153

RED-NECKED PHALAROPE

Phalaropus lobatus

One of the world's smallest pelagic birds, the Red-necked Phalarope is also the smallest, most abundant and most widely distributed of the three phalarope species. This bird spends up to nine months of the year at sea. During winter and migration, flocks may number in the tens to hundreds of thousands. Most Red-necked Phalaropes migrate to and from their arctic summering grounds via the Atlantic and Pacific coasts, but every year, small flocks, more numerous in fall than in spring, pass through Illinois. • When foraging on the water with other shorebirds, phalaropes can be identified by their habit of spinning and whirling in tight circles, stirring up tiny crustaceans, mollusks and other aquatic invertebrates. As prey funnels toward the water's surface, these birds daintily pluck it from the water with their needlelike bills. • "Phalarope" is the Greek word for "coot's foot."

nonbreeding

ID: thin, black bill; long, gray legs; lobed toes. *Breeding female:* chestnut brown stripe on neck and throat; white "chin"; blue black head; incomplete, white eye ring; white belly; 2 rusty buff stripes on back. *Breeding male:* white "eyebrow"; less intense colors than female. *Nonbreeding:* white underparts; dark nape; black "cap"; broad, dark band from eye to ear; white wing stripes; dark legs. *Juvenile:* bold, buff stripes on dark back; white underparts.
Size: *L* 7 in; *W* 15 in.
Status: rare spring migrant; locally uncommon in fall; occurs from mid-May to early June and from late July to early October.
Habitat: open water bodies, including ponds, lakes, marshes and sewage lagoons; rarely in flooded fields.

Nesting: does not nest in Illinois.
Feeding: whirls in tight circles in shallow or deep water to bring prey to the water's surface; eats aquatic insects, worms and small crustaceans; also small insect larvae including mosquitoes and midges.
Voice: often noisy in migration; soft *krit krit krit.*
Similar Species: *Wilson's Phalarope* (p. 153): longer, thinner bill; breeding female has gray "cap" and wide, black band from base of bill through eye, down side of neck and onto back; nonbreeding has white face, gray nape and gray, unstreaked back. *Red Phalarope* (p. 155): heavy, thicker bill; breeding has reddish brown neck, breast and underparts, buff to orange markings on black back, blackish crown and yellow bill; dark line behind eye in nonbreeding.
Best Sites: L. Chautauqua.

RED PHALAROPE

Phalaropus fulicarius

The Red Phalarope, also known as the Gray Phalarope over much of its circumpolar breeding range, is the least common of the three phalarope species in Illinois. It is seen most commonly during the fall season in its nonbreeding plumage. At this time, it can be extremely difficult to distinguish this bird from its more common cousin, the Red-necked Phalarope. A combination of traits including an unstreaked back, slightly thicker bill and slightly larger size may help identify the Red Phalarope. • The most pelagic of the three phalarope species, the Red Phalarope spends most of the nonbreeding season floating on open ocean waters feeding on plankton, small fish, jellyfish and crustaceans. Flocks may number into the tens of thousands, but Illinois birders are lucky if they see one Red Phalarope a year. It's often the latest of the phalarope species to arrive in fall in Illinois. • Red Phalaropes breed mostly above the Arctic Circle and winter as far south as the coast of Chile, thus many spend most of their lives in daylight.

nonbreeding

ID: *Breeding female:* chestnut red throat, neck and underparts; white "cheek"; black crown, forehead and throat; black-tipped, yellow bill; buff to orange markings on dark back. *Breeding male:* duller face and underparts. *Nonbreeding:* white face, neck and underparts; blue gray upperparts; mostly dark bill; dark nape; broad, dark patch extends from eye to ear. *Juvenile:* similar to nonbreeding, but is buff-colored overall with dark streaking on upperparts.
Size: *L* 8 in; *W* 17 in.
Status: very rare but regular migrant; only recorded singly in the state; mostly seen in fall; occurs from late August to mid-November.

Habitat: lakes, large wetlands and sewage lagoons.
Nesting: does not nest in Illinois.
Feeding: small crustaceans, mollusks, insects and other invertebrates; rarely takes vegetation or small fish; gleans from the water's surface, usually while swimming in tight, spinning circles.
Voice: usually silent; calls include a shrill, high-pitched *wit* or *creep* and a low *clink clink*.
Similar Species: *Red-necked Phalarope* (p. 154): smaller; thinner bill; breeding lacks all-red underparts; juvenile has buff stripes on upperparts. *Wilson's Phalarope* (p. 153): breeding lacks all-red underparts; nonbreeding lacks dark "mask"; no white wing stripe, but shows white rump in flight.
Best Sites: L. Michigan shoreline; L. Chautauqua; Carlyle L.; Rend L.

POMARINE JAEGER
Stercorarius pomarinus

Jaegers are powerful, swift predators of the open seas. They spend most of their lives in the air, occasionally resting on the ocean's surface and only seeking land during the nesting season. • This is the largest of the three jaeger species seen in Illinois. Keen fall and early winter Illinois birders patrolling large downstate reservoirs probably have the best chance of seeing a migrant juvenile Pomarine, which looks like a dark, falconlike gull. Roughly only 6 percent of jaegers flying over Lake Michigan are identified as Pomarines; over 90 percent are Parasitic Jaegers. • Knowing the subtleties of plumage, wingbeat rhythm and wing breadth are important in distinguishing between the three jaeger species that are seen in Illinois. • Scientists speculate that this jaeger is nomadic, moving around the Arctic during the nesting months to find places where a sufficient number of lemmings are available. When lemming populations are large, more young Pomarines make it to adulthood. Many years, these jaegers do not even attempt to nest because of low lemming populations.

*immature
light morph*

ID: *Juvenile:* light morph most often seen in Illinois; large bill compared to other jaeger species; brownish to light-colored, barrel-chested body, darker on back; variable dark barring on under-wings and underparts. *In flight:* wings are wide at base of body; powerful, steady wingbeats; 2 white wing flashes at base of underside of primaries.
Size: *L* 20–23 in; *W* 4 ft.
Status: rare migrant from early October to late November.
Habitat: large downstate reservoirs.
Nesting: does not nest in Illinois.
Feeding: snatches fish from the water's surface while in flight; chases down small birds such as phalaropes and sandpipers; may also take small mammals and nestlings; pirates food from gulls.
Voice: generally silent; may give a sharp *which-yew,* a squealing *weak-weak* or a squeaky whistled note in migration.
Similar Species: *Parasitic Jaeger* (p. 157): light-morph juvenile has smaller body, less barrel-chested appearance, smaller bill and most have rufous tones, especially on nape. *Long-tailed Jaeger:* light-morph juvenile is smaller, grayer and lighter-colored, slimmer overall, smaller bill, more rounded head, more buoyant flight and rapid wingbeats, wings proportionally slimmer and narrower at base.
Best Sites: L. Springfield; L. Chautauqua; Carlyle L.

PARASITIC JAEGER

Stercorarius parasiticus

Although "jaeger" is a German word for "hunter," "parasitic" more aptly describes this bird's foraging tactics. "Kleptoparasitism" is the scientific term for the jaeger's pirating ways, and of the three jaeger species, the Parasitic is the most adept at this technique. Parasitic Jaegers will harass and intimidate terns and gulls until they regurgitate their partially digested meals. As soon as the food is ejected, these aerial pirates snatch it out of midair or pick it from the water's surface in a swooping dive. However, fewer than 25 percent of these chases are successful. • The Parasitic Jaeger is the most numerous bird of prey on its arctic breeding grounds. It is also the most abundant jaeger in the world and the most commonly seen in Illinois, though still very rare. As with the other jaeger species, juveniles are most often seen in Illinois, but nonbreeding adults have occasionally been found.

immature light morph

ID: *Light-morph juvenile:* relatively small bill; medium to dark brown overall, often with much barring, including on underwing; often some rufous tones on nape and other parts of body. *In flight:* white flash at base of primaries on under- and uppersides (other 2 jaeger species mostly only show white flash on undersides).

Size: *L* 15–20½ in; *W* 3 ft.

Status: rare migrant from early September to late November.

Habitat: large rivers and lakes, especially L. Michigan.

Nesting: does not nest in Illinois.

Feeding: pirates, scavenges and hunts for food; takes fish, eggs, large insects and small birds and mammals; also eats carrion and some berries while on land; may pirate fish from gulls, terns and other birds.

Voice: generally silent; may make shrill calls in migration.

Similar Species: *Pomarine Jaeger* (p. 156): light-morph has larger bill, more barrel-chested body, variable dark barring on underwings and underparts; in flight, wings are wide at base of body, has power-ful, steady wingbeats and 2 white wing flashes on underside of primaries. *Long-tailed Jaeger:* light-morph is smaller, grayer and lighter-colored overall, has more rounded head, more buoyant flight and rapid wingbeats, wings proportionally slimmer and narrower at base.

Best Sites: L. Michigan shoreline; 2½-mile strip along L. Michigan from Gillson Park in Wilmette south to Northwestern University in Evanston; L. Springfield; L. Chautauqua; Carlyle L.; downstate reservoirs.

LAUGHING GULL
Larus atricilla

L ife has not always been easy for the Laughing Gull. In the late 19th century, high commercial demand for egg collections and feathers for use in women's head-dresses caused the extirpation of this gull as a breeding species in many parts of its Atlantic Coast range. Today, populations on the East Coast are gradually assuming their former abundance. • In Illinois, the first documented Laughing Gull occurred in Chicago in 1935. • This bird is typically seen singly, but larger numbers have been documented in the state more recently for reasons that are unclear. • Laughing Gulls, like many other gull species, are voracious scavengers; one industrious Laughing Gull can reliably be found foraging, especially on french fries, outside a certain fast-food restaurant in Chicago. • While the laughing call explains this bird's common name, the Latin name *atricilla* refers to a black band present only on the tails of immature birds.

nonbreeding

breeding

ID: *Breeding:* black head; broken, white eye ring; red bill droops slightly at tip; relatively dark gray mantle. *1st-winter:* white forehead with dark patch behind eye and on nape; broad, dark tail band; gray back with brown scapulars, tertials and wing coverts; all-black primaries; black bill.
Size: *L* 15–17 in; *W* 3 ft.
Status: rare migrant from April to mid-November; often occurs in summer, but does not breed in Illinois.
Habitat: lakes and rivers.
Nesting: does not nest in Illinois.
Feeding: omnivorous; gleans inverte-brates, spiders and small fish from the

ground or water while flying, wading, walking or swimming; may steal food, eggs and nestlings from other birds; scavenges at landfills.
Voice: loud, high-pitched, laughing call: *ha-ha-ha-ha-ha-ha.*
Similar Species: *Franklin's Gull* (p. 159): more common; smaller; shorter, slimmer bill; slightly paler mantle; breeding has white tips on outer primaries; 1st-winter and nonbreeding birds have black "hood." *Bonaparte's Gull* (p. 161): much more common; reddish to pinkish legs; slimmer, black bill; lighter mantle; white wedge on upper leading edge of wing; black "hood" in breeding does not extend over nape. *Little Gull* (p. 160): rarer; much smaller; paler mantle; reddish legs; dainty black bill; no eye ring.
Best Sites: L. Michigan shoreline; L. Springfield; Clinton L.; Carlyle L.; Rend L.

FRANKLIN'S GULL
Larus pipixcan

The Franklin's Gull is not a typical "seagull." It spends a large part of its life inland on its traditional nesting territories in the Canadian prairie provinces and in the north-central U.S. • Sometimes called "Prairie Dove," this gull has a dovelike profile and often follows tractors across Illinois' agricultural fields, snatching up insects. • In fall, flocks of migrating Franklin's Gulls arrive in Illinois and are more common inland. Numbers in a flock of this species can vary annually from dozens to hundreds depending on the wind strength and direction. • The Franklin's Gull is one of only two gull species that migrate long distances between breeding and wintering grounds—the majority of these gulls winter along the Pacific coast of Peru and Chile.

nonbreeding

breeding

ID: dark gray mantle; broad, broken, white eye ring; large, white primary tips. *Breeding:* black head; orange red bill and legs; narrow black bill tip; breast may have pinkish tinge. *Nonbreeding:* white head with extensive "hood"; all-black bill. *1st-winter:* lacks obvious white primary tips; incomplete black terminal tail band; brownish wash on wings.
Size: *L* 13–15 in; *W* 3 ft.
Status: occasional spring and uncommon fall migrant; larger flocks in fall; occurs from late March to early June and from late July to late November.
Habitat: agricultural fields, marshlands, rivers and lakes.
Nesting: does not nest in Illinois.
Feeding: very opportunistic; eats insects, flying invertebrates, small fish and some crustaceans.

Voice: mewing, shrill *weeeh-ah weeeh-ah* while feeding and in migration.
Similar Species: *Laughing Gull* (p. 158): rarer; larger; longer, heavier bill; nonbreeding bird lacks black "hood." *Bonaparte's Gull* (p. 161): more common; slightly smaller; black bill; white wedge on forewing; bright red orange legs; immature has narrow, dark "M" on upperwing, small dark spot behind eye on white head, pink legs and complete black tail band. *Little Gull* (p. 160): much rarer; much smaller; paler mantle; breeding bird lacks broken white eye ring and white nape; nonbreeding has black spot behind eye; immature has bold, black "M" on upperwing and complete black tail band.
Best Sites: L. Springfield; Clinton L.; Carlyle L.; Rend L.; Crab Orchard NWR.

159

LITTLE GULL
Larus minutus

This common Eurasian bird was first identified in North America around 1820 from a specimen collected on the first Franklin expedition. It was considered an exceptionally rare vagrant until 1962, when the first documented nest in the New World was discovered in Ontario, Canada. • Little Gulls never nest at a given site for more than a few years. In North America, they have been found nesting primarily in the Great Lakes region and the Hudson Bay Lowlands in Canada. The closest and most recent breeding colony to Illinois was in Manitowoc County, Wisconsin, about 100 miles north of the state border. • A rare bird in Illinois, usually seen singly, it may be separated from its cousin, the Bonaparte's Gull, by its dark underwings. • The number of migrating Little Gulls may be declining in Illinois. This is possibly linked to the decreasing breeding populations in Wisconsin.

nonbreeding

breeding

ID: gray back and wings; orange red feet and legs; black bill. *Breeding:* black head; white tail. *Non-breeding:* dark ear spot and smudgy "cap"; white tail. *Immature:* pinkish legs; brown and black on wings; dark terminal tail band. *In flight:* white wing tips and trailing edge of wing; dark underwings.
Size: *L* 10–11 in; *W* 24 in.
Status: rare and decreasing migrant from early April to late May; more common in fall, occurring from late October to early December.
Habitat: larger lakes, especially L. Michigan.
Nesting: does not nest in Illinois

Feeding: gleans insects from the ground or from the water's surface; may also take small mollusks, fish, crustaceans, marine worms and spiders.
Voice: repeated *kay-ee;* low *kek-kek-kek.*
Similar Species: *Bonaparte's Gull* (p. 161): much more common; dark tips and white leading edge to primaries; broken, white eye ring in breeding plumage; nonbreeding bird has white "cap." *Franklin's Gull* (p. 159): more common; larger; black tips on primaries; darker mantle; breeding bird has broken, white eye ring and brighter red bill; nonbreeding has black "hood." *Laughing Gull* (p. 158): somewhat more common; much larger; much larger bill with slightly drooped tip; black wing tips; darker mantle; blackish legs; breeding bird has broken, white eye ring.
Best Sites: L. Michigan, especially Evanston-Wilmette; large downstate reservoirs; Clinton L.; Carlyle L.; L. Springfield.

BONAPARTE'S GULL

Larus philadelphia

The almost ternlike, graceful and dainty Bonaparte's Gull is Illinois' most common small, hooded gull. It can be identified at almost any distance by a white wedge in the outer wing. • In Illinois, the Bonaparte's usually feeds in flocks that hover just above the water to catch small fish. These engaging birds will sometimes even tip up like dabbling ducks to catch small invertebrates in the shallows. When a flock of Bonaparte's Gulls spies a school of fish or an intruder, they utter soft, scratchy calls. • Unlike other gulls and terns, Bonaparte's Gulls nest in coniferous trees, often spruce. • In years when mild winter weather prevails, some of these gulls remain in Illinois; however, they do not frequent landfills like other gulls and rarely stand on ice. • Bonaparte's Gull was named after Napoleon's nephew, naturalist Charles-Lucien Bonaparte, who made significant contributions to the study of ornithology in the 1800s.

nonbreeding

breeding

ID: black bill; gray mantle; white tail. *Breeding:* black head; incomplete, white eye ring; orange legs. *Nonbreeding:* white head; dark ear patch. *Immature:* black edge to tail. *In flight:* white forewing wedge; black tips to primaries.
Size: *L* 11½–14 in; *W* 33 in.
Status: common to abundant migrant from early March to early June and from late July to mid-December; rare, nonbreeding summer resident; rare winter resident in southern Illinois.
Habitat: lakes, rivers and flooded fields.
Nesting: does not nest in Illinois.
Feeding: dabbles and tips up for aquatic invertebrates, small fish and tadpoles;

gleans the ground for terrestrial invertebrates; also captures insects in the air; most often seen diving for small fish.
Voice: scratchy, soft *ear ear* while feeding.
Similar Species: *Franklin's Gull* (p. 159): less common; slightly larger; lacks white upper forewing wedge; darker mantle; breeding bird has orange bill; nonbreeding has black "hood." *Little Gull* (p. 160): much rarer; smaller; daintier bill; dark underwing diagnostic; breeding bird's black "hood" extends over nape; nonbreeding has white "cap." *Sabine's Gull* (p. 170): much rarer; black forewing wedge; black legs; yellow-tipped bill; forked tail; "scaly" brown back; immature has brownish crown, "cheek" and nape. *Black-legged Kittiwake* (p. 171): much rarer; dark legs; all-white head; yellow bill; black "collar" on immature is diagnostic.
Best Sites: L. Michigan.

RING-BILLED GULL

Larus delawarensis

The Ring-billed is the most common gull in Illinois. • This species was first found breeding in Illinois at Lake Calumet in 1975, where observers counted 800 birds, including 71 young. The number of breeding gulls has since grown into the thousands. • In 2001, the Ring-billed Gull was documented nesting on a rooftop in Illinois for the first time in the city of Des Plaines. Nesting Ring-billed Gulls are considered a nuisance in some suburban areas, for example, Waukegan. Ring-billed Gulls are heavy nest predators, wreaking havoc for some breeding waterbirds. • Ring-billed Gulls feed on midges and other insect swarms over Lake Michigan as well as downstate reservoirs, mainly in fall.

nonbreeding

breeding

ID: 3-year gull; white head; yellow bill and legs; black ring around bill tip; pale gray mantle; yellow eyes; white underparts; black primaries tipped with 2 white spots. *Nonbreeding:* brown-streaked head. *Immature:* varying amounts of brown and gray on head, back and underparts; black to brown, subterminal tail band; pinkish legs; darkish or 2-tone bill; all-black wing tips.
Size: *L* 18–20 in; *W* 4 ft.
Status: common to abundant migrant and year-round resident; numbers increase southward as rivers and lakes freeze.
Habitat: *Breeding:* sparsely vegetated natural and mainly human-made islands; rooftops; Chicago breakwalls. *In migration*

and *winter:* lakes, rivers, landfills, agricultural lands; suburban and urban environments such as parks and golf courses.
Nesting: colonial; in a shallow scrape on the ground lined with plants, debris, grass and sticks; pair incubates 2–4 brown-blotched, gray to olive eggs for 23–28 days.
Feeding: gleans the ground for garbage, spiders, insects, rodents, earthworms, grubs and some waste grain; scavenges for carrion; surface-tips for aquatic invertebrates and fish.
Voice: high-pitched *kakakaka-akakaka;* also a low, laughing *yook-yook-yook.*
Similar Species: *Herring Gull* (p. 164) and *Thayer's Gull* (p. 165): larger; pinkish legs; lack bill ring; red spot near tip of lower mandible. *California Gull* (p. 163): much rarer; larger; slightly darker mantle, one red and one smaller black spot on bill; dark iris. *Mew Gull* (p. 356): rare vagrant; slightly smaller; dark eye; all-yellow bill; rounder head and darker mantle; extensive white mirrors on primaries in flight.
Best Sites: *Summer:* large lakes and rivers statewide; mainly L. Michigan; widespread in migration.

CALIFORNIA GULL

Larus californicus

Finding an adult California Gull in Illinois can be difficult; the species is rare and looks similar to several of its cousins, including the Herring Gull and Ring-billed Gull. However, some key identifying factors include a dark iris, a bill that has both red and black markings and greenish yellow legs. California Gulls typically mingle with Herrings and Ring-bills, allowing for close comparison. As optics and birders improve, the presence of California Gulls has become more apparent in Illinois. • California Gulls appear annually as individuals in our prairie state and there have been sightings along Lake Michigan and at landfills, among other places. • The Western Gull probably should have been called the California Gull, because it lives year-round in California. The so-called California Gull only winters there.

nonbreeding

nonbreeding

ID: 4-year gull; yellow bill with red and black spots; yellow green legs; dark eyes; medium gray mantle; black wing tips. *Breeding:* white head; white underparts. *Nonbreeding:* dark spotting on head. *Immature:* highly variable; mottled brown to dark brown overall; gray, pink and blackish legs; pale bill with black tip.
Size: *L* 18–20 in; *W* 4 ft.
Status: rare but annual visitor; more common in fall; occurs from early March to mid-April and from early October to early December; very rare summer and winter resident.

Habitat: large lakes and reservoirs; landfills.
Nesting: does not nest in Illinois.
Feeding: gleans the ground for terrestrial invertebrates, especially grasshoppers, earthworms and cutworms; scavenges at landfills; surface-tips for aquatic invertebrates.
Voice: high-pitched, nasal *kiarr-kiarr,* most often heard at breeding colonies.
Similar Species: *Ring-billed Gull* (p. 162): much more common; light eyes; black ring around bill; lighter mantle; immature is lighter overall. *Mew Gull* (p. 356): rarer; smaller; all-yellow bill; breeding has extensive white "mirrors" in primaries in flight.
Best Sites: L. Michigan; L. Springfield.

163

HERRING GULL

Larus argentatus

Like many of the larger *Larus* gull species, the Herring Gull has a small red spot on its lower mandible, which serves as a target for nestling young. When a downy chick pecks at the red spot, the parent recognizes the cue and regurgitates its meal. Many juveniles continue to beg for food into the winter. • The increasing number of this species has caused a subsequent decrease in tern and other waterbird populations because Herring Gulls feed on their eggs. Herring Gulls often nest in large colonies, though relatively few nest in Illinois. • Unlike Ring-billed Gulls, Herring numbers increase in Illinois in winter as lakes and rivers freeze. They can be found loafing where ice meets open water. • The Herring Gull's scientific name *argentatus* means "plated with silver."

breeding

nonbreeding

ID: large, 4-year gull; pink legs: yellow bill with red spot on lower mandible; light eyes; pale gray mantle; white head and underparts during breeding season, otherwise washed with brown; single, white spot on wing tip. *Immature:* variable; 2-tone bill; varying degrees of mottled brown overall.
Size: *L* 23–26 in; *W* 4 ft.
Status: common year-round resident along L. Michigan; regular, local breeder in northeastern Illinois; rare summer visitor elsewhere; abundant winter resident along L. Michigan; uncommon to common winter resident elsewhere.
Habitat: lakes, rivers and landfills; in winter, prefers places where ice and open water meet.
Nesting: singly or colonially, often with other gulls; on the ground in a shallow

scrape lined with plants and sticks; pair incubates 3 darkly blotched, olive to buff eggs for 31–32 days.
Feeding: surface-tips for aquatic invertebrates and fish; gleans the ground for insects and worms; scavenges at landfills; eats other birds' eggs and young.
Voice: loud, buglelike *kleew-kleew;* also an alarmed *kak-kak-kak.*
Similar Species: *Ring-billed Gull* (p. 162): smaller; black bill ring; yellow legs. *Glaucous Gull* (p. 168): rarer; larger; paler mantle; lacks black in wings. *Iceland Gull* (p. 166): rarer; slightly smaller; paler mantle; lacks black in wings. *Thayer's Gull* (p. 165): rarer; smaller bill; breeding has slightly darker mantle; more white on outer primaries. *Lesser Black-backed Gull* (p. 167): rarer; smaller; darker mantle; yellow legs.
Best Sites: L. Michigan shoreline year-round; Starved Rock lock and dam, Peoria L. and locks and dams along the Mississippi R. in winter.

THAYER'S GULL

Larus thayeri

The Thayer's Gull is part of a group of recently evolved gulls that have similar traits and, therefore, may potentially interbreed. It was actually once considered a subspecies of the very similar-looking Herring Gull, and some ornithologists dispute the decision to grant this bird full species status. Alternatively, other ornithologists believe that the Thayer's Gull is merely a subspecies of the Iceland Gull. • Many Illinois records are of adult or first-winter birds since they are the easiest to identify. This species breeds on rocky shores and islands along the arctic coast and visits Illinois in winter. • John Eliot Thayer was a Boston philanthropist in the late 19th and early 20th centuries who assembled a large collection of birds and a comprehensive ornithological library. He also provided financial backing for a number of natural history expeditions.

nonbreeding

nonbreeding

ID: 4-year gull; relatively slim bill; brown-flecked head, neck and upper breast; white-spotted, black wing tips; dark eyes; yellow bill with red spot at tip of lower mandible; dark pink legs. *Immature:* variable, mottled white-and-brown plumage; generally pale primaries.
Size: *L* 22–25 in; *W* 4½ ft.
Status: regular migrant and winter resident in small numbers from mid-October to late May.
Habitat: open water on large lakes and rivers; landfills.
Nesting: does not nest in Illinois.
Feeding: eats small fish, crustaceans, mollusks, carrion and human food waste; gleans from the water's surface while in flight.

Voice: various raucous and laughing calls, much like the Herring Gull's *kak-kak-kak*.
Similar Species: *Herring Gull* (p. 164): much more common; black wing tips; light eyes; usually darker mantle. *Iceland Gull* (p. 166): smaller; light eyes; more white than dark gray on wing tips. *Glaucous Gull* (p. 168): larger; longer, heavier bill; light eyes; pure white wing tips; lighter pink legs. *Ring-billed Gull* (p. 162): much more common; smaller; dark ring on yellow bill; yellow legs.
Best Sites: L. Michigan lakefront, especially Winthrop Harbor, Wilmette and Evanston; O'Brien lock and dam; Starved Rock lock and dam; Peoria L.; L. Springfield; locks and dams along the Mississippi R., especially from Quad Cities to Alton; Illinois R.; Clinton L.; Carlyle L.

ICELAND GULL
Larus glaucoides

The pale Iceland Gull can be seen in small numbers each winter in Illinois, usually among large flocks of more common wintering gulls. They gather where ice meets open water and at landfills where they scavenge. • The Iceland Gull comes in two slightly different forms; the *kumlieni* subspecies is the most common in Illinois. • On Baffin Island in Canada, this subspecies occasionally interbreeds with the Thayer's Gull. An ongoing debate continues on the status of these gulls and some scientists believe that the Thayer's Gull is really just a subspecies of the Iceland Gull. • This bird nests on cliffs in the Canadian Arctic Archipelago and close to Greenland. It has a circumpolar distribution and also breeds in Norway and Sweden.

nonbreeding

ID: 4-year gull; relatively short, yellow bill with red spot on lower mandible; brown-streaked head and breast; rounded head; yellow to brownish eyes with red orbital ring; white wing tips sometimes with small amounts of dark gray; pink legs; pale gray mantle. *Immature:* dark eyes; black bill; white or paler gray overall; light pink legs.
Size: *L* 22 in; *W* 4½ ft.
Status: rare to locally uncommon, regular winter resident from late November to early May, occasionally, birds do not arrive until ice appears in late December or January; most depart by March; maximum count at any one location is 2–4 birds.
Habitat: where open water meets ice on lakes and rivers; landfills.
Nesting: does not nest in Illinois.
Feeding: eats mostly fish; may also take crustaceans, mollusks, carrion, seeds and human food waste; scavenges at landfills and in harbors.
Voice: high, screechy calls, much less bugling than other large gulls.
Similar Species: *Herring Gull* (p. 164): much more common; larger bill; nonbreeding has darker, more extensive gray on primaries; much more streaking on head and neck. *Thayer's Gull* (p. 165): nonbreeding bird has darker gray mantle, more black on upperwing tips, some black on tips of underwing and usually has dark eyes; immature is darker overall with darker primaries and tail. *Glaucous Gull* (p. 168): larger; lighter mantle; longer, heavier bill; pure white wing tips; immature has distinctive bicolored bill.
Best Sites: L. Michigan, especially Winthrop Harbor, Wilmette and Evanston; O'Brien lock and dam; Starved Rock lock and dam; Pekin lock and dam; L. Springfield; locks and dams along the Mississippi R., especially from Quad Cities to Alton; Illinois R. and large downstate reservoirs.

LESSER BLACK-BACKED GULL

Larus fuscus

Equipped with long wings for long-distance flights, increasing numbers of Lesser Black-backed Gulls are being observed annually in Illinois. • The Lesser Black-backed Gull is a Eurasian species and a relative newcomer to North America. It was first recorded in September 1934 at Beach Haven, New Jersey; however, this species wasn't documented in Illinois until 1980, with reports increasing dramatically beginning the winter of 1988–89. • The *graellsii* subspecies, which breeds in Iceland and Europe, occurs in Illinois. • This species will eat the young of its own kind as well as other seabird young, including cormorants and alcids.

nonbreeding

breeding

ID: 4 year gull; dark gray mantle; brown-streaked head and neck; one white "mirror" on black wing tip; yellow bill with red spot on lower mandible; yellow eyes; yellow legs. *Immature:* dark or light eyes; bill has various colors; plumage variable; dark brownish in 1st year, becoming increasingly lighter below and grayer above; pinkish legs.
Size: *L* 20½ in; *W* 4½ ft.
Status: increasing; uncommon, local migrant and winter resident; arrives in early April from south of Illinois and departs by early May; occurs in small numbers in September and October, peaking in early to mid-November with most departing by late March; few summer records.
Habitat: landfills, large lakes and rivers, especially at locks and dams.

Nesting: does not nest in Illinois.
Feeding: eats mostly fish, crustaceans, mollusks, insects, small rodents, carrion, seeds and human food waste; scavenges at landfills and harbors; opportunistically preys on other birds, especially young.
Voice: screechy call is like a lower-pitched version of the Herring Gull's.
Similar Species: *Herring Gull* (p. 164): much more common; lighter mantle; pink legs. *Great Black-backed Gull* (p. 169): rarer, especially downstate; much larger; more massive head and bill; black mantle; pale pinkish legs; 2 white "mirrors" in outer 2 primaries.
Best Sites: L. Michigan shoreline, especially Winthrop and Montrose Harbors; L. Calumet; Carlyle L.; Starved Rock lock and dam; L. Springfield; locks and dams along the Mississippi R.

167

GLAUCOUS GULL
Larus hyperboreus

The Glaucous Gull's mostly white underparts and very pale gray mantle camouflage it against the cloud-filled skies of winter as it flies over Lake Michigan and the ice- and snow-covered landscape. Its pale plumage and very large size also help birders to distinguish it from other, more numerous, wintering gull species. • The Glaucous Gull traditionally fished for its meals or stole food from smaller gulls or even fast-flying Gyrfalcons. More recently, however, wintering Glaucous Gulls have traded the rigors of hunting for the job of defending plots of garbage at various landfills. • Fortunately, immatures are light enough that they can be easily distinguished from the darker immatures of other gull species. Immatures also have distinct, pale pink bills with dark tips. • In summer, while other gulls are strolling along local beaches or hanging out in fast-food restaurant parking lots, the Glaucous Gull is far away breeding in the arctic wilderness. • The subspecies seen in Illinois is *L. h. hyperboreus*.

1st winter

nonbreeding

ID: heavy-bodied; massive head and bill; pure white tips to primaries; pink legs. *Nonbreeding:* yellow bill with red spot on lower mandible; flattened crown; very pale gray mantle; brown-streaked head, neck and breast; pure white wing tips; yellow eyes usually with yellow orbital ring. *Immature:* dark eyes; pale, black-tipped bill; plumage varies from almost pure white to brown flecking throughout.
Size: *L* 27 in; *W* 5 ft.
Status: uncommon, regular winter resident along L. Michigan; rare but regular downstate on large lakes and rivers; very rare elsewhere; occurs from September to mid-November; some stay until late May, especially on L. Michigan.

Habitat: large lakes and rivers, especially at locks and dams; landfills; appears on downstate lakes and rivers as ice forms.
Nesting: does not nest in Illinois.
Feeding: mainly preys on live seabirds, ducks, starfish and sea urchins; in Illinois, mainly eats carrion or pirates fish from other gulls; scavenges at landfills.
Voice: high, screechy calls similar to Herring Gull's *kak-kak-kak*.
Similar Species: *Thayer's Gull* (p. 165) and *Iceland Gull* (p. 166): less heavy bodied; smaller heads and bills; darker mantles. *Herring Gull* (p. 164): much more common; smaller; less heavy bodied; less massive head and bill; much darker mantle.
Best Sites: L. Michigan shoreline, especially Winthrop Harbor; O'Brien lock and dam; Starved Rock lock and dam; L. Springfield; locks and dams along the Illinois R. and Mississippi R.

GREAT BLACK-BACKED GULL

Larus marinus

The Great Black-backed Gull's commanding size enables it to dominate other gulls, giving it first pick of prey, whether it is fresh fish or a meal from a landfill. No other gull species except the Glaucous Gull is as domineering. • In recent years, the Great Black-backed Gull has begun nesting along the Great Lakes in a few locations, although not in Illinois. • This gull was documented in Illinois as far back as the late 1800s and has since been a rare migrant, though its numbers did increase in the 1980s. In the 21st century, however, numbers seem to be decreasing here for unknown reasons, just as numbers of its smaller cousin, the Lesser Black-backed Gull, seem to be increasing. • The Great Black-backed Gull is a "four-year gull," meaning that it goes through various plumage stages until its fourth winter, when it develops its full adult plumage.

breeding

ID: largest North American gull; 4-year gull; massive bill; pinkish legs; *Nonbreeding:* all white except for gray underwings and black mantle; light-colored eyes; large, yellow bill with red spot at tip of lower mandible; may have light streaking on nape. *Immature:* variable, mottled gray brown, white and black with much white throughout; marbled underwings; black to 2-tone bill. *In flight:* 2 large "mirrors" at tip of primaries.
Size: *L* 30 in; *W* 5½ ft.
Status: very rare to rare migrant and winter resident; arrives in late September, with most arriving in November or later; departs by late April through late May; few summer records.

Habitat: landfills and open water on large lakes and rivers, especially at locks and dams.
Nesting: does not nest in Illinois.
Feeding: opportunistic feeder; eats fish, eggs, birds, small mammals, berries, carrion, mollusks, crustaceans and insects; scavenges at landfills.
Voice: a harsh *kyow*.
Similar Species: *Lesser Black-backed Gull* (p. 167): somewhat more common; much smaller; lighter mantle; yellow legs; 1 white "mirror" on outer primaries.
Best Sites: most common along L. Michigan shoreline, especially Winthrop Harbor and Waukegan; O'Brien lock and dam; locks and dams from Quad Cities to Alton along Illinois R. and Mississippi R.; L. Springfield.

SABINE'S GULL

Xema sabini

This attractive, ternlike gull is a rarity in Illinois, best observed in mid-September when it heads south from the Arctic. It is usually seen singly or in very small numbers and in its juvenile plumage. • Like the terns of the genus *Sterna*, the Sabine's Gull features a buoyant, dipping flight pattern and is the only gull in the United States with a forked tail. These characteristics have earned this bird the distinctive genus name *Xema* and taxonomic placement between the *Larus* gulls and the terns. • This gull often feeds while in flight, gently dipping down to the water's surface to snatch prey without landing. Illinois birders take annual "pelagic" boat trips in September on downstate Carlyle Lake, Illinois' largest inland reservoir, hoping to spot this rarity. Only a narrow corridor of time exists in which to see this bird in Illinois. Occasionally, one or two of these gulls are seen on Lake Michigan.

1st winter

ID: 2-year gull; gray "hood" with black lower border; black bill with yellow tip; red eye ring. *Juvenile:* nearly all birds seen in Illinois are immatures; soft gray brown crown and nape; brownish back edged in black and white; all-dark bill; dark tail band; pinkish legs. *In flight:* distinctive 3-tone wing: gray at base, then white, then black at tip; shallowly forked tail; immature has more muted wing color, with brown replacing gray.
Size: *L* 13–14 in; *W* 35 in.
Status: very rare to rare fall migrant; occurs as early as mid-August and as late as early November; most birds seen in September; only 2 spring records exist;

small flocks of 3–7 birds have been observed; most birds found singly.
Habitat: mainly large lakes and reservoirs.
Nesting: does not nest in Illinois.
Feeding: runs on mudflats like a plover to find food; gleans the water's surface while swimming or flying; eats mostly insects, fish and crustaceans.
Voice: ternlike *kee-kee*; not frequently heard in migration.
Similar Species: *Bonaparte's Gull* (p. 161): much more common; lacks black wedge to outer wing edge; breeding has lighter mantle, all-black head and bill, white eye ring and red legs; rounded tail in flight. *Franklin's Gull* (p. 159): more common; lacks 3-tone wing pattern; breeding has black head with broad, broken, white eye ring, red bill with small black ring near tip and reddish legs; rounded tail in flight.
Best Sites: Carlyle L.; Chicago lakefront; Springfield L.

BLACK-LEGGED KITTIWAKE

Rissa tridactyla

The Black-legged Kittiwake is more closely associated with the marine environment than any other North American gull. Most of the small population of Black-legged Kittiwakes that move through Illinois are well offshore over the open waters of Lake Michigan. Lucky birders may occasionally spot them flying close to shore. • Even during the most violent storms, Black-legged Kittiwakes remain in open water, floating among massive freshwater swells that remind them of their saltwater homes. Unlike other gulls, but similar to more pelagic species such as petrels and shearwaters, kittiwakes will only drink salt water. As a result, these birds have evolved ways in which to excrete excess salt from their bodies. • The Black-legged Kittiwake feeds almost solely on fish, rather than foraging at landfills like the majority of gulls in Illinois. It spends nearly all its life on water, returning in March to nesting colonies situated on narrow ledges of vertical sea cliffs. • The creation of large inland reservoirs has created more habitat for pelagic species like the kittiwake.

breeding

1st winter

nonbreeding

ID: 2-year gull; slightly forked tail; black legs. *Breeding:* gray mantle; all-white head and underparts; yellow bill. *Juvenile:* gray mantle; black "collar"; mostly white head with dark ear patch; darkish bill. *In flight:* black triangular wing tips; juvenile has bold black "M" on wings.
Size: *L* 16–18 in; *W* 35 in.
Status: very rare spring migrant; rare but regular late fall migrant, arriving in mid-November; most gone by mid-December; very rare winter resident.
Habitat: large lakes and reservoirs.

Nesting: does not nest in Illinois.
Feeding: prefers small fish; also takes crustaceans, insects and mollusks; dips to the water's surface to snatch prey; may plunge under the water's surface or glean from the surface while swimming.
Voice: calls are *kittewake* and *kekekek.*
Similar Species: *Bonaparte's Gull* (p. 161): much more common; smaller; rounded tail; breeding has black "hood," partial white eye ring, black bill and red legs; nonbreeding and immature have white head with black ear patch and pink legs; immature has narrow, rather than wide, dark "M" on upperwings in flight.
Best Sites: L. Michigan shoreline, especially at Gillson Park in Wilmette; Clinton L.; Carlyle L.; L. Springfield.

CASPIAN TERN

Sterna caspia

I n size and habits, the Caspian Tern bridges the gulf between smaller terns and gulls. It is the largest tern in North America with wingbeats that are slower and more gull-like than most other terns; the Caspian can even soar like a gull. • This bird's distinctive, heavy, coral red bill and forked tail help reveal its identity. The juveniles can be easily separated from the adults by their distinctive calls—those of the young are much higher in pitch. • These terns are often seen with gulls on shoreline sandbars and mudflats in migration. The Caspian Tern is a common migrant in Illinois, wintering on the Gulf of Mexico. • These waterbirds feed their young during migration, therefore, Illinoisans who observe this behavior should not assume that the bird nested in the state. Hopefully this species, which lingers into June, may one day begin nesting in our prairie state. • This species was first collected from the Caspian Sea, hence its name. The Caspian Tern only nests on islands and can be found nesting in Eurasia, Africa and even Australia.

breeding

ID: *Breeding:* black "cap"; heavy, coral red bill with faint black tip; light gray mantle; black legs; shallowly forked tail; white underparts; long, frosty, pointed wings; dark gray on underside of outer primaries. *Nonbreeding:* black "cap" streaked with white; black legs. *In flight:* dark primary underwing patch.
Size: *L* 19–23 in; *W* 4–4½ ft.
Status: common migrant from early April to late May and from late August to early October; some linger into early November.

Habitat: wetlands and shorelines of large lakes and rivers.
Nesting: does not nest in Illinois.
Feeding: hovers over water and plunges headfirst after small fish; may take tadpoles and aquatic invertebrates; also gleans at the water's surface; occasionally pirates food; sometimes eats the eggs or young of other terns and gulls.
Voice: low, harsh *ca-arr;* loud *kraa-uh;* juvenile answers with a high-pitched whistle.
Similar Species: *Common Tern* (p. 173) and *Forster's Tern* (p. 174): much smaller; daintier bills; much more deeply forked tails; breeding have orange legs; lack dark primary underwing patch in flight.
Best Sites: L. Michigan shoreline; large downstate lakes and reservoirs.

COMMON TERN

Sterna hirundo

The Common Tern has never been a common breeder in Illinois, and its nesting population began declining as early as the 19th century. Egg-collecting, habitat destruction, disturbance and the slaughter of these birds for the millinery trade contributed to the decline. Today, this species has little of its sand and gravel bar habitat left in Illinois upon which to breed. Intensive management at the Common Tern's last-known nesting site on the Great Lakes Naval Training Center may keep this bird from becoming extirpated in Illinois. • Tern colonies are noisy and chaotic. Should an intruder approach a nest, the parent will dive repeatedly. • Downstate, the similar-looking Forster's Tern far outnumbers and is more frequently seen than the Common Tern.

breeding

ID: *Breeding:* black "cap"; thin, orange red, black-tipped bill; red legs; gray body and back; white face; white, forked tail with dark outer edges, gray wings with narrow, dark edge to outer primaries in flight.
Nonbreeding: black nape; white forehead; black bill; black legs.
Immature: similar to nonbreeding; much more black throughout wing. *In flight:* dark carpal bar; more extensive dark wedge on primaries.
Size: *L* 13–16 in; *W* 30 in.
Status: state-endangered; abundant spring migrant and common fall migrant along L. Michigan; largest numbers from mid- to late May and from early July to late October, with regular stragglers in November; very rare, local breeder; only breeding location is at Great Lakes Naval Training Center.
Habitat: *Breeding:* islands, breakwaters and beaches. *In migration:* lakes and rivers.
Nesting: colonial; on an island with non-vegetated, open areas; in a small scrape lined sparsely with pebbles, vegetation or

shells; pair incubates 1–3 variably marked eggs for up to 27 days.
Feeding: hovers over the water and plunges headfirst after small fish and aquatic invertebrates.
Voice: high-pitched, drawn-out *keee-are* is most commonly heard at colonies, but also in foraging flights.
Similar Species: *Forster's Tern* (p. 174): breeding has orange bill with black tip, all-white underparts contrasting with dark mantle, longer, gray tail with white outer web, silvery white primaries and tail often projects beyond wing tips; nonbreeding has black blotch extending from dark eye, white crown and nape and orange legs. *Caspian Tern* (p. 172): much larger overall; much heavier, red orange bill; very dark primary underwing patch.
Best Sites: *Summer:* Great Lakes Naval Training Center. *In migration:* L. Michigan shoreline, especially Winthrop Harbor; Waukegan Beach; L. Springfield.

173

FORSTER'S TERN

Sterna forsteri

The Forster's Tern closely resembles the Common Tern, but the careful observer can use several clues to separate the two, including wing color, especially in breeding birds, and head pattern in nonbreeding and immature birds. Unlike the Common Tern, the Forster's winters in the United States and most of its migration is inland. • This state-endangered bird breeds on undisturbed islands and in wetlands near lakes. The Forster's Tern has always been a rare breeder in the state and in the past decade, was almost extirpated as a breeder with just a few pairs nesting on various sites on and around the expansive Chain O'Lakes State Park. Causes for the decline include habitat loss and boat traffic that eroded the islands upon which the terns nested. Various agencies worked to create an artificial dredge island to help the terns, and in the summer of 2003, dozens of pairs of Forster's Terns successfully fledged young at Grass Lake on the Chain.

nonbreeding

breeding

Nesting: colonial; in cattail marshes, atop floating vegetation; pair incubates 3 brown-marked, buff to olive eggs for 23–25 days.
Feeding: hovers above the water and plunges headfirst after small fish and aquatic invertebrates; catches flying insects; snatches prey from the water's surface.
Voice: flight call is a short nasal *keer keer;* also a grating *tzaap.*
Similar Species: *Common Tern* (p. 173): breeding has red orange, black-tipped bill, gray underparts and white forked tail with dark outer edges; nonbreeding has black crown and nape, black legs and white forked tail with dark outer edges. *Caspian Tern* (p. 172): much larger overall; much heavier, red orange bill; very dark primary underwing patch.
Best Sites: *Summer:* Chain O'Lakes SP. *In migration:* L. Michigan shoreline, especially Great Lakes Naval Training Center and Evanston; downstate lakes and Illinois R. and Mississippi R.

ID: *Breeding:* black "cap" and nape; thin, orange, black-tipped bill; orange legs; light gray mantle; pure white underparts; white rump; gray tail with white outer edges. *Nonbreeding:* lacks black "cap"; black band through eyes. *In flight:* forked, gray tail; long, pointed wings.
Size: *L* 14–16 in; *W* 31 in.
Status: state-endangered; common migrant from early April to mid-May and from early July to mid-October; very rare, local breeder; most common tern away from L. Michigan.
Habitat: *Breeding:* marshes bordering lakes. *In migration:* lakes, rivers, ponds, sewage lagoons and marshes.

174

LEAST TERN

Sterna antillarum

This species was listed as federally endangered in 1985. Development, human disturbance and flooding have caused breeding habitat to decline dramatically throughout this bird's range. Additionally, predation, as well as severe weather, have caused the deaths of adults and young and nest failure. • Few breeding sites for this species are left in Illinois. Intensive management may be required if the Least Tern is to remain a breeder in our state. • When water levels are high along the Mississippi River, these birds search for and will occasionally use alternate nesting sites, including sandy agricultural fields in the Mississippi River floodplain and the edges of dry-ash slurry ponds near power plants. • The subspecies in Illinois is *S. a. athalassos.*

breeding

ID: relatively long, very narrow wings; short, forked tail. *Breeding:* black "cap" and nape; white forehead with black line through eye; unique yellow bill; yellow legs; light gray upperparts; white underparts; narrow black edge on upperwing. *Nonbreeding:* white on forehead; black bill. *Immature:* dark carpal bar at shoulder; more extensive black in primaries while perched and in flight. *In flight:* dashing, rapid wing strokes.

Size: *L* 9 in; *W* 20 in.

Status: federal and state-endangered; very rare migrant; local summer resident and breeder; occurs in May and from mid-August to mid-September; rare local summer resident in southern Illinois.

Habitat: *Breeding:* river sandbars and adjacent bottomlands. *In migration:* mudflats along large rivers, lakes and reservoirs.

Nesting: colonial; on undisturbed flat ground near water; nest is a shallow, scraped-out depression often lined with pebbles, grasses or debris; pair incubates 1–3 darkly marked, buff to pale olive eggs for 20–22 days.

Feeding: hovers above water before plunging to or below the surface; eats mostly fish and invertebrates; will take insects on the wing.

Voice: call is a loud, high-pitched *chirreek* and *kip kip kip.*

Similar Species: *Common Tern* (p. 173) and *Forster's Tern* (p. 174): much more common; larger; breeding birds lack white forehead and have longer, more deeply forked tails and red bills. *Black Tern* (p. 176): nonbreeding has much darker gray back and wings; shallower forked tail; black spot behind eye; reddish legs.

Best Sites: *Breeding:* sandbars, wetlands and mudflats in and adjacent to Ohio R., Wabash R. and Mississippi R., especially Horseshoe Lake CA; Union, Jackson and Massac counties; flooded fields south of Beall Woods, Wabash Co. *In migration:* Horseshoe L.; Madison Co.; Carlyle L.; Rend L.

BLACK TERN

Chlidonias niger

During spring migration, Black Terns are routinely found, often in groups, flying about just before and after a storm; not long after the storm subsides, the terns are gone. • Wheeling about in foraging flights, Black Terns pick small minnows from the water's surface or catch flying insects in midair. • The state-endangered Black Tern has very specific habitat requirements for nesting. Slight changes in the water level or in vegetation, often because of human disturbance, may drive them away from historic nesting places. This selectiveness has contributed to a significant decline in populations over recent decades and only a few breeding sites remain in Illinois for this species. Commitment to restoring and protecting valuable wetland habitats may help this bird to continue breeding in Illinois. • The Black Tern winters in Central and South America.

breeding

nonbreeding

ID: *Breeding:* black head and underparts; white from lower belly to undertail; dark gray back, tail and wings; white undertail coverts; black bill; reddish black legs. *Nonbreeding:* white underparts and forehead; dark bar on side of breast in flight. *Immature:* similar to nonbreeding; more orangy legs; back feathers edged in black and brown. *In flight:* long, pointed wings; shallowly forked tail.
Size: *L* 9–10 in; *W* 24 in.
Status: state-endangered; common migrant; occurs from May to early June and from early July to September, with some lingering into early October; very rare, local summer resident in northeastern Illinois.
Habitat: shallow, freshwater cattail marshes, wetlands, lake edges, rivers and sewage ponds with emergent vegetation.

Nesting: loosely colonial; flimsy nest of dead plant material is built on floating vegetation, a muddy mound or a muskrat house; pair incubates 3 darkly blotched, olive to pale buff eggs for 21–22 days.
Feeding: takes insects from the air and from the water's surface; also makes shallow dives to catch small fish; follows farmers plowing fields near marshes to snatch insects.
Voice: greeting call is a shrill, metallic *kik-kik-kik-kik-kik;* typical alarm call is *kreea.*
Similar Species: *Other terns* (pp. 172–75): plumages are light, rather than dark.
Best Sites: *Breeding:* Broberg Marsh in Wauconda. *In migration:* L. Michigan shoreline; Hennepin L.; Arcola Marsh, especially in spring; L. Springfield; L. Chautauqua; Carlyle L.

ROCK PIGEON

Columba livia

Rock Pigeons are believed to have been domesticated from Eurasian birds in about 4500 BC as a source of meat. Since their domestication, these birds have been used as message couriers, as scientific subjects and even as pets. They are one of the most intensively studied birds, and much of our understanding of bird migration, avian flight mechanics, endocrinology, orientation and navigation and sensory perception derives from experiments involving Rock Pigeons. • These birds were introduced to North America in the 17th century by colonists who brought domestic pigeons with them from Europe. Now feral, though never far from human habitation, Rock Pigeons have settled wherever cities, towns and farms are found. • All members of the pigeon family, including doves, feed their young "milk." Because birds lack mammary glands, it is not true milk, but a nutritious liquid produced by glands in the bird's crop. The chicks insert their bills down the adult's throat to eat the thick, protein-rich fluid. • No other "wild" bird varies as much in coloration—a result of semi-domestication and extensive inbreeding. This bird was formerly known as the "Rock Dove."

ID: colors are iridescent, blue gray, red, white or tan; usually has white rump and orange feet; dark-tipped tail. *In flight:* holds its wings in a deep "V" while gliding. **Size:** *L* 12–13 in; *W* 28 in. **Status:** abundant statewide.
Habitat: urban and suburban areas, railroad yards, agricultural areas.
Nesting: on ledges of barns, cliffs, bridges, buildings and towers; also in abandoned buildings; flimsy nest of sticks, grass and assorted vegetation; pair incubates 2 white eggs for 16–19 days; pair feeds the young "pigeon milk"; may raise broods year-round.
Feeding: gleans the ground for waste grain, seeds and fruits; occasionally eats insects.
Voice: soft, cooing *coorrr-coorrr-coorrr.*
Similar Species: *Mourning Dove* (p. 179): smaller; slimmer; brown plumage; gray underwings; long, pointed tail and wings; distinctive black dots on wings; outer tail feathers edged in black and white. *Eurasian Collared-Dove* (p. 178): slimmer; pale gray tan overall; black nape band; broadly white-tipped tail.
Best Sites: widespread.

177

EURASIAN COLLARED-DOVE
Streptopelia decaocto

A century ago, this dove was found primarily in India, with a range that extended into Europe and Turkey. That range expanded farther in the early 1900s and by 1950, it had reached the British Isles. Today, there are Eurasian Collared-Doves living above the Arctic Circle in Scandinavia. Once introduced to the Bahamas, the species colonized much of Florida and is now rapidly spreading northward and westward. This dove was documented in southern Illinois in 1997 and it has recently been accepted on the official state checklist. It has become well established in some Illinois communities in the lower two-thirds of the state where it is successfully breeding. Few observations have come from northern Illinois; a pair recently attempted to breed at Chicago's Montrose Harbor. Only time will tell us whether this lovely bird has a negative impact on North America's increasingly threatened native avifauna. • The similar Ringed Turtle-Dove, a caged bird hybrid introduced into the wild, can easily be confused with this species.

ID: gray plumage tinged with brown on upper-wings; black "collar" on nape; black eye with red eye ring; wide, white edges on tail.
Size: *L* 10–12 in; *W* 22 in.
Status: rare to uncommon local year-round resident.
Habitat: small, rural communities, often near grain elevators.
Nesting: flimsy stick platform is built in a tree, shrub or on a building; pair alternates incubation of 1–4 white or pale buff eggs over 13–14 days.

Feeding: eats mostly seeds with some berries and fruits; mainly forages on ground; young are fed "pigeon milk."
Voice: plain, loud cooing call: *coo-coo-coo*.
Similar Species: *Mourning Dove* (p. 179): browner overall; slimmer, pointed tail; distinctive black spots on wings; lacks black "collar." *Rock Pigeon* (p. 177): stockier; most birds darker overall, except for white variants; lacks black "collar" and white tips to outer tail feathers.
Best Sites: Newton, Carlyle, Nokomis and Metropolis; often seen feeding at grain elevators.

MOURNING DOVE

Zenaida macroura

The soft cooing of the Mourning Dove that filters through broken woodlands, farmlands, suburban parks and gardens can be confused with the sound of a hooting owl, but the pitch is higher and more sorrowful. • The Mourning Dove is one of the most abundant and widespread native birds in North America and one of the most popular game birds. Seventy million Mourning Doves are shot annually. • This number is greater than the annual harvest of all other migratory game birds combined. • This species has benefited from human-induced changes to the landscape and its numbers and distribution have increased since the continent was settled. Dramatic increases in range and numbers occurred in New England and southern Canada between the 1950s and 1980s. • The Mourning Dove is a swift, direct flyer, traveling at speeds up to 56 miles per hour. Its wings often whistle as they cut through the air, clapping above and below the bird's body. • Although somewhat sedentary, Illinois birds do migrate south and southwest as far as Florida and Texas, mainly from mid-August through October. • This bird's common name reflects its sad, cooing song.

ID: brown plumage; gray underwings; small head; long, white-trimmed, tapering tail; sleek body; dark patch below ear; iridescent area on nape; dull red legs; dark bill; pale rosy underparts; black spots on upperwing. **Size:** *L* 11–13 in; *W* 18 in.

Status: abundant, year-round resident statewide.
Habitat: open or riparian woodlands, woodlots, forest edges, agricultural and suburban areas; open parks and shrublands.

Nesting: in the fork of a shrub or tree, rarely on the ground; female builds a flimsy, shallow platform nest from twigs supplied by the male; pair incubates 2 white eggs for 14 days; young are fed "pigeon milk"; nests have been found as early as January and as late as October in Illinois.
Feeding: gleans the ground and vegetation for seeds; visits feeders.
Voice: mournful, soft, slow *oh-woe-woe-woe-woe-woe.*
Similar Species: *Rock Pigeon* (p. 177): stockier; white rump; shorter tail. *Eurasian Collared-Dove* (p. 178): much rarer; larger and bulkier; lighter overall; black "collar"; square tail with wide, white edges; lacks black spots on wings.
Best Sites: widespread.

MONK PARAKEET
Myiopsitta monachus

Originally from South America, the Monk Parakeet has been introduced throughout the world, mostly by irresponsible pet owners. The boom of the exotic pet industry in the late 1960s led to the introduction of this bird to North American urban parks. Illinois' first sighting was in 1968. Unlike most parrots, this bird originated in the more temperate regions of South America and therefore can survive in the North American climate. It is considered an agricultural pest in its native regions, and American attempts to eradicate the bird in the 1970s failed. In 1999, the Monk Parakeet was added to the Illinois state checklist. • It is the only species in the parrot family to nest communally. Other parrots use nest cavities, while Monk Parakeets build a condominium of sticks and grass for the entire flock atop a utility pole.

ID: green upperparts; gray white throat, chest and forehead; yellow green belly; blue outer-wings; thick, pink, hooked bill; long, green tail. *Juvenile:* green patch on forehead.
Size: *L* 11½ in; *W* 19 in.
Status: introduced; local year-round resident in some Chicago neighborhoods; breeding pairs recently established at Carlyle L.
Habitat: urban neighborhoods and parks; visits feeders in winter.
Nesting: on a pole or high up in a tree; nests also found in Illinois atop power transformers; a group of parakeets builds a large, multi-compartment nest of twigs, sticks and grass where each pair will have an "apartment"; male and female incubate 6–8 white eggs for 25–30 days; may have 2 broods each year; juveniles may stay to help with new broods.
Feeding: uses feeders; also eats large insects, cracked corn, pine seeds, suet, acorns, apples, cherries, grapes, crabapples, grass seeds and fruits from ornamental trees and shrubs.
Voice: very vocal; emits screeches and squawks and chatters almost constantly near the nest.
Similar Species: none in Illinois.
Best Sites: Hyde Park and Jackson Park in Chicago; Addison Rd. and Armitage Rd. in town of Addison; town of Burnham near Calumet City; grain elevator in town of Carlyle.

BLACK-BILLED CUCKOO
Coccyzus erythropthalmus

Shrubby field edges, hedgerows, tangled riparian thickets and abandoned, over-grown fields provide the elusive Black-billed Cuckoo with its preferred nesting grounds. Although this bird is not rare in Illinois, it can be difficult to locate, especially if one is unfamiliar with its soft *cu-cu-cu* call. This species seems to be declining in numbers, both as a migrant and breeder in the state. Arriving in May, this cuckoo hops slowly and deliberately, skulking through low, dense deciduous vegetation searching for caterpillars. • The Black-billed Cuckoo and its cousin, the Yellow-billed Cuckoo, are two of the few birds that thrive on hairy caterpillars, particularly tent caterpillars. Cuckoo populations may even increase when a caterpillar infestation occurs. In spring, in Illinois, the Black-billed Cuckoo typically arrives at least a few days before the Yellow-billed. Both cuckoo species commonly call at night, but the Yellow-billed is much more vocal and has a wider song repertoire. • The Black-billed Cuckoo, a neotropical migrant, winters as far south as northwestern South America.

ID: brown upperparts; white underparts; long, gray undertail feathers with white tips edged in black; downcurved, dark bill; reddish eye ring. *Juvenile:* buff eye ring; may have buff tinge on throat and undertail coverts; gray tail with small, pale tips on underside.
Size: *L* 11–13 in; *W* 17½ in.
Status: uncommon migrant; occurs from early May to mid-June and from mid-August through late September, with some lingering into October; rare to uncommon breeder from central Illinois northward.
Habitat: dense second-growth woodlands, shrubby areas and thickets; often in tangled riparian areas and abandoned farmlands with low deciduous vegetation and adjacent open areas.
Nesting: in a shrub or small deciduous tree; flimsy nest of twigs is lined with grass and other vegetation; occasionally lays eggs in other birds' nests, including Yellow-billed Cuckoo; pair incubates 2–5 blue green, occasionally mottled, eggs for 10–14 days.
Feeding: gleans hairy caterpillars from leaves, branches and trunks; also eats other insects and berries.
Voice: fast, repeated *cu-cu-cu* or *cu-cu-cu-cu-cu;* also a series of *ca, cow* and *coo* notes.
Similar Species: *Yellow-billed Cuckoo* (p. 182): yellow on bill; bright rufous tinge to primaries; larger, more prominent, white undertail spots; lacks red eye ring.
Best Sites: none.

YELLOW-BILLED CUCKOO
Coccyzus americanus

The Yellow-billed Cuckoo is much more widely distributed in Illinois and throughout its range compared to the Black-billed. Most of the time, the Yellow-billed Cuckoo negotiates its tangled home in forested understories and edges in silence. Occasionally, the male cuckoo issues a barrage of loud, rhythmic calls used for courtship and to warn its mate that danger may be nearby. • This species is often called "Rain Crow" because it tends to sing and call when rain is imminent. • In Illinois, this species can be locally common when a temporary abundance of cicadas creates an easily gathered food supply. • Distantly related Eurasian cuckoos only lay their eggs in other birds' nests. Neither of the North American cuckoos is considered to be an obligate nest parasite; however, both will lay eggs in each other's as well as other bird species' nests, including those of the Northern Cardinal, Cedar Waxwing and Mourning Dove.

ID: fawn brown upperparts; white underparts; downcurved bill with yellow, mostly on lower mandible; yellow eye ring; long tail with brown on upperside and large white spots on jet black feathers on underside; bright rufous in wings, very noticeable in flight. *Juvenile:* similar to adult except much more subtle tail pattern, with gray replacing jet black.
Size: *L* 11–13 in; *W* 18 in.
Status: common migrant statewide from early May to June; early fall migrants difficult to distinguish from local breeders; most are gone by mid- to late September, with some lingering into November; common to locally abundant breeder in southern Illinois decreasing northward.
Habitat: semi-open to large, closed-canopy deciduous woods; dense tangles

and thickets at the edges of orchards, suburban parks and agricultural fields.
Nesting: in a deciduous shrub or small tree up to 30 ft high; builds a flimsy platform of twigs often lined with catkins and roots; pair incubates 3–4 pale bluish green eggs for 9–11 days.
Feeding: gleans insect larvae, especially hairy caterpillars and cicadas; also eats berries, small fruits, small amphibians and occasionally the eggs of small birds.
Voice: much more variable and louder than Black-billed; long series of deep, hollow *kuks,* slowing near the end: *kuk-kuk-kuk-kuk kuk kop kow kowlp kowlp.*
Similar Species: *Black-billed Cuckoo* (p. 181): all-black bill; lacks rufous tinge on primaries; less prominent, white undertail spots; red rather than yellow eye ring; juvenile has buff eye ring and may have buff wash on throat and undertail coverts; migrates earlier in spring.
Best Sites: *Summer:* Shawnee NF.

BARN OWL
Tyto alba

Up until the early 1950s, small towns and most farms in Illinois had Barn Owls. Several factors contributed to this bird's rapid decline. Pesticides killed its rodent prey and even the owls themselves. The chemicals also caused the birds' eggs to crack before they hatched or to not hatch at all. As well, humans indiscriminately shot these owls and converted much of their favorite hayfield feeding grounds to sterile corn and soybean fields. • Strictly nocturnal, the Barn Owl can easily catch prey in absolute darkness. Its asymmetrically placed ear openings, along with its heart-shaped facial disc, help it zero in on prey without having to see. • Although Barn Owls are somewhat migratory, especially at the northern edge of their range, which includes Illinois, most nesting pairs in the state live here year-round; however, extremely cold temperatures can cause mortality.

ID: heart-shaped, white facial disc; dark eyes; pale bill; golden brown upper parts suffused with black and gray; creamy white, black-spotted underparts; long, mostly featherless legs; white underwings; mothlike flight.
Size: *L* 12½–18 in; *W* 3–4 ft.
Status: state-endangered; extremely rare, year-round, local resident in southern Illinois; found statewide, although most records come from central and southern Illinois.
Habitat: roosts and nests in hollow trees, barns and other unoccupied buildings; requires grasslands and other open areas for hunting.
Nesting: in a natural or artificial cavity, often in a sheltered, secluded ledge of a building; may use an artificial nest box; no nest is built; pair may reuse nest site; female incubates 3–8 whitish eggs for 29–34 days; number of eggs depends on prey abundance; young hatch asynchro-

nously and are raised on a bed of disintegrated owl pellets; male feeds incubating female.
Feeding: eats mostly small mammals, especially voles, mice and rats; also takes snakes, lizards, birds and large insects; rarely takes frogs and fish; regurgitates pellets, indigestible parts of prey including bones and feathers.
Voice: wide repertoire, including metallic clicking, squeaks and screams; most common calls include harsh, raspy screeches and hisses.
Similar Species: *Short-eared Owl* (p. 189): yellow eyes; vertical streaks on breast and belly; legs are feathered to toes; black "wrist" patches in flight; lacks heart-shaped face; similar, mothlike flight.
Best Sites: abandoned buildings near large grasslands in southern Illinois.

EASTERN SCREECH-OWL
Megascops asio

The diminutive Eastern Screech-Owl is a year-round resident of deciduous woodlands, but its presence is rarely detected by humans. Most screech-owls sleep during the day inside tree cavities, artificial nest boxes or conifers, especially small red cedars. • An encounter with an Eastern Screech-Owl is usually the result of a sound cue. Chickadees, titmice, nuthatches and woodpeckers, which also nest in tree cavities, mob screech-owls when members of their tribe are preyed upon, alerting a birder to an owl's presence during the day. More commonly, you will find this owl by listening for the male's eerie, horse "whinny" courtship call and loud trills and tremolos at night. • Unique among the owls found in our region, Eastern Screech-Owls are polychromatic: they show red or gray color morphs. Parent morph combinations can produce young of either color. • Two subspecies are found in Illinois: *M.a. naevius* in the northern and central part of the state, though it wanders south in winter, and *M. a. asio* in the south.

gray morph

ID: "ear" tufts; reddish or grayish overall; dark breast streaking; yellow eyes; pale grayish to greenish bill; obvious white spots on wings.
Size: *L* 8–9 in; *W* 20–22 in.
Status: common year-round resident statewide.
Habitat: mature deciduous forests, open deciduous woodlands, riparian woodlands, orchards and shade trees, including trees with natural cavities in suburban neighborhoods; where successional woodlands meet a field or meadow traversed by a stream.
Nesting: in a natural cavity or artificial nest box, especially Wood Duck box; no lining is added; female incubates 4–5 white

eggs for about 26 days; male brings food to the female during incubation.
Feeding: feeds at dusk and at night; eats small mammals such as mice, moles, chipmunks and flying squirrels; also takes earthworms and larger birds, including American Woodcocks and American Kestrels; eats insects, including beetles, cicadas and crickets in flight.
Voice: horselike "whinny" that rises and falls; responds readily to imitations of its call, either via tape or human voice.
Similar Species: *Northern Saw-whet Owl* (p. 190): mostly winter resident; lacks "ear" tufts; long, reddish streaks on white underparts; large spots on wings; head has fine, heavy streaking.
Best Sites: common where favorable habitat exists.

GREAT HORNED OWL

Bubo virginianus

This formidable, primarily nocturnal hunter uses its acute hearing, exceptional vision and huge talons to hunt a wide variety of prey. Almost any small creature that moves is fair game for the Great Horned Owl. However, it has a poorly developed sense of smell, which might explain why it is the only consistent predator of skunks. • Great Horned Owls often begin their courtship as early as December, at which time their hooting calls make them quite conspicuous. A courting pair hoots back and forth; the female's hoot is lower and deeper in pitch. By February and March, females are already incubating their eggs. The pair continues to feed the young, both in and out of the nest, well into autumn. • The large eyes of an owl are fixed in place, so to look up, down or to the side, the bird must move its entire head. An owl can swivel its neck 270 degrees to either side and 90 degrees up and down. • The breeding subspecies of the Great Horned Owl in Illinois is *B. v. virginianus* and is the most common and widespread large owl in the state.

ID: yellow eyes; dark bill; large "ear" tufts set wide apart; fine, horizontal barring on breast; facial disc is outlined in black and is often rusty orange; white "chin"; heavily mottled gray, brown and black upperparts; overall plumage varies from light gray to dark brown; huge feet and talons; strong, direct flight.

Size: *L* 18–25 in; *W* 3–5 ft.

Status: common, year-round resident.

Habitat: fragmented and mature forests, especially near agricultural areas, meadows and other open habitats; riparian woodlands; wooded suburban parks.

Nesting: in the abandoned stick nest of a hawk or crow or in a squirrel nest; may also use a tree cavity or, occasionally, even an abandoned building; adds little or no nest material; female incubates 2–3 dull, whitish eggs for 28–35 days; young hatch asynchronously.

Feeding: mostly nocturnal, but also hunts at dusk or by day in winter; usually swoops from a perch; eats small mammals, birds, snakes, amphibians and even fish.

Voice: 4–6 deep hoots during the breeding season: *hoo-hoo-hoooo hoo-hoo;* male gives higher-pitched hoots; loud screeches of young heard well after fledging.

Similar Species: *Long-eared Owl* (p. 188): mostly seen in winter; much smaller; thinner; vertical breast streaks; smaller feet; "ear" tufts are closer together; lacks white "chin"; mothlike flight. *Barred Owl* (p. 187): somewhat smaller; yellow bill; browner overall; dark eyes; vertical streaks on breast; lacks "ear" tufts.

Best Sites: widespread in appropriate habitat.

SNOWY OWL
Bubo scandiacus

Each winter, Illinois birders scout the Lake Michigan shoreline to search for Harry Potter's favorite owl, the Snowy Owl. These birds also use agricultural fields in winter, where they are camouflaged against the flat, open, snow-covered landscape. • One of the world's largest and North America's heaviest owl, the Snowy visits Illinois annually in winter, typically remaining in the northern half of the state. Most birds seen are the darker females or immatures. During what are known as "irruptive" years, the Snowy has been found as far south as Carlyle Lake and Union County Conservation Area. Irruptions often occur in regular cycles, for instance, when lemming and vole populations in the Snowy Owl's arctic home crash, forcing the owls to move south to search for food. One of the more recent Snowy Owl invasions in Illinois occurred during the winter of 1996–97, when at least 73 individuals were found. • Snowy Owls, usually the larger females, may remain on the same territory in Illinois all winter, while others, often the smaller males, disappear after a day or two. • This circumpolar species often pairs for life.

ID: female is larger than male; predominantly white; yellow eyes; black bill and talons; no "ear" tufts; completely feathered legs and toes. *Male:* almost entirely white with very little dark flecking. *Female:* prominent dark barring or flecking on breast and upperparts. *Immature:* heavier barring than adult female; immature females sometimes more black than white. *In flight:* strong, direct flight.
Size: *L* 20–27 in; *W* 4½–6 ft.
Status: rare but regular winter resident from November to mid- to late March, with some lingering into April.

Habitat: open country, including croplands, meadows, airports and lakeshores; industrial areas near towns; often perches on fence posts, buildings and utility poles.
Nesting: does not nest in Illinois.
Feeding: swoops from a perch, often punching through the snow, to take mice and voles; along Chicago lakefront where many records occur, eats mostly waterbirds such as gulls and ducks, as well as rats; also hovers while hunting.
Voice: quiet in winter.
Similar Species: *Short-eared Owl* (p. 189): often mistaken because of its light undersides in flight, but mothlike flight and much browner upperparts help distinguish it.
Best Sites: Waukegan Beach; Chicago lakefront; Meigs Field is likely best area in state.

BARRED OWL
Strix varia

The sound of courting Barred Owls echoes through the wet woodlands of Illinois. The escalating laughs, hoots and monkeylike howls reinforce the bond between pairs. • Barred Owls tend to be more vocal when the moon is full and the air is calm. They also frequently call during the day, especially when it is overcast. • Compared to Great Horned Owls, Barred Owls have relatively weak talons; therefore, they prey on smaller animals such as voles, small birds and even smaller owls. • This owl's preferred swamp and bottomland woods habitat in Illinois offers a diet of reptiles, amphibians, fish, snails and cray-fish. • The Barred Owl population is largest in southern Illinois, where their familiar calls ring through the cypress swamps. Barred Owls often nest in tree cavities and will also use old hawk nests.

ID: dark eyes; horizontal barring around neck and upper breast; vertical brown streaking on white belly; no "ear" tufts; gray facial disc; brown back and wings covered with white dots and smudges; strong, direct flight.
Size: L 17–24 in; W 3½–4 ft.
Status: common year-round resident, decreasing northward; rarest in heavily urbanized northeastern part of state.
Habitat: mature deciduous and mixed-wood forests, especially in dense, older stands near swamps, streams, rivers and lakes; also upland woods; uses conifers for roosting, especially in winter.
Nesting: in a natural tree cavity, broken treetop or abandoned stick nest; adds very

little material to the nest; female incubates 2–3 white eggs for 28–33 days; male feeds the female during incubation.
Feeding: nocturnal; swoops from a perch to pounce on prey; eats mostly mice and voles; also takes foxes, weasels, bats and small birds; also eats amphibians and aquatic creatures.
Voice: most characteristic of all the owls; loud, hooting, rhythmic, laughing call is heard mostly in spring but also throughout the year: *Who cooks for you? Who cooks for you all?* also, a nasal, repeated *hoo*, rising in pitch and volume.
Similar Species: *Great Horned Owl* (p. 185): larger; more widespread; "ear" tufts; orange facial disc; yellow eyes; much larger feet and talons; white "chin"; densely barred underparts; grayer overall.
Best Sites: Union County CA; Horseshoe Lake CA; larger rivers statewide.

187

LONG-EARED OWL
Asio otus

A winter visitor to Illinois, the Long-eared Owl remains hidden during the day, most often in conifers, but also in oaks and other deciduous trees that retain their leaves. • To hide from an intruder, the Long-eared Owl flattens its feathers and compresses itself into a long, thin, vertical form, often against a tree trunk. This skittish bird will also flush upon eye contact. Some researchers think the "ear" tufts, not used for hearing, help the owl to resemble a broken-off branch or tree stump for camouflaging. • A rare nesting species in Illinois and formerly state-endangered, the Long-eared Owl is not often found during the breeding season. Searching for winter roosts affords the birder the best chance to find this bird in Illinois. Roosts typically consist of several to a few dozen birds. One of the largest roosts, discovered at the Morton Arboretum in 1955, contained at least 200 birds. Winter birds can usually be found by locating extensive accumulations of whitewash and pellets, bits of indigestible food, underneath the roosting trees. Most owls regurgitate one pellet daily. • The eastern subspecies, *A. o. wilsonianus*, is found in Illinois and also in Europe and Asia.

Nesting: often in an abandoned hawk or more commonly a crow nest; female incubates 2–6 white eggs for 26–28 days; male feeds the female during incubation.

Feeding: nocturnal; flies low, pouncing on prey from the air; eats mostly voles; also takes other rodents, especially shrews and bog lemmings, and a variety of small birds.

Voice: breeding call is a low, soft, ghostly *quoo-quoo;* alarm call is *weck-weck-weck;* also a dovelike *coo;* often issues various shrieks, hisses, whistles, barks and hoots, especially near the nest.

Similar Species: *Great Horned Owl* (p. 185): much more common and widespread; larger; "ear" tufts are set farther apart; rounder face; white "chin"; orange facial disc lacks dark vertical stripe through eye; densely barred underparts; more powerful, direct flight. *Short-eared Owl* (p. 189): lacks long "ear" tufts; nests and roosts on the ground in more open areas; hunts over grasslands.

Best Sites: Bartel and Orland Grasslands in Cook Co.; Middlefork State Fish and WA; cedar groves at Carlyle L.

ID: long, relatively close-set "ear" tufts; slim body; vertical belly markings; rusty brown facial disc; mottled brown plumage; yellow eyes; white around bill; mothlike flight.

Size: *L* 13–16 in; *W* 3–4 ft.

Status: uncommon migrant and winter resident; occurs from late October through mid- to late April; some birds may stay longer to try and nest; very rare breeder.

Habitat: *Breeding:* dense coniferous, mixed and riparian forests. *Winter:* old cedar groves and pine plantations; woodlots, dense riparian woodlands and hedgerows; isolated tree groves in meadows, fields and cemeteries.

SHORT-EARED OWL
Asio flammeus

This state-endangered grassland bird can be difficult to find in summer when females sit tightly on their ground nests. The Short-eared Owl was probably once one of the most abundant owl species in the state, but its grassland habitat has virtually disappeared in Illinois. • As with many other predators, Short-eared Owl populations grow and decline in response to dramatic fluctuations in prey availability. Cold weather and decreases in small mammal populations occasionally force large numbers of these owls, especially immatures, to become temporary nomads, searching for food outside their normal range. • Short-eared Owls often form colonial winter roosts in large grasslands. They are more active at dawn and dusk, but occasionally hunt during the day.

ID: yellow eyes set in black sockets; heavy vertical streaking on buff belly; straw-colored upperparts; short "ear" tufts are inconspicuous. *In flight:* dark "wrist" crescents; deep wingbeats; low, coursing, mothlike flight or high, more direct flight.
Size: *L* 13–17 in; *W* 3–4 ft.
Status: state-endangered; rare to uncommon migrant and winter resident; occurs from late September to late April, with a few lingering in early May; rare local breeder.
Habitat: *Breeding:* large grasslands; drier portions of wetlands. *In migration* and *winter:* wet meadows, agricultural fields, grassy ditches and airports.
Nesting: slight depression is sparsely lined with grass; female incubates 4–7 white

eggs for 24–31 days; male feeds the female during incubation.
Feeding: forages while flying low over marshes, wet meadows and tall vegetation; pounces on prey from the air; eats mostly voles and other small rodents; also takes insects, small birds and amphibians.
Voice: generally quiet; produces a soft *toot-toot-toot* during the breeding season; also squeals and barks in winter, often when leaving the roost or being pursued.
Similar Species: *Long-eared Owl* (p. 188): prominent "ear" tufts; much darker overall; orange facial disc; roosts in trees. *Snowy Owl* (p. 186): much rarer; much larger; much lighter, especially on upperparts; more powerful, direct flight.
Best Sites: Illinois Beach SP; Pratt's Wayne Woods; Prairie Ridge SNA; Pyramid Lake SP; Cypress Creek NWR; Grassy Slough NP.

NORTHERN SAW-WHET OWL

Aegolius acadicus

In Illinois, the Northern Saw-whet Owl, a nocturnal winter resident, feeds almost exclusively on deer mice and white-footed mice. It will also take small birds. • The Northern Saw-whet Owl was named for its shrill, raspy call that resembles the sound of a saw being sharpened on an old-fashioned whetstone. This owl can be remarkably tame, remaining still and quiet on its winter roost even when closely approached, relying on its camouflage. Some careful researchers have even been able to lift it out of its roost. When alarmed, this owl will elongate its body and raise feathers on its head. • Certain clues may give away this bird's location in winter: look for an accumulation of whitewash and pellets at the bases of trees—this species habitually uses the same roost perch for days, if not weeks. • A northern boreal forest breeder, the Saw-whet has nevertheless been documented breeding in Illinois. • The subspecies found in Illinois is *A. a. acadicus.*

ID: small body; small, rounded head; light, unbordered facial disc; dark bill; yellow eyes; vertical, rusty streaks on otherwise white underparts; white-spotted, brown upperparts; white-streaked forehead; short, brown to black tail.
Immature: very rarely seen in Illinois; white patch between eyes; rich brown head and breast; buff brown belly.
Size: *L* 7–9 in; *W* 17–22 in.
Status: rare to uncommon migrant and winter resident from early October, but in some years may not arrive until mid-November or December; departs by mid-March, with some lingering into April; very rare, local breeder.
Habitat: mixed woodlands; often in red cedars, white pines, hemlocks and yews;

roosts singly in dense foliage, especially evergreens or in vine tangles.
Nesting: in an abandoned woodpecker cavity or natural hollow in a tree, often an aspen or poplar; female incubates 5–6 white eggs for 27–29 days; male feeds the female during incubation.
Feeding: swoops down from a perch; eats mostly mice in Illinois; also eats larger insects, songbirds, shrews, moles and occasionally amphibians.
Voice: whistled, evenly spaced notes repeated about 100 times per minute: *whew-whew-whew-whew* or *toot-toot-toot;* also a catlike whine or yelp rising in pitch; will respond to other owl calls.
Similar Species: *Eastern Screech-Owl* (p. 184): much more common; overall gray or rufous; "ear" tufts; vermiculated streaks on breast; facial disc outlined in black.
Best Sites: Colored Sands Bluff NP; Morton Arboretum; Middlefork State Fish and WA; Eldon Hazlet SP.

COMMON NIGHTHAWK
Chordeiles minor

Beginning in late April or the first few days of May, Illinois birders look to the sky for the return of these strictly insectivorous birds. During early summer, lucky Illinois birders may even experience the aerial courtship dance of the male as he makes dives to the ground while thrusting his wings forward to create a hollow booming sound that attracts potential mates. • Pesticide use for mosquito control has reduced this bird's population throughout the eastern United States. Also, new buildings constructed with tarred or rubber-clad roofs overheat the eggs. • In fall, hundreds to thousands of nighthawks may be seen in Illinois as they fly south for winter. • Like other members of the nightjar family, the Common Nighthawk funnels insects into its large, gaping mouth, which is surrounded by bristles. At least one fourth of this bird's diet consists of flying ants with one record of more than 2000 ants in one bird's stomach.

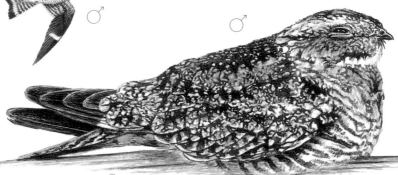

ID: mottled black, gray and brown plumage; barred underparts; primaries project beyond tail tip. *Male:* white throat. *Female:* buff throat. *In flight:* bold, white "wrist" patches on long, pointed wings; shallowly forked, barred tail; erratic flight.
Size: *L* 8½–10 in; *W* 24 in.
Status: fairly common spring migrant from late April to late May; common fall migrant from mid-August to early October; fairly common breeder.
Habitat: *Breeding:* on gravel rooftops; grasslands with sparse cover or bare patches. *In migration:* anywhere large numbers of flying insects are found; around lights in parking lots or in rural grasslands and hayfields.
Nesting: on bare ground or on a gravel rooftop; no nest is built; female incubates

2 well-camouflaged eggs for about 19 days; both adults feed the young.
Feeding: primarily at dawn or dusk; flies around street lights at night to catch prey attracted to the light.
Voice: frequently repeated, nasal *peent;* also makes a deep, hollow *vroom* with its wings during courtship flight.
Similar Species: *Whip-poor-will* (p. 193): less common and found in more remote, well-forested areas; best identified by voice; shorter, rounder wings; rounded tail with white or buff at tip; dark throat with white "necklace" on male and buff "necklace" on female. *Chuck-will's-widow* (p. 192): rare, except in southern Illinois; larger body; found in more remote, well-forested areas; best identified by voice; more rufous to buff overall; buff brown throat with white "necklace."
Best Sites: widespread.

CHUCK-WILL'S-WIDOW

Caprimulgus carolinensis

This bird's core range lies in the hot, humid southeastern United States. • You would be lucky to see this perfectly camouflaged bird during the day, roosting on the furrowed bark of a tree limb or sitting among scattered leaves on the forest floor. You would be even luckier to observe the fascinating courtship display of the male as he claps his wings together over his head, droops his wings, spreads his tail and appears to swell to twice his size. • The Chuck-will's-widow belongs to a group of birds called "nightjars," once known as "goatsuckers," because it was thought that they used their huge mouths, as wide as 2 inches, to suck milk from goats and other animals at night. • Today, people applaud nightjars for their ability to eat copious amounts of mosquitoes, moths and other flying insects.

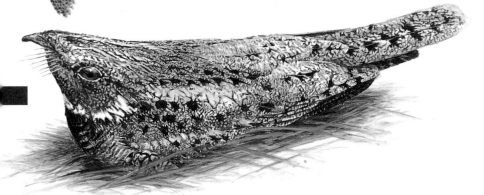

ID: best identified by voice; mottled brown-and-buff body with rufous overall; pale brown to buff throat; whitish "necklace"; darkish breast; long, rounded tail; inner webs of outer tail feathers are white, outlined in buff.
Size: *L* 11–13 in; *W* 24–25 in.
Status: uncommon to locally common migrant and breeder in extreme southern Illinois; very rare, sporadic breeder elsewhere; migrants arrive in mid- to late April; a few migrate annually to central and northern Illinois; most are gone from southern Illinois by mid-September.
Habitat: upland woods, often near or in pine plantations.
Nesting: on bare ground; no nest is built; female incubates 2 heavily blotched,

creamy white eggs for about 21 days and raises the young alone.
Feeding: catches insects on the wing or by hawking; eats beetles, moths, flying ants, flies, damselfies, dragonflies, crickets, grasshoppers and cicadas; occasionally eats small birds, including swallows and wrens.
Voice: 4 loud syllables paraphrased as *chuck-will's-widow;* a deep *quok,* probably an alarm note often given in flight.
Similar Species: *Whip-poor-will* (p. 193): much more common; much smaller; less heavily spotted; grayer overall; white "necklace"; black throat; male shows more white in tail feathers; female's dark tail feathers are bordered with buff on outer tips. *Common Nighthawk* (p. 191): much more common; smaller; forked tail; white patches on wings; male has white throat; female has buff throat.
Best Sites: Fern Clyffe SP; Lake Murphysboro SP; Shawnee NF.

WHIP-POOR-WILL
Caprimulgus vociferus

In early April, on a warm evening, birders in southern Illinois may hear the first spring Whip-poor-will call its name or see it perched alongside a road with its glowing red eyes. • Whip-poor-wills call in Illinois from April to August, and sometimes for a short time in September. The most vocal of Illinois' three nightjars, the Whip-poor-will calls once per second, sometimes repeated 50 to 100 times. • Within days of hatching, young Whip-poor-wills scurry away from their nest to find protective cover. Until they are able to fly, about 20 days later, the parents feed them regurgitated insects. • When disturbed at the nest, the female performs various distraction displays, including flying around the nest site while giving repeated alarm calls or feigning injury by fluttering her wings on the ground. • This species seems to be decreasing in Illinois and other parts of its range, possibly because of forest fragmentation and human disturbance.

ID: mottled, brown gray overall with black flecking; reddish tinge on rounded wings; black throat; long, rounded tail. *Male:* white "necklace"; extensive white on outer tail feathers. *Female:* buff "necklace."
Size: *L* 9–10 in; *W* 16–20 in.
Status: fairly common migrant and breeder, decreasing northward; arrives in southern Illinois in late March, leaving by late September, although some linger into October.
Habitat: open, deciduous and pine woodlands; often along forest edges.
Nesting: on the ground, sometimes in leaf or pine needle litter; no nest is built; mostly the female incubates 2 whitish eggs, blotched brown and gray, for 19–21 days; both adults raise the young.

Feeding: almost entirely nocturnal; forages by hovering or sallies from a perch; flies along treetops and high in the air; eats flying insects, particularly moths; some grasshoppers are swallowed whole; may feed on the ground; may eat grit.
Voice: far-carrying, frequently repeated *whip-poor-will*, with emphasis on the *will;* most often calls at dusk and through the night; if disturbed at nest, often utters a soft *quirt, quirt.*
Similar Species: *Common Nighthawk* (p. 191): longer, pointed wings with white "wrist" patches; shallowly forked, barred tail. *Chuck-will's-widow* (p. 192): best distinguished by voice; larger body; pale brown to buff throat with white "necklace"; dark breast; more rufous overall; much less white on male's tail.
Best Sites: Little Red Schoolhouse Nature Center; Forest Glen FP; Sand Ridge SF; Giant City SP; Trail of Tears SF; Shawnee NF.

193

CHIMNEY SWIFT

Chaetura pelagica

Chimney Swifts feed, drink, bathe, collect nesting material and sometimes even mate while in flight. • In spring, Chimney Swifts perform an aerial courtship display, holding their wings in a V-shape. • These birds historically nested in natural tree cavities and woodpecker excavations, and can still be found doing so in the Cache River bottomlands of southern Illinois. However, elsewhere, they now more commonly nest and roost in chimneys. There are several designs available for chimney swift towers that you can erect near your home. • This bird's eastern North American populations appear to be declining because of habitat loss. • Strong claws allow swifts to cling to vertical surfaces. In fall, migrating flocks of hundreds, and sometimes more than a thousand, swifts may be seen funneling like a tornado into large chimneys to roost.

ID: sooty brown overall; slim body and long, thin, pointed wings; square tail. *In flight:* boomerang-shaped profile; erratic flight pattern; rapid, shallow wingbeats.
Size: *L* 5–5½ in; *W* 12–13 in.
Status: common to abundant migrant and breeder; migrants arrive from mid-April to May; breeders congregate in September and early October; most birds are gone by mid-October; often joined or replaced by returning migrants from the north.
Habitat: forages over cities and towns; roosts and nests in chimneys; nests in tree cavities in more remote areas.

Nesting: often colonial; nests deep in the interior of a chimney, tree cavity or in the attic of an abandoned building; pair fixes a half-saucer nest of short, dead twigs to a vertical wall with saliva; pair incubates 4–5 white eggs for 19–21 days; both adults feed the young; young fledge in 30 days, nearly twice as long as the typical songbird; a third adult often assists in rearing young.
Feeding: flying insects are swallowed whole during continuous flight.
Voice: rapid, chirping call is given in flight: *chitter-chitter-chitter;* also gives a rapid series of *chip* notes.
Similar Species: *Swallows* (pp. 231–36): broader, shorter wings; smoother flight pattern; most have forked or notched tails.
Best Sites: in towns during breeding season.

RUBY-THROATED HUMMINGBIRD
Archilochus colubris

Ruby-throated Hummingbirds feed on the energy-rich nectar of flowers, pollinating them in turn. A study in central Illinois showed that hummingbirds deposited 10 times as much pollen per stigma per visit as did bees. • Weighing about as much as a nickel, a hummingbird can fly vertically as well as in reverse and beats its wings up to 80 times per second in forward flight. Its heart beats up to 1200 times per minute. • Each year, these hummingbirds migrate across the Gulf of Mexico—an incredible, nonstop journey of more than 500 miles. Those that remain in Illinois to breed often begin as the wild columbines are blooming. The nest, built only by the female, is about the size of a walnut shell. • If nighttime temperatures get too low on the hummingbird's northern breeding grounds, it may go into a state of torpor, slowing its heartbeat to conserve energy.

ID: tiny; long bill; iridescent, green back; light underparts; dark tail. *Male:* ruby red throat; thin, black "chin." *Female* and *immature:* fine, dark throat streaking.
Size: *L* 3½–4 in; *W* 4½ in.
Status: fairly common to common migrant and breeder; migrants occur from mid-April to early June and from early to mid-August to early November or after frost.
Habitat: open, mixed woodlands, flower gardens and backyards with blooming shrubs, trees, wildflowers and feeders.
Nesting: female selects site, usually near the tip of a downsloping branch; tiny, deep cup nest of plant down and fibers is held together with spider silk and covered with lichens; female incubates 2 white eggs for 13–16 days; female feeds the young.
Feeding: uses its long bill and tongue to probe blooming flowers for nectar and sugar-sweetened water from feeders; feeds in the blooms of Ohio buckeye, tulip tree and nonnative mimosa in spring; also eats small insects and spiders.
Voice: wings buzz softly in flight; loud *chick* and other high squeaks.
Similar Species: *Rufous Hummingbird* (p. 196): very rare; variable plumage especially in fall; male has rufous on flanks, back and tail; female may have orange red spots on throat and rufous flanks; juvenile has greenish back and light rufous on sides.
Best Sites: Shawnee NF in breeding season; bottomlands with extensive jewelweed patches in early fall.

RUFOUS HUMMINGBIRD

Selasphorus rufus

Once considered hypothetical in Illinois, the Rufous Hummingbird now makes an appearance nearly every fall at some well-kept feeder in the state. The reasons for more sightings could be because the bird is changing its migration route and has more food sources as hummingbird feeding becomes more popular. In addition, birders have also become more advanced in separating hummingbird species. • Illinois' first confirmed record and specimen of the Rufous Hummingbird occurred on October 14, 1993, at a feeder in Olympia Fields near Chicago. The immature male stayed, but was discovered dead not far from the feeder on November 12. At least eight Rufous Hummingbirds have been documented in Illinois, the latest two in Mt. Vernon and Pinckneyville in the fall of 2002. All Illinois records of Rufous Hummingbirds are from the fall; a few include the brightly colored adult males. • This western montane species ranges farther north than any other North American hummingbird, breeding in Alaska and the southern Yukon Territory of Canada. It winters mainly in southern Mexico.

VAGRANT

ID: long, thin, black bill; mostly rufous tail. *Male:* rufous back, tail and flanks; scaled, scarlet throat; green crown; white breast and belly. *Female:* green back with some rufous; rufous base to tail feathers; sometimes red-spotted throat; rufous flanks; light underparts. *Juvenile:* distinctive tail feather shape upon close observation; greenish back; light rufous on sides.
Size: *L* 3¼ in; *W* 4½ in.
Status: very rare late fall and early winter migrant; probably more common than records indicate; typically found in November with birds often lingering at the same feeder for weeks; no spring records exist.
Habitat: suburban and rural hummingbird feeders.
Nesting: does not nest in Illinois.
Feeding: hover-probes mostly red flowers for nectar and sugar water at feeders; also eats small insects and sap.
Voice: call is a gentle *chewp chewp;* also, makes a fast buzz: *zeee-chuppity-chup.*
Similar Species: *Ruby-throated Hummingbird* (p. 195): much more common; male has ruby red throat, green back and crown; female and immature have greenish backs and dark throat streaking; may also have red spots on throat; shade of spots is more scarlet red.
Best Sites: hummingbird feeders in late fall.

BELTED KINGFISHER

Ceryle alcyon

When perched on a bare branch overlooking water or when flying across open water, the Belted Kingfisher gives its telltale rattling call. With a precise headfirst dive, this species can catch fish at depths of up to 2 feet or snag a frog immersed in only a few inches of water. Kingfishers may even dive into water to elude avian predators. • During the breeding season, a pair of kingfishers takes turns excavating a nest burrow. They use their bills to chip away at an exposed sandbank, and then kick loose material out of the tunnel with their feet, forming two well-defined troughs with a ridge in the middle. • You can easily identify the female Belted Kingfisher from the male by noting the red band across her belly. In other kingfisher species, this pattern is reversed, with the male more colorful than the female. • Open water entices kingfishers to remain in winter and southern Illinois Christmas bird counts can yield up to a dozen or more of these birds.

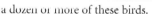

ID: bluish upperparts; shaggy crest; blue gray breast band; white "collar"; long, straight bill; short legs; white underwings; small, white patch in front of eye. *Male:* no "belt." *Female:* rust-colored "belt."

Size: *L* 11–14 in; *W* 20 in.

Status: year-round resident where water remains unfrozen; migrants difficult to detect; uncommon to common breeder; rare to uncommon winter resident depending on ice cover; birds mostly seen singly or in pairs.

Habitat: rivers, large streams, lakes, marshes and beaver ponds, especially near exposed soil banks, gravel pits or bluffs.

Nesting: in a cavity at the end of an earth burrow, often up to 6 ft long, dug by the pair; pair incubates 6–7 white eggs for 22–24 days; both adults feed the young.

Feeding: dives headfirst into water, either from a perch or from hovering flight; eats mostly small fish, tadpoles and other aquatic invertebrates; crushes some prey such as crayfish before eating; also takes small mammals, lizards, young birds, insects and berries; captures moths and butterflies on the wing.

Voice: fast, loud, repetitive rattle.

Similar Species: none in Illinois.

Best Sites: rivers, lakes and ponds with open water and well-stocked with fish.

RED-HEADED WOODPECKER
Melanerpes erythrocephalus

The Red-headed Woodpecker prefers open woodlands, including savannas and flooded bottomlands with standing dead trees, where it can sally from perches to catch its prey. With a habitat frequently found close to roads, these birds are susceptible to being killed by vehicles. Habitat loss and degradation from fire suppression and competition with the nonnative European Starling and House Sparrow have caused this species to decline rapidly. Many of Illinois' historic oak-hickory forests have been overtaken by maple trees, causing a loss of the Red-headed Woodpecker's mainstay in winter, acorns. If acorns are plentiful, this bird can be locally abundant in oak bottomland woods in southern Illinois during the winter. A walk along the Union County Conservation Area during one recent Christmas bird count revealed several Red-headed Woodpeckers every quarter of a mile, giving their *kweer* calls and chasing one another as they vied for feeding territories. • Restoration of oak woodlands may help this species in Illinois, although it is likely that it will never return to its historic numbers.

ID: bright red head, chin, throat and "bib" with thin, narrow, black border; black back, wings and tail; white breast, belly, rump and lower back; large, prominent, white wing patches. *Juvenile:* brown head; black back, wings and tail; slight brown streaking on white underparts; also has prominent, white wing patches, but with black near edges of secondaries.
Size: *L* 9–9½ in; *W* 17 in.
Status: fairly common migrant from early March to mid-May and from late August to mid-October; uncommon to locally common breeder; rare in northeastern Illinois; uncommon to locally common some years in winter, especially in southern Illinois.
Habitat: open deciduous woodlands, especially oak woodlands, suburban parks and river bottomlands, especially with snags.
Nesting: male excavates a nest cavity in a dead tree or limb; pair incubates 4–5 white eggs for 12–13 days; both adults feed the young.
Feeding: catches insects in midair or sallies from a perch; eats mostly insects, especially cicadas, ants and beetles; also eats earthworms, corn, grubs, spiders, nuts, berries, seeds and fruit; may also eat some young birds and eggs.
Voice: loud *kweer* or *kwrring* notes; also a chattering *kerr-r-ruck;* drums softly in short bursts.
Similar Species: *Red-bellied Woodpecker* (p. 199): whitish face and underparts; black-and-white barring on back.
Best Sites: Union County CA; Horseshoe Lake CA; Cypress Creek NWR. *Summer:* Palos Preserves; Iroquois County CA; Momence Wetlands; Milan Bottoms along Mississippi R.; Sanganois CA; L. Chautauqua.

RED-BELLIED WOODPECKER

Melanerpes carolinus

The Red-bellied Woodpecker issues noisy, rolling *churr* calls, which sound similar to those of both the Golden-fronted Woodpecker and the Red-headed Woodpecker. Unlike most woodpeckers, which eat mostly insects, Red-bellies also consume large amounts of plant material. An opportunistic feeder, this bird will even eat a tree frog if it's within easy grasp. • Red-bellied Woodpecker populations are expanding northward and westward. Though considered a year-round resident in Illinois, these birds have been noticed in apparent migration along Lake Michigan in May and in October and November. • The Red-bellied Woodpecker does have a reddish belly, but it is only a small area that is difficult to see in the field. Novice birders may get confused and think the Red-bellied is a Red-headed Woodpecker, however, upon closer observation, they are easy to distinguish. The Red-headed's entire head down to its neck is bright red; the Red-bellied has a ladder-back appearance and only has red on its crown and nape.

ID: black-and-white barring on back; white patches on rump and topside base of primaries; reddish tinge on belly. *Male:* red nape extends to forehead and forms "collar" around half of neck. *Female:* gray crown; red nape. *Juvenile:* limited orangy nape; gray crown.
Size: *L* 9–10½ in; *W* 16 in.
Status: common year-round resident.
Habitat: deciduous woodlands; remote wilderness areas; wooded residential areas; backyard bird feeders in winter.
Nesting: in a cavity; female selects one of several nest sites excavated by the male; pair incubates 4–5 white eggs for 12–14 days; male often incubates at night; both adults raise the young.
Feeding: forages in trees, on the ground or occasionally in flight; eats insects, seeds, nuts and fruit; may also eat tree sap, small amphibians, bird eggs or small fish; eats suet and sunflower seeds at feeders.
Voice: call is a soft, rolling *churr*; drums in second-long bursts.
Similar Species: *Northern Flicker* (p. 203): yellow underwings; gray crown and nape; black "mustache"; brown face; brown back with dark barring; black breast band; spotted rather than white underparts. *Red-headed Woodpecker* (p. 198): all-red head; unbarred, black back and wings; white rump; prominent, white wing patches.
Best Sites: widespread in most woodlands.

YELLOW-BELLIED SAPSUCKER

Sphyrapicus varius

Lines of parallel holes freshly drilled in tree bark are a sure sign that sapsuckers are nearby. The holes fill with sweet, sticky sap, attracting insects. Sapsuckers eat both the bugs and sap, but do not actually suck sap; they lap it up with their long tongues. • Early in the season when flying insects, fruits and nectar are scarce, hummingbirds, kinglets, waxwings and warblers, especially the Cape May Warbler, and waxwings benefit from Yellow-bellied Sapsucker holes. • The most migratory of Illinois' woodpeckers, some sapsuckers winter as far south as Panama. Illinois lies at the southern edge of the Yellow-bellied Sapsucker's breeding range and the northern edge of its wintering range. • Sapsucker nests have been found fairly regularly in Illinois since 1854. • In the far south of Illinois, wintering sapsuckers join mixed flocks of foraging birds.

ID: black "bib"; red fore-crown; black-and-white face, back, wings and tail; large, white wing patch; yellow wash on lower breast and belly. *Male:* red "chin." *Female:* white "chin." *Juvenile:* brownish overall; large, clearly defined, white wing patches.
Size: *L* 7–9 in; *W* 16 in.
Status: common migrant from mid- to late March to early May and from early September to mid-November; rare but regular breeder in extreme northwestern corner of the state; very rare and sporadic breeder elsewhere in central and northern Illinois; fairly common winter resident in southern Illinois, decreasing northward.

Habitat: upland and bottomland deciduous and mixed woods. *Winter:* residential areas, cemeteries and parks with pine and spruce.
Nesting: in a cavity; usually in a live poplar or birch tree with heart rot; often lines the cavity with wood chips; pair incubates 5–6 white eggs for 12–13 days; male often incubates at night.
Feeding: hammers trees for insects; drills holes in live trees to collect sap and trapped insects; also flycatches for insects; eats beetles, ants, wasps, hornets, mayflies and moths, small fruits and suet at feeders.
Voice: nasal, catlike *meow;* territorial and courtship hammering has a distinctive, 2-speed quality; soft *vee-ooo* when alarmed.
Similar Species: *Downy Woodpecker* (p. 201) and *Hairy Woodpecker* (p. 202): white barring on black backs; lack large, white wing patch and red forecrown.
Best Sites: *Summer:* Lost Mound NWR; Mississippi Palisades SP. *In migration:* Chicago lakefront parks. *Winter:* Shawnee NF; Cache River Biosphere Reserve.

DOWNY WOODPECKER

Picoides pubescens

The Downy Woodpecker is the smallest and most common woodpecker in Illinois. The only other species that looks and sounds similar is the larger Hairy Woodpecker, though it is much less often seen in backyards. • Like other members of the woodpecker family, the Downy has evolved a number of features that help cushion the repeated shocks of hammering. These characteristics include a strong bill, strong neck muscles, a flexible, reinforced skull and a brain that is tightly packed in its protective cranium. Stiff, pointed tail feathers, help woodpeckers brace themselves while hammering on trees and climbing. Downies and other woodpeckers also have feathered nostrils, which filter the sawdust produced when hammering. • From fall through spring, Downy Woodpeckers commonly feed on corn borers in harvested and unharvested stalks in corn fields. These industrious feeders also glean dormant wasps and other insects that live within tall forbs, especially goldenrod, in winter.

ID: clear white belly and back; black wings barred with white, broad, black eye line and crown; short, stubby bill; mostly black tail; white outer tail feathers spotted with black. *Male:* small, red patch on back of head. *Female:* no red patch.
Size: L 6–7 in; W 12 in.
Status: common year-round resident.
Habitat: woodlots and woodlands of any size; shrublands; open fields and agricultural areas; also common in suburban and urban yards.
Nesting: pair excavates a cavity in a dying or decaying tree trunk or limb and lines it with wood chips; pair incubates 4–5 white eggs for 11–13 days; both adults feed the young and may bring them to feeders.
Feeding: forages on trunks and branches in saplings and shrubs; chips and probes for ants and beetles, grasshopper eggs and other insect eggs; eats cocoons, larvae and adults of moths and butterflies; visits feeders with suet, peanuts and sunflower seeds; often feeds on corn and poison ivy berries in Illinois.
Voice: long, unbroken, descending trill; calls are a sharp *pik* or *ki-ki-ki* or whiny *queek queek;* drums more and at a higher pitch than the Hairy Woodpecker.
Similar Species: *Hairy Woodpecker* (p. 202): larger; bill is as long as head is wide; no spots on white outer tail feathers; louder, shriller call. *Yellow-bellied Sapsucker* (p. 200): large, white wing patch; red forecrown; red throat on male; lacks red head patch and clean white back.
Best Sites: widespread.

201

HAIRY WOODPECKER

Picoides villosus

The secret to woodpeckers' feeding success is hidden in their skulls. Most woodpeckers have very long tongues—in some cases more than four times the length of the bill—made possible by twin structures that wrap around the perimeter of the skull. These structures store the tongue in much the same way that a measuring tape is stored in its case. Besides being long and maneuverable, the tip of the tongue is sticky with saliva and is finely barbed to help seize reluctant wood-boring insects. • Woodpeckers have zygodactyl feet, with two toes facing forward and two facing backward. Sometimes, the outer rear toe rotates to the side for even better climbing. • The Hairy Woodpecker has many subspecies, which range throughout almost all wooded regions from Alaska to Central America. The Illinois subspecies is *P. v. villosus.* • The Hairy Woodpecker characteristically peels strips of bark off trees as it searches for bark beetles and other insects.

Habitat: mature woodlands; usually does not venture into open fields.

Nesting: pair excavates a nest site in a live or decaying tree trunk or limb; cavity is lined with wood chips; pair incubates 4–5 white eggs for 12–14 days; both adults feed the young.

Feeding: forages on tree trunks and branches; chips, hammers, probes and peels away bark for insect eggs, cocoons, larvae and adults; also eats nuts, fruit and seeds; attracted to feeders with suet, peanuts and sunflower seeds, especially in winter.

Voice: loud, sharp *peek peek;* long, unbroken trill: *keek-ik-ik-ik-ik;* drums less regularly and at a lower pitch than the Downy Woodpecker.

Similar Species: *Downy Woodpecker* (p. 201): smaller; shorter bill; dark spots on white outer tail feathers; softer, less shrill call. *Yellow-bellied Sapsucker* (p. 200): large, white wing patch; red forecrown; lacks red head patch and clean white back.

Best Sites: large tracts of forest, especially at Palos Preserves, Pere Marquette SP, Shawnee NF along the Illinois R. and Mississippi R.

ID: pure white belly; black wings spotted with white; black "cheek" and crown; bill is about as long as head is wide; black tail with unspotted, white outer feathers. *Male:* small red patch on back of head. *Female:* no red patch. *Juvenile:* more indistinct patterning with brown instead of black.

Size: *L* 8–9½ in; *W* 15 in.

Status: locally rare to fairly common year-round resident; winter numbers may include migrants from the north.

NORTHERN FLICKER
Colaptes auratus

Unlike other woodpeckers, the Northern Flicker spends much of its time on mowed lawns and grassy meadows, feeding on ants and other insects. • The flicker eats more ants than any other bird: one record showed a flicker stomach that contained more than 5000 ants! The flicker scratches the ground to locate ant nests, then digs into the nest with its long bill and laps up the insects. • Flickers bathe in dust to absorb oils and bacteria from their feathers. They also squash ants and preen themselves with the remains in a process called "anting." Ants produce formic acid, which kills small parasites on the flicker's skin and feathers. • The northern subspecies, *C. a. borealis,* occurs as a migrant and winter resident in Illinois. The western or "red-shafted" form, *C. a. cafer,* has rarely been found in the state. • The flicker performs a lively courtship ritual; three or more birds of both sexes face each other, dancing, nodding, bowing and swaying.

ID: barred, brown back and wings; white underparts with uniform black spotting; black "bib"; yellow underwings and undertail; white rump; long bill; brownish to buff face; gray neck and crown. *Male:* black "mustache" stripe; red nape crescent. *Female:* no "mustache."
Size: *L* 12½–13 in; *W* 20 in.
Status: common migrant and breeder; migrants occur from mid-March through May and from late August to early November; common winter resident, decreasing northward.
Habitat: *Breeding:* open woodlands. *In migration* and *winter:* corn fields, shrublands, pastures, open woodlands, mowed lawns and parks.

Nesting: pair excavates a cavity in a dead or dying deciduous tree; will also use a nest box; lines the cavity with wood chips; pair incubates 5–8 white eggs for 11–16 days; both adults feed the young.
Feeding: forages for ants, beetles, wasps, grasshoppers and crickets; also takes berries of dogwood, Virginia creeper, poison ivy, sumac, hackberry, pokeberry, mulberry, blackberry, wild cherry, wild grape; probes bark; occasionally flycatches; visits suet feeders.
Voice: loud, laughing, rapid *kick-kick-kick-kick-kick-kick; wicka-wicka-wicka* during courtship.
Similar Species: *Red-bellied Woodpecker* (p. 199): black-and-white pattern on back; more red on head; dark underwings.
Best Sites: found throughout state in appropriate habitat.

PILEATED WOODPECKER

Dryocopus pileatus

W ith its flaming red crest, swooping flight and loud, maniacal call, this impressive deep-forest dweller easily attracts the attention of a birder. Using its powerful, dagger-shaped bill, the Pileated Woodpecker chisels distinctively shaped, large, oblong cavities while searching for grubs and ants, especially carpenter ants. • A pair of breeding Pileated Woodpeckers requires more than 100 acres of mature forest. They often choose large, tall trees, especially sycamore, tulip tree, beech, cottonwood, hackberry or cypress, for nesting. Like most other woodpecker species in Illinois, the Pileated begins laying eggs in April. • Other birds and even mammals depend on the activities of this woodpecker— Wood Ducks, American Kestrels, screech-owls and even flying squirrels frequently nest in abandoned Pileated Woodpecker cavities. • There are two subspecies of the Pileated Woodpecker in Illinois. The northern *D. p. abieticola* subspecies may now be extirpated in the state, but the southern *D. p. pileatus* is still a resident. As forests mature in northern Illinois, especially along major rivers, this bird may return to its historical breeding grounds.

ID: predominantly black; white wing linings; shiny red crest; yellow eyes; stout, black, blunt-tipped bill; white stripe runs from bill to shoulder; white "chin." *Male:* scarlet "mustache"; red crest extends from forehead to crest. *Female:* no scarlet "mustache"; red crest starts on crown. *In flight:* large, white patches on front half of upper side of wings.
Size: *L* 16–19 in; *W* 29 in.
Status: uncommon year-round resident; very rare or absent in northeastern Illinois.
Habitat: extensive tracts of mature deciduous or mixed forest, especially bottomland forests.
Nesting: pair excavates a cavity in a tree trunk; excavation can take 3–6 weeks; lines the cavity with wood chips; pair incubates 4 white eggs for 15–18 days; both adults feed the young.
Feeding: hammers the base of rotting trees, creating large oblong or rectangular holes; eats carpenter ants, wood-boring beetle larvae, acorns, beech nuts and berries, including hackberry, smilax vine, poison ivy and sassafras; occasionally visits suet feeders.
Voice: loud, fast, laughing, rolling *yucka-yucka-yucka;* long series of *kuk* notes; diagnostic, loud resonant drumming tapers off at end.
Similar Species: *Other woodpeckers* (pp. 198–203): much smaller. *American Crow* (p. 228): lacks white underwings and flaming red crest.
Best Sites: Illinois R. and Mississippi R. valleys; Forest Glen Preserve; Shawnee NF; Beall Woods; Pere Marquette SP; Cache River Biosphere Reserve.

Flycatchers

Shrikes & Vireos

Jays & Crows

Larks & Swallows

Chickadees, Nuthatches & Wrens

Kinglets, Bluebirds & Thrushes

Mimics, Starlings & Waxwings

Wood Warblers & Tanagers

Sparrows, Grosbeaks & Buntings

Blackbirds & Orioles

Finchlike Birds

Passerines are also commonly known as songbirds or perching birds. Although these terms are easier to comprehend, they are not as strictly accurate, because some passerines neither sing nor perch, and many nonpasserines do sing and perch. In a general sense, however, these terms represent passerines adequately: they are among the best singers, and they are typically seen perched on a branch or wire.

It is believed that passerines, which all belong to the order Passeriformes, make up the most recent evolutionary group of birds. Theirs is the most numerous of all orders, representing about 46 percent of the bird species in Illinois, and nearly three-fifths of all living birds worldwide.

Passerines are grouped together based on the sum total of many morphological and molecular similarities, including such things as the number of tail and flight feathers and reproductive characteristics. All passerines share the same foot shape: three toes face forward and one faces backward, and no passerines have webbed toes. Also, all passerines have a tendon that runs along the back side of the bird's knee and tightens when the bird perches, giving it a firm grip.

Some of our most common and easily identified birds are passerines, such as the Black-capped Chickadee, American Robin and House Sparrow, but the passerines also include some of the most challenging and frustrating birds to identify, until their distinct songs and call are learned.

OLIVE-SIDED FLYCATCHER

Contopus cooperi

Q*uick-three-beers!* This interpretation of the male Olive-sided Flycatcher's courtship song is surprisingly accurate. Illinois birders only hear this song for a short time in late spring, when the Olive-sided Flycatcher pauses on its way to its breeding grounds in northern coniferous forests and mountainous regions, as well as bogs and muskegs at lower elevations. Once you hear the song, look for an olive-vested songbird perched high atop a bare branch at the edge of a woodland. Then, watch as it quickly flies out to snatch flying insects in midair before returning to its original perch. • This species is such a late spring arrival that ornithologists once thought it bred in Illinois. • The Olive-sided Flycatcher winters in mountainous regions from southern Mexico to South America. Since 1966, the Olive-sided Flycatcher population has declined by 67 percent, likely a result of deforestation in its Andean wintering range, although land practices on its breeding grounds may also play a role.

ID: dark olive gray "vest"; light throat and belly; olive gray to olive brown upperparts; white tufts on sides of rump; dark upper mandible; dull yellow orange base to lower mandible; inconspicuous eye ring.
Size: *L* 7–8 in; *W* 13 in.
Status: uncommon migrant from mid- to late May through mid-June and from early to mid-August through late September.
Habitat: high, open perches in woodlands and woodland edges; often in large snags.
Nesting: does not nest in Illinois.

Feeding: flycatches insects from a perch; eats winged insects, such as beetles, butterflies, moths and gadflies.
Voice: *Male:* lively *quick-three-beers,* with the 2nd note highest in pitch; descending *pip-pip-pip.*
Similar Species: *Eastern Wood-Pewee* (p. 207): smaller; lacks white rump tufts; gray breast; 2 faint wing bars. *Eastern Phoebe* (p. 213): smaller; lacks white rump tufts; all-dark bill; often wags its tail. *Eastern Kingbird* (p. 216): lacks white rump tufts; all-dark bill; white-tipped tail.
Best Sites: woodland edges with snags near water.

EASTERN WOOD-PEWEE
Contopus virens

Perched on an exposed tree branch in a suburban park or woodlot edge, the male Eastern Wood-Pewee whistles his plaintive *pee-ah-wee pee-oh* all day long, even on the hottest days throughout the summer. Some males will even sing late into the evening, long after most birds have become quiet. European Starlings are particularly adept at imitating the pewee's song. • Like other flycatchers, the Eastern Wood-Pewee flies out from exposed perches to snatch flying insects in midair, a technique referred to as "hawking." • Males fight quite vociferously during mating season, hovering in a clearing, then chasing one another with squeaking sounds, until one bird lands on a perch to rest. • This bird's well-camouflaged nest looks like a knot on a horizontal, dead tree branch. • At the nest site, Eastern Wood-Pewees will drive away gray squirrels and birds larger than themselves, particularly Blue Jays, Acadian Flycatchers, Common Grackles and American Robins. • Pewees winter in Central and South America.

ID: olive gray to olive brown upperparts; 2 narrow, white wing bars; whitish throat; gray breast and sides; whitish or pale yellow belly, flanks and undertail coverts; dark upper mandible; dull yellow orange base to lower mandible; weak eye ring.
Size: *L* 6–6½ in; *W* 10 in.
Status: common migrant and breeder; migrants occur from late April or early May through early to mid-June and from September to mid-October.
Habitat: all forested areas.
Nesting: on a horizontal deciduous branch well away from the trunk; open cup of grass, plant fibers, and lichen, bound with spiderwebs; female incubates 3 darkly blotched, whitish eggs for 12–13 days; rarely parasitized by Brown-headed Cowbird.

Feeding: flycatches insects from a perch; may also glean insects from foliage, especially while hovering; eats mainly flies, gnats and small beetles.
Voice: a *chip* call. *Male:* clear, slow, plaintive *pee-ah-wee,* with the 2nd note lower, sometimes followed by a downslurred *pee-oh,* given with or without intermittent pauses; different early morning and twilight song with rising inflections: *ahhhh-dih-dee.*
Similar Species: *Olive-sided Flycatcher* (p. 206): larger; white rump tufts; olive gray "vest"; lacks conspicuous white wing bars. *Eastern Phoebe* (p. 213): all-dark bill; lacks conspicuous white wing bars; often pumps its tail. *Eastern Kingbird* (p. 216): larger; black head; white-tipped tail; brighter white underparts; all-dark bill. Empidonax *flycatchers* (pp. 208–12): smaller; more conspicuous wing bars; eye rings.
Best Sites: widespread in all forested habitat.

YELLOW-BELLIED FLYCATCHER

Empidonax flaviventris

In late spring and early summer, the Yellow-bellied Flycatcher, on the way to its northern boreal forest breeding grounds, passes through Illinois almost unnoticed. It is much more common than birders realize, but because of its secretive habits and soft, subtle vocalizations, it can be more difficult to find than the other flycatchers. Its song somewhat resembles and may be mistaken for that of the Least Flycatcher or the Eastern Wood-Pewee. Listen for a *che-bunk* or soft, liquid *per-wee* in late spring to locate the Yellow-bellied Flycatcher. • Illinois offers fine opportunities for birders to develop their *Empidonax* flycatcher identification skills. Key identification clues include yellow undersides and a yellow eye ring. • Unlike its brethren, this flycatcher avoids perching in the open, preferring to remain well concealed in dense tangles. • Because its nest is sunk in moist habitat and very difficult to find, little is known about this species' nesting habits. No other North American flycatcher species nests on the ground. • As it flies from perch to perch, the Yellow-bellied Flycatcher quickly lowers and raises its wings and tail. • The Yellow-bellied Flycatcher winters in eastern Mexico and Central America.

ID: olive green upperparts; 2 whitish wing bars; yellowish eye ring; white throat; yellow underparts; pale olive breast. *Juvenile:* buff wing bars.
Size: *L* 5–6 in; *W* 8 in.
Status: uncommon to locally common migrant from mid-May to mid-June and from mid-August to late September; a few linger into October.
Habitat: dense woodlands, especially wet woods.
Nesting: does not nest in Illinois.
Feeding: flycatches for insects at low to middle levels of the forest; gleans vegetation for larval and adult inverte-

brates while hovering; diet consists of ants, spiders, beetles, bees, wasps, butterflies and caterpillars.
Voice: calls include a chipper *pe-wheep, preee, pur-wee* or *killik;* also, a soft, flat *che-bunk.*
Similar Species: *Acadian* (p. 209), *Willow* (p. 211), *Alder* (p. 210) and *Least* (p. 212) *flycatchers:* white eye rings; all lack extensive yellow wash from throat to belly; different songs; all but the Acadian have browner upperparts. *Acadian Flycatcher* (p. 209): juvenile has buff wing bars like Yellow-bellied, but is not as yellowish underneath.
Best Sites: dense, wet woodlands in spring.

ACADIAN FLYCATCHER

Empidonax virescens

One of the keys to identifying a flycatcher is to listen for its distinctive song. The Acadian Flycatcher's signature song is a quick, forceful *peet-sa* or *pizza*, as some birders say. • Learning to identify this bird is only half the fun. Its speedy aerial courtship chases and the male's hovering flight displays are sights to behold. • Maple and beech trees provide preferred nesting sites for the Acadian Flycatcher in Illinois. The female builds the nest on a horizontal branch 6 to 30 feet above the ground, using loose material that often dangles from the nest, giving it a sloppy appearance. This species often builds its nest over streambeds, trails and even paved roads through forests. • Flycatchers are members of the family Tyrannidae or "Tyrant Flycatchers," so named because of their feisty, aggressive behavior.

ID: narrow, yellowish eye ring; 2 buff to yellowish wing bars; large bill has dark upper mandible and pinkish yellow lower mandible; white throat; faint olive yellow breast; yellow belly and undertail coverts; olive green upperparts; very long primaries. *Immature:* greenish head and back have buff edges, creating a "scaly" effect; yellow wash on underparts may extend onto throat.
Size: *L* 5½–6 in; *W* 9 in.
Status: common to abundant migrant and breeder in southern Illinois, decreasing northward; migrants occur from late April through early June and from mid-August to late September.
Habitat: mature deciduous uplands, riparian woodlands and bottomland swamps.
Nesting: in a beech or maple tree; female builds a loose, sloppy-looking cup nest with vegetation and spider silk; female incubates 3 brown spotted, creamy white eggs

for 13–15 days; both adults raise the young; occasionally parasitized by the Brown-headed Cowbird.
Feeding: forages by hawking or gleaning while hovering; takes insects and insect larvae including wasps, bees, spiders and ants; may also eat berries and small fruits.
Voice: best identified by its forceful *peet-sa* or *pizza* song; call is a softer *peet;* may issue a loud, flickerlike *ti-ti-ti-ti-ti* during the breeding season.
Similar Species: *Alder Flycatcher* (p. 210): narrower, white eye ring is often inconspicuous; browner overall; smaller head relative to its body; song is *fee-bee-o*. *Willow Flycatcher* (p. 211): browner overall; smaller head; very faint eye ring; song is an explosive *fitz-bew*. *Least Flycatcher* (p. 212): prominent, white eye ring; rounded head; shorter wings; song is a clear *che-bek*. *Yellow-bellied Flycatcher* (p. 208): yellow wash from throat to belly; song is a liquid *che-bunk* or *per-wee*.
Best Sites: Mississippi Palisades SP; Starved Rock SP; Fox Ridge SP; Siloam Springs SP; Shawnee NF; Cache River Biosphere Reserve.

ALDER FLYCATCHER

Empidonax alnorum

The Alder Flycatcher is virtually indistinguishable from other *Empidonax* fly-catchers until it opens its small, bicolored beak and utters a hearty *fee-bee-o* to reveal its identity. • This bird is well named because it is often found in alder and dogwood thickets, which can be important in its identification. The Alder Flycatcher is thought to breed in very small numbers in extreme northern Illinois, however, it has yet to be confirmed as a breeder here. • Many young birds must learn their songs and calls, but Alder Flycatchers instinctively know the simple phrase of their species. Even if a young bird is isolated from other Alders, it can produce its *fee-bee-o* call when it matures. • The Willow Flycatcher is a very close relative of the Alder Flycatcher and, until 1973, these two species were grouped together as a single species known as "Traill's Flycatcher." The Alder breeds farther north than the Willow and it builds its nest substantially lower, on average. • The Alder Flycatcher's scientific name *alnorum* is Latin and means "of the alders."

ID: olive brown upper-parts; 2 dull white to buff wing bars; faint, whitish eye ring; dark upper mandible; orange lower mandible; long tail; white throat; pale olive breast; pale yellowish belly.
Size: *L* 5½–6 in; *W* 8½ in.
Status: fairly common migrant from mid- to late May into mid-June and from late August through a few days of October; possibly very rare breeder; records exist for July.
Habitat: *Breeding:* alder, willow or dogwood thickets almost always near water, often in wetter areas than Willow Flycatcher. *In migration:* shrubby fields near upland woods.
Nesting: in a dense bush or shrub, usually less than 3 ft above the ground; small cup nest is loosely woven from plant materials, often up to several inches deep; female incubates 3–4 darkly spotted, white eggs for 12–14 days; both adults feed the young.
Feeding: flycatches from a perch for beetles, bees, wasps, aphids and other flying

insects; also eats spiders, moths, caterpillars, berries and seeds.
Voice: song is *fee-bee-o;* call is a *pit.*
Similar Species: *Eastern Wood-Pewee* (p. 207): found in woodlands; larger; darker overall; lacks eye ring and conspicuous wing bars. *Least Flycatcher* (p. 212): found in woodlands; bolder, white eye ring; greener upperparts; pale gray white underparts; song is a clear *che-bek. Acadian Flycatcher* (p. 209): found in woodlands; yellowish eye ring; greener upperparts; yellower underparts; song is a forceful *peet-sa* or *pizza. Yellow-bellied Flycatcher* (p. 208): found in woodlands; yellowish eye ring; greener upperparts; yellower underparts; song is a liquid *che-bunk* or *perwee. Willow Flycatcher* (p. 211): virtually identical; best identified by *fitz-bew* song.
Best Sites: common in appropriate habitat statewide. *Summer:* Volo Bog; Illinois Beach SP; Plum Creek FP.

WILLOW FLYCATCHER

Empidonax traillii

Upon arriving in a suitable shrubby area with thick willows and tangled shrubbery, male Willow Flycatchers utter their characteristic, sneezing *fitz-bew* call to battle vocally over preferred territories. Although closely related and very similar to the Alder Flycatcher, no hybridization between these two species has been documented. • The Willow Flycatcher's cup-shaped nest resembles that of a Yellow Warbler, which often shares similar breeding and feeding habitat. • Populations of the southwestern subspecies, *E. t. extimus*, found in Illinois, have declined dramatically; it has almost been extirpated from portions of its range in Arizona and California. This subspecies was placed on the federally endangered species list in 1995. • Willow Flycatchers winter from Mexico to northern South America.

ID: olive brown upper parts; 2 whitish wing bars; no eye ring; white throat; yellowish belly; pale olive breast.
Size: *L* 5½–6 in; *W* 8½ in.
Status: common migrant from early to mid- May (a week or so before Alder Flycatcher) to early June and from late August to first few days of October; relatively common breeder, decreasing southward.
Habitat: shrubby areas, usually along streams or near ponds, often containing dogwood and willow; also in dry, overgrown fields and pastures.
Nesting: in a dense shrub, usually 3–7 ft above the ground; female builds an open cup nest with grass, bark strips and plant fibers and lines it with down; female incubates 3–4 brown-spotted, whitish to pale buff eggs for 12–15 days; rarely parasitized by the Brown-headed Cowbird.

Feeding: flycatches insects; also gleans insects from vegetation, usually while hovering.
Voice: call is a quick *whit. Male:* quick, sneezy *fitz-bew* that drops off at the end, repeated up to 30 times a minute.
Similar Species: *Eastern Wood-Pewee* (p. 207): larger; lacks eye ring and conspicuous wing bars. *Least Flycatcher* (p. 212): bolder, white eye ring; greener upperparts; pale gray white underparts; song is a clear *che-bek. Acadian Flycatcher* (p. 209): yellowish eye ring; greener upperparts; yellower underparts; song is a forceful *peet-sa. Yellow-bellied Flycatcher* (p. 208): yellowish eye ring; greener upperparts; yellower underparts; song is a liquid *che-bunk* or *perwee. Alder Flycatcher* (p. 210): virtually identical; best identified by 3-syllable *fee-bee-o* song.
Best Sites: *Summer:* L. Calumet; Shabbona Lake SP; Iroquois County CA; Pyramid Lake SP.

LEAST FLYCATCHER

Empidonax minimus

Usually the first "empid" to arrive in Illinois in spring, the Least Flycatcher gives its two-part *che-bek* call to signal its arrival. Intense song battles normally eliminate the need for physical aggression, but feather-flying fights are occasionally required to settle disputes over territory and courtship privileges. • The Least Flycatcher is the most common and widespread *Empidonax* flycatcher in Illinois. • This bird may have been more common historically as an Illinois breeder before open oak woodlands became overgrown and degraded. These birds often fall victim to nest parasitism by the Brown-headed Cowbird, whose hatched young often smother the much smaller Least Flycatcher nestlings. • *Empidonax* flycatchers are aptly named: the literal translation is "mosquito king" and refers to their insect-hunting prowess.

ID: olive brown upperparts; 2 white wing bars; bold, white eye ring; fairly long, narrow tail; mostly dark bill has yellow orange lower base; white throat; gray breast; gray white to yellowish belly and undertail coverts.
Size: *L* 4½–6 in; *W* 7½ in.
Status: common migrant from late April to early to mid-June and from mid-August to early October; rare breeder in northern and, occasionally, central Illinois.
Habitat: *Breeding:* open deciduous or mixed woodlands; forest openings and edges; often in second-growth woodlands and occasionally near human habitation. *In migration:* most types of woodlands and shrublands.
Nesting: in a small tree or shrub, commonly 15–40 ft above the ground; female builds a small cup nest with plant fibers and bark and lines it with fine grass, plant down and feathers; female incubates 4

creamy white eggs for 13–15 days; both adults feed the young.
Feeding: flycatches bees, wasps, moths and butterflies; gleans trees and shrubs for insects while hovering; also eats some fruit and seeds.
Voice: constantly repeated, dry *che-bek*.
Similar Species: *Eastern Wood-Pewee* (p. 207): larger; lacks eye ring and conspicuous wing bars. *Alder Flycatcher* (p. 210): faint eye ring; usually found in wetter areas; song is *fee-bee-o*. *Willow Flycatcher* (p. 211): lacks eye ring; greener upperparts; yellower underparts; song is *fitz-bew*. *Acadian Flycatcher* (p. 209): yellowish eye ring; greener upperparts; yellower underparts; song is *peet-sa* or *pizza*. *Yellow-bellied Flycatcher* (p. 208): yellowish eye ring; greener upperparts; yellower underparts; song is a liquid *che-bunk* or *perwee*.
Best Sites: *Summer:* Lowden-Miller SF and Castle Rock SP. *In migration:* woodlands and shrublands.

EASTERN PHOEBE

Sayornis phoebe

The first of the flycatchers to arrive in Illinois in spring, the Eastern Phoebe has even begun to overwinter in very small numbers in the southern part of the state. By mid- to late March, even the phoebes in northern Illinois are defending territory with their two-syllable *phoebe* song and the constant pumping of their tails. Once limited to nesting on natural cliffs and fallen riparian trees, this flycatcher has adapted to nesting on buildings and bridges, typically near water. Some can still be found nesting on cliffs in southern Illinois. • Though the Eastern Phoebe is mostly insectivorous, like its other flycatching cousins, it can survive on fruit and even small fishes from shallow water. • Since Eastern Phoebes winter farther north than most other North American flycatchers, they may have periodic population setbacks, as many birds perish during severe weather.

ID: gray brown upperparts; white underparts with gray wash on breast and sides; belly may be washed with yellow in fall; no eye ring; no obvious wing bars; all-black bill; dark legs; frequently pumps its tail.
Size: *L* 6½–7 in; *W* 10½ in.

Status: common migrant and breeder; migrants arrive in March and depart by mid-May; fall migrants occur from late August to early November, with some lingering into Christmas bird count season; rare but regular winter resident in the south.

Habitat: open deciduous woodlands, forest edges and clearings; usually near water; often near bridges.

Nesting: under the ledge of a building, picnic shelter, shed, outhouse, culvert, bridge, cliff or well; nests both inside and outside buildings; may use an old Barn Swallow nest; cup-shaped mud nest is lined with moss, grass, fur and feathers; female incubates 4–5 white eggs for 14–16 days; both adults feed the young; often has 2 broods, which is rare in Illinois for flycatchers; frequently parasitized by Brown-headed Cowbird.

Feeding: flycatches flying beetles, flies, wasps, grasshoppers, mayflies, airborne spiders and other insects; plucks aquatic invertebrates and small fish from the water's surface.

Voice: loud, buzzy, repeated *fee-bee,* the 2nd syllable lower in pitch; call is a distinctive, flat *chip.*

Similar Species: *Eastern Wood-Pewee* (p. 207): pale wing bars; bicolored bill; rarely pumps its tail. *Olive-sided Flycatcher* (p. 206): less common; later spring migrant; larger; dark "vest"; white, fluffy patches border rump. *Empidonax flycatchers* (pp. 208–12): most have eye ring and conspicuous wing bars. *Eastern Kingbird* (p. 216): white-tipped tail; black upperparts.

Best Sites: abundant at Trail of Tears SF and Giant City SP.

GREAT CRESTED FLYCATCHER
Myiarchus crinitus

Unlike most other flycatchers, the Great Crested Flycatcher nests in natural tree cavities, abandoned woodpecker nests and sometimes even in nest boxes intended for bluebirds. It often outcompetes the Northern Flicker and Red-headed Woodpecker for nest sites, but is no match for the nonnative European Starling. • Often, this large flycatcher decorates the entrance of its nest with a shed snakeskin, translucent plastic wrap or even onion skin. Its sharp *wheeep* whistle is a distinct sound of Illinois forests in summer. • This flycatcher is a subtropical or tropical bird of Central and South America that visits North America only briefly to raise its young before returning home. It is the only regularly occurring *Myiarchus* flycatcher east of the Mississippi River. • The Great Crested Flycatcher spends a lot of time in the forest canopy and seems to slip away unnoticed during fall migration.

ID: bright yellow belly and undertail coverts; gray throat, back and upper breast; some reddish brown in tail and wing; large, gray, peaked, "crested" head; dark olive brown upperparts; heavy, large, black bill.
Size: *L* 8–9 in; *W* 13 in.

Status: common migrant and breeder; migrants occur from mid-April to late May; fall migrants difficult to detect, but typically occur from late August to early October.
Habitat: mature deciduous forests in upland and bottomland woods; needs open areas for sallying.
Nesting: in a tree cavity, nest box or other artificial cavity; nest is often lined with grass, bark strips, fur and feathers; female

incubates 5 creamy white to pale buff eggs, marked with lavender, olive and brown for 13–15 days; rarely parasitized by Brown-headed Cowbird.
Feeding: often flycatches in the upper branches of deciduous trees; eats flying insects such as bees, wasps, butterflies, moths and cicadas; also eats crickets, caterpillars and occasionally fruit.
Voice: loud, whistled *wheep!* and a rolling *prrrrreet!*
Similar Species: *Eastern Kingbird* (p. 216): black head with no crest; all-dark back; white at tail tip. *Western Kingbird* (p. 215): very rare; all-gray head, neck and breast; darker tail with white outer margins; lacks head crest.
Best Sites: *Summer:* Palos Preserves; Lost Mound NWR; Kankakee River SP; Sanganois CA; Shawnee NF; Cache River Biosphere Reserve.

WESTERN KINGBIRD

Tyrannus verticalis

A bird of the western prairies, the Western Kingbird is a rare but regular visitor and breeder in Illinois and has been recorded statewide. During the 20th century, this species expanded its range eastward and has nested near East St. Louis since the mid-1980s. • The Western Kingbird sits on fence posts, power lines or utility poles to scout for prey. When a kingbird spots an insect, it may chase it for up to 50 feet before capturing it. • Once you have witnessed the kingbird's brave attacks against much larger birds, you'll understand why this bird was awarded the name "kingbird." Its scientific name *verticalis* refers to its hidden, red crown patch, which is flared during courtship displays and while in combat with rivals. This red patch, however, is not a good field mark because it is rarely visible. • The Western Kingbird performs a tumbling, aerial courtship display. The male twists and turns as he rises to heights of 65 feet above the ground, then stalls before tumbling, flipping and twisting his way back to earth.

ID: gray head and breast; yellow belly and undertail coverts; black tail; white edge to outer tail feathers; white "chin"; black bill; ashy gray upperparts; faint, dark gray "mask"; thin, orange red crown is rarely seen.
Size: *L* 8–9 in; *W* 15½ in.

Status: rare migrant and local breeder; migrants occur from early May to early June and from early August to early October; breeding birds disappear the first week in August and the first migrants appear.
Habitat: open areas with scattered trees or tree rows; often feeds from utility lines along roadsides.
Nesting: near the trunk of a deciduous tree; often in a power line transformer; bulky cup nest of grass, weeds and twigs is lined with fur, plant down and feathers; female incubates 3–5 whitish, heavily blotched eggs for 18–19 days.
Feeding: sallies out to catch flying insects, including bees, wasps, butterflies, moths and flies; also eats grasshoppers, caterpillars, crickets and spiders; occasionally eats berries.
Voice: chatty, twittering *whit-ker-whit;* also a short *kit* or extended *kit-kit-keetle-dot.*
Similar Species: *Eastern Kingbird* (p. 216): much more common; black upperparts; white underparts; white-tipped tail. *Great Crested Flycatcher* (p. 214): much more common; slightly crested head; brownish upperparts; reddish brown tail and primaries; yellowish wing bars; lacks white edges to outer tail feathers.
Best Sites: *Summer:* towns of East St. Louis and Granite City in discrete locations near the Mississippi R; also on golf course in Springfield.

EASTERN KINGBIRD

Tyrannus tyrannus

Although it is named "Eastern Kingbird," this species has the most extensive breeding range of any North American flycatcher, reaching to the Pacific Coast. • The Eastern Kingbird attacks crows, hawks, vultures and even humans that come too close to its territory. Males vigorously pursue intruders, pecking and plucking feathers or fur from them. While intolerant of most species, the kingbird often allows Baltimore Orioles and Orchard Orioles to nest in the same tree. • In spring and again in fall, you may find loose flocks of 20 to 30 birds in scattered locations. • While migrating to and from their Central and South American wintering areas, Eastern Kingbirds mix with flocks of Scissor-tailed Flycatchers and Western Kingbirds. Though many songbirds migrate at night, kingbirds and other related species often migrate during the day.

ID: dark gray to black upperparts; white underparts; white-tipped tail; black bill; small head crest; thin, orange red crown patch is rarely seen; no eye ring; black legs.
Size: L 8½ in; W 15 in.
Status: common migrant and breeder from mid-April to late May and from mid-August to late September.
Habitat: *Breeding:* rural fields and pastures with scattered, tall trees or hedgerows, parks, open roadsides, burned areas and near human settlements. *In migration:* flocks perch on corn stubble stalks in fields or in tops of tall trees in forested areas.
Nesting: usually well out on a horizontal tree limb 15–50 ft high; often near water; pair builds a bulky cup nest of weeds, twigs and grass and lines it with root fibers, fine grass and fur; female incubates

3–4 darkly blotched, white to pinkish white eggs for 14–18 days; rarely parasitized by Brown-headed Cowbird.
Feeding: hovers low to ground before dropping on prey; sallies out from an exposed perch or flycatches; eats over 200 kinds of insects; hovers above shrubs or trees to pick berries, including sassafras.
Voice: call is a quick, loud, chattering *kit-kit-kitter-kitter;* also a very rapid, sputtering, buzzy *dzee-dzee-dzee,* often repeated several times.
Similar Species: *Olive-sided Flycatcher* (p. 206): 2 white tufts above rump; lacks white-tipped tail and all-white underparts. *Eastern Wood-Pewee* (p. 207): found in less open, forested habitats; smaller; bicolored bill; lacks white-tipped tail and all-white underparts. *Western Kingbird* (p. 215): rare; yellow belly and undertail coverts; white edges to outer tail feathers; lacks white-tipped tail.
Best Sites: statewide in open habitats with scattered trees.

SCISSOR-TAILED FLYCATCHER
Tyrannus forficatus

Endowed with the refined, long tail feathers of a tropical bird of paradise, the Scissor-tailed Flycatcher remains one of the top birds on most "must-see" lists. Once a rare vagrant in Illinois, this bird is now seen every year, often in both spring and fall, with at least 85 existing records dating back to 1865. To the delight of Illinois birders, this species could be expanding its breeding range northeastward. The Scissor-tailed Flycatcher has recently been documented as a breeder in the southwestern edge of the state near the Mississippi River. In 2001, a pair of birds nested in a large, lone pecan tree near the Union County Conservation Area. • The Scissor-tailed Flycatcher gets its name from the male's habit of opening and closing the gap between its long tail feathers during its roller-coaster courtship flight, which often includes backward somersaults. Like its close kingbird relatives, this bird aggressively defends its nest, giving shrill, piercing calls and attacking much larger birds such as jays, crows and hawks.

VAGRANT

Habitat: open, grassy areas with scattered trees and shrubs.

Nesting: in a tree or shrub or on a utility pole; female builds a bulky, messy nest cup of twigs, vegetation and animal hair; female incubates eggs; both adults raise the young.

ID: dark wings; extremely long outer tail feathers give forked appearance in flight; female's tail about one third as long as male's; whitish to grayish head, back and breast; salmon pink underwing linings, flanks and lower underparts; bright pink "wing pits." *Immature:* duller, shorter-tailed version of adult with brownish back.

Size: *L* 10–15 in; *W* 15 in.

Status: very rare migrant and breeder; migrants occur from mid-April to early June and from mid-August to late October.

Feeding: typically catches insects by hawking; may also catch insects on the ground, in flight or by gleaning from foliage while hovering; eats mainly grasshoppers, beetles and crickets; also takes bees, wasps, moths, dragonflies and occasionally small fruits.

Voice: calls include a repeated *ka-leap* and a sharp, harsh *kek*.

Similar Species: none in Illinois.

Best Sites: *Summer:* Randolph Co., Monroe Co. and Union Co., especially along Mississippi R. levee roads.

LOGGERHEAD SHRIKE
Lanius ludovicianus

The "Butcher Bird" resembles a Northern Mockingbird in body shape and color, but the Loggerhead's method of hunting is quite different. This shrike interacts with many species in its habitat, dominating aggressive species such as kingbirds and mockingbirds. Males also display their hunting prowess by impaling prey on thorns or barbed wire. This behavior also serves as a means of storing excess food items. Mockingbirds, caracaras and Burrowing Owls have been known to steal from the shrike's caches of food. • Populations of the Loggerhead Shrike, as well as other shrike species worldwide, have declined drastically. Reasons include pesticide use in Illinois in the 1950s and earlier, and loss and degradation of thorny shrubs, especially the introduced osage orange. Also, habitat loss on the bird's wintering grounds in the southern United States may be contributing to its decreased numbers.

ID: black tail and wings; black bill; gray crown and back; white underparts; wide, black "mask" extends above hooked bill onto forehead. *Juvenile:* brownish gray, barred upperparts. *In flight:* white wing patches; white-edged tail; undulating flight with rapid wingbeats and sailing; usually swoops upward to perch.
Size: *L* 9 in; *W* 12 in.
Status: state-threatened; uncommon year-round resident in southern Illinois; uncommon migrant; rare breeder (formerly common) in eastern part of central and northern Illinois; arrives mid- to late March and departs by mid- to late October, with some stragglers in November; very rare winter resident in central and northern Illinois.
Habitat: grazed pastures and marginal and abandoned farmlands with scattered hawthorn shrubs, osage orange hedgerows, fence posts and barbed wire fences.
Nesting: low in a thorny shrub or small tree; bulky cup nest of large twigs is lined with animal hair, feathers, plant down and rootlets; female incubates 5–6 darkly spotted, pale buff to grayish white eggs for 15–17 days; nesting may begin late March or early April.
Feeding: swoops down on prey or attacks in pursuit; follows farmers plowing their fields; takes mostly spiders and large insects, including beetles and grasshoppers; regularly eats rodents, shrews and small birds, such as House Sparrows and Dark-eyed Juncos; also eats carrion, small snakes and amphibians.
Voice: *Male:* liquid trill; also clear, musical notes; infrequently a harsh *shack-shack* year-round.
Similar Species: *Northern Shrike* (p. 219): usually darker gray overall; longer, more hooked bill; paler lower mandible, especially on juvenile; fine barring on sides and breast; black "mask" does not extend above hooked bill. *Northern Mockingbird* (p. 261): slimmer overall; slim bill with no hook; no "mask"; paler wings and longer tail; larger white wing patch; yellow eyes; different flight pattern.
Best Sites: Midewin National Tallgrass Prairie; Lost Mound NWR; Prairie Ridge SNA; Cypress Creek NWR; southeastern Illinois, especially Pope Co., Hardin Co. and Gallatin Co.

NORTHERN SHRIKE

Lanius excubitor

L ike the Snowy Owl and other birds of prey, the Northern Shrike appears in Illinois each winter in unpredictable and highly variable numbers. Research shows that Northern Shrikes in the eastern United States appear in large numbers on roughly eight-year cycles. One of the largest incursions in Illinois occurred in the 1999–2000 winter season, when 105 Northern Shrikes were seen in 32 counties. • Northern Shrikes occupy large territories during the breeding and winter seasons; one shrike had at least a 2½-square-mile territory. • Shrikes possess extremely acute vision. One trained bird spotted flying bumblebees at least 100 yards away. • The Northern Shrike's habit of impaling its prey on thorns and barbs has earned it the name "Butcher Bird." A shrike may gulp down prey whole and then later disgorge pellets containing indigestible food parts such as matted feathers and small pieces of bone. Northern Shrikes have also been documented killing other birds for pure sport, with no intention of eating them.

ID: dark gray overall; black tail and wings; pale lower mandible, especially on juvenile; pale gray upperparts; finely barred, light underparts; black "mask" does not extend above hooked bill. *Juvenile:* faint "mask"; light brown upperparts; brown or gray barring on underparts. *In flight:* white wing patches; white-edged tail; undulating flight with periods of rapid wingbeats and sailing; usually swoops upwards to perch.
Size: *L* 10 in; *W* 14½ in.
Status: very rare to uncommon winter resident in northern and central Illinois, extremely rare to absent in southern Illinois; arrives in mid- to late October, departs by mid- to late March.
Habitat: large, open grassy areas with scattered trees and bushes, often near marshes or wet, grassy areas.
Nesting: does not nest in Illinois.

Feeding: swoops down on prey or chases prey through the air; may also hover or walk around bushes flashing its white wing patches to scare out prey; regularly eats small birds, shrews and large insects; may also take carrion, snakes, frogs, large beetles and grasshoppers.
Voice: song, sometimes heard in winter, includes *caws, mews,* scraping notes, liquid trills and whistles of various lengths.
Similar Species: *Loggerhead Shrike* (p. 218): shorter bill with less-hooked tip; "mask" is wider and extends above eye and bill onto forehead; lacks barring on underparts; juvenile has barred underparts, crown and back. *Northern Mockingbird* (p. 261): more common; slimmer overall; slim bill with no hook; no "mask"; paler wings and longer tail; larger, white wing patch; yellow eyes; different flight pattern.
Best Sites: Illinois Beach SP; Paul Douglas FP; Greene Valley FP; Goose Lake Prairie SNA; Midewin National Tallgrass Prairie; Clinton L.

WHITE-EYED VIREO

Vireo griseus

L ike most vireo species, the White-eyed Vireo can be a challenge to spot as it sneaks through dense tangles of branches and foliage searching for insects. • Even more secretive than the bird itself is the location of its nest. Intricately woven from grass, twigs, bark, lichens, moss, plant down, leaves and the fibrous paper from a wasp nest, the vireo's nest is hung between the forking branches of a tree sapling or shrub. Both parents remain near the nest even when approached closely. • A single White-eyed Vireo can have a repertoire of a dozen or more songs and might also mimic the calls of other bird species. Its variable songs ring in spring, summer and even in September in southern Illinois. • As this bird's name implies, the iris of the adult bird's eye is white; however, it is brown in the immature bird.

ID: yellow "spectacles"; olive gray upperparts; white underparts with yellow sides and flanks; 2 whitish wing bars; dark wings and tail; blue gray legs; white iris; juvenile has dark eyes.

Size: *L* 5 in; *W* 7½ in.

Status: common migrant from early April to late May and from early September to early October, with a few lingering into November and December; common breeder, decreasing northward.

Habitat: dense shrubby undergrowth and thickets in open, swampy or wet deciduous woodlands, overgrown fields, young, second-growth woodlands, woodland clearings and along woodlot edges.

Nesting: in a deciduous shrub, often a viburnum, or small tree; cup nest made mainly of strips of inner bark and grasses hangs from a horizontal fork; pair incubates 4 lightly speckled, white eggs, laid as early as late April, for 13–15 days; both adults feed the young; frequently parasitized by Brown-headed Cowbird.

Feeding: gleans insects, including caterpillars, butterflies, bees, wasps and flies from branches and foliage; often hovers while gleaning.

Voice: loud, variable 3–9-note song, usually beginning and ending with *quick* or *pick: pick-up-your-beer-check-quick.*

Similar Species: *Pine Warbler* (p. 281): thinner bill; yellow throat; dark eyes; olive streaks on flanks; white in outer tail feathers. *Yellow-throated Vireo* (p. 222): bright yellow throat and breast. *Blue-headed Vireo* (p. 223): much grayer overall, especially on head; very little yellow tone; white "spectacles"; dark eyes.

Best Sites: Forest Glen Preserve; Fox Ridge SP; Shawnee NF; Giant City SP; Cache River Biosphere Reserve.

BELL'S VIREO
Vireo bellii

The Bell's Vireo can easily be mistaken for a number of other vireos, especially the Warbling Vireo, and a few warblers with similar, subtle colors and markings. These tough-to-spot songsters will boldly sing right near their nest; males may even sing while incubating eggs. The call of the Bell's Vireo is distinctive and much less musical than that of other vireos. • Like other vireos, the Bell's has a slight hook at the tip of a flattened bill, probably designed for easier feeding. • Illinois lies near the northeastern edge of this species' breeding range. The Bell's Vireo population decline is widespread—formerly unmanaged orchard habitat along with increased pesticide use has limited the number of nesting sites available in Illinois for this and many other species. The Bell's Vireo is mostly absent from northeastern Illinois. • The western form of the Bell's Vireo is much grayer than the eastern form found in Illinois. One subspecies, the Least Bell's Vireo, was recently designated as a federally endangered species.

ID: gray to green upperparts; white to yellow underparts; 2 white wing bars, upper bar is usually faint if present; whitish "eyebrow"; whitish eye ring or whitish lores or both; blue gray legs. *Eastern Midwest species:* olive green upperparts; yellow underparts.
Size: *L* 4½ –5 in; *W* 7 in.
Status: rare migrant; uncommon to locally common breeder; occurs from late April to mid- to late September.
Habitat: brushy fields, second-growth scrub; hedgerows; favors reclaimed strip mine areas and gravel pits, especially with dense growth of introduced autumn olive; preferred native species include hazel, dogwood and wild plum.
Nesting: male builds dummy nests; female builds small hanging cup of woven vegetation suspended along the outer edge of a shrub, usually within 6 ft or less of the ground and well concealed from above; pair incubates 3–5 darkly dotted, white eggs, for about 14 days; both adults feed

the young; heavily parasitized by Brown-headed Cowbird.
Feeding: gleans insects from foliage by hawking or hovering; also eats spiders and some berries.
Voice: song is a distinctive, rapid, nonmusical, short series of harsh notes, increasing in volume and often ending with an upward or downward inflection on the last note: *chu-chee-chu-chee-chu-chee-chu-chi-chi-chee-chu.*
Similar Species: *Tennessee Warbler* (p. 268): whitish line above eye; bright, green back; breeding birds lack yellow wash on flanks; black legs; slimmer, bill lacks hook on tip. *Pine Warbler* (p. 281): more robust; yellow throat and breast; blurry streaks on sides and breast; yellow "spectacles"; no hook on bill; pale legs; 2 bold wing bars; white in outer tail feathers. *Ruby-crowned Kinglet* (p. 250): uniformly colored; tiny bill; white eye ring; yellow feet on black legs; frequently hovers.
Best Sites: Midewin National Tallgrass Prairie; Pyramid Lake SP; L. Shelbyville; Prairie Ridge SNA.

221

YELLOW-THROATED VIREO

Vireo flavifrons

The Yellow-throated Vireo breeds in mature deciduous woodlands with little or no understory and favors tall oaks and maples. • Males sing their buzzy, two-syllable song that sounds like *three eight, three eight* as they search for nest sites, often placing a few pieces of nest material in several locations. When a female appears, the male leads her on a tour of potential nest sites within his large territory. If a bond is established, they will mate and build an intricately woven, hanging nest in the forking branches of a deciduous tree. A devoted helper, the male assists the female in all stages of building the nest and raising the young. Yellow-throated Vireos breed in small densities compared with other breeding vireo species in the state. • This species is one of North America's most colorful vireos. The Latin name *flavifrons* means "yellow front."

Feeding: forages by slowly and methodically inspecting branches and foliage in the upper canopy; eats mostly insects, such as butterflies, moths, leafhoppers, beetles and cicadas, but will also feed on seasonally available berries.

ID: bright yellow "spectacles," chin, throat and breast; olive upperparts, except for gray rump and dark wings and tail; 2 white wing bars; white belly and undertail coverts; blue gray legs.
Size: *L* 5½ in; *W* 9½ in.
Status: uncommon migrant and breeder; migrants occur from early April to late May and from the end of August to early October.
Habitat: mature deciduous woodlands.
Nesting: in a deciduous tree 15–60 ft above ground; pair builds a hanging cup nest of plant fibers and spider silk decorated with moss and lichens; pair incubates 4 darkly spotted, creamy white to pinkish eggs for 14–15 days; both parents raise young; commonly parasitized by Brown-headed Cowbird.

Voice: song is a series of hoarse phrases with long pauses in between: *three-eight, three-eight;* alarm call is a harsh, descending series of notes: *chi-chi-cha-cha-chu-chu-chu.*
Similar Species: *Pine Warbler* (p. 281): olive yellow rump; thinner bill; faint, darkish streaking along sides; yellow belly; fainter "spectacles" in spring plumage; pale legs; white in outer tail feathers; lacks hook on tip of bill. *White-eyed Vireo* (p. 220): usually low to ground; white "chin" and throat; grayer head and back; white eyes; yellow wash on lower flanks. *Blue-headed Vireo* (p. 223): blue gray head; white "spectacles" and throat.
Best Sites: Palos Preserves; Forest Glen Preserve; Shawnee NF; Cache River Biosphere Reserve.

BLUE-HEADED VIREO
Vireo solitarius

As the trees begin to leaf out in spring, one of the first vireos to pass through Illinois woodlands is the dapper Blue-headed Vireo. This species often sings its soft, liquid, repeated phrases during migration. The Blue-headed occurs singly during migration, but other vireos, such as the Red-eyed, may travel in groups of several to a dozen birds. In a day of birding during spring migration, you would be doing well to observe three or four Blue-headed Vireos. • Like other vireos, the Blue-headed is a slow, deliberate feeder—this characteristic, along with the slightly hooked bill, help separate vireos from warblers. • Though this bird is also found in deciduous habitats, it is the only vireo that commonly occupies coniferous forests. The few that have bred in Illinois have often chosen pine plantations. • A "tame" bird, the female Blue-headed Vireo will often allow a close approach to her nest, even sitting still as a human strokes her feathers. • Until 1997, the Blue-headed, Cassin's *(V. cassinii)* and Plumbeous *(V. plumbeus)* vireos were lumped together as one species, the Solitary Vireo.

ID: white "spectacles"; blue gray head; 2 white wing bars; olive green upperparts; white underparts; yellow sides and flanks; 2 whitish bars on dark wings; stout bill; blue gray legs. **Size:** *L* 5–6 in; *W* 9½ in.

Status: uncommon migrant; occurs from mid-April to late May and from early September to late October, with some lingering well into November; extremely rare breeder.

Habitat: *Breeding:* primarily remote, mixed coniferous-deciduous forests; also pine plantations. *In migration:* woodlands.

Nesting: in a coniferous tree or tall shrub; hanging, basketlike cup nest is made of grass, roots, plant down, spider silk and cocoons; pair incubates 3–5 lightly spotted, whitish eggs for 12–14 days; commonly parasitized by Brown-headed Cowbird.

Feeding: gleans branches for insects, including caterpillars, moths and butterflies; also eats stink bugs, beetles, wasps, ants, bees and spiders; frequently hovers to pluck insects from vegetation; also eats berries from viburnum and dogwood.

Voice: *churr* call; male has slow, purposeful, slurred, robinlike notes with moderate pauses in between: *chu-wee, taweeto, toowip, cheerio, teeyay;* similar to Red-eyed Vireo, but sweeter, slightly softer and slightly more separated phrases.

Similar Species: *White-eyed Vireo* (p. 220): yellow "spectacles"; white eyes. *Yellow-throated Vireo* (p. 222): greenish head; yellow "spectacles," throat and breast; gray rump.

Best Sites: woodlands throughout state.

WARBLING VIREO
Vireo gilvus

By early May, the Warbling Vireo's bubbling voice fills local parks, lakesides, rural backyards and woodland edges. • These drab, leafy green birds, which remain high in the trees especially during breeding season, are difficult to find. • To court a female, the male spreads his wings and tail and struts in circles around her, warbling sweetly. Like the Red-eyed Vireo, the Warbling exhibits an odd, swaying motion both during courtship and after the young are fledged. Like other vireos, the male often sings from the nest while incubating. In Illinois, this species prefers cottonwoods, silver maples and willows for both foraging and nesting.

breeding

ID: plain-looking face, sometimes with pale lores; olive gray upperparts; slightly yellowish flanks; white to pale gray underparts; gray crown; blue gray legs.
Size: *L* 5–5½ in; *W* 8½ in.
Status: common migrant and breeder; migrants occur from early to mid-April through late May, with a few lingering into June, and from late August to early October.
Habitat: open deciduous woodlands and parks and gardens with deciduous trees, especially cottonwoods and silver maples.
Nesting: in a deciduous tree or shrub, 20–90 ft above ground; hanging, basketlike cup nest is made of grass, roots, plant down, spider silk and a few feathers; pair incubates 4 darkly speckled, white eggs for 12–14 days; frequently parasitized by Brown-headed Cowbird.

Feeding: gleans foliage for insects, including caterpillars, butterflies, moths, ladybird beetles, dragonflies and ants; occasionally hovers to snatch insects from vegetation; also eats elderberries and pokeberries.
Voice: long, musical warble of slurred whistles, typically 7–25 notes; call note similar to that of Red-eyed Vireo, but has a slightly upward inflection.
Similar Species: *Bell's Vireo* (p. 221): slightly smaller; bright yellow wash to flanks; green back; 2 wing bars, usually one is faint; found low in shrubs; best identified by song. *Red-eyed Vireo* (p. 226): blue gray crown; dark stripe through red eye; green back; brighter white underparts. *Tennessee Warbler* (p. 268): slimmer, sharp-pointed bill lacks hook on tip; brighter overall; faint wing bars. *Orange-crowned Warbler* (p. 269): slimmer, sharp-pointed bill lacks hook; yellow underparts with some streaking; grayish upperparts; greenish rump; yellow undertail coverts; pale legs.
Best Sites: especially numerous along Illinois R., Mississippi R. and other large rivers.

PHILADELPHIA VIREO
Vireo philadelphicus

The Philadelphia Vireo breeds farther north than any other vireo and is one of the last to migrate through Illinois. This vireo sometimes feeds like a chickadee, hanging upside down from a cluster of leaves while picking insects. It may also forage by hover-gleaning like a kinglet. • Though the Philadelphia Vireo is the only North American vireo with a combination of no bars on its wings and yellow underparts, this bird is still easily confused with the Warbling Vireo or Red-eyed Vireo. • Like several other passerine species, including those of the vireo family, the female Philadelphia occasionally sings, especially while on the nest. • This vireo prefers various types of successional forest, both for breeding and migration. Like other small passerines, this vireo migrates at night, frequently colliding with TV towers and other tall structures. • The Philadelphia Vireo bears the name of the city in which the first specimen was collected.

breeding

ID: gray "cap"; full, dark eye line bordered by bold, white "eyebrow"; dark olive green upperparts; pale yellow breast, sides and flanks; white belly; underparts may be completely yellow in fall; blue gray legs.
Size: *L* 4½–5 in; *W* 8 in.
Status: fairly common migrant from late April to end of May and from end of August through early to mid-October.
Habitat: open broadleaf and mixed woodlands with aspen, willow and alder; second-growth on burns and cutovers; occasionally in gardens and parks.
Nesting: does not nest in Illinois.
Feeding: gleans for spiders and insects, including caterpillars, wasps, bees, flies, butterflies, moths and beetles, especially ladybird beetles; frequently hover-gleans; eats small amounts of fruit, including wild grapes and rose hips.

Voice: like that of the Red-eyed Vireo, but usually slower, softer, sweeter and not as variable: *look-up way-up tree-top see-me*.
Similar Species: *Red-eyed Vireo* (p. 226): longer, bulkier bill; blue gray "cap"; red eyes; lacks yellow breast; song is very similar. *Warbling Vireo* (p. 224): yellow restricted to flanks; longer tail; pale lores. *Tennessee Warbler* (p. 268): blue gray "cap" and nape; olive green back; slimmer, sharp-pointed bill lacks hook at tip; pale legs; faint wing bars; lacks yellow breast. *Orange-crowned Warbler* (p. 269): slimmer, sharp-pointed bill lacks hook on tip; underparts with some streaking; grayish upperparts; greenish rump; yellow undertail coverts; pale legs.
Best Sites: none.

225

RED-EYED VIREO
Vireo olivaceus

The Red-eyed Vireo is the undisputed champion of vocal endurance. In spring and early summer, males sing continuously throughout the day, carrying on long after most songbirds have curtailed their courtship melodies. One particularly vigorous Red-eyed Vireo male holds the record for the most songs delivered in a single day: approximately 22,000 in 10 hours. • The Red-eyed Vireo adopts a particular stance when feeding. It is more hunched over than other songbirds and hops with its body turned diagonally to the direction of travel. • Red-eyed Vireos are very unusual among songbirds. Red eyes tend to prevail in nonpasserines, such as accipiters and grebes. • This is the most common and widespread vireo in Illinois. The Brown-headed Cowbird frequently lays its eggs in a Red-eyed Vireo nest and the Red-eyed Vireo will often respond by either abandoning the nest or raising the cowbird young with its own. Only the female builds the nest, although the male follows and watches. • The Red-eyed Vireo is one of the most common victims of collisions with TV towers in Illinois.

ID: red eyes; dark eye line; white "eyebrow"; blue gray crown with black border; olive green upperparts; olive "cheek"; white to pale gray underparts; may have yellow wash on sides, flanks and undertail coverts, especially in fall; no wing bars; blue gray legs.

Size: *L* 6 in; *W* 10 in.

Status: common to abundant migrant and breeder; migrants occur from late April to early June and from late August through early to mid-October.

Habitat: deciduous woodlands with a shrubby understory; shade trees and shrubbery in urban parks and gardens.

Nesting: in a deciduous tree or shrub; hanging, basketlike cup nest is made of bark strips, grass, roots, spider silk and decorated with lichens and whitish silk from cocoons; built 6–60 ft above ground often in a sugar maple; female incubates 4 darkly spotted, white eggs for 11–14 days; frequently parasitized by cowbirds.

Feeding: gleans foliage for insects, especially caterpillars and moths; often hovers; eats more fruit than other vireos, including elderberries and berries from dogwood, spicebush, Virginia creeper and sassafras; almost half of fall diet consists of wild fruit.

Voice: scolding call is a nasal, *quay* or *quee;* song is continuous with quick, short phrases and distinct pauses: *look-up, way-up, tree-top, see-me, here-I-am!*

Similar Species: *Philadelphia Vireo* (p. 225): shorter, stubbier bill; grayish back; yellow breast; white "eyebrow" lacks black outline; lacks red eyes; song is very similar, but sweeter and softer. *Warbling Vireo* (p. 224): different song; plainer face; grayer overall; lacks red eyes. *Tennessee Warbler* (p. 268): smaller overall; dark eyes; blue gray "cap" and nape; thinner, sharp-pointed bill lacks hook at tip; pale legs; faint wing bars.

Best Sites: common throughout most woodlands; abundant in summer in Shawnee NF.

BLUE JAY

Cyanocitta cristata

With its raucous *jay-jay-jay* calls and conspicuous deep blue plumage, the Blue Jay makes its presence known. This adaptable bird is common at backyard feeding stations maintained with sunflower seeds and peanuts. After a day of watching House Sparrows eat your birdseed, a Blue Jay can be a welcome sight. Blue Jays cache food from feeders in trees and other places for later use. In fall and winter, flocks may congregate in corn fields as well as oak woodlands if acorns are abundant. • The Blue Jay embodies the resourceful traits and aggressive qualities of the corvid family, which includes magpies, crows and ravens. • Whether on its own or in a mob, the Blue Jay often drives away smaller birds, squirrels or even cats. Groups of Blue Jays, along with American Crows, will even harass a Great Horned Owl, dive-bombing it until it flies off to another grove of trees.

ID: blue crest; black "necklace"; blue upperparts; white underparts; white bar and flecking on wings; dark bars and white corners on blue tail; black bill.
Size: *L* 11–12½ in; *W* 16 in.
Status: common year-round resident; migratory along L. Michigan and river valleys; breeding birds are often not the same birds present in winter.
Habitat: mixed deciduous forests, agricultural areas, scrubby fields and towns.
Nesting: in a tree or tall shrub; pair builds a bulky stick nest and incubates 4–5 greenish, buff or pale blue eggs, spotted with

gray and brown, for 16–18 days; birds are quiet and inconspicuous during breeding season, especially near their nests.
Feeding: moves in groups to search for food in winter; forages on the ground and among vegetation for nuts, berries, eggs, nestlings and birdseed; also eats insects and carrion.
Voice: noisy, screaming *jay-jay-jay;* nasal *queedle queedle queedle-queedle* sounds like a muted trumpet; often imitates various sounds, including calls of the Red-tailed Hawk and Red-shouldered Hawk.
Similar Species: *Eastern Bluebird* (p. 252): smaller; no crest; male has blue back with red on breast.
Best Sites: *In migration:* suburban backyards, fields, lakeshores and river valleys.

AMERICAN CROW

Corvus brachyrhynchos

Wary and intelligent, American Crows have flourished because of their ability to adapt to many different habitats. • Crows are common to abundant statewide. They form wintering flocks in the hundreds to tens of thousands, often beginning as early as September. Some birds from these flocks may travel 20 miles or more one way daily to forage. Flocks begin disbanding in February as birds pair bond for breeding. • A favorite pastime for American Crows is to gather in small groups and call loudly while mobbing a Great Horned Owl or other raptor. Aggregations of crows are known as "murders." • This species appears to be particularly susceptible to the West Nile virus, which has recently spread into the state. • Crows are impressive mimics, able to whine like a dog, cry like a child, squawk like a hen and laugh like a human. Some crows in captivity can repeat simple, spoken words. • At some crow nests, young from the previous year will help their parents raise nestlings. • *Corvus brachyrhynchos* is Latin for "raven with the small nose."

ID: all-black body; square-shaped tail; black bill and legs; slim, sleek head and throat.
Size: *L* 17–21 in; *W* 37 in.
Status: common to locally abundant year-round resident; West Nile virus has decreased numbers.
Habitat: widespread.
Nesting: in a coniferous or deciduous tree where the bulky nest can be hidden; large stick and branch nest is lined with fur and soft plant materials; female incubates 4–6 gray green to blue green eggs, blotched with brown and gray, for about 18 days.

Feeding: opportunistic; feeds on carrion, small vertebrates, other birds' eggs and nestlings, berries, seeds, invertebrates and human food waste.
Voice: distinctive, far-carrying, repetitive *caw-caw-caw*.
Similar Species: *Fish Crow* (p. 229): restricted to extreme southern Illinois and the Mississippi R. valley north to St. Louis; slightly smaller; proportionally longer tail; best distinguished by nasal, 2-syllable, squeaky call.
Best Sites: downtown Danville in winter, where more than 100,000 congregate annually at dusk; woodlands statewide in smaller numbers year-round.

FISH CROW
Corvus ossifragus

The Fish Crow is best distinguished from the American Crow by its nasal, two-note, *uh-uh* call. The Fish Crow glides more than the American Crow and has wingbeats that are somewhat quicker. In Illinois, the Fish Crow can only be found along large rivers and their floodplains, especially the Illinois, Ohio and Mississippi Rivers in the southern half of the state. • Although most common in extreme southern Illinois, the Fish Crow could be extending its range northward in the state along these rivers. This southern Illinois species often hovers while searching for food and catches small minnows with its feet. • Only a few nests have been found of this rare breeder. The first was discovered in Massac County in 1992, and the second was documented in 1993 about 40 feet high in a tall, spindly ash tree along the Union County Wildlife Refuge dike road. • Calls of newly fledged American Crows are often mistaken for the Fish Crow.

ID: virtually identical to American Crow, though slightly smaller; best identified by voice.
Size: *L* 15½ in; *W* 36 in.
Status: uncommon spring migrant beginning in early March; fall migration less clear; most gone by early to mid-October, with some lingering into November; locally common breeder; very rare winter resident.
Habitat: river valleys and riparian woodlands.
Nesting: often nests in small, loose colonies; both adults probably help to build a bulky stick nest in the fork of a tree or large shrub; female incubates 2–6 pale bluish green eggs with brown markings for 16–19 days, but both adults probably help raise young.
Feeding: omnivorous scavenger; feeds on a wide variety of foods including carrion, fish, crayfish, crabs, insects, shrimp, turtle eggs, bird eggs (especially herons), seeds, nestling birds, berries and human food waste; typically forages by walking along shorelines, in shallow water and on fields.
Voice: single or double call note has a nasal sound: *uh-uh*.
Similar Species: *American Crow* (p. 228): slightly larger; proportionally shorter tail; best distinguished by call note: *caw*.
Best Sites: Union County CA; Heron Pond and Little Black Slough SNA; Oakwood Bottoms; Horseshoe Lake CA; Mermet L., Jackson, Alexander, Pulaski, Massac, Pope counties; common in major river valleys.

HORNED LARK
Eremophila alpestris

All year long, but especially in early spring, Horned Larks give a bubbling *tsee-titi* or *zoot* while they feed in Illinois' agricultural fields. Sometimes before the snow is gone, Horned Larks have already begun breeding. • The male performs his courtship display, flying in circles up to 800 feet high. After singing in the air, he closes his wings and plummets in a high-speed dive that he aborts just before reaching the ground. By early April, young are often fledged in central Illinois. They look much different than their parents and can be mistaken for longspurs or pipits. • When agricultural fields replaced tall-grass prairies, Horned Lark numbers temporarily grew. Today, Horned Lark populations in Illinois may be decreasing as farm fields become housing and commercial developments. • In migration and winter, these open-country inhabitants congregate in flocks at the edges of roads, frequently accompanied by Snow Buntings and Lapland Longspurs.

ID: *Male:* small, black "horns," rarely raised; black line under eye extends from bill to "cheek"; light yellow to white face; dull brown upperparts; black breast band; dark tail with white outer tail feathers; light throat. *Female:* less distinctively patterned; duller plumage overall.
Size: *L* 7 in; *W* 12 in.
Status: common year-round resident, although birds in winter are not necessarily those that breed in the state.
Habitat: *Breeding:* open areas, including pastures, croplands, sparsely vegetated fields and airfields; needs very short vegetation, often bare ground. *In migration* and *winter:* croplands and fields.
Nesting: on the ground; often in rows of corn or soybean stubble; in a shallow scrape lined with grass, plant fibers and roots; female chooses the nest site and incubates 3–4 brown-blotched, pale gray to greenish white eggs for 10–12 days; early

nests often lost to spring plowing and late winter storms.
Feeding: gleans the ground for seeds, grain and insects; type of food varies with the seasons; picks off grass seeds while perched, as opposed to longspurs and buntings, which alight on the plant to feed.
Voice: call is a tinkling *tsee-titi* or *zoot;* song, often given in flight, is a long series of tinkling, twittered whistles.
Similar Species: *Sparrows* (pp. 304–27) and *longspurs* (pp. 325–26): all lack distinctive facial pattern, "horns" and solid black breast band. *American Pipit* (p. 264): smaller than juvenile Horned Lark; paler lower mandible; much more white on outer tail feathers; darker brown overall with streaks on back rather than spotting; buffier underparts with distinct dark spotting or streaking on breast. *Sprague's Pipit:* very similar to juvenile Horned Lark, but very rare; white wing bars; yellow legs; extensive white in outer tail feathers; "necklace" of streaks on breast.
Best Sites: agricultural fields of central Illinois.

PURPLE MARTIN

Progne subis

Purple Martins once nested in natural tree hollows, in cliff crevices at forest edges or near wooded ponds and beaver marshes. Now, nearly all of these birds in the eastern United States, including Illinois, nest in birdhouses. In the West, however, Purple Martins still nest almost exclusively in natural cavities, often woodpecker holes. • A "condo complex" for this species should be placed high on a pole in a large, open area, preferably near water. It should be cleaned and removed every winter, to keep the more aggressive, nonnative House Sparrows and European Starlings from invading. • Griggsville, in the west-central part of the state, is known as the Purple Martin capital of the world. Purple Martin houses can be found on nearly every street and a 600-apartment Purple Martin high-rise graces the town center. • With insects as an essential part of the martin's diet, weather, especially late cold snaps in spring, can substantially affect local populations of this species.

ID: largest swallow species in Illinois; dark blue, glossy body; slightly forked tail; pointed wings; small bill. *Male:* dark underparts. *Female:* sooty gray underparts.
Size: *L* 8 in; *W* 18 in.
Status: common migrant and locally common breeder; arrives in mid- to late March; most depart by early to mid-September.
Habitat: semi-open areas, often near water.
Nesting: in an apartment-style birdhouse or hollowed-out gourd; nest materials include feathers, grass, catalpa pods, rags, string, straw; cow manure and mud used to form a sloping wall from the entrance to the rear of the box; fresh, green leaves brought to nest and throughout nest cycle; female incubates 4–5 white eggs for 15–18 days.

Feeding: strictly insectivorous; eats mostly while in flight; takes flies, ants, bugs, damselflies, dragonflies, wasps, grasshoppers and beetles; also spiders, moths, mosquitoes and other flying insects; picks up small bits of gravel for digestion; drinks on the wing.
Voice: rich *pew-pew,* often heard in flight; calls include low whistles and a descending *cherr.*
Similar Species: *Barn Swallow* (p. 236): smaller; deeply forked tail; buff orange to reddish brown throat; whitish to cinnamon underparts. *Tree Swallow* (p. 232): smaller; metallic blue green back; white underparts; female underparts totally white. *Cliff Swallow* (p. 235): beige rump; chestnut face and throat; white patch on forehead.
Best Sites: *Summer:* Griggsville; late summer roosts at Waukegan Beach and Lincoln Park. *In migration:* L. Chautauqua.

TREE SWALLOW
Tachycineta bicolor

The hardy and abundant Tree Swallow is the earliest swallow to return to Illinois in spring. • Tree Swallows nest in natural tree hollows or woodpecker cavities in standing dead trees, but also readily use nest boxes designed for bluebirds. Placing two bluebird houses next to each other helps keep Tree Swallows from using all the houses. • Tree Swallows defend their territories vigorously and readily dive-bomb intruders. Males often have more than one mate. The female swallow uses duck and goose feathers to line her nest. As with other swallow species, Tree Swallows engage in interesting feather play. One swallow tosses a feather in the air and the other catches the feather before it reaches the ground. • When conditions are favorable, these birds may return to their young 10 to 20 times per hour. • Most Tree Swallows migrating through Illinois continue north to nest. • Unlike other North American swallows, female Tree Swallows do not acquire their full adult plumage until their second or third year. • Tree Swallows form huge flocks, in the tens to hundreds of thousands in late summer. A high count of 300,000 Tree Swallows was reported on October 2, 1999, at Carlyle Lake.

ID: iridescent, dark blue or green head and upperparts; white underparts; dark rump; small bill; long, pointed wings; shallowly forked tail. *Female:* slightly duller. *1st-year female* and *immature:* brown upperparts; white underparts.

Size: *L* 5½ in; *W* 14½ in.

Status: common to abundant migrant; common breeder, decreasing southward; arrives in late February to early March; most are gone by mid- to late November; a few linger into Christmas bird count season.

Habitat: open areas, along marshes, lakeshores, field fencelines and open fields with nest boxes.

Nesting: in a tree cavity or nest box lined with weeds, grass and many feathers; female incubates 4–6 eggs for up to 19 days.

Feeding: catches flies, midges, mosquitoes, beetles, dragonflies and ants on the wing; also takes stoneflies, mayflies and caddisflies over water; eats berries and seeds, especially when cold, early spring weather limits insect supply; drinks on the wing.

Voice: call is a rapidly repeated *silip;* song is a liquid, chattering twitter.

Similar Species: *Purple Martin* (p. 231): male is dark blue overall; female has sooty gray underparts. *Bank Swallow* (p. 234) and *Northern Rough-winged Swallow* (p. 233): brown upperparts; Bank Swallow has brown chest band and Northern Rough-winged has brownish breast and throat compared with 1st-year female and juvenile Tree Swallow. *Barn Swallow* (p. 236): buff orange to reddish brown throat; deeply forked tail.

Best Sites: Clinton L., L. Chautauqua and Carlyle L. in fall.

NORTHERN ROUGH-WINGED SWALLOW

Stelgidopteryx serripennis

The Northern Rough-winged Swallow nests in banks along rivers and streams, sometimes alongside a colony of Bank Swallows. The length of the nest burrow depends on the soil type; tunnels can reach 4 to 5 feet in length. • This adaptable species also nests in holes, the sides of wooden buildings, adobe walls, quarries and caves, under bridges, culverts and wharves, and in gutters, drainpipes and sewer pipes. It also will readily use an old kingfisher burrow or the home of a ground squirrel or other small mammal. • Young swallows may perish from heavy infestations of nest parasites, black rat snake predation and flooding of burrows. • Unlike other swallows, male Northern Rough-wings have curved barbs along the outer edge of their primary wing feathers, which may be used to produce sound during courtship. The ornithologist who named this bird must have been very impressed with its wings: *Stelgidopteryx* means "scraper wing" and *serripennis* means "saw feather."

ID: brown upperparts; light brownish gray underparts; small bill; dark "cheek"; dark rump. *Juvenile:* may have cinnamon wing bars. **Size:** *L* 5½ in; *W* 14 in. **Status:** common migrant and breeder; arrives in late March and departs by late September to early October. **Habitat:** ponds, lakes and streams; open and semi-open areas, including fields and open woodlands, usually near water. **Nesting:** occasionally in small colonies; at the end of a burrow lined with leaves, dry grass and feathers; sometimes uses a kingfisher burrow, rodent burrow or human-made crevice; mostly the female incubates 4–8 white eggs for 12–16 days. **Feeding:** catches flying insects on the wing; occasionally eats insects from the ground; drinks on the wing. **Voice:** a burry *brrrtt;* usually 2–3 notes. **Similar Species:** *Bank Swallow* (p. 234): smaller; dark breast band; shallower, more rapid wingbeats; longer, rapid series of call notes; nest burrow holes are generally rounder. *Tree Swallow* (p. 232): 1st-year female and juvenile have clean white underparts. *Cliff Swallow* (p. 235): brown-and-blue upperparts; white forehead; buff rump patch. **Best Sites:** L. Chautauqua and Mark Twain NWR in fall.

BANK SWALLOW

Riparia riparia

Overwintering in South America, Bank Swallows are one of the last swallows to arrive in Illinois during spring and the first to depart in fall. • These birds nest in colonies that range in size from 20 to 2000 nests. They usually excavate their own nest burrows, first using their small bills and later digging with their feet. Most nestlings are safe from predators deep within their nest chamber, which is typically 2 to 4 feet in length. • Bank Swallow populations have declined in some states because of habitat loss. These birds have found sand and gravel pits to mimic their natural nesting habitat; however, the transitory nature of these habitats makes it difficult for the Bank Swallow to complete the nesting cycle. Some states such as California are working with gravel pit owners to lower the incidence of swallow nests that get destroyed. During the Mississippi River flood of 1993, large sand deposits created temporary nesting sites for these birds in Alexander County. • In fall, large mixed flocks of Bank and other swallows annually create an impressive sight as they perch on utility lines along the edges of Lake Chautauqua.

ID: brown upperparts; light underparts; brown breast band; long, pointed wings; shallowly forked tail; white throat; dark "cheek"; small legs. **Size:** *L* 5½ in; *W* 13 in.
Status: common migrant, uncommon to common, local breeder; arrives in mid- to late April; departs by early to mid-September, with some lingering into early October.
Habitat: steep banks, lakeshore bluffs and open areas, such as sand or gravel pits, even sawdust piles.
Nesting: colonial; pair excavates or reuses a long burrow in a steep earthen bank or cliff; nest holes usually at top of bank; the

end of the burrow is lined with grass, rootlets, weeds, straw and feathers; pair incubates 4–5 white eggs for 14–16 days.
Feeding: catches flying insects; drinks on the wing.
Voice: twittering chatter: *speed-zeet speed-zeet.*
Similar Species: *Northern Rough-winged Swallow* (p. 233): larger; lacks dark, defined breast band; deeper, slower wingbeats; voice is a few short, burry notes. *Tree Swallow* (p. 232): iridescent, dark bluish to greenish upperparts; lacks dark breast band. *Cliff Swallow* (p. 235): brown-and-blue upperparts; white forehead; buff rump; lacks dark breast band.
Best Sites: *Summer:* Dallas City along the Mississippi R. *In fall migration:* L. Chautauqua.

CLIFF SWALLOW
Petrochelidon pyrrhonota

Cliff Swallows roll mud into balls with their bills and press the pellets together to form their characteristic nests. • Cliff Swallows are brood parasites— females often lay one or more eggs in the nests of neighboring Cliff Swallows, who will care for them as if they were their own. Birds such as House Wrens and House Finches use old Cliff Swallow nests to raise their own families; bats use old Cliff Swallow nests for roosting. • In Illinois, Cliff Swallow numbers declined drastically as the introduced House Sparrow population rose. One House Sparrow may clean out 15 Cliff Swallow nests before selecting one. These sparrows will also destroy many eggs in a colony. Even so, within the past decade, Cliff Swallow numbers have slowly begun to rebound in Illinois for unknown reasons.

ID: buff orange rump; white forehead; deep blue crown and back; rusty "cheek," buff nape and breast; dark throat; white belly; spotted undertail coverts; nearly square tail. *In flight:* slants wings downward.
Size: *L* 5½ in; *W* 13½ in.
Status: fairly common migrant; rare to locally common breeder; arrives in mid- to late April; most migrants are gone by late September.
Habitat: steep banks, cliffs, bridges and buildings near watercourses; forages over water, fields, marshes and a wide variety of other habitats.
Nesting: colonial; under a bridge or on a cliff or building; pair builds a gourd-shaped mud nest with a small opening near the bottom; pair incubates 4–5 brown-spotted,

white to pinkish eggs for 14–16 days; parasitized by Brown-headed Cowbird.
Feeding: catches flying insects, including flies, beetles and wasps, on the wing; feeds in flocks on insect swarms; drinks exclusively on the wing, trapping water with its lower mandible.
Voice: twittering chatter: *churrr-churrr;* also an alarm call: *nyew.*
Similar Species: *Barn Swallow* (p. 236): deeply forked tail; dark rump; usually has rust-colored underparts and forehead. *Other swallows* (pp. 231–35): lack white forehead and buff rump patch.
Best Sites: *Summer:* Apple River Canyon SP; Smithland Dam in Pope Co.; I-24 bridge near Metropolis; Mary's R. bridge, I-51 bridge and near Front Street in town of Chester. *In migration:* L. Chautauqua.

BARN SWALLOW

Hirundo rustica

Although Barn Swallows do not occur in the mass colonies in which some other Illinois swallows do, they are probably the most well known because of their propensity for building their nests on human-made structures and following farmers mowing hayfields. • The Barn Swallow is the most abundant swallow in the state during the breeding season. Since the early 1900s, this species has shifted its Illinois breeding range from the north to the south. • Barn Swallows once nested on cliffs and in the entrances to caves, but now they more commonly build their cup-shaped mud nests under house eaves, in barns and boathouses, under bridges or on other structures that can provide shelter from predators and inclement weather. The Barn Swallow returns to the same nest site every year, repairing or rebuilding it to raise another season's young. • This species uses tail length for mate selection; a longer tail often means more reproductive success. • The most widely distributed swallow in the world, the Barn Swallow breeds over much of North America, Europe, Asia and Africa and winters throughout the Southern Hemisphere.

ID: long, deeply forked tail; rust-colored throat and forehead; blue black upperparts; rust- to buff-colored underparts; long, pointed wings.
Size: *L* 7 in; *W* 15 in.
Status: common to abundant migrant; common breeder; arrives in late March to early April and departs by early to mid-October, with a few November stragglers.
Habitat: in open rural and urban areas where bridges, culverts and buildings are found near rivers, lakes, marshes or ponds.

Nesting: singly or in small, loose colonies; pair builds half or full cup nest made of mud, grass and straw and lines it with feathers; female often waits 2 weeks after nest is built to lay eggs; pair incubates 4–7 brown-spotted, white eggs for 13–17 days; often has 2 broods.
Feeding: highly insectivorous; catches flying insects, mostly flies; also takes beetles, bees and wasps on the wing.
Voice: continuous twittering chatter: *zip-zip-zip;* also *kvick-kvick.*
Similar Species: *Cliff Swallow* (p. 235): nearly square tail; buff rump; white forehead; pale underparts. *Purple Martin* (p. 231): larger; shallowly forked tail; male is completely blue black; female has sooty gray underparts. *Tree Swallow* (p. 232): iridescent, blue to green back; clean white underparts; slightly notched tail.
Best Sites: L. Chautauqua in fall; rural farms statewide.

CAROLINA CHICKADEE

Poecile carolinensis

Separating the Carolina Chickadee and Black-capped Chickadee by plumage alone is difficult, if not impossible. Generally, the Carolina Chickadee is found in the extreme southern areas of Iroquois County and southwest into Madison County. The Black-cappeds are usually found farther north. • Carolina Chickadees readily come to feeders with suet and sunflower seeds. These common backyard birds grow more feathers in winter to help them maintain body heat. Muscles in the skin allow the chickadee to fluff its feathers on cold winter days to trap the warmth from its own body. Like other birds, the chickadee uses its beak to coat its feathers with oil from a gland near its tail. • As with many passerines, the life expectancy for the chickadee is usually a year or less, but if a juvenile survives its first year, it can live up to 10 years.

ID: black "cap" and "bib"; white "cheek"; gray upperparts; white underparts; buffy flanks.
Size: *L* 4¾ in; *W* 7½ in.
Status: common year-round resident in its range.
Habitat: deciduous and mixed forests, riparian woodlands, groves and isolated shade trees.
Nesting: pair excavates or enlarges interior of a natural tree cavity; may also use a nest box, woodpecker cavity or rotten tree stub; often builds one side of the nest higher than the other; nest is lined with soft plant material, mainly green moss, milkweed, thistledown, animal hair, fur and feathers; female incubates 5–8 white

eggs with reddish brown speckling and splotches; male feeds female on the nest; both parents raise young.
Feeding: gleans a variety of insects, seeds and berries from vegetation; may hawk for insects and hang upside down on branches; also gleans while hovering; often visits feeders for seed and suet.
Voice: whistling song has 4 clear notes: *fee-bee fee-bay;* call is a faster, higher version of the Black-capped Chickadee's *chick-a-dee-dee-dee.*
Similar Species: *Black-capped Chickadee* (p. 238): almost identical; lower edge of black "bib" is not as defined; secondaries and wing coverts have broad, white edgings; may interbreed with Carolina Chickadee where their ranges overlap.
Best Sites: widespread in its range.

BLACK-CAPPED CHICKADEE

Poecile atricapillus

In winter, Black-capped Chickadees often join the company of kinglets, nuthatches, creepers and small woodpeckers to feed; in spring and fall, they join mixed flocks of vireos and warblers. • Black-capped Chickadees eat seeds and berries, readily visiting feeders. Their diet mainly consists of caterpillars, spiders and insects, including eggs and larvae. They have specialized leg muscles so they can feed while hanging upside down, giving them a chance to grab something another bird might not get. Chickadees also store or cache food for retrieval later in winter. They may move in from more northern states or move from the north of Illinois to the south if food becomes scarce. • Most songbirds have both songs and calls. The chickadee gives its *fee-bee* song mostly during courtship. Its *chick-a-dee-dee-dee* call maintains contact between flock members and keeps flocks together. • On a very cold winter day, the Black-capped Chickadee increases its heartbeat to 1000 beats per minute to raise its body temperature. While sleeping in a tree cavity during the night, it can lower its heart rate to 500 beats per minute. • The Black-capped Chickadee ranges as far south as Tennessee, but it lives at higher elevations than its cousin, the Carolina Chickadee.

ID: black "cap" and "bib"; white "cheek"; gray back and wings; white underparts; light buff sides and flanks; dark legs; conspicuous white edging on wing feathers. **Size:** *L* 5–6 in; *W* 8 in. **Status:** common year-round resident in its range; sometimes moves into southern Illinois in winter.
Habitat: deciduous and mixed forests, woodlots, riparian woodlands, birch stands, wooded urban parks and backyards with bird feeders.
Nesting: pair excavates a cavity in a soft, rotting stump or tree; also uses nest boxes, fence posts and even iron pipes used for clotheslines; female builds a nest with fur, feathers, moss, grass and cocoons; female incubates 6–8 white eggs, with reddish brown speckles and splotches, for 12–13 days.
Feeding: hovers, hangs, probes, gleans and hawks; eats small insects and spiders; visits backyard feeders; also eats conifer seeds and invertebrate eggs; during breeding season mostly eats animal matter, largely caterpillars; rarely eats food where found, instead carries it away to eat elsewhere.
Voice: call is a chipper, whistled *chick-a-dee-dee-dee;* song is a slow, whistled *fee-bee.*
Similar Species: *Carolina Chickadee* (p. 237): almost identical; neater lower edge of black "bib"; lacks broad, white edgings on secondaries and wing coverts; may interbreed with Black-capped Chickadee where their ranges overlap.
Best Sites: widespread in its range.

TUFTED TITMOUSE
Baeolophus bicolor

L ike other members of its tribe, the dexterous Tufted Titmouse strikes its dainty bill repeatedly against a seed's hard outer coating while holding it between its feet, exposing the inner core. • Tufted Titmice maintain pair bonds year-round. The titmouse family bond is so strong that the young from one breeding season will often stay with their parents long enough to help with nesting and feeding duties the following year. • In late winter, mating pairs break from their flocks to search for nesting cavities and soft lining material, including mammal hair. A female titmouse was observed pulling hair from live squirrels, woodchucks and even a man's head and beard. • During Christmas bird counts in southern Illinois, the Tufted Titmouse, along with nuthatches, chickadees, creepers, woodpeckers and kinglets, will respond readily to Eastern Screech-Owl calls, often inspecting tree holes where it thinks the owl is lurking. • During the past 50 years, this species' population has increased in its North American range, possibly because of an increase in bird feeding and climatic warming.

ID: gray crest and upperparts; black forehead; white underparts; buffy flanks.
Size: *L* 6–6½ in; *W* 10 in.
Status: common year-round resident, decreasing northward.
Habitat: deciduous woodlands; groves and suburban parks with large, mature trees.
Nesting: in a tree 20–90 ft high; in a natural cavity or woodpecker hole lined with soft vegetation such as mosses and grasses, bark strips, shed snakeskins and animal hair; male feeds female from courtship to time of hatching; female incubates 5–6

finely dotted, white eggs for 12–14 days; both adults and occasionally a "helper" raise the young.
Feeding: forages on the ground and in trees, often hanging upside down like a chickadee; eats insects, including copious amounts of caterpillars, beetles, ants, wasps, bees and insect egg cases; also eats seeds and suet from feeders, nuts and fruits, including acorns from oak trees.
Voice: noisy, scolding call, like that of a chickadee; song is a whistled *peter peter* or *peter peter peter;* also emits a thin, high-pitched, repeated *see* when alarmed.
Similar Species: none.
Best Sites: widespread in its range.

RED-BREASTED NUTHATCH

Sitta canadensis

The Red-breasted Nuthatch, along with its cousin, the White-breasted Nuthatch, has the unusual habit of going headfirst down tree trunks. Its distinctive nasal call sounds like a toy horn being blown. • Red-breasted Nuthatches tend to make large-scale migrations every two years, perhaps because conifers on their breeding grounds fail to produce enough cones. In such years, they often join groups of other foraging songbirds in woodlands. These birds cache food in winter, which may help to perpetuate coniferous species. • This mainly boreal species is a very rare breeder in northern Illinois. It smears the entrance of its nest cavity with pitch from pine or spruce trees. This sticky doormat may inhibit ants and other animals from entering the nest chamber. Invertebrates can be the most serious threat to nesting success, because they transmit fungal infections or parasitize nestlings. • The Red-breasted Nuthatch is more closely related to other conifer-dwelling Old World nuthatches than it is to the White-breasted Nuthatch.

ID: rusty underparts; gray blue upperparts; white "eyebrow"; black eye line; black "cap"; straight bill; short tail; white "cheek." *Male:* deeper rust on breast; black crown. *Female:* light red wash on breast; dark gray crown. **Size:** *L* 4½ in; *W* 8½ in.

Status: uncommon to locally common some years; can be almost nonexistent in other years; spring migrants occur from mid- to late April to mid- to late May; very rare summer resident and local breeder; wintering birds arrive in late August.

Habitat: *Breeding:* extensive evergreen plantations. *In migration* and *winter:* mainly pine and other evergreen plantations; also in mixed woodlands.

Nesting: unmated males or mated pairs may begin excavating several cavities or choose an abandoned woodpecker nest; female typically does most of excavation and male brings her food; smears pitch at entrance; nest is made of bark shreds, grass and fur; female incubates 5–6 white eggs, spotted with reddish brown, for about 12 days; male roosts with female in nest cavity.

Feeding: forages down trees while probing under loose bark for larval and adult invertebrates, especially beetles, in breeding season; eats pine and spruce seeds in winter; often visits feeders.

Voice: call is a slow, continually repeated, nasal *yank-yank-yank* or *rah-rah-rah-rah;* also a short *tsip.*

Similar Species: *White-breasted Nuthatch* (p. 241): larger; lacks black eye line and red underparts; nasal call is louder and deeper.

Best Sites: Illinois Beach SP; Morton Arboretum; Lowden-Miller SF; White Pines Forest SP; Sand Ridge SF; Crab Orchard NWR.

WHITE-BREASTED NUTHATCH

Sitta carolinensis

Giving its familiar *ank ank* call and moving headfirst down a tree trunk, the White-breasted Nuthatch probes and chips away bark to reveal insect larvae hidden in crevices. The bird's long claws are an adaptation that allows the nuthatch to grasp the bark of trees firmly while upside down. • White-breasted Nuthatches store nuts in bark crevices and under branches in trunks of large trees. They often cover the food with a piece of bark, rotten wood, lichens, snow or moss. • The male White-breasted Nuthatch courts the female, giving a *werwerwer* song while bobbing his head up and down. He also feeds her during courtship. • White-breasted Nuthatches nest in cavities high in trees. A pair of nuthatches will sweep crushed insects that secrete chemicals with a distinct odor onto the inside and outside of the nest site to deter predators. White-breasted Nuthatches also have large black and white areas on their underwings, which may appear as "eyes" to confuse predators. • In fall and winter, nuthatches follow chickadees and titmice in feeding flocks, then chase them away from the food source.

ID: white underparts; white face; gray blue back; rusty undertail coverts; short tail; straight bill; short legs. *Male:* black "cap." *Female:* dark gray "cap." **Size:** *L* 5½–6 in; *W* 11 in. **Status:** common year-round resident.
Habitat: deciduous and mixedwood forests, woodlots and backyards with large trees.
Nesting: in a natural cavity, especially a knothole or an abandoned woodpecker nest in a large, deciduous tree; female lines the cavity with bark, grass, fur and feathers; female incubates 5–8 white eggs, spotted with reddish brown, for 12–14 days.
Feeding: forages for larval and adult invertebrates; also eats many nuts and seeds; regularly visits feeders; in fall and winter, eats mostly acorns, beech nuts and sunflower seeds.
Voice: song is a frequently repeated *werwerwerwer;* calls are *ha-ha-ha ha-ha-ha, ank ank* and *ip.*
Similar Species: *Red-breasted Nuthatch* (p. 240): smaller; black eye line; rusty underparts; softer, higher pitched call.
Best Sites: widespread in appropriate habitat.

BROWN CREEPER

Certhia americana

The Brown Creeper feeds by slowly spiraling up a tree trunk, searching for hidden invertebrates, propping itself up with its long, stiff tail feathers. Unlike nuthatches, it does not move down and sideways along tree trunks; it works its way up only. Creepers also sometimes hop backward for a short distance to reinspect feeding sites. • Although a state-threatened species, the Brown Creeper is probably a more common breeder than birders realize. Its soft, sibilant song and preference for flooded bottomland forests makes it difficult to find. In far southern Illinois, it prefers cypress-tupelo swamps for nesting; elsewhere, it can be found in mature, flooded bottomland forests along major river valleys. Extensive flooding along the Mississippi and other big rivers between 1993 and 1995 temporarily provided copious habitat for breeding creepers. • During courtship, creepers chase one another, spiraling upward around a tree. They place their nests behind peeling bark and thus need large, mature trees for breeding. • In winter, creepers join feeding flocks of chickadees, titmice, nuthatches, kinglets and other small birds. Adults will also roost communally in a hollow limb.

hammock of mosses, twigs, shredded bark, spider silk and cocoons is lined with feathers; female incubates 5–6 whitish eggs, dotted with reddish brown, for 14–17 days.

ID: brown back is heavily streaked with buffy white; white "eyebrow"; white underparts; downcurved bill; long, pointed tail feathers; rusty rump.
Size: *L* 5–5½ in; *W* 7½ in.
Status: common migrant; rare but regular breeder in small numbers statewide; fairly common winter resident, decreasing northward; wintering birds arrive in mid-September and depart by early to mid-May.
Habitat: mature deciduous, coniferous and mixed forests and woodlands, especially in wet areas with large, dead trees.
Nesting: under loose bark usually against the trunk of a dead tree; crescent-shaped

Feeding: probes loose bark on tree trunks for adult and larval invertebrates, including ants, caterpillars and spiders; visits suet feeders.
Voice: song is a short, sibilant, musical series of notes; call is a high *seee*.
Similar Species: *Red-breasted Nuthatch* (p. 240) and *White-breasted Nuthatch* (p. 241): gray blue backs; straight or slightly upturned bills; move down and sideways along trees, rather than upward.
Best Sites: *Summer:* Sanganois CA; Calhoun Point Waterfowl Management Area; Long I. in the Gardner Division of Mark Twain NWR; Heron Pond SNA and other cypress-tupelo swamps in far southern Illinois. *In migration* and *winter:* widespread in appropriate habitat.

CAROLINA WREN
Thryothorus ludovicianus

Even on a cold winter day, the Carolina Wren often gives its loud, melodious *tea-kettle tea-kettle tea-kettle* song. Pairs may perform lively duets year-round. The highest densities of this wren in Illinois occur in bottomland woods in the southern part of the state. • During mild winters, Carolina Wren populations remain stable; however, a prolonged snow or ice event makes it difficult for them to secure food and can drastically reduce their numbers. Populations usually recover within a few years. • Carolina Wrens maintain pair bonds year-round, unlike most other wren species. • In Illinois, Carolina Wrens have been found roosting in old Wood Thrush nests in the summer and old Barn Swallow nests inside barns in winter.

ID: long, prominent, white "eyebrow"; rusty brown upperparts; rich buff-colored underparts; white throat; slightly downcurved bill.
Size: *L* 5½ in; *W* 7 in.
Status: common year-round resident, decreasing northward; rare in northeastern Illinois; populations may fluctuate greatly depending on weather conditions.
Habitat: dense forest undergrowth, especially shrubby tangles and thickets.
Nesting: on or near the ground; in a nest box, natural cavity, among vegetation or in some type of unused receptacle; male often builds multiple nests; both adults fill nest with twigs and vegetation and line it with finer materials; often builds a "ramp" entrance into nest; female incubates 4–5 brown-blotched, white eggs for 12–16 days; both adults feed the young; has 2 broods.
Feeding: usually forages in pairs on the ground and among vegetation, especially brush piles; eats mostly insects and spiders; takes berries, fruits and seeds; also lizards,

frogs and snakes; occasionally visits bird feeders for peanuts and suet.
Voice: song is a loud, repetitious *tea-kettle tea-kettle tea-kettle* heard at any time of the day or year; female often chatters while the male sings.
Similar Species: *House Wren* (p. 245): lacks prominent, white "eyebrow"; paler grayish brown overall. *Winter Wren* (p. 246): lacks prominent, white "eyebrow"; smaller body, bill and tail; strongly barred underparts. *Marsh Wren* (p. 248): black, triangular back patch is streaked with white; bold streaking on back; prefers marsh habitat. *Sedge Wren* (p. 247): dark crown and back are streaked with white; pale, indistinct "eyebrow"; prefers wet meadows and sedges. *Bewick's Wren* (p. 244): much rarer; white to grayish belly; lighter brown back; buffy "eyebrow" not outlined in black; long tail twitches from side to side.
Best Sites: Shawnee NF; Cache River Biosphere Reserve.

BEWICK'S WREN

Thryomanes bewickii

A state-endangered species, the Bewick's Wren flits about and waves its long tail from side to side. • Bewick's Wren populations in the West are more stable than those in the East, where numbers have declined dramatically. A century ago, the Bewick's Wren was common in Illinois, but as the House Wren expanded its range, the Bewick's Wren population declined. The House Sparrow, Carolina Wren and European Starling also outcompeted the Bewick's Wren for nesting sites. Loss of habitat, severe winters and the use of pesticides have also taken their toll on this bird. • Today, most Bewick's Wrens found in Illinois are near human habitat; one bird recently nested in a charcoal grill in a state park and another nested in the end of an upturned canoe on a patio. • The Bewick's Wren, a western species, expanded eastward into Illinois when extensive logging was done in the mid- to late 1800s.

ID: long, bold, white "eyebrow"; very long tail trimmed with white spots; brown to gray brown upperparts; clean, whitish underparts; slender, downcurved bill.
Size: *L* 5¼ in; *W* 7 in.
Status: state-endangered; very rare migrant from late March to early April through early to mid-May; most birds depart by late September or early October; very rare, local breeder mostly in southern and western Illinois.
Habitat: open woodlands and thickets.
Nesting: once nested in natural cavities or abandoned woodpecker nests; now mostly uses human-made structures; cup nest, sometimes domed, of sticks and grass is lined with feathers, snakeskin or cellophane; female incubates 5–7 finely speckled, white eggs for about 14 days.
Feeding: gleans vegetation and dead leaves on ground for insects, especially caterpillars, grasshoppers, beetles, wasps and spiders.
Voice: song is bold and clear *chick-click for me-eh for you;* alarm call is a *dzeeeb* or *knee-deep.*
Similar Species: *Marsh Wren* (p. 248): more common; heavy white streaking on black back; shorter tail; browner overall. *House Wren* (p. 245): much more common; some streaking on back; lacks white "eyebrow." *Winter Wren* (p. 246): smaller; shorter tail and bill; faint buff "eyebrow"; more uniformly colored overall. *Carolina Wren* (p. 243): much more common; more rufous tones overall; white "eyebrow" bordered by black; buffy underparts; lacks white spots on tail.
Best Sites: Siloam Springs SP.

244

HOUSE WREN
Troglodytes aedon

One of the best-known songbirds in North America, the House Wren announces its arrival to your backyard with its bubbly song. A small cavity in a standing dead tree or a nest box might attract these birds to your yard. • House Wrens can create problems for other birds by taking over Eastern Bluebird boxes or outcompeting the much rarer Bewick's Wren for nest sites. They also puncture and remove eggs from many species' nests within their territories. Cavity nesters, including Prothonotary Warblers, Black-capped Chickadees, Eastern Bluebirds and Tree Swallows are particularly susceptible to this destruction. • Abundant across most of its range and tolerant of human activity, this species has been studied a great deal. The House Wren has expanded its range ever since the clearing of forests in the late 1800s. • In far southern Illinois, House Wrens are only found in towns and along the Mississippi River and Ohio River bottomlands.

ID: brown upperparts; fine, dark barring on upperwings and lower back; faint, pale "eyebrow" and eye ring; short tail is finely barred with black and held upraised; whitish throat; whitish to buff underparts; faintly barred flanks.

Size: *L* 4½–5 in; *W* 6 in.

Status: common migrant and breeder; occurs from mid-April through mid- to late October, with some lingering into Christmas bird count season in southern Illinois; very rare winter resident.

Habitat: thickets and shrubby openings in or at the edges of deciduous or mixed woodlands; often in shrubs and thickets near buildings.

Nesting: in a natural cavity or abandoned woodpecker nest; also in a nest box or other artificial cavity such as a fish creel or old boot; nest of sticks and grass is lined with feathers, fur and other soft materials; female incubates 6–8 white eggs, heavily dotted with reddish brown, for 13–15 days.

Feeding: gleans the ground and vegetation for insects, especially grasshoppers and crickets; also eats caterpillars, spiders, leafhoppers, flies and snails.

Voice: call is a harsh, scolding rattle; song is a smooth, running, bubbly warble: *tsi-tsi-tsi-tsi oodle-oodle-oodle-oodle,* lasting about 2–3 seconds.

Similar Species: *Winter Wren* (p. 246): smaller; not found in summer; prefers tangly undergrowth in woodlands; darker overall; much shorter, stubby tail; prominent, dark barring on flanks. *Sedge Wren* (p. 247): faint, white streaking on dark crown and back; prefers wet meadows. *Bewick's Wren* (p. 244): much rarer; white "eyebrow"; lacks streaking on back. *Carolina Wren* (p. 243): prominent, white "eyebrow"; much more rufous tones overall.

Best Sites: widespread in appropriate habitat.

WINTER WREN

Troglodytes troglodytes

O ne of the most varied and beautiful bird songs comes from the Winter Wren—its melodious, bubbly, tinkling series of notes, can last for 10 seconds, with up to 113 tones. Recordings of Winter Wren songs played back at half speed show that this bird can sing more than one note at a time. • Winter Wrens skulk like mice through the damp forest understory, creeping about woodpiles and brush heaps, quietly probing the myriad nooks and crannies for invertebrates. • *Troglodytes* is Greek for "creeping in holes" or "cave dweller." • This bird has a habit of bobbing its entire body up and down as if it were doing push-ups. • The Winter Wren is the only North American wren that is also found across Europe and Asia, where it is a common garden bird known simply as a "Wren."

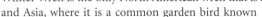

ID: short, stubby, upraised tail; fine, pale buff "eyebrow"; brownish overall with lighter throat; prominent, dark barring on flanks.
Size: *L* 4 in; *W* 5½ in.
Status: common migrant from early to mid-March through early to mid-May and from early to mid-September to early to mid-November; possibly very rare breeder in northern Illinois; rare to uncommon winter resident, increasing southward.
Habitat: brushy wet areas of bottomland woods, near streams in upland woods; often found in dense, tangly branches.
Nesting: no concrete records of nesting in Illinois.
Feeding: forages on the ground and in trees for wood-boring insects, including

bark beetles, weevils and other invertebrates.
Voice: *Male:* song is a warbled, tinkling series of trills and twitters; call is a sharp *chip-chip*.
Similar Species: *House Wren* (p. 245): larger; longer tail; less conspicuous barring on flanks; paler overall. *Carolina Wren* (p. 243): long, bold, white "eyebrow"; much larger; long tail. *Marsh Wren* (p. 248): white streaking on black back; bold, white "eyebrow." *Sedge Wren* (p. 247): white streaking on black back and crown; longer tail; paler underparts.
Best Sites: *In fall migration:* Jackson Park, Chicago. *Winter:* Shawnee NF and Cache River Biosphere Reserve.

SEDGE WREN
Cistothorus platensis

L ike most wrens, the Sedge Wren is secretive and difficult to observe. It remains concealed in dense stands of sedges and tall, wet grass, and is usually identified by its short, strident song that sounds like a sewing machine. Sedge Wrens occasionally sing at night. • Most Sedge Wrens that come through Illinois in spring, continue north to breed; some remain, however, to breed in the few sedge meadows and grasslands left in the state. They also make use of drier edges near marshes. • As with many wren species, the male Sedge Wren builds several incomplete nests throughout his territory. These "dummy" nests often serve as dormitories for young and adult birds later in the season. • The scientific name *platensis* refers to the Rio de la Plata in Argentina, where an isolated population of this wren is found.

ID: short, narrow tail, often upraised; faint, pale "eyebrow"; dark crown and back are faintly streaked with white; barring on wing coverts; whitish underparts with buff orange sides, flanks and undertail coverts.
Size: *L* 4–4½ in; *W* 5½ in.

Status: uncommon migrant and breeder; migrants arrive in late April to early May, departing by mid- to late May; another wave arrives in late June to early July; most are gone by mid-October, with some November stragglers; very rare winter resident in far southern Illinois.
Habitat: sedge meadows, grassy fields.
Nesting: male builds unlined dummy nests, usually less than 3 ft from the ground; well-built globe nest with a side entrance is woven from sedges and grasses; female incubates 4–8 unmarked, white eggs for about 14 days.
Feeding: forages low in dense vegetation, where it probes for adult and larval insects, including caterpillars, moths, crickets, grasshoppers and beetles; also eats spiders and flying insects.

Voice: song is a few short, staccato notes followed by a rattling trill: *chap-chap chap-chap, churrr;* call is a sharp, staccato *chat* or *chep.*
Similar Species: *Marsh Wren* (p. 248): broad, conspicuous, white "eyebrow"; prominent white streaking on black back; unstreaked crown; prefers cattail marshes. *Winter Wren* (p. 246): darker overall; shorter, stubby tail; unstreaked crown. *House Wren* (p. 245): unstreaked, dark brown crown and back; lacks buffy underparts.
Best Sites: Moraine Hills SP; Fermilab; Goose Lake Prairie SNA; Midewin National Tallgrass Prairie; Iroquois County CA; Richardson Wildlife Foundation; Green River CA; Prairie Ridge SNA.

247

MARSH WREN
Cistothorus palustris

Fueled by aquatic insects, the Marsh Wren zips about in short bursts through tall stands of cattails and bulrushes, remaining hidden in its dense marshland habitat. A patient observer might be rewarded with a brief glimpse of a Marsh Wren, which often cocks its tail at a steep angle. Its distinctive song, reminiscent of an old-fashioned sewing machine, will more likely alert you to its presence. Males may learn 50 to 200 song variations and sing vociferously to defend territories. • Marsh Wrens will destroy the nests and eggs of other Marsh Wrens as well as those of other marsh-nesting songbirds, such as the Red-winged Blackbird. Other birds are usually prevented from doing the same because the Marsh Wren's globe nest keeps the eggs well hidden and up to six "dummy" nests help to divert predators and attract mates. Marsh Wrens are polygynous, meaning that the male takes more than one mate.

ID: white "chin" and belly; white to light brown upperparts; black triangle on upper back is streaked with white; bold, white "eyebrow"; unstreaked dark crown; fairly long, thin, down-curved bill.
Size: *L* 5 in; *W* 6 in.

Status: uncommon migrant, decreasing southward; occurs from mid- to late April through mid- to late May and from early to mid-September to mid-November; rare to uncommon, local breeder in the northern quarter of the state; common in northeastern Illinois; very rare winter resident.
Habitat: cattail and bulrush marshes interspersed with open water.
Nesting: in a marsh among cattails or tall emergent vegetation; globelike nest is woven from cattails, bulrushes, weeds and grass and lined with cattail down; female incubates 4–6 white to pale brown eggs, heavily dotted with dark brown, for 12–16 days.

Feeding: gleans vegetation and flycatches for larval aquatic invertebrates including those of dragonflies and damselflies; also eats aphids, flies, beetles, mites, bees, ants, wasps and spiders; forages on or near the marsh floor and among vegetation.
Voice: *Male:* rapid, rattling, staccato warble sounds like an old-fashioned sewing machine; call is a harsh *chek*.
Similar Species: *Sedge Wren* (p. 247): streaked crown; lacks dark back; lacks bold white "eyebrow" contrasting with dark crown. *House Wren* (p. 245): faint "eyebrow"; lacks white streaking on black back; different habitat. *Carolina Wren* (p. 243): larger, bulkier bill; lacks white streaking on black back; buff underparts.
Best Sites: *Summer:* Chain O'Lakes SP; Moraine Hills SP; L. Calumet. *In migration:* Arcola Marsh; Horseshoe Lake SP.

GOLDEN-CROWNED KINGLET

Regulus satrapa

Before the trees have unfurled their leaves in spring, tiny, migratory Golden-crowned Kinglets flit among bare branches, giving their high-pitched *see-see-see-see* call. This common migrant breeds in northern coniferous forests, but at least one breeding record was confirmed in northern Illinois when young successfully fledged in 1988 at the Morton Arboretum. The species returned to nest the following year in the same location. • In winter, these kinglets join mixed-species flocks of Black-capped Chickadees, Red-breasted Nuthatches and Brown Creepers when they use both conifers and deciduous trees. Golden-crowned Kinglets survive cold temperatures by roosting together in groups or in empty squirrel nests. Like chickadees, these birds can lower their body temperature at night to conserve energy. Nonetheless, harsh winters can cause die-offs of these small birds.

ID: olive back; darker wings and tail; light underparts; dark "cheek"; 2 white wing bars; black eye line; white "eyebrow;" black border around crown. *Male:* reddish orange crown. *Female:* yellow crown. **Size:** *L* 4 in; *W* 7 in.

Status: common migrant; very rare, local breeder; common winter resident, decreasing northward; occurs from mid-September through mid-April to early May.

Habitat: *Breeding:* conifer plantations. *In migration* and *winter:* coniferous, deciduous and mixed forests and woodlands.

Nesting: usually in a spruce or conifer; Illinois nest was 45 ft high in a spruce;

hanging nest is made of moss, lichens, twigs and leaves; female incubates 8–9 whitish to pale buff eggs, spotted with gray and brown, for 14–15 days.

Feeding: feeds from tips of branches, tufts of conifer needles and trunks of spruce, fir and pine; hovers and gleans in canopy; eats gnats, butterfly caterpillars, aphids and their eggs, ladybird beetles, spiders, mites and flies; occasionally eats berries and sap.

Voice: call is a faint, high-pitched, accelerating *see-see-see-see.*

Similar Species: *Ruby-crowned Kinglet* (p. 250): bold, broken, white eye ring; lacks black border around crown.

Best Sites: *In migration:* widespread throughout state. *Winter:* southern Illinois.

249

RUBY-CROWNED KINGLET
Regulus calendula

In spring, the long, musical, rising and falling pitches of the song of the Ruby-crowned Kinglet echo through the deciduous woodlands. If you're lucky you might see the male kinglet expose his brilliant, red crown as he defends territory. • During migration, Ruby-crowned Kinglets regularly mingle with a colorful assortment of warblers and vireos. They can be separated from other tiny songbird species by their hovering technique and wing-flicking, which probably startle insects into movement. • Sometimes becoming entangled in the burs of burdock, the Ruby-crowned Kinglet feeds lower than its cousin, the Golden-crowned. It also winters farther south, breeds farther north, arrives later in spring and departs earlier in fall than the Golden-crowned Kinglet. Like the Golden-crowned Kinglet, Ruby-crown populations are also susceptible to winter storms.

ID: bold, broken eye ring; 2 bold, white wing bars; olive green upperparts; whitish to yellowish underparts; dark wings; short, dark tail. *Male:* small, red crown is usually hidden.
Size: *L* 4 in; *W* 7½ in.
Status: common migrant from mid- to late March through mid-May and from early to mid-September through mid- to late November; uncommon winter resident in southern Illinois.
Habitat: upland and bottomland woods; forested edges, shrublands and conifer plantations, especially in winter in southern Illinois.
Nesting: does not nest in Illinois.

Feeding: gleans and hovers for insect eggs, wasps, ants, leafhoppers, beetles, flies and spiders; will also eat very small amounts of seeds and berries.
Voice: song is an accelerating and rising *tea-tea-tea-tew-tew-tew look-at-Me, look-at-Me, look-at-Me;* call is a short, explosive, double-noted call: *cha-rat;* sometimes a harsh chattering.
Similar Species: *Golden-crowned Kinglet* (p. 249): dark "cheek"; black border around crown; male has orange crown with yellow border; female has yellow crown. *Orange-crowned Warbler* (p. 269): no eye ring; yellow undertail coverts.
Best Sites: *In migration:* widespread. *Winter:* Shawnee NF and Cache River Biosphere Reserve.

BLUE-GRAY GNATCATCHER
Polioptila caerulea

The active Blue-gray Gnatcatcher inhabits woodlands, looking like a tiny mock-ingbird, cocking its tail like a wren and giving a high-pitched buzzy *spee* as it gleans insects from branches and leaves. • During courtship, the male gnat-catcher follows his prospective mate around his territory. Once a bond is established, the pair is inseparable. Male Blue-gray Gnatcatchers take a greater part in nesting and raising the young than males of closely related species. • Blue-gray Gnatcatchers occa-sionally tear up their cup nests and use the material to begin another one elsewhere, possibly as a defense against predators. When completed, the nest often looks like a knot on the limb because of the lichens used to decorate it. In Illinois, gnatcatchers often nest in oaks and walnuts. • Populations of the seven subspecies of the Blue-gray Gnatcatcher have been expanding northward in the past 25 years. Like other species that have a limited breeding distribution north of Illinois, it's dif-ficult to detect fall migration for the Blue-gray Gnatcatcher.

breeding

♂

ID: blue gray upperparts; very long tail; white eye rIng; pale gray under-parts; black uppertail with white outer tail feathers; dark legs. *Breeding male:* black forehead. *Juvenile:* similar to adult; pale bill; brown-washed upper-parts. *In flight:* broad-wings; long, fan-shaped tail with flashy white outer feathers.
Size: *L* 4½ in; *W* 6 in.
Status: common migrant from early April to end of September; abundant breeder in southern Illinois, decreasing northward.
Habitat: mature and successional decidu-ous woodlands, often along streams, ponds, lakes and swamps; also in orchards, shrub-lands, woodland edges and oak savannas.
Nesting: pair builds nest on a branch 6–70 ft above ground; cup nest of plant fibers and bark chips is decorated with lichens and attached to its foundation with spider silk; lined with fine vegetation, hair and feathers; pair incubates 3–5 pale bluish

white eggs, dotted with reddish brown, for 11–15 days; frequently parasitized by Brown-headed Cowbirds; often abandons nest when parasitized.
Feeding: gleans, hovers and sallies; moves up and down through foliage, flicking its tail constantly, possibly to flush prey into view; eats small insects, spiders, moths and their larvae; eats very little, if any, plant matter.
Voice: high-pitched, nasal, buzzy *spee* notes or a short series of *mewing* or chat-tering notes; can mimic several species.
Similar Species: none.
Best Sites: *Summer:* Palos Preserves; Forest Glen Preserve; Shawnee NF and Cache River Biosphere Reserve.

EASTERN BLUEBIRD
Sialia sialis

The Eastern Bluebird lost valuable cavity-nesting habitat when House Sparrows and European Starlings were introduced to North America. Humans worked to perfect the design and placement of bluebird nesting boxes that would deter competitors and predators. Today, bluebirds commonly breed in Illinois. • Most of the state's bluebirds live in the southern third of the state, especially in winter. • Although most bluebird pairs are monogamous, males or females sometimes have more than one mate. Young sometimes help at the nest. • Migratory bluebirds return to Illinois quite early, often in February, and sometimes perish in late winter storms. A cold spell in April can also freeze eggs and may kill adults sitting on nests. • House Wrens and Tree Swallows also use bluebird boxes and wrens frequently pierce and remove bluebird eggs.

♂

ID: chestnut red "chin," throat, breast and sides; white belly and undertail coverts; dark bill and legs. *Male:* deep blue upperparts. *Female:* thin, white eye ring; gray brown head and back tinged with blue; blue wings and tail; paler chestnut on underparts. *Immature:* spotted breast.
Size: *L* 7 in; *W* 13 in.
Status: common migrant and breeder; arrives in late February and leaves by late November; fairly common winter resident, decreasing northward.
Habitat: cropland fencelines, meadows, fallow and abandoned fields, pastures, forest clearings and edges, golf courses and cemeteries.

Nesting: in an abandoned woodpecker cavity, natural cavity, fence post or nest box, which should be cleaned yearly; mostly the female incubates 4–5 pale blue, sometimes white, eggs for 13–16 days; 2 broods; pair may move to different nest for second brood.
Feeding: often swoops from a perch to snatch prey; eats cutworms, cicadas, beetles, crickets and grasshoppers; eats fruits in winter such as mistletoe, grapes, sumac and holly.
Voice: song is a rich, warbling *turr, turr-lee, turr-lee;* call is a chittering *pew.*
Similar Species: *Blue Jay* (p. 227): larger; crested head; lacks red on breast.
Best Sites: *Summer:* Morton Arboretum; Kennekuk County Park. *Winter:* widespread in appropriate habitat in southern Illinois.

VEERY
Catharus fuscescens

Anorthern United States breeder, the Veery has a flutelike, downward spiraling song that rings through some select northern and occasionally central Illinois woodlands in summer. Like many other songbirds, Veeries migrate mostly at night. Data from tracking radio-tagged Veeries show that these birds begin migrating within 30 minutes after sundown. Cold fronts abruptly stop them on their migration, which can bring a fall-out at some stopover sites. Otherwise they fly for three to eight hours, up to 178 miles at a time, flapping their wings constantly. • The Veery population could be declining because of habitat loss on wintering and breeding grounds. Northern Illinois is at the southern edge of the Veery's breeding range.

ID: reddish to chocolate brown upperparts; very thin, grayish eye ring; faintly spotted, buff throat and upper breast; light underparts; gray flanks and face patch.
Size: *L* 7 in; *W* 12 in.
Status: common migrant; much less common in fall, especially in western and southern Illinois; occurs from late April to early June and from late August through mid- to late September; rare to uncommon breeder in northern third of state; very rare breeder in central Illinois.
Habitat: cool, moist deciduous and mixed forests and woodlands with a dense understory of shrubs and ferns.
Nesting: on the ground or in a shrub, often gooseberry; female builds a bulky nest of leaves, weeds, bark strips and rootlets; female incubates 3–4 pale greenish blue eggs for 10–15 days; frequently parasitized by Brown-headed Cowbird.
Feeding: gleans, hovers and hawks the ground and lower vegetation for insects;

also eats fruits such as honeysuckle berries, blackberries, wild cherries, elderberries and dogwood berries; mostly eats insects in summer and fruits in fall; occasionally takes small frogs and salamanders.
Voice: song is a flutelike, descending *vee-ur, vee-ur, vee-ur, veer, veer, veer;* call is a high, whistled *veer.*
Similar Species: *Swainson's Thrush* (p. 255): buffy eye ring; olive brown upperparts; darker spotting on throat and upper breast. *Hermit Thrush* (p. 256): reddish brown tail contrasts with olive brown upperparts; white eye ring; large, dark spots on throat and breast; raises and lowers tail. *Gray-cheeked Thrush* (p. 254): gray brown upperparts; dark breast spots; gray "cheek."
Best Sites: *Summer:* Swallow Cliff FP; Lowden-Miller SF; Castle Rock SP; Mississippi Palisades SP. *In migration:* Des Plaines River Corridor; Palos Preserves; Shawnee NF.

GRAY-CHEEKED THRUSH
Catharus minimus

The Gray-cheeked Thrush winters as far south as Peru and regularly spends summers in the Arctic—farther north than any other North American thrush. Each spring and fall, the Gray-cheeked Thrush migrates through Illinois, with some interesting population variations. For example, fall migrant numbers are lower than in spring, except in east-central Illinois where these birds remain common. • In fall migration, Gray-cheeked Thrushes, like Swainson's Thrushes, are frequent victims of collisions with TV towers. Gray-cheeks represent roughly 11 percent of birds that fly into TV towers. • Gray-cheeked Thrushes sing less frequently in spring than do Swainson's Thrushes or Veeries; their songs are just as beautiful and flutelike, but a bit softer. • Until 1995, the Gray-cheeked Thrush and the very similar-looking Bicknell's Thrush *(C. bicknelli)* were classified as a single species.

ID: gray brown upperparts; gray "cheek"; inconspicuous eye ring may not be visible; heavily spotted breast; light underparts; brownish gray flanks.
Size: *L* 7–8 in; *W* 13 in.
Status: uncommon to common spring migrant and uncommon fall migrant, although more common in east-central Illinois; occurs from late April or early May to early June and from late August to early October.
Habitat: deciduous and mixed woodlands; prefers upland woods.
Nesting: does not nest in Illinois.
Feeding: hops along the ground; eats mostly insects; ants constitute half of diet;

also eats caterpillars, crane flies and their larvae, beetles and mollusks; feeds on berries, including elderberries and pokeberries in fall.
Voice: flutelike, ending with a clear, usually 3-part, whistle, with the middle note higher pitched: *wee-o, wee-a, titi wheeee;* call is a downslurred *wee-o.*
Similar Species: *Swainson's Thrush* (p. 255): prominent buffy eye ring; lacks gray "cheek." *Hermit Thrush* (p. 256): reddish brown tail contrasting with olive brown upperparts; lacks gray "cheek"; raises and lowers tail. *Veery* (p. 253): reddish brown upperparts; weakly spotted breast; lacks gray "cheek."
Best Sites: parks along L. Michigan shoreline; Forest Glen Preserve; Shawnee NF.

SWAINSON'S THRUSH

Catharus ustulatus

On a quiet, clear evening during migration, thrushes call to one another as they fly, possibly as a way to keep in contact. With some practice, a birder may even separate some of the thrush species by their migratory calls. The Gray-cheek and the Veery give an *eer* sound; Swainson's Thrush gives a *whoit*, like a drop of water in a barrel. • In Illinois, one of the most common calls heard from the night sky in May and September is that of the Swainson's Thrush. On the ground, it gives an upward spiraling courtship song, like a Veery singing backward. • Swainson's is the most common migrant thrush in Illinois, sometimes appearing in backyards and parks. • Most thrushes feed on the ground, but the Swainson's Thrush can also find food high in the trees, briefly hover-gleaning like a warbler or vireo. • This is one of the most common songbird species killed in collisions with TV towers. • Swainson's Thrush was once known as the "Olive-backed Thrush."

ID: gray brown upperparts; conspicuous buff eye ring; buff wash on "cheek" and upper breast; spots arranged in streaks on throat and breast; white belly and undertail coverts; brownish gray flanks.
Size: *L* 7 in; *W* 11½ in.

Status: common to locally abundant migrant, especially in spring; occurs from mid- to late April to early June and from late August through early to mid-October.
Habitat: deciduous and mixed woodlands.
Nesting: does not nest in Illinois.
Feeding: gleans vegetation and forages on the ground for invertebrates, including ants, caterpillars, beetles, bees, wasps and crickets; also eats berries, mostly in fall, such as grapes, wild cherries, pokeberries, Virginia creeper, elderberries and blackberries.
Voice: song is a slow, rolling, rising spiral; call is a sharp *witt*.

Similar Species: *Gray-cheeked Thrush* (p. 254): gray "cheek"; less or no buff wash on breast; lacks buffy eye ring. *Hermit Thrush* (p. 256): reddish brown tail and rump contrast with gray body; grayish brown upperparts; darker breast spotting on whiter breast; raises and lowers tail. *Veery* (p. 253): upperparts reddish brown overall; faint breast spots; lacks bold eye ring.
Best Sites: parks along L. Michigan; Des Plaines River Corridor, including Ryerson Woods; Palos Preserves; Pine Hills–LaRue Ecological Area; Giant City SP; Trail of Tears SF.

HERMIT THRUSH
Catharus guttatus

The Hermit Thrush undoubtedly has one of the most beautiful songs of all woodlands species, but Illinoisans rarely get to hear it sing during migration. It's the first thrush, besides the robin and bluebird, to arrive in spring. Its Illinois spring migration coincides with the emergence of many beetle species. You'll recognize this thrush by its reddish brown tail, which it habitually raises and lowers. • Birds banded in northeastern Illinois in fall have been recovered in winter and early spring in Mississippi, Arkansas, southeastern North Carolina and south-central Texas. Along with robins and bluebirds, the Hermit Thrush is the only thrush species that winters in our state; most wintering birds are found in far southern Illinois. During harsher winters, like the bluebird, they are more susceptible to higher mortality rates. • The scientific name *guttatus* is Latin for "spotted" or "speckled," in reference to this bird's breast. • Unlike its relatives, Hermit Thrushes are rarely killed in collisions with TV towers.

ID: reddish brown tail and rump; olive brown upperparts; black-spotted throat and breast; light underparts; gray flanks; thin, whitish eye ring; habitually raises and lowers tail.
Size: *L* 7 in; *W* 11½ in.
Status: common migrant, arriving in late March to early April, with most departing by early May; fall migrants occur from late September through early to mid-November; overwinters in small numbers, mostly in southern Illinois.
Habitat: deciduous and mixed woodlands.
Nesting: does not nest in Illinois.
Feeding: forages on the ground and gleans vegetation for ants, beetles, butterflies and moths; also eats spiders, grasshoppers and wild fruits such as pokeberries,

serviceberries, wild grapes, blackberries, berries from dogwood, Virginia creeper, sumac and poison ivy.
Voice: song is a series of ethereal, flutelike notes, rising and falling in pitch; a small questioning note may precede the song; calls include a faint *chuck*.
Similar Species: *Other thrushes* (pp. 252–59): do not raise and lower tail. *Swainson's Thrush* (p. 255): buff eye ring; grayish brown back and tail. *Veery* (p. 253): lightly spotted upper breast; reddish brown overall with little contrast between tail and upperparts. *Gray-cheeked Thrush* (p. 254): gray "cheek"; lacks conspicuous eye ring. *Fox Sparrow* (p. 317): stockier build; conical bill; brown breast spots.
Best Sites: *In migration:* Chicago lakefront parks; Shawnee NF, especially in pine plantations in winter.

WOOD THRUSH
Hylocichla mustelina

The resonant, flutelike *eeolay* notes of the Wood Thrush once resounded through many Illinois woodlands, but forest fragmentation and urban sprawl have eliminated much of this bird's nesting habitat. • The Wood Thrush winters from southeastern Mexico to Panama, and makes its way northward each spring, breeding primarily in the eastern United States, from the Gulf Coast to southern Canada. This neotropical migrant's population has decreased significantly over much of its range since the late 1970s. Heavily parasitized by the Brown-headed Cowbird, a Wood Thrush nest often holds two, and often more, nonhost eggs in Illinois. • Naturalist and author Henry David Thoreau considered the Wood Thrush to have the most beautiful song of any bird.

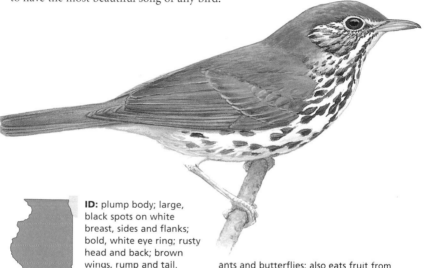

ID: plump body; large, black spots on white breast, sides and flanks; bold, white eye ring; rusty head and back; brown wings, rump and tail.
Size: *L* 8 in; *W* 13 in.
Status: uncommon to locally common migrant from mid-April to late May and from early September to mid-October; common breeder.
Habitat: moist, mature and preferably undisturbed deciduous woodlands and mixed forests.
Nesting: low in a deciduous tree; often in spicebush, American hornbeam and American beech saplings; female builds a bulky cup nest with various vegetation and mud; often includes pieces of plastic; nest is lined with softer materials; female incubates 3–4 pale greenish blue eggs for 13–14 days; parasitized by Brown-headed Cowbird; has 2 broods.
Feeding: forages on the ground and gleans vegetation for insects and other invertebrates, including millipedes, beetles,

ants and butterflies; also eats fruit from spicebush, Virginia creeper, pokeberry, jack-in-the-pulpit, black cherry, elderberry and black gum in late summer.
Voice: bell-like phrases of 3–6 notes, *eeo-lay,* each at a different pitch and followed by a trill; often sings high in a tree; calls include *pit pit.*
Similar Species: *Ovenbird* (p. 291): much smaller and browner; black and russet crown stripes. *Other thrushes* (pp. 252–59): less chunky; much less bold and extensive spotting on underparts; lack bold, white eye ring and rusty "cap" and back. *Fox Sparrow* (p. 317): seen only during migration; stockier build; conical bill; brown breast spots; reddish tail.
Best Sites: *Summer:* Lake County FP woodlands; Deer Grove FP; Palos Preserves; Hanover Bluff Nature Preserve; Forest Glen Preserve; Shawnee NF; Cache River Biosphere Reserve.

257

AMERICAN ROBIN

Turdus migratorius

Although many American Robins migrate, some overwinter in Illinois, especially where berries are plentiful. • A robin in spring with its bill stuffed full of earthworms and grubs is often a sign that hungry young are nearby. This species has been found nesting on window sills, inside sheds and in leftover Christmas wreaths and planters. They nest from mid-March to early September and often return to their place of birth. • North American thrushes migrate during the day and possibly at night. • Robins sing from January through November in Illinois and can be heard at dusk and during the night, especially in spring. American Robins form large winter roosts; the largest in Illinois was 8000 at Rend Lake in 2001; a roost of 300,000 was observed in Missouri during a Christmas bird count.

ID: gray brown back; dark head; white throat streaked with black; incomplete white eye ring; yellow, black-tipped bill. *Male:* deep brick red breast; black head. *Female:* light red orange breast; dark gray head. *Immature:* heavily spotted breast.
Size: *L* 10 in; *W* 17 in.
Status: abundant migrant and breeder; uncommon to locally common winter resident, especially in southern Illinois; migrants arrive in early to mid-February and depart by late November or early December.
Habitat: residential lawns and gardens, pastures, parks, woodlands, shrublands and woodland edges.

Nesting: in a tree or shrub; sturdy cup nest is built of grass, moss and loose bark and is cemented with mud; female incubates 4 light blue eggs for 11–16 days; may have 2, sometimes 3, broods; rarely parasitized by Brown-headed Cowbird.
Feeding: forages on the ground and among vegetation for larval and adult insects, earthworms and other invertebrates; eats fruit, including wild grape, black cherry, hackberry, dogwood and others.
Voice: song is an evenly spaced warble: *cheerily cheer-up cheerio;* call is a rapid *tut-tut-tut.*
Similar Species: *Varied Thrush* (p. 259): extremely rare; black breast band; 2 orange wing bars.
Best Sites: widespread.

VARIED THRUSH
Ixoreus naevius

Though a common bird in the moist coniferous woods of the Northwest, the Varied Thrush has wandered as far east as New England in the winter. • This lovely bird with a dark breast band, orange wing bars and an orange stripe above the eye occurs in Illinois almost every winter. Most records come from the northern part of the state, with only one record ever from southern Illinois and 10 from central Illinois. A Varied Thrush will arrive at a feeder in December in Illinois and often stay for several weeks, sometimes months, if the food supply is abundant. • Varied Thrushes eat berries, fruits, seeds, nuts, acorns and suet from feeders. They particularly like oranges; those who are lucky enough to find a Varied Thrush in their backyard may have to put out fresh oranges and other fruit daily to keep the bird around. • The scientific name *naevius* is Latin for "spotted" or "varied."

VAGRANT

ID: dark upperparts; orange "eyebrow"; orange throat and belly; 2 orange wing bars. *Male:* black breast band; blue black upperparts. *Female:* brown upperparts; faint breast band.
Size: *L* 9½ in; *W* 16 in.
Status: very rare winter resident in northern and occasionally central Illinois; occurs singly nearly every year, mostly in the north; dates of recorded sightings range from October 29 to May 1.
Habitat: suburban yards with well-stocked feeders.

Nesting: does not nest in Illinois.
Feeding: forages on the ground and among vegetation for insects, seeds and berries; takes a variety of foods at feeders, including suet and oranges.
Voice: rarely vocal in Illinois; song is a series of notes delivered at five different pure tones, with a lengthy pause between each note; call is a quiet *tuck*.
Similar Species: *American Robin* (p. 258): much more common; seen year-round; lacks black breast band and orange "eyebrow," throat and wing bars.
Best Sites: backyard feeders in winter, mostly in northern Illinois.

GRAY CATBIRD

Dumetella carolinensis

Upon arrival in spring, the Gray Catbird begins giving its familiar *mew* call, as well as a series of squeaks, chatters and whistles that seem to have no pattern. • A member of the family Mimidae, meaning "mimics," the Gray Catbird can sing two notes at once because both sides of the syrinx can operate independently. • The Gray Catbird builds its loose cup nest within tangles, brambles and thorny thickets. If appropriate habitat exists, a catbird will even nest in a backyard. Finding this bird or its nest during breeding season is difficult, but if a human gets too close, the catbird will scream, assume a defense posture and even attempt to hit the intruder. Catbirds will destroy the eggs and nestlings of other songbirds, including the Chipping Sparrow, American Robin and Eastern Wood-Pewee. • The Brown-headed Cowbird parasitizes catbird nests, but the female catbird often removes the cowbird eggs immediately, a learned skill in the species. Only very rarely do catbirds raise cowbird young. • A nighttime migrant, the Gray Catbird is often a victim of collisions with TV towers.

ID: dark gray overall; black "cap"; long tail may be dark gray to black; chestnut undertail coverts; black eyes, bill and legs.
Size: *L* 8½–9 in; *W* 11 in.
Status: common migrant and breeder from mid- to late April to mid-September through mid- to late November, with some lingering into December; very rare winter resident.
Habitat: dense thickets, brambles, shrubby or brushy areas and hedgerows, often near water.

Nesting: in a dense shrub or thicket; bulky cup nest is loosely built with twigs, leaves and grass and is lined with fine material, often grapevine bark; female incubates 4 greenish blue eggs for 12–15 days.
Feeding: mostly gleans vegetation; forages on the ground and in shrubs for ants, beetles, grasshoppers, caterpillars, moths, craneflies, dragonflies and spiders; also eats berries, including those from dogwood, cherry, wild grape, mulberry, elderberry and pokeberry; may even eat some tree flowers early in breeding season.
Voice: calls include a catlike *meoow* and a harsh *check-check;* song is a variety of warbles, squeaks and mimicked phrases, sometimes interspersed with the *meoow* call.
Similar Species: *Northern Mockingbird* (p. 261): light gray upperparts; white underparts, undertail coverts and outer tail feathers; gray "cap"; large, white wing patches.
Best Sites: widespread in appropriate habitat.

NORTHERN MOCKINGBIRD
Mimus polyglottos

I n northern and sometimes in central Illinois, birders rarely get the chance to see a Northern Mockingbird; this species is much more at home in southern Illinois where its vast repertoire of songs fills the spring and summer mornings. One bird may sing more than 150 different song types, which change and may increase in number as the bird gets older. The mockingbird imitates bird songs and calls, barking dogs, even musical instruments. Mockingbirds, especially males, sing at night. • When walking or hopping on the ground, Northern Mockingbirds flash their wings, showing off their white wing patches. Scientists think this display may be used to stir up insects, deter predators or defend territory. • This species dispersed northward with the introduction of the non-native multiflora rose, a thorny shrub that mockingbirds often use for nesting and for a source of berries in winter. • Some mockingbird pairs have been known to stay together for eight years. • Like the Eastern Bluebird and the Carolina Wren, populations of this species are susceptible to harsh winters.

ID: gray upperparts; dark wings; 2 thin, white wing bars; long, dark tail with white outer tail feathers; light underparts. *Immature:* paler overall; spotted breast. *In flight:* large, white patch at base of black primaries. **Size:** *L* 10 in; *W* 14 in.

Status: common year-round resident in southern half of state; migrants occur from early April to late May; fall migrants difficult to detect; very rare breeder, migrant and winter resident in northeastern Illinois.
Habitat: hedges, suburban gardens, old, overgrown fields and orchard margins.
Nesting: often in a small shrub or small tree; cup nest is built with twigs, grass, fur and leaves; female incubates 3–4 brown-blotched, bluish gray to greenish eggs for 12–13 days; often has 2 broods.
Feeding: gleans vegetation and forages in short grass for beetles, ants, wasps and grasshoppers; also eats berries and other wild fruits; visits feeders for suet and raisins.

Voice: song is a medley of mimicked phrases, often a series of other bird songs; phrases often repeated 3 times or more; calls include a harsh *chair* and *chewk*.
Similar Species: *Northern Shrike* (p. 219) and *Loggerhead Shrike* (p. 218): thicker, hooked bills; black "masks"; much less common, with Northern Shrikes appearing mostly in the northern part of the state and only in winter. *Gray Catbird* (p. 260): gray overall; black "cap"; chestnut undertail coverts; lacks white outer tail feathers and white wing patches.
Best Sites: Midewin National Tallgrass Prairie and Kankakee Sands in northern Illinois; suburban or rural homesteads in southern Illinois.

261

BROWN THRASHER

Toxostoma rufum

Early in the breeding season, the male Brown Thrasher issues his lengthy, complex song with its twice-repeated phrases. • Because this bird nests on or close to the ground, its eggs and nestlings are particularly vulnerable to predation by snakes, weasels, skunks and other animals. Brown Thrashers defend their nests defiantly, attacking large snakes and flying close to humans, calling loudly. • The Brown Thrasher is more likely to be parasitized by the Brown-headed Cowbird than Illinois' other two mimics, the Northern Mockingbird and the Gray Catbird, but the cowbird young in the thrasher's nest often do not survive. • The Brown Thrasher also breeds in more remote places than the mockingbird and catbird and is much less frequently found in backyards. • Fox squirrels in northern Illinois and black rat snakes in southern Illinois prey on thrasher eggs and nestlings.

ID: reddish brown upperparts; pale underparts with heavy, brown streaking; long, downcurved bill; orange yellow eyes; long, rufous tail; 2 white wing bars.
Size: *L* 11½ in; *W* 13 in.
Status: common migrant and breeder; migrants arrive in mid- to late March; fall migrants depart by early to mid-November; regular winter resident in small numbers in southern third of Illinois; very rare to rare winter resident elsewhere.
Habitat: dense shrubs and thickets, overgrown pastures, especially those with hawthorns and osage orange, woodland edges and brushy areas.
Nesting: usually in a low shrub, especially osage orange, hawthorn and large multiflora roses; sometimes on the ground; cup

nest of grass, twigs and leaves is lined with fine vegetation; pair incubates 4 bluish white to pale blue eggs, dotted with reddish brown, for 11–14 days.
Feeding: gleans the ground and vegetation for invertebrates; eats beetles and earthworms; also eats seeds, berries, grains and occasionally salamanders and tree frogs; eats nuts and sunflower seeds at feeders.
Voice: sings a large variety of phrases, with each phrase usually repeated twice: *dig-it dig-it, hoe-it hoe-it, pull-it-up, pull-it-up;* calls include a loud crackling note, a harsh *shuck*, a soft *churr* and a whistled, 3-note *pit-cher-ee.*
Similar Species: *Wood Thrush* (p. 257): heavily spotted underparts; dark eyes; pale eye ring; much shorter tail; prefers woodlands.
Best Sites: common in appropriate habitat.

EUROPEAN STARLING
Sturnus vulgaris

In the early 1890s, roughly 100 European Starlings were released into New York's Central Park, a plan by the local Shakespeare society to introduce all the birds mentioned in their favorite author's writings. The European Starling easily established itself across the continent, often at the expense of native cavity-nesting birds, such as the Eastern Bluebird, Northern Flicker and Red-headed Woodpecker. The first European Starlings recorded in Illinois occurred in the winter of 1922. By 1957, an estimated 11 million starlings existed in the state. • European Starlings mimic many bird songs, including those of Killdeers, Red-tailed Hawks, Soras and meadowlarks. • Highly social and gregarious birds, European Starlings form enormous flocks numbering into the thousands or hundreds of thousands from fall through early spring. When attacked by falcons or other predators, starlings form a large ball in the air as a deterrent.

breeding

ID: short, squared tail; dark eyes; pale reddish to pinkish legs; walks with a waddle. *Breeding:* iridescent, blackish plumage; speckled, yellow bill; spangling on back and wings. *Nonbreeding:* blackish wings; feather tips are heavily spotted with white and buff; white speckles on head, breast and belly; golden spangling on back and wings.
Size: *L* 8½ in; *W* 16 in.
Status: abundant year-round resident.
Habitat: agricultural areas, towns, woodland and forest edges, landfills and roadsides.
Nesting: in a tree, nest box or other artificial cavity; nest is made of grass, twigs and straw; mostly the female incubates 4–6 bluish to greenish white eggs for 12–14 days.
Feeding: forages mostly on the ground; diverse diet includes many invertebrates, berries, corn and other grains, seeds and human food waste; eats cutworms, Japanese beetles and other destructive agricultural pests.
Voice: variety of whistles, squeaks and gurgles; imitates other birds throughout the year; gives a call like a wolf whistle.
Similar Species: *Blackbirds* (pp. 333–43): longer tails; thinner appearance. *Brown-headed Cowbird* (p. 341): male's brown head contrasts with dark, metallic body; female is brownish overall. *Rusty Blackbird* (p. 338): migrant only; lacks speckling; light eyes; dark legs; dark bill. *Brewer's Blackbird* (p. 339): much rarer; lacks speckling; light eyes in male only; dark legs; dark bill; female is brown overall. *Common Grackle* (p. 340): much larger; pale eyes; longer, keel-shaped tail; lacks speckling.
Best Sites: widespread, especially in towns at landfills and in rural areas near farm animals and grain elevators.

AMERICAN PIPIT
Anthus rubescens

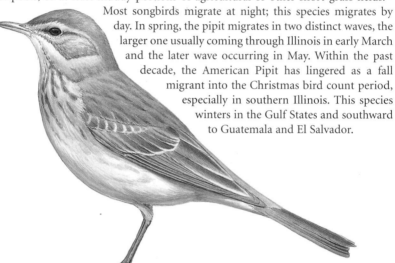

Each spring and fall, wet agricultural fields and mudflats attract this migratory species because they resemble the American Pipit's arctic tundra nesting grounds. • Flocks of pipits may go unnoticed to untrained eyes, because their brown-and-buff plumage blends perfectly with the landscape. Also, birders do not frequent their favorite habitat. Keen observers, however, recognize pipits' white outer tail feathers and habit of bobbing their tails as well as their distinctive, two-syllable *pip-it* calls, usually given in flight. • Formerly known as "Water Pipit," this species prefers wet pools, or at least muddy portions of agricultural or other short-grass fields. • Most songbirds migrate at night; this species migrates by day. In spring, the pipit migrates in two distinct waves, the larger one usually coming through Illinois in early March and the later wave occurring in May. Within the past decade, the American Pipit has lingered as a fall migrant into the Christmas bird count period, especially in southern Illinois. This species winters in the Gulf States and southward to Guatemala and El Salvador.

ID: bold, white eye stripe; lightly streaked "necklace" on upper breast; streaked sides and flanks, more prominent in fall; gray brown upperparts; buff-colored upperparts in spring; dark tail with white outer tail feathers; dark legs; slim bill and body.
Size: *L* 6–7 in; *W* 10½ in.
Status: uncommon to common migrant from late February to early March through mid-May; fall migrants occur from mid-September to mid-November, with a few lingering into early winter, especially in far southern Illinois.
Habitat: agricultural fields, especially wet spots in plowed or short-grass situations; also mudflats.

Nesting: does not nest in Illinois.
Feeding: gleans the ground and vegetation for terrestrial and freshwater invertebrates, including mayflies, caddisflies, stoneflies and dragonflies, especially their larvae; also eats seeds; in summer, almost exclusively eats animal matter.
Voice: familiar flight call is *pip-it;* also a harsh, sharp *tsip-tsip* or *chiwee.*
Similar Species: *Horned Lark* (p. 230): black "horns"; black markings on yellowish face; does not bob tail. *Smith's Longspur* (p. 326) and *Lapland Longspur* (p. 325): chunkier overall; black-streaked, brownish backs; conical, finchlike bills; rattlelike call notes.
Best Sites: *In migration:* agricultural areas; sod farms and dried-up lake beds in fall; L. Chautauqua; H&E Sod Farms in McHenry Co.; Momence Sod Farms; Union County CA and Horseshoe Lake CA in late fall and early winter.

CEDAR WAXWING

Bombycilla cedrorum

Flocks of handsome Cedar Waxwings feast on berries from bushes or trees in late summer and fall. Waxwings can digest a wide variety of berries, some of which are inedible or even poisonous to humans. If the fruits have fermented, these birds may show signs of tipsiness, flying erratically or even flopping around on the ground. • During courtship, the male first lands slightly away from the female and then hops toward her and offers her a berry. The female accepts the berry and hops away from the male, then she stops, hops back and offers him the berry. This ritual can last for several minutes. Native berry-producing trees and shrubs planted in your backyard will attract Cedar Waxwings and may even encourage them to nest in your neighborhood. • This species spends winter in Illinois where sufficient berries can sustain it. Wintering flocks can number into the hundreds. Some waxwings have orange rather than yellow-tipped tails, perhaps because of their different diets.

ID: cinnamon crest; brown upperparts; black "mask"; yellow wash on belly; gray rump; yellow terminal tail band; white undertail coverts; small red "drops" on wings. *Juvenile:* no "mask"; streaked underparts; gray brown body.
Size: *L* 7 in; *W* 12 in.
Status: common migrant; spring migrant wave occurs from late January or early February through early April; second wave occurs from late April to early June; fall migrants occur from early August through early to mid-November; fairly common breeder; uncommon winter resident.
Habitat: wooded urban parks and gardens, overgrown fields, forest edges, second-growth, riparian and open woodlands.

Nesting: in a tree or shrub; bulky, unkept cup nest of twigs, grass, moss and lichens is often lined with fine grass; female incubates 3–5 pale gray to bluish gray eggs, with fine dark spotting, for 12–16 days.
Feeding: catches flying insects on the wing or gleans vegetation; also eats large amounts of berries and wild fruit including cedar berries, especially in fall and winter.
Voice: faint, high-pitched, trilled whistle: *tseee-tseee-tseee.*
Similar Species: *Bohemian Waxwing* (p. 357): much larger; chestnut undertail coverts; small white, red and yellow markings on wings.
Best Sites: *In migration:* Illinois Beach SP. *Winter:* Klehm Arboretum, Rockford; common statewide in appropriate habitat.

BLUE-WINGED WARBLER
Vermivora pinus

Like many other warblers, the Blue-winged Warbler does not warble, but rather has a fast, trilly chatter ending in a *buzz*, sounding more like an insect than a bird. The most familiar is the two-syllable song that sounds like the bird is inhaling on the first note and exhaling on the second. • The Blue-winged is one of the earlier warblers to return to the Prairie State in spring. It winters in Mexico and northern Central America. • The species name *pinus* is a misnomer because the Blue-winged does not breed in, nor does it prefer, pines. *Pinus* probably came from "Pine Creeper," a name early American ornithologists gave to the Blue-winged. • In overlapping ranges, this Illinois nester regularly interbreeds with the Golden-winged, the Kentucky and the Mourning warblers.

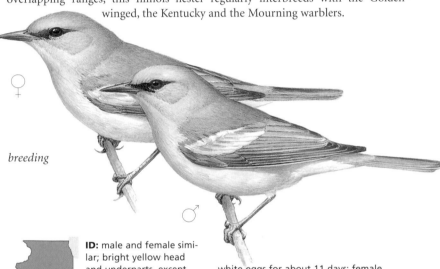

breeding

ID: male and female similar; bright yellow head and underparts, except for white to yellowish undertail coverts; olive yellow upperparts; bluish gray wings and tail; 2 white wing bars; black line through eye; thin, dark bill; white spots on underside of tail.
Size: *L* 4½–5 in; *W* 7½ in.
Status: fairly common migrant and breeder, decreasing northward; migrants arrive in early to mid-April, most depart by mid- to late September.
Habitat: second-growth woodlands, willow swamps, shrubby, overgrown fields, pastures, woodland edges and woodland openings.
Nesting: on or near the ground, concealed by vegetation; female builds a narrow, inverted, cone-shaped nest of grass, leaves and bark strips and lines it with soft materials; female incubates 5 brown-spotted,

white eggs for about 11 days; female remains on the nest even when intruders approach; parasitized by Brown-headed Cowbird.
Feeding: gleans insects and spiders from the lower branches of trees and shrubs; often hangs upside down or hovers to search and probe leaf clumps for insects.
Voice: buzzy, 2-note song: *beee-bzzz*.
Similar Species: *Prothonotary Warbler* (p. 289): blue gray legs and feet; lacks black line through eye and white wing bars; white outer tail feathers, broadly edged in black, in flight. *Yellow Warbler* (p. 272): all yellow; lacks black line through eye; male has orange stripes on breast and appearance of yellow wing bars against darker wing.
Best Sites: *Summer:* Cherry Hill Woods FP, Cook Co.; Forest Glen Preserve, Vermilion Co.; Cypress Creek NWR; War Bluff Audubon Sanctuary. *In migration:* Palos Preserves and Des Plaines River Corridor.

GOLDEN-WINGED WARBLER

Vermivora chrysoptera

The Golden-winged Warbler looks different than the Blue-winged Warbler, but has extremely similar habitat requirements and breeding biology. Where their ranges overlap, a distinctive, fertile hybrid known as the "Brewster's Warbler" exists. This hybrid tends to be grayish overall, like the Golden-winged, but it retains the thin, black eye line and the touch of yellow on the breast from its Blue-winged parent. In rare instances when two of these hybrids reproduce successfully, a second-generation hybrid, the "Lawrence's Warbler," occurs. The Lawrence's is yellowish overall, like the Blue-winged, but has the black "mask," "chin" and throat of the Golden-winged. • The Golden-winged Warbler may be losing habitat to its colonizing relative, the Blue-winged Warbler, which appears to be outcompeting the Golden-wing through hybridization. • The Golden-winged Warbler is a very rare northern Illinois breeder. It winters from the Yucatan south to Columbia and Venezuela.

breeding

ID: yellow forecrown and wing patch; black "chin," throat and "mask" over eye bordered by white; bluish gray upperparts and flanks; white undersides; white spots on underside of tail. *Female* and *immature:* duller overall with gray throat and "mask."

Size: *L* 4½–5 in; *W* 7½ in.

Status: uncommon to fairly common migrant from April to mid- or late May and from late August to late September; very rare breeder in northern Illinois.

Habitat: shrubby fields, woodland edges and early-succession forest clearings.

Nesting: on the ground, concealed by vegetation; female builds an open cup nest of grasses, leaves and grapevine bark and lines it with softer materials; female incubates 5 pinkish to pale cream eggs, marked with brown and lilac, for about 11 days.

Feeding: gleans insects and spiders from trees and shrubs; often hangs upside down to search leaf clumps and even hovers to pick insects from leaves; also probes in dead leaf clumps; eats copious amounts of caterpillars during migration.

Voice: buzzy song begins with a higher note: *zee-bz-bz-bz;* call is a sweet *chip.*

Similar Species: *Black-capped Chickadee* (p. 238) and *Carolina Chickadee* (p. 237): shorter bills; lack any yellow in plumage.

Best Sites: *In migration: Des Plaines River Corridor; Palos Preserves; Atwood Ridge, Shawnee NF.*

TENNESSEE WARBLER
Vermivora peregrina

Other than the Yellow-rumped, the Tennessee is the most numerous migratory warbler in Illinois. At the height of migration, the Tennessee Warbler's loud, three-part song rings throughout woodlands, suburban and even urban yards. • Migrating Tennessee Warblers often sing and forage for insects high in the forest canopy. This bird breeds in the boreal forest; during spruce budworm outbreaks one pair may produce more than seven young in a single brood. • Early ornithologist Alexander Wilson first saw this bird along the Cumberland River in Tennessee and named it after the state. It is only a migrant in Tennessee, however, and breeds in Canada, northern New England, northern Minnesota and Michigan's Upper Peninsula. • Tennessee Warblers winter as far south as Central and South America, choosing open second-growth forests, edges, coffee plantations and gardens with tall trees. In fall, these nocturnal migrants are common victims of collisions with TV towers.

breeding

Habitat: woodlands, urban and suburban areas; anywhere with trees.
Nesting: does not nest in Illinois.
Feeding: gleans foliage and buds for small insects, caterpillars and other invertebrates; also eats berries and sucks nectar; often forages high in forest canopy by hanging upside down on branches.
Voice: male's song is a rapid, loud, sharp, accelerating *ticka-ticka-ticka swit-swit-swit-swit chew-chew-chew-chew-chew;* call is a sweet *chip.*
Similar Species: *Vireos* (pp. 220–26): larger and stouter; thicker, slightly hooked bills. *Warbling Vireo* (p. 224): much less green on upperparts. *Philadelphia Vireo* (p. 225): yellow breast and sides. *Red-eyed Vireo* (p. 226): white "eyebrow" bordered by black line above and below; blue gray feet and legs; duller green back compared with adult male Tennessee Warbler. *Nashville Warbler* (p. 270): bold, white eye ring; lacks eye stripe; breeding male is bright yellow underneath than 3.
Best Sites: *In migration:* widespread in various habitats.

ID: *Breeding male:* blue gray "cap"; olive green back, wings and tail edgings; white "eyebrow"; black eye line; clean, white underparts; thin bill; black legs. *Breeding female:* yellow wash on breast and "eyebrow"; olive gray "cap"; black legs. *Nonbreeding:* olive yellow upperparts; yellow "eyebrow"; yellow underparts except for white undertail coverts; male may have white belly.
Size: *L* 4½–5 in; *W* 8 in.
Status: common to abundant migrant from late April to late May and from mid-August to mid-October.

ORANGE-CROWNED WARBLER

Vermivora celata

The Orange-crowned Warbler breeds most commonly in the western and northwestern parts of the continent and eastward across Canada. In Illinois, it is an early spring and late fall migrant. Its drab appearance makes it easily overlooked and the small, orange crown patch that gives it its name is rarely visible. • This bird's infrequent, rapid, chipping song can be difficult to separate from the songs of several other species that breed in or migrate through Illinois. The Orange-crowned usually forages high in trees in spring and forages low in shrubby, forb-covered fields in fall as well as on its wintering grounds in the southern U.S., Mexico and Central America. • Separating the Orange-crowned from other female and immature warblers in fall can be challenging. This hardy bird is one of the few Illinois warbler species that can occasionally be found in winter, visting pine plantations and suet feeders.

ID: dull, olive yellow to olive gray body; Illinois subspecies has bluish head; faintly streaked underparts; bright yellow undertail coverts; thin, faint, dark eye line; sometimes slight, broken eye ring and light "eyebrow"; thin bill; faint orange crown patch (rarely seen).
Size: *L* 5 in; *W* 7 in.
Status: uncommon spring migrant from mid-April through mid-May; fairly common fall migrant from mid-September to early November; very rare winter resident.
Habitat: woodlands, woodland edges, shrublands and overgrown fields.
Nesting: does not nest in Illinois.
Feeding: gleans foliage for invertebrates, including insect larvae, beetles, ants, spiders and caterpillars; often hover-gleans; eats berries; pierces flower bases for nectar; regularly feeds on sap from old sapsucker holes; eats suet at feeders.
Voice: song is a faint trill that breaks downward halfway through, fading at the end; call is a clear, sharp *chip*.
Similar Species: *Yellow Warbler* (p. 272): female and immature brighter yellow and lack streaking on sides. *Common Yellowthroat* (p. 297): female and immature have grayish "cheek" patch and lack streaking on sides; yellow throat contrasts with whiter belly. *Nashville Warbler* (p. 270): bold, white eye ring; usually distinct separation between blue gray head, green back and yellow underparts. *Pine Warbler* (p. 281): nonbreeding has less pointed bill, white undertail coverts, green upperparts, yellow underparts, distinct white wing bars and white outer tail feathers. *Tennessee Warbler* (p. 268): white undertail coverts; brighter green above and whiter below.
Best Sites: widespread in migration.

NASHVILLE WARBLER

Vermivora ruficapilla

The Nashville Warbler has two widely separated summer populations: one in eastern North America and the other in the West. These populations may have developed thousands of years ago when a single core population split during continental glaciation. • Nashville Warblers migrate through Illinois on their way north to and from their boreal breeding grounds. It has only been documented as a breeder in northern Illinois a few times. • Considered rare in the 1800s, the Nashville Warbler, like the Chestnut-sided Warbler, has benefited from the clearing of old-growth forests for timber and agriculture. • This bird was first described near Nashville, Tennessee, but it does not breed in that state. The Tennessee, Cape May and Connecticut warblers also bear names that misrepresent their breeding distributions. The Nashville Warbler winters mainly in Mexico.

ID: bold, white eye ring; yellow green upperparts; yellow underparts; white between legs. *Male:* blue gray head; rarely shows small, chestnut red crown. *Female* and *immature:* duller colors overall; light eye ring; olive gray head; blue gray nape.

Size: *L* 4½–5 in; *W* 7½ in.

Status: common migrant from mid- to late April through late May and from mid- to late August through mid- to late October; extremely rare, local breeder.

Habitat: *Breeding:* second-growth mixed or deciduous woodlands; overgrown steep slopes and upland forest with nearby marsh thickets. *In migration:* various habitats, woodlands, shrublands and suburban areas.

Nesting: on the ground under a fern, sapling or shrubby cover; female builds a cup nest of grass, bark strips, ferns and

moss and lines it with conifer needles, fur and fine grasses; female incubates 4–5 brown-spotted, white eggs for 11–12 days.

Feeding: mostly insectivorous; gleans foliage for insects such as caterpillars, flies, aphids, leafhoppers, young grasshoppers, locusts, wood-boring beetles and spruce budworms; forages in tassels of flowering trees and undersides of leaves; occasionally catches flies on the wing.

Voice: song begins with a thin, high-pitched *see-it see-it see-it see-it,* followed by a trilling *ti-ti-ti-ti-ti,* similar to Tennessee Warbler but in two parts; call is a metallic *chink.*

Similar Species: *Common Yellowthroat* (p. 297) and *Wilson's Warbler* (p. 299): females lack grayish head and bold, white eye ring. *Tennessee Warbler* (p. 268): white underparts; lacks white eye ring. *Connecticut Warbler* (p. 295) and *Mourning Warbler* (p. 296): grayish to brownish throat and breast; yellow feathering against pinkish legs.

Best Sites: widespread during migration.

NORTHERN PARULA

Parula americana

Young Northern Parulas spend the first few weeks of their lives enclosed in a fragile, socklike nest often hidden in dense tree foliage. • The Northern Parula, one of the smallest North American warblers, usually lives in older forests where it finds mature lichens and mosses for nest building during the breeding season. In Illinois, however, the Northern Parula uses dense clusters of leaves and grapevine tangles as an alternative. Males spend most of their time singing their buzzy trills and foraging among the tops of tall trees, especially sycamores. • Interestingly, extensive populations of Northern Parulas breed north of Illinois in Canada, Wisconsin and Michigan, but not in northern Illinois, possibly because of the lack of sycamores there.

breeding

ID: blue gray upperparts; olive patch on back; 2 white wing bars; white eye crescents; yellow "chin," throat and breast; white lower belly and flanks. *Male:* 1 black and 1 orange breast band. **Size:** *L* 4½ in; *W* 7 in.
Status: common migrant and breeder, decreasing northward; migrants occur from early April through mid- to late May and from mid- to late August through early October; rarely overwinters in pine plantations.
Habitat: moist coniferous forests, humid riparian woodlands and swampy deciduous woodlands, especially where lichens hang from branches.
Nesting: usually 15–75 ft high in cottonwoods, sycamores, oaks and other trees near streams and rivers; female uses dense clusters of leaves, grapevine tangles and other material in Illinois; uses *Usnea* lichens (old man's beard) or Spanish moss

elsewhere; pair incubates 4–5 brown-marked, whitish eggs for 12–14 days.
Feeding: gleans mostly for spiders, caterpillars and beetles; hovers at the tips of branches; occasionally eats berries, seeds and nectar.
Voice: song is a rising, buzzy trill ending with an abrupt, lower-pitched *zip;* a second, less frequent song is a rising series of buzzy notes with a sharp, slurred ending.
Similar Species: *Cerulean Warbler* (p. 286) male has cerulean blue upperparts; white throat extends behind "cheek"; single blue gray to black breast band only; white underparts with blue and black streaking on flanks; lacks white eye crescents. *Yellow-throated Warbler* (p. 280): yellow lores; black, triangular "mask" outlined in white continues as black streaks along flanks; broad, white eye stripe; white lower eye crescent; lacks green back and orange and black breast bands.
Best Sites: *Summer:* Middlefork State Fish and WA; Sanganois SCA; Pere Marquette SP; Giant City SP; Cache River Biosphere Reserve.

271

YELLOW WARBLER

Dendroica petechia

In Illinois, Yellow Warblers arrive with the first main wave of spring warblers, issuing their *sweet, sweet, sweet, sweeter than sweet* calls in shrubby areas. Their variable song can sometimes be confused with that of the Chestnut-sided Warbler. • The Yellow Warbler, the most widely distributed member of its family, is a common breeder in Illinois. • Brown-headed Cowbirds frequently parasitize this species, but Yellow Warblers can recognize the foreign eggs and will abandon their nests or build another nest atop the old eggs. These warblers are persistent and will sometimes create multilayered, high-rise nests over parasitized nests. • The Yellow Warbler consists of 43 subspecies of three groups, which include the "Golden Warbler" and "Mangrove Warbler."

breeding

ID: bright yellow body; black bill and eyes; yellow tail edged in dark olive; pinkish legs. *Breeding male:* reddish orange breast streaks.
Size: *L* 5 in; *W* 8 in.
Status: common migrant and breeder; arrives in mid- to late April; fall migrants occur from late July through mid-September.
Habitat: usually near water in moist, successional, open woodlands with dense, low scrub; also shrubby meadows, willow tangles and riparian thickets.
Nesting: low in a deciduous tree or shrub, including young cottonwoods and willows; female builds a compact cup nest of grass, weeds and shredded bark and lines it with plant down and fur; nest often has a silvery appearance; female incubates 4–5 speckled, greenish white eggs for 11–12 days; frequently parasitized by Brown-headed Cowbird.
Feeding: gleans foliage and vegetation for invertebrates, especially caterpillars, inchworms, beetles, aphids and cankerworms; occasionally hover-gleans.
Voice: song is a fast, frequently repeated *sweet-sweet-sweet sweeter than sweet.*
Similar Species: *Orange-crowned Warbler* (p. 269): darker olive plumage overall; lacks reddish breast streaks of male. *American Goldfinch* (p. 350): black wings and tail; male often has black forehead. *Wilson's Warbler* (p. 299): shorter, darker tail; male has black "cap"; female has darker crown and upperparts. *Common Yellowthroat* (p. 297): darker face and upperparts; female lacks yellow highlights in wings. *Prothonotary Warbler* (p. 289): large, dark eyes; long bill; olive green back; blue gray legs; unmarked, bluish gray wings, rump and tail on perched bird.
Best Sites: widespread in appropriate habitat.

CHESTNUT-SIDED WARBLER
Dendroica pensylvanica

Chestnut-sided Warblers favor early-succession forests and shrublands, which have become abundant over the past century. While clear-cut logging and prescribed forest burns have adversely affected other warbler species, these practices have created suitable habitat for the Chestnut-sided Warbler. Today, birders can easily see more of this species in a single day in the appropriate season than John J. Audubon saw in his entire life—he reportedly saw only one. • In fall, warblers acquire their nonbreeding plumage, which can make identification confusing. The Chestnut-sided Warbler undergoes one of the more dramatic changes, sporting unusual yellowish green upperparts in fall and winter. • Males sing two "song classes," one before the female arrives and the other during the nesting cycle. • In Illinois, the Chestnut-sided is a frequent victim of collisions with television towers.

breeding

ID: *Breeding:* chestnut brown streaks on sides; white underparts; yellow "cap"; black legs; yellowish wing bars; black "mask"; male has bold colors. *Female:* paler colors; dark streaking on yellow "cap." *Nonbreeding:* yellowish green crown, nape, rump and back; white eye ring; gray face and sides; white underparts. *Immature:* similar to fall adult, but with brighter yellow wing bars.
Size: *L* 5 in; *W* 8 in.
Status: common migrant; arrives in late April and early May; departs by late May; fall migrants occur from mid-August to early October; rare to locally uncommon breeder in northern Illinois; very rare breeder elsewhere.
Habitat: *Breeding:* shrubby, second-growth, deciduous woodlands and abandoned fields and orchards; especially in successional areas, including those regenerating after logging or fire. *In migration:* various woodlands.

Nesting: low in a shrub or sapling; small cup nest is made of bark strips, grass, roots and weed fibers and lined with fine grasses, plant down and fur; female incubates 4 brown-marked, whitish eggs for 11–12 days; frequently parasitized by Brown-headed Cowbird.
Feeding: searches undersides of leaves on trees and shrubs at midlevel for insects, mostly larvae of butterflies and moths, as well as some adults; also eats spiders, seeds and fruit; on wintering grounds, one quarter of diet may consist of fruit.
Voice: loud, clear song: *so pleased, pleased, pleased to MEET-CHA;* second song lacks accented last syllable; musical *chip* call.
Similar Species: *Bay-breasted Warbler* (p. 284): spring male has black face; dark chestnut hindcrown, upper breast, throat and sides; buff belly and undertail coverts; white wing bars; darker upperparts in fall.
Best Sites: *Summer:* Swallow Cliff FP; Lowden-Miller SF. *In migration:* widespread.

273

MAGNOLIA WARBLER
Dendroica magnolia

F amous ornithologist Alexander Wilson gave this bird its inappropriate name when he first collected it from a magnolia tree in 1810. This species is not habitually found in magnolia trees, but rather breeds in coniferous forests containing spruces, hemlocks and other evergreens. • This species' short, variable song can be confused with that of the Yellow Warbler and Chestnut-sided Warbler. • Large numbers of Magnolia Warblers and other songbirds, which migrate at night, frequently die from collisions with TV towers and other tall structures. • This species nests in hidden, dense areas of small conifers; as a result, much remains to be learned about its breeding habits and life history.

breeding

ID: *Breeding male:* yellow underparts with bold, black streaks; black "mask"; white "eyebrow"; blue gray crown; dark upperparts; white wing bars often blend into larger patch. *Female* and *nonbreeding male:* duller overall; light "mask"; 2 distinct white wing bars; streaked olive back. *In flight:* yellow rump; white tail patches.
Size: *L* 4½–5 in; *W* 7½ in.
Status: common migrant from late April to late May and from late August to mid-October, with some lingering into late October.
Habitat: woodlands and shrubby patches.
Nesting: does not nest in Illinois.

Feeding: gleans vegetation and buds for insects; occasionally flycatches for beetles, flies, wasps, caterpillars and other insects; sometimes eats berries; often feeds closer to the ground than other warblers.
Voice: song is a quick, rising *pretty pretty lady* or *wheata wheata wheet-zu;* call is a *clank.*
Similar Species: *Yellow-rumped Warbler* (p. 277): white throat, breast and belly; yellow shoulder patches and crown during breeding season. *Cape May Warbler* (p. 275): chestnut "cheek" patch on yellow face; streaked breast extends onto throat. *Canada Warbler* (p. 300): blue gray upperparts; complete white eye ring; black streaking on throat only; much less extensive black on face; yellow legs; lacks wing bars and white in tail feathers.
Best Sites: widespread during migration.

CAPE MAY WARBLER
Dendroica tigrina

Cape May Warblers have a strong affinity for spruces, often using those in suburban Illinois settings during migration. • In years of spruce budworm outbreaks on their northerly breeding grounds, Cape May Warblers can successfully fledge more young. The use of pesticides to control budworms and the cutting of old-growth forests may adversely affect populations of this species. • The Cape May uses its tubular tongue, unique among wood-warblers, to feed on nectar and fruit juices during migration and on its tropical wintering grounds. In Illinois, the Cape May Warbler feeds on the blossoms of tulip trees, hawthorns and crab apples. It also defends small territories around trees with sapsucker holes. • Many Cape May Warblers go unnoticed during migration because their high-pitched song is hard to hear and they often feed high in the trees. Most high counts for this fairly uncommon migrant are in the Chicago region and extreme east-central Illinois, especially in fall.

ID: combination of yellow rump, bold, extensive streaking on entire underparts and large, white wing patch is diagnostic in males. *Breeding male:* chestnut brown "cheek" on yellow face; dark crown. *Female:* paler overall; 2 faint, thin, white wing bars; grayish "cheek" patch on yellowish face; grayish crown. *Nonbreeding:* dull grayish overall with extensive streaking on flanks; yellow "collar" extending to nape.
Size: *L* 5 in; *W* 8 in.
Status: uncommon migrant downstate; locally common migrant along Chicago lakefront; occurs from early to late May and from mid- to late August through early to mid-October, with some lingering until early November.
Habitat: woodlands, especially those dominated by oaks, spruces and spring-flowering trees and shrubs.
Nesting: does not nest in Illinois.
Feeding: gleans treetop branches and foliage for spruce budworms and other insects; occasionally hover-gleans; probes sapsucker holes and flowers for sap or nectar; visits suet feeders in winter.

Voice: song is a very high-pitched, soft *see see see see;* call is a very high-pitched *tsee.*
Similar Species: *Blackburnian Warbler* (p. 279): nonbreeding has streaking confined to flanks, dark facial marking, darker blackish crown, yellow throat; female has white wing bars. *Magnolia Warbler* (p. 274): nonbreeding has less extensive streaking, blue gray crown, nape and "cheek" and usually yellow throat. *Yellow-rumped Warbler* (p. 277): nonbreeding has much less streaking, male is more brownish overall. *Blackpoll Warbler* (p. 285): nonbreeding lacks yellow rump, yellow feet and gray "collar"; male has thinly streaked crown. *Pine Warbler* (p. 281): nonbreeding lacks yellowish rump and has less pronounced blurry streaks.
Best Sites: *In fall migration:* Jackson, Lincoln and Grant Parks in Chicago.

275

BLACK-THROATED BLUE WARBLER

Dendroica caerulescens

O f the migrant warblers that nest north of Illinois, the Black-throated Blue is by far the rarest. Black-throated Blue Warblers enter the United States from the southeast in spring, heading toward their main breeding range in the northeastern U.S. and southeastern Canada. The birds seen in Illinois are from a relatively thin breeding population west of this region, in northern Wisconsin and northeastern Minnesota. • Male and female Black-throated Blue Warblers are so different in plumage that early naturalists, including John J. Audubon, initially thought they were two different species. In warblers, this occurrence is the exception to the rule. • The Black-throated Blue Warbler retains its breeding plumage in fall, making the male one of the easiest fall warblers to identify.

breeding

ID: *Male:* black face, throat, upper breast and sides; dark blue upper-parts; clean white under-parts and wing patch. *Female:* olive brown upperparts; unmarked buff underparts; pale "eye-brow" on darkish face; small buff to whitish wing patch (may not be visible).
Size: *L* 5–5½ in; *W* 7½ in.
Status: uncommon migrant in northeast-ern Illinois; very rare to rare migrant else-where; occurs from early May to late May and from late August to early October; slightly more common and widespread statewide in fall.
Habitat: *In migration:* mainly deciduous and mixed forests with a dense understory of deciduous saplings and shrubs.
Nesting: does not nest in Illinois.

Feeding: gleans the understory for cater-pillars, moths, other insects and spiders; often hover-gleans or snatches prey in flight; occasionally eats seeds and berries.
Voice: song is a slow, wheezy or buzzy *I am soo lay-zeee;* call is a short *tip.*
Similar Species: male and white wing mark in female are distinctive. *Mourning Warbler* (p. 296) and *Connecticut Warbler* (p. 295): females and fall immatures have greener backs, yellower underparts, partial white eye rings (complete in Connecticut), lack dark ear patches and have pink feet and lower mandibles. *Common Yellow-throat* (p. 297): female and immature have browner upperparts with contrasting yel-low throat, yellow undertail coverts and pink legs.
Best Sites: Montrose Point, Jackson Park (Chicago); other L. Michigan parks; Des Plaines and Skokie River Corridors; Champaign-Urbana parks and residential areas.

YELLOW-RUMPED WARBLER

Dendroica coronata

I ts generalist feeding and habitat requirements have likely led to the Yellow-rumped Warbler's widespread and abundant status in Illinois and North America. Among the first warblers to return in spring, the Yellow-rump is fairly common in winter in southern Illinois, surviving on wintering insects and berries, especially poison ivy. Winter populations vary and numbers may depend on poison ivy fruit supplies. Small flocks of Yellow-rumps roost together in winter in pine plantations. • During migration, the highest densities of migrant Yellow-rumps occur in southern Illinois pine plantations and in bottomland forests elsewhere. • Though confined to coniferous breeding habitats, Yellow-rumps forage during migration in a wide variety of habitats. • The "Myrtle Warbler," found in the northern and eastern United States, and "Audubon's Warbler," found in the West, were once considered two separate species. The "Audubon's Warbler," rarely seen in Illinois, has a yellow throat compared with the "Myrtle's" white throat.

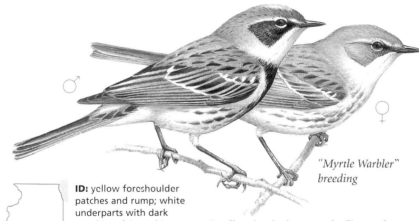

"Myrtle Warbler" breeding

ID: yellow foreshoulder patches and rump; white underparts with dark streaking; faint, white wing bars; thin "eyebrow." *Male:* yellow crown; blue gray upperparts with black streaking; black "cheek" and breast band. *Female:* gray brown upperparts with dark streaking. *Nonbreeding:* less yellow and more brown than black.
Size: *L* 5–6 in; *W* 9 in.
Status: abundant migrant and fairly common winter resident decreasing northward; migrants occur from late March to early April through late May and mid-September to late November.
Habitat: upland, especially pine plantations in southern Illinois; bottomland forests statewide; also forest edges, shrublands, fallow and cultivated fields.
Nesting: does not nest in Illinois.

Feeding: hawks, hovers and sallies out for beetles, flies, wasps, caterpillars, moths and other insects; also gleans vegetation; eats berries and suet at feeders in winter.
Voice: variable song is a tinkling trill, often given in 2-note phrases that rise or fall at the end; call is a sharp *chip* or *check*.
Similar Species: *Magnolia Warbler* (p. 274): yellow underparts; yellow throat; bold, white "eyebrow"; white patches on tail; lacks yellow crown. *Chestnut-sided Warbler* (p. 273): chestnut brown sides on otherwise clean white underparts; lacks yellow rump. *Cape May Warbler* (p. 275): heavily streaked yellow throat, breast and sides; lacks yellow crown. *Yellow-throated Warbler* (p. 280): yellow throat; bold, white "eyebrow," ear patch and wing bars; lacks yellow crown and rump. *Palm Warbler* (p. 283): nonbreeding has greenish rump; incessantly wags tail.
Best Sites: widespread in migration.

277

BLACK-THROATED GREEN WARBLER

Dendroica virens

I n spring, birders aren't likely to miss the Black-throated Green Warbler's buzzy, distinctive *zee-zee-zee-zoo-zee* song as migrants forage in mid- to high-level canopies. When researchers heard the song in the summer of 1984 at Lowden-Miller State Forest, they realized they may have discovered the state's first confirmed breeding Black-throated Green Warbler. In late June, they found a nest of fledglings in a white pine. Fifteen singing males were recorded there as well; some may have been unmated. • The Black-throated Green Warbler is the eastern representative of a group that includes the federally endangered Golden-cheeked Warbler, as well as the Hermit Warbler and Townsend's Warbler. These closely related species were probably isolated periodically during times of glaciation. The Black-throated Green Warbler consists of two subspecies: one breeds over most of its range and the other, a smaller population, breeds in cypress swamps in the southeastern United States.

breeding

ID: yellow face; may show faint dusky "cheek" or eye line; black upper breast band; streaking along sides; olive crown, back and rump; dark wings and tail; 2 bold, white wing bars; white lower breast, belly and undertail coverts. *Male:* black throat. *Female:* yellow throat with black "bib"; thinner wing bars. *Nonbreeding female:* whitish throat with some darkish streaks.
Size: *L* 4½–5 in; *W* 7½ in.
Status: common migrant from mid-April to late May or early June and from late August to mid-October; very rare local breeder in northern Illinois.
Habitat: *Breeding:* pine plantations. *In migration:* coniferous, deciduous and mixed woodlands.

Nesting: usually in a conifer; compact cup nest of grass, weeds, twigs, bark, lichens and spider silk is lined with moss, fur, feathers and plant fibers; female incubates 4–5 scrawled and spotted, creamy white to gray eggs for 12 days.
Feeding: gleans vegetation and buds for beetles, flies, wasps, caterpillars and other insects; sometimes takes berries; frequently hover-gleans.
Voice: fast *zee-zee-zee-zoo-zee* or *zoo-zee-zoo-zoo-zee;* call is a fairly soft *tick.*
Similar Species: black on throat, yellow "cheek" and olive crown in spring and fall are distinctive in Illinois, except for imma-ture warblers. *Blackburnian Warbler* (p. 279): fall immature has yellow to orange throat, paler yellow in face and streaked back. *Blackpoll Warbler* (p. 285): fall immature has whitish or dull "cheek," gray nape, yellow feet and more faintly streaked sides.
Best Sites: *Summer:* Lowden-Miller SF. *In migration:* widespread.

BLACKBURNIAN WARBLER
Dendroica fusca

High among coniferous and deciduous trees lives the Blackburnian Warbler, its fiery orange throat ablaze in spring. Different species of wood-warblers coexist with the help of specific feeding strategies and the partitioning of foraging niches. Some warblers inhabit high treetops, a few feed and nest along outer tree branches at different levels. Others restrict themselves to inner branches and tree trunks. Blackburnians have found their niche predominantly in the outermost branches of the crowns of mature trees. • During migration, Blackburnians are more partial to mature woodlands than other warbler species. They tend to migrate farther east in fall than in spring, and so are more numerous in spring in coastal Texas and more numerous in fall in Florida. • On their breeding grounds, populations of Blackburnian Warblers may decline as populations of Cape May Warblers and Bay-breasted Warblers, with whom they share some feeding niches, increase.

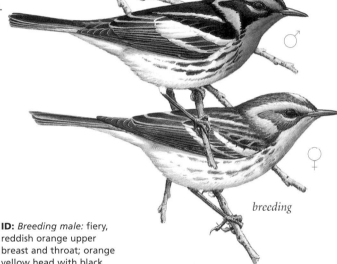

breeding

ID: *Breeding male:* fiery, reddish orange upper breast and throat; orange yellow head with black markings; blackish upperparts; large, white wing patch; yellowish to whitish underparts; dark streaking on sides and flanks. *Female:* brown version of male; upper breast and throat are more yellowish than male's. *Nonbreeding:* yellow throat on male; dusky throat on female; both have white wing bars or patches and streaking on sides of pale underparts.
Size: *L* 5–5½ in; *W* 8½ in.
Status: fairly common migrant from early to late May and from late August to late September; more numerous in eastern Illinois.

Habitat: woodlands, particularly mature pine forests.
Nesting: does not nest in Illinois.
Feeding: forages on the uppermost branches, gleaning budworms, flies, beetles and other invertebrates; occasionally hover-gleans.
Voice: song is a soft, faint, high-pitched *ptoo-too-too-too-tititi-zeee* or *see-me see-me see-me see-me*, often ending in a high-pitched *squeak;* call is a short *tick.*
Similar Species: *Black-throated Green Warbler* (p. 278): fall immature has brighter yellow face, lacks streaked back.
Best Sites: fairly common in appropriate habitat.

279

YELLOW-THROATED WARBLER
Dendroica dominica

For unknown reasons, this bird began to retreat southward in the early 1900s from its southern Michigan and northern Ohio breeding grounds. Since the 1940s, it has slowly begun reoccupying its former territory. • In Illinois, Yellow-throats breed in dry, upland pine plantations or wet, lowland forests, especially along rivers. They show a distinct preference for sycamores statewide and cypress trees in southern Illinois. They prefer to feed and nest in the upper canopy. • The Yellow-throated Warbler forages more like a creeper or nuthatch than a warbler, inserting its unusually long, thin bill into cracks and crevices in bark, pine needles and pine cones. • In southern Illinois, the Yellow-throated Warbler shares breeding habitat with the much less common Pine Warbler, and may adapt its foraging strategies to coexist peacefully. Its breeding range and habitat also overlap with the Northern Parula.

breeding

ID: fall and spring plumages similar; yellow throat and upper breast; triangular black "mask"; black forehead; bold, white "eyebrow" and ear patch; white underparts with black streaking on sides; 2 white wing bars; bluish gray upperparts.

Size: *L* 5–5½ in; *W* 8 in.

Status: common migrant and breeder in southern Illinois, decreasing northward; occurs from late March to late September.

Habitat: upland pine plantations; bottomland forests with sycamores or cypress.

Nesting: saddled on a horizontal branch in a deciduous or pine tree, well away from the trunk; female builds a cup nest of fine grasses, weed stems, bark shreds and plant fibers and lines it with plant down and feathers; female incubates 4 pale greenish or grayish white eggs, spotted and blotched with purple, gray and dark red, for about 12 days.

Feeding: gleans insects from tree trunks and foliage; forages on undersides of branches; often flycatches insects in midair; probes pine needles, pine cones and tree crevices; occasionally visits suet feeders.

Voice: boisterous song is a series of down-slurred whistles with a final rising note: *tee-ew tee-ew tee-ew tew-wee;* call is a soft *chip.*

Similar Species: *Magnolia Warbler* (p. 274): black "necklace" across yellow breast, which extends to lower belly; wide, white wing panel; black back; lacks white ear patch. *Kentucky Warbler* (p. 294): entirely yellow underparts; olive green upperparts; yellow "eyebrow" stripe and spectacles; lacks wing bars and bold, black streaking; pinkish legs.

Best Sites: *Summer:* Sugar River FP; Middlefork SFWA, Vermilion Co.; Pere Marquette SP; Little Black Slough Nature Preserve; Pine Hills–LaRue Ecological Area.

PINE WARBLER

Dendroica pinus

Pine Warblers usually forage near the tops of tall, mature pine trees, frequently building nests there. Their unmusical trill resembles that of Chipping Sparrows and Worm-eating Warblers, making them difficult to identify by song alone. • Unlike most wood-warblers, the Pine Warbler breeds in Canada and the eastern U.S. and winters almost exclusively in the southern U.S. In southern Illinois, the Pine Warbler nests in loblolly, white and shortleaf pines. • This warbler behaves like a Brown Creeper when it forages, probing furrowed bark or tree trunks, searching for hidden insects. It also probes in clusters of pine needles at the tips of branches. • The Pine Warbler resembles some immature and fall-plumaged vireos and warblers, forcing birders to obtain a good, long look before making a positive identification.

breeding

ID: *Male:* olive green head and back; dark grayish wings and tail; whitish to dusky wing bars; yellow throat and breast; faded dark streaking or dusky wash on sides of breast; white undertail coverts and belly; faint yellow spectacles; a little duller in fall. *Female:* similar to male, but duller, especially in fall.
Size: *L* 5–5½ in; *W* 8½ in.
Status: rare to uncommon migrant from early to mid-April through mid-May and from late August to mid-October; locally common breeder in pine plantations in southern Illinois; rare, local breeder elsewhere; uncommon, regular winter resident in extreme southern Illinois.
Habitat: *Breeding:* open, mature pine woodlands and plantations or mixed and deciduous woodlands, especially oak trees. *In migration:* large, mature pines.
Nesting: toward the end of a pine limb; average 30–50 ft or more above ground; female builds a deep, open cup nest of twigs, bark, weeds, grasses, pine needles and spider webs and lines it with feathers;

pair incubates 3–5 brown-speckled, whitish eggs for about 10 days.
Feeding: eats mostly insects, berries and seeds; gleans from the ground or foliage; may hang upside down on branch tips; eats suet and sunflower seeds at feeders.
Voice: song is a short, musical trill; call note is a sweet *chip*.
Similar Species: *Blackpoll Warbler* (p. 285): nonbreeding has streaking on back, gray side of neck contrasts with green back and head, lacks distinct eye ring. *Orange-crowned Warbler* (p. 269): nonbreeding has more pointed bill, yellow undertail coverts, grayer overall, less distinct wing bars and lacks white outer tail feathers. *Yellow-throated Vireo* (p. 222): bright yellow "spectacles"; gray rump and lower back; lacks streaking on sides; stouter bill with slightly hooked tip; blue gray legs and feet.
Best Sites: *Summer* and *Winter:* Crab Orchard NWR; Trail of Tears SF; Lusk Creek Wilderness, Pope Co.

PRAIRIE WARBLER

Dendroica discolor

The inappropriately named Prairie Warbler occupies early successional areas and upland fields with short trees and scattered vegetation. Once rare over much of its current breeding range, its numbers grew as North America was colonized. Today, populations may be declining because of reforestation. • A male Prairie Warbler may return each year to a favored nest site until the vegetation in that area grows too tall and dense. Nests have been found in winged elms and, less frequently, in red cedars, which are both widespread in this species' habitat in southern Illinois. • Although this bird regularly nests as far north as Vermilion County in east-central Illinois, most of the state's breeding population of Prairie Warblers is confined to Jackson, Williamson, Union, Johnson and Pope counties in southern Illinois. The species is rare or absent from western Illinois. • The Prairie Warbler is one of the most thoroughly studied North American songbirds.

breeding

ID: *Male:* bright yellow face and underparts, except for white undertail coverts; dark "cheek" patch and eye line; black streaking on sides; olive gray upperparts; somewhat inconspicuous chestnut streaks on back; 2 faint yellowish wing bars. *Female* and *immature:* similar to male, but duller.
Size: *L* 4½–5 in; *W* 7 in.
Status: rare migrant; fairly common breeder in southern Illinois, decreasing northward; arrives in early April; most birds depart by mid-September, with some lingering into early October; fall migration goes largely undetected.
Habitat: shrubby, old fields; early successional habitat; young pine plantations.

Nesting: female selects nest site, typically 1–10 ft above ground, in a winged elm; builds stiff, cuplike nest of spider webs, hair, feathers and plant fibers in upright fork or vertical branch; female incubates 3–5 creamy white eggs, dotted with brown and gray, for 12–13 days; parasitized by Brown-headed Cowbird; occasionally tears nest apart and rebuilds elsewhere.
Feeding: gleans, hover-gleans and occasionally hawks for prey, including beetles, moths, butterflies, ants, bees and wasps; also eats spiders, berries and tree sap.
Voice: buzzy song is an ascending series of *zee* notes, getting faster; call is sweet *chip*.
Similar Species: most birds distinctive in adult plumage.
Best Sites: *Breeding:* Giant City SP; Fern Clyffe SP; Lusk Creek Wilderness and War Bluff Sanctuary, Pope Co.; Forest Glen Preserve, Vermilion Co.

PALM WARBLER
Dendroica palmarum

The Palm Warbler was apparently named to indicate its subtropical winter range. It could just as easily have been named "Bog Warbler," because it breeds in the northern bogs and fens of sphagnum moss and black spruce. The Palm Warbler nests farther north than all other wood-warblers, except the Blackpoll. • In Illinois, Palm Warblers commonly forage on the ground in cattail marshes, on beaches, along the edges of ponds and lakes, in wet agricultural fields and in the low vegetation of woodlands and shrublands. This bird also feeds in niches as high as the upper canopy in woodland areas. • The Palm Warbler incessantly bobs its tail; a good identifying characteristic, particularly in fall when its colors are more subdued. • The subspecies found in Illinois is the western *D. p. palmarum*. Records of the eastern or "yellow" Palm Warbler, *D. p. hypochrysea*, in Illinois are rare. When side by side in the field, they can easily be separated. During migration, Palm Warblers and Yellow-rumped Warblers often travel together; both are hardy, moving north early in spring and south late in fall.

breeding

ID: chestnut "cap," may be inconspicuous in fall; yellow "eyebrow," throat and undertail coverts; yellow or white breast and belly; dark streaking on breast and sides; olive brown upperparts; may show dull yellowish rump; frequently bobs tail.
Size: *L* 4–5½ in; *W* 8 in.
Status: common to very common migrant from early April to mid-May and from late August to late October, with birds regularly lingering into November; occasionally recorded on Christmas bird counts.
Habitat: low vegetation in a wide variety of habitats where one would expect to find sparrows; also, high in trees in woodlands.

Nesting: does not nest in Illinois.
Feeding: feeds while perched or hovering; gleans the ground and vegetation for a wide variety of insects, including grasshoppers, beetles, moths and butterflies; eats berries and seeds; sometimes hawks.
Voice: song is a weak, buzzy trill with a quick finish; call is a sharp *sup* or *check*.
Similar Species: *Yellow-rumped Warbler* (p. 277): nonbreeding has bright, yellow green rump and does not bob tail. *American Pipit* (p. 264): nonbreeding has bold, white or buff eye line, much more heavily streaked underparts and white undertail coverts.
Best Sites: widespread during migration.

283

BAY-BREASTED WARBLER
Dendroica castanea

The Bay-breasted Warbler's populations fluctuate with the cyclical rise and fall of spruce budworms on its breeding grounds in northern spruce forests. The death of spruce forests and the use of pesticides to control the budworms may be contributing to this warbler's declining numbers. On their wintering grounds in Panama and Colombia, Bay-breasted Warblers eat mostly fruit. • Though easy to distinguish in spring, fall-plumaged Bay-breasted Warblers and Blackpoll Warblers look very similar. These closely related species have sometimes hybridized. One of the later migrating warblers in Illinois, the Bay-breasted wastes no time when it arrives on its breeding grounds to begin nesting; it will lay six to eight eggs during spruce budworm outbreaks, compared with other years when it lays four to five eggs.

breeding

ID: *Breeding male:* black face and "chin"; chestnut crown, throat, sides and flanks; creamy yellow belly, undertail coverts and neck patch; 2 white wing bars; dark legs. *Breeding female:* paler overall; dusky face; whitish underparts and neck patch; faint chestnut "cap"; rusty wash on sides and flanks. *Nonbreeding:* yellow olive head and back; dark streaking on crown and back; whiter underparts; males show rufous on flanks; females have buffy wash on flanks.
Size: *L* 5–6 in; *W* 9 in.
Status: common migrant from early May to early June and from late August to mid-October.
Habitat: mainly upland forests during migration.

Nesting: does not nest in Illinois.
Feeding: usually forages at the midlevel of trees; gleans vegetation and branches for spruce budworms, caterpillars and adult invertebrates, such as spiders and flies.
Voice: song is an extremely high-pitched series of notes varying little in pitch: *set-seee-seesee-seetse-seeee;* call is a high *see.*
Similar Species: *Cape May Warbler* (p. 275): chestnut brown "cheek" on yellow face; dark streaking on mostly yellow underparts; lacks reddish flanks and crown. *Chestnut-sided Warbler* (p. 273): yellow crown; white "cheek" and underparts; non-breeding has white eye ring, unmarked whitish face and underparts and lacks bold streaking on yellow green upperparts. *Blackpoll Warbler* (p. 285): nonbreeding and immature have dark streaking on breasts and sides, light-colored legs and white undertail coverts; lack chestnut on sides and flanks.
Best Sites: woodlands.

BLACKPOLL WARBLER

Dendroica striata

Weighing less than a wet teabag, the Blackpoll Warbler has been known to fly nonstop from the eastern coast of North America, south over the Atlantic Ocean to the northern coast of Venezuela, a flight that can last for three days. In a single year, a Blackpoll Warbler may fly up to 15,000 miles! • The Blackpoll Warbler breeds in Canadian and Alaskan spruce forests. During migration, these birds prefer oaks for feeding. They can be found in bottomland forests in southern Illinois where several species of oak trees such as the swamp, overcup, cherrybark, Shumard, pin and swamp chestnut grow. In northern Illinois, they frequent upland oak woodlands. In central and southern Illinois, this species is more common in spring than in fall. Among spring migrants, Blackpoll Warblers are among the most commonly killed in collisions with TV towers, lighthouses and other structures.

breeding

ID: 2 white wing bars; black streaking on white underparts; white undertail coverts. *Breeding male:* black "cap" and "chin" stripe; white "cheek"; black-streaked, olive gray upperparts; white underparts; orange legs. *Breeding female:* streaked, yellow olive head and back; small, dark eye line; pale "eyebrow." *Nonbreeding:* olive yellow head, back, rump, breast and sides; yellow "eyebrow"; light-colored legs.
Size: *L* 5–5½ in; *W* 9 in.
Status: common spring migrant statewide; common fall migrant in northeastern Illinois; uncommon fall migrant elsewhere; occurs from late April to early June and from late August to early to mid-October.
Habitat: oaks in upland woods in northern Illinois; oaks in upland and bottomland woods in southern Illinois.
Nesting: does not nest in Illinois.

Feeding: gleans buds, leaves and branches for aphids, mosquitoes, beetles, canker worms, wasps, spiders, caterpillars and many other insects; often flycatches; takes some fruit during fall migration; eats nectar and pollen on wintering grounds.
Voice: song is an extremely high-pitched, uniform trill: *tsit tsit tsit;* call is a loud *chip.*
Similar Species: *Black-and-white Warbler* (p. 287): dark legs; black-and-white-striped crown; male has black "chin," throat and "cheek" patch. *Bay-breasted Warbler* (p. 284): nonbreeding and immature lack dark streaking on underparts and most show some rufous on flank; all have dark legs. *Pine Warbler* (p. 281): nonbreeding has eye ring and somewhat less distinct white wing bars, lacks streaking on sides and back. *Black-capped Chickadee* (p. 238): completely different bill; black "chin" and throat; lacks wing bars and black streaking on underparts.
Best Sites: upland and bottomland woods with oaks.

CERULEAN WARBLER

Dendroica cerulea

The Cerulean Warbler may be added to the federally threatened species list and the state endangered species list for Illinois. Its numbers have drastically declined throughout its range, especially in Illinois. Only a few historical breeding places remain in the Prairie State, including mature bottomland forests with high densities of large, mature box elder in which these birds build their nests. Once a fairly common breeder in the oak woodlands at Chain O'Lakes State Park, the Cerulean Warbler is now difficult to find there in summer. Cowbird parasitism, predation and forest fragmentation are likely contributing to the decline. This bird requires a rather specific habitat for breeding— woodlands with large trees and several herbaceous layers including canopy, subcanopy, shrub and ground cover. This species is one of the earlier warblers to return in spring.

breeding

ID: white undertail coverts, wing bars and tail spots. *Male:* bright, cerulean blue upperparts; white underparts; narrow black "necklace"; black streaks along sides and back. *Female:* blue green upperparts; yellowish white underparts; pale blue crown; white or yellowish line over eye.
Size: *L* 4½–5 in; *W* 8 in.
Status: rare to uncommon migrant and breeder from mid-April to mid-September.
Habitat: mature deciduous hardwood forests and extensive woodlands with several layers of understory; particularly drawn to bottomland forests; usually stays high in canopy.
Nesting: on the end of a branch high in a deciduous tree; female builds an open cup nest of bark strips, weeds, grass, lichen and spider silk and lines it with fur and moss; female incubates 3–5 brown-spotted, gray to creamy white eggs for about 12–13 days; frequently parasitized by Brown-headed Cowbird.
Feeding: gleans or hawks for insects such as caterpillars from upper canopy foliage and branches.
Voice: song is a rapid, accelerating sequence of buzzy notes leading into a higher trilled note; call is a sharp *chip;* song can sometimes be confused with that of Northern Parula.
Similar Species: none.
Best Sites: Sugar River FP; Mississippi Palisades SP; Castle Rock SP; Cave Creek and Cedar Creek drainage areas near Pomona.

BLACK-AND-WHITE WARBLER
Mniotilta varia

Black-and-whites behave like creepers and nuthatches—a distantly related group of birds. These warblers methodically creep up and down tree trunks, probing bark crevices for food. They also join mixed flocks of other warblers gleaning food from leaves. • The Black-and-white Warbler has rictal bristles around its mouth, which may help it to catch flying insects; the Canada Warbler and American Redstart also have these long bristles. • A keen ear helps to identify this forest-dweller, whose high-pitched song sounds like rapid inhaling and exhaling. • One of the first warblers to arrive in spring, the Black-and-white Warbler also begins breeding early. This bird may have nests well underway while other migrating warblers are still passing through. Because of this, some breeding Black-and-white Warblers may be overlooked in Illinois. • This species has been known to feed the young of other ground-nesting warblers such as the Ovenbird and Worm-eating Warbler, which have similar striped head patterns.

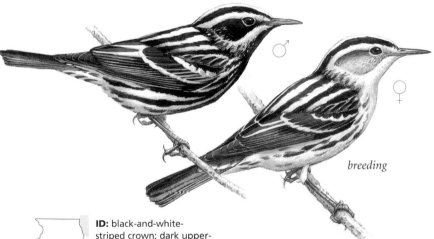

breeding

ID: black-and-white-striped crown; dark upperparts with white streaking; 2 white wing bars; white underparts with black streaking on sides, flanks and undertail coverts; black legs. *Breeding male:* black "cheek" and throat. *Breeding female:* gray "cheek"; white throat.
Size: *L* 5 in; *W* 8 in.
Status: common migrant from early April to late May or early June and from mid-August to early October, with a few lingering into early November; rare breeder.
Habitat: *Breeding:* deciduous or mixed forests with wooded ravines and hillsides. *In migration:* woodlands.
Nesting: usually on the ground next to a tree, log or large rock; in a shallow scrape,

often among a pile of dead leaves; female builds a cup nest with grass, leaves, bark strips, rootlets and pine needles and lines it with fur and fine grasses; female incubates 5 brown-flecked, creamy white eggs for 10–12 days.
Feeding: gleans insect eggs, larval insects, bark beetles, spiders and other invertebrates while creeping along tree trunks and branches; also routinely gleans leaves.
Voice: song is a series of high, thin, 2-syllable notes: *weetsee weetsee weetsee weetsee weetsee weetsee;* call is a sharp *pit* and a soft, high *seet*.
Similar Species: *Blackpoll Warbler* (p. 285): breeding male has solid black "cap" and clean white undertail coverts.
Best Sites: *Summer:* Shawnee NF. *In migration:* widespread statewide.

AMERICAN REDSTART

Setophaga ruticilla

One of Illinois' most common migrant warblers, the American Redstart flashes its boldly colored, fan-shaped tail, appearing like a butterfly in the forest. The male has contrasting black-and-orange plumage; females and young are yellow and black. Breeding American Redstarts in Illinois favor young, successional bottomland forests along streams, rivers and swamps, especially where vines grow entangled in trees. Their variable, high-pitched, lisping, trilly songs alert birders to their presence in their small, loose nesting colonies. • These active birds respond readily to "pishing." Acrobatic and constantly on the move, redstarts have rictal bristles around their mouths, which aid in the aerial capture of insects. • On its Central American wintering grounds, the American Redstart is called *candelita*, meaning "little candle."

ID: *Male:* black overall; red orange foreshoulder, wing and tail patches; white belly and undertail coverts. *Female* and *immature:* olive brown upperparts; gray head; yellow foreshoulder, wing and tail patches; dirty white underparts.
Size: *L* 5 in; *W* 8½ in.
Status: common migrant and locally common breeder from mid- to late April to mid-October.
Habitat: *Breeding:* bottomland, riverine and swamplike woods with secondary growth. *In migration:* widespread.

Nesting: in the fork of a shrub or sapling, usually 3–30 ft above the ground; female builds an open cup nest of plant down, bark shreds, grass and rootlets and lines it with feathers; female incubates 4 whitish eggs, marked with brown or gray, for 11–12 days.
Feeding: actively gleans foliage and hawks for insects and spiders on leaves, buds and branches; often hover-gleans.
Voice: song is a highly variable series of *tseet* or *zee* notes, often given at different pitches; call is a sharp, sweet *chip*.
Similar Species: none.
Best Sites: *Summer:* Lowden-Miller SF; Castle Rock SP; Milan Bottoms, Rock Island Co.; Thomson Causeway Unit of the Upper Mississippi Wildlife and Fish Refuge; Newell Road near L. Vermilion; Union County CA levee; Pomona region of the Shawnee NF.

PROTHONOTARY WARBLER
Protonotaria citrea

A bird of southern Illinois swamps and major river valleys farther north, the Prothonotary is one of only two North American warbler species that nests in cavities. In spring and summer, you'll often hear the rich, loud *sweet, sweet, sweet, sweet* song of this warbler near stagnant, swampy water where dead trees and stumps can be found. Prothonotary Warblers also nest in artificial cavities, including old tin cups or old water pump handles. A few thousand Prothonotary Warblers have used nest boxes made of milk cartons placed in southern Illinois swamps in a multi-year study of the species. • Illinois is at the northern part of its breeding range, therefore, fall migration is difficult to detect.

breeding

ID: large, dark eyes; long bill; unmarked, orangy yellow head; yellow underparts except for white undertail coverts; olive green back; blue gray legs; unmarked, bluish gray wings, rump and tail on perched bird. *In flight:* white outer tail feathers, broadly edged in black.
Size: *L* 5½ in; *W* 8½ in.
Status: common migrant and breeder in southern Illinois; locally rare to uncommon elsewhere in the state; occurs from early April to early September.
Habitat: wooded, deciduous swamps; prefers backwater sloughs, swamps and slowly moving rivers.
Nesting: in a cavity in a standing dead tree, rotten stump, birdhouse or abandoned woodpecker nest, from water level to 10 ft above the ground; often returns to the same nest site; female chooses one of the male's moss-filled cavities and lines it with soft plant material; female incubates 4–6 brown-spotted, creamy to pinkish eggs

for 12–14 days; often parasitized by Brown-headed Cowbird.
Feeding: forages for a variety of insects and small mollusks; gleans from vegetation; may hop on floating debris or creep along tree trunks.
Voice: song is a loud, ringing series of *sweet* or *zweet* notes issued on a single pitch; flight-song is *chewee chewee chee chee;* call is a brisk *tink*.
Similar Species: *Blue-winged Warbler* (p. 266): greenish rump; white wing bars; black eye line; blackish legs; outer tail feathers lack black border in flight. *Yellow Warbler* (p. 272): yellow undertail coverts; mostly yellow wings; male has reddish streaking on breast and the appearance of yellow wing bars against darker wings; pinkish legs. *Hooded Warbler* (p. 298): female has yellow undertail coverts, yellow olive head and nape, greenish rump and tail and pinkish legs.
Best Sites: McHenry Dam, Milan Bottoms in Rock Island Co.; L. Chautauqua; Stump L. at Mark Twain NWR; Horseshoe Lake CA; Mermet L.; Oakwood Bottoms; Union County CA; Cypress Creek NWR; LaRue Swamp.

289

WORM-EATING WARBLER

Helmitheros vermivorus

During breeding season in extreme southern Illinois, the rapid, single-pitched notes of the Worm-eating Warbler ring from the wooded ravines. Along with the Kentucky, the Worm-eating is one of the most common breeding warblers in this kind of habitat. Finding this bird, however, can be difficult. Its subdued colors allow it to blend in with the decomposing twigs, roots and leaves that litter the forest floor. • John J. Audubon and Alexander Wilson never found a nest of this species, and Audubon assumed that the Worm-eating Warbler nested in a shrub. Instead, the Worm-eating is one of a small group of eastern warbler species that nest on the ground. The Worm-eating chooses steep slopes on which to build its nest. A female becomes completely still if approached while on the nest, relying on her striped crown for concealment. If flushed, the female may flutter off the nest and feign a broken wing by dragging it on the ground.

with reddish brown, for about 13 days; frequently parasitized by Brown-headed Cowbird and predated by snakes.

Feeding: forages on the ground and in trees and shrubs; often forages in dead, curled leaves hanging from trees; eats mostly spiders and slugs early in the season and mostly caterpillars and small insects in summer.

ID: black stripes on buff orange head; uniform brownish olive upperparts; rich buff breast; whitish undertail coverts.
Size: *L* 5 in; *W* 8½ in.
Status: rare to uncommon migrant; common breeder in southern Illinois; rare and local breeder in central and northern Illinois; absent from northeastern Illinois; occurs from mid-April to mid-September; fall migration difficult to detect.
Habitat: steep, deciduous woodland slopes and ravines with shrubby understory cover.
Nesting: on a hillside or ravine bank; on the ground at the base of a tiny sapling or fallen, decaying tree limbs; female builds a cup nest of decaying leaves and lines it with fine grass, moss stems and hair; female incubates 3–5 white eggs, speckled

Voice: song is a buzzy trill, similar to that of a Chipping Sparrow, but lower pitched and with an abrupt ending; call is a buzzy *zeep-zeep.*
Similar Species: *Louisiana Waterthrush* (p. 293) and *Northern Waterthrush* (p. 292): darker upperparts; bold, white or yellowish "eyebrow"; dark streaking on white breast; lack striped head. *Ovenbird* (p. 291): bold streaking on breasts and flanks; orangy brown central stripe on head; bold, white eye ring. *Swainson's Warbler* (p. 358): extremely rare; rusty-colored crown; lacks distinct, black eye stripe and buffy tinge to head and undersides.
Best Sites: Siloam Springs SP; Trail of Tears SF; Fox Ridge SP; Pine Hills–LaRue Ecological Area; Giant City SP; War Bluff Sanctuary, Pope Co.

OVENBIRD

Seiurus aurocapilla

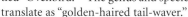

While this common migrant is fairly easy to find in spring, pinpointing its exact location in summer is more difficult. Two neighboring males may counter sing, one beginning its song just as the other finishes, causing an echo effect in the woods. • The name "Ovenbird" refers to this bird's unusual, oven-shaped ground nest. An incubating female nestled within her well-camouflaged woven dome will sit tight rather than fleeing when approached. However, forest grazing by cattle and hog farming are causing problems for ground-nesting species, including the Ovenbird. • This species is a common victim of collisions with TV towers. • Robert Frost was so inspired by the Ovenbird's songs that he dedicated a poem to them entitled "Ovenbird." • The genus and species names together translate as "golden-haired tail-waver."

ID: olive brown or greenish upperparts; white eye ring; heavy, dark streaking on white breast, sides and flanks; orange crown bordered with black; pink legs; white undertail coverts; no wing bars.
Size: *L* 6 in; *W* 9½ in.
Status: common migrant; uncommon to locally common breeder; occurs from mid-April to mid-October, with some lingering into November; fall migrants arrive in late August.
Habitat: *Breeding:* undisturbed, mature deciduous upland forests with a closed canopy and very little understory, but sufficient ground cover; pine plantations, especially in southern Illinois. *In migration:* wooded areas and pine plantations.
Nesting: on the ground; female builds a well-camouflaged, oven-shaped, domed nest of grass, weeds, bark, twigs and dead leaves and lines it with animal hair; female incubates 4–5 white eggs, spotted with gray and brown, for 11–13 days; parasitized by Brown-headed Cowbird.

Feeding: gleans the ground for worms, snails, insects, inchworms and occasionally seeds.
Voice: song is a loud, distinctive *tea-cher tea-cher tea-CHER tea-CHER,* increasing in speed and volume; night song is an elaborate series of bubbly, warbled notes, often ending in *teacher-teacher;* call is a brisk *chip, cheep* or *chock.*
Similar Species: *Northern Waterthrush* (p. 292) and *Louisiana Waterthrush* (p. 293): bold, yellowish or white "eyebrow"; darker upperparts; brownish backs; lack orange crown and bold white eye ring. *Worm-eating Warbler* (p. 290): lacks streaking, orange crown and bold, white eye ring. *Thrushes* (pp. 252–59): much larger; lack orange crown outlined in black.
Best Sites: *Summer:* Deer Grove FP; Palos Preserves; Lowden-Miller SF; Mississippi Palisades SP; Trail of Tears SF; Giant City SP; Lusk Creek Wilderness, Pope Co. *In migration:* widespread in woodlands.

NORTHERN WATERTHRUSH

Seiurus noveboracensis

The Northern Waterthursh and the Louisiana Waterthrush are not thrushes, but wood-warblers. The similarly plumaged birds share certain behaviors, but they can be distinguished by song, habitat and feeding strategies. The Northern Waterthrush can be found in almost any wet woodland in Illinois during migration, but most occur in bottomland forests, swamps and bogs. The Louisiana Waterthrush prefers upland woods with ravines, but will occasionally use forested swamps as well. • The Northern Waterthrush's breeding range begins in central Wisconsin and extends, northward, while the Louisiana's is mostly restricted to southern Wisconsin and southward. Both breed in the Appalachian Mountains. • Waterthrushes bob their tails while walking on logs over water or along shorelines and on forest vegetation. This habit is similar to that of Spotted Sandpipers and perhaps intended to disturb ground- and water-dwelling insects.

ID: pale yellowish to buff "eyebrow" and under-parts; dense, dark streaking on underparts; finely spotted throat; olive brown upperparts; frequently bobs its tail.
Size: *L* 5–6 in; *W* 9½ in.
Status: common migrant from mid-April to late May and from mid-August to mid-October; early to mid-July arrivals not uncommon.
Habitat: bottomland forests, swamps and boggy areas; rarely far from water.
Nesting: does not nest in Illinois.
Feeding: gleans foliage and the ground for invertebrates, including larval and adult insects, spiders and stoneflies; frequently tosses aside ground litter with its bill; may also take aquatic invertebrates such as snails, small clams and small fish from shallow water.
Voice: song is a loud, 3-part *sweet sweet sweet, swee wee wee, chew chew chew chew;* call is a brisk *chip* or *chuck.*
Similar Species: *Louisiana Waterthrush* (p. 293): occurs in summer; broader, white "eyebrow"; unspotted, white throat; less dense streaking on breast. *Ovenbird* (p. 291): distinctly greenish back; orange crown bordered with black stripe; white eye ring; unspotted throat; lacks pale "eyebrow." *Thrushes* (pp. 252–59): larger; more robust; breast usually spotted instead of streaked; lack "eyebrow" stripe; do not bob or wag tails.
Best Sites: widespread during migration in appropriate habitat.

LOUISIANA WATERTHRUSH
Seiurus motacilla

The earliest warbler to return to Illinois in spring is the Louisiana Waterthrush. It gives its varied, mellifluous song from the rivulets and streams flowing through ravines of upland forests. Both waterthrush species bob their heads and move their tails up and down as they walk, but the Louisiana Waterthrush bobs its tail more slowly and sways it from side to side. • The Louisiana Waterthrush has long, linear breeding territories, which may encompass several adjacent ravines. A southern Illinois study showed that at least one pair of birds was incubating a full clutch of eggs by April 19, with the last pair incubating on May 13—while many other migrant birds haven't yet made it to their final destination, the Louisiana Waterthrushes are well into their breeding season. • Cowbird parasitism, flooding of breeding grounds or predation may encourage these birds to attempt a second nest.

ID: brownish upperparts; long bill; white underparts; long, dark streaks on breast and sides; bicolored, buff-and-white "eyebrow"; clean white throat.
Size: *L* 6 in; *W* 10 in.
Status: common migrant and breeder in southern Illinois, decreasing northward; occurs from late March to mid-September; most birds gone by the end of August.
Habitat: moist, forested ravines alongside fast-flowing, often rocky, streams; sometimes, cypress swamps.
Nesting: in a tangle of tree roots or cavities along a streambed in a ravine; pair builds a cup nest of leaves, bark strips, twigs and moss and lines it with animal hair, ferns and rootlets; female incubates 3–6 creamy white eggs, spotted with brown and purple gray, for about 14 days; frequently parasitized by Brown-headed Cowbird.
Feeding: gleans terrestrial and aquatic insects and crustaceans from rocks and

debris in or near shallow water; debris submerged in water may be flipped and probed for hidden invertebrates; occasionally catches flying insects over water.
Voice: song begins with 3–4 distinctive, shrill, slurred notes followed by a warbling twitter; call is a brisk *chick* or *chink*.
Similar Species: *Northern Waterthrush* (p. 292): yellowish "eyebrow"; denser streaking on breast and throat. *Ovenbird* (p. 291): distinctly greenish back; lacks pale "eyebrow." *Thrushes* (pp. 252–59): larger; more robust; lack "eyebrow" stripes; breast usually spotted rather than streaked; lack tail bobbing and wagging.
Best Sites: Palos Preserves; Starved Rock SP; Mississippi Palisades SP; Forest Glen Preserve; Pere Marquette SP; Giant City SP; Trail of Tears SF; Pine Hills–LaRue Ecological Area; Bell Smith Springs; Heron Pond.

293

KENTUCKY WARBLER
Oporornis formosus

The Kentucky Warbler is one of three *Oporornis* species seen in Illinois. Members of this genus exhibit shy, skulking behavior and walk and feed on the ground among dense thickets where they are difficult to see. A Kentucky Warbler hops or flutters from the ground into the air to catch insects from the undersides of leaves and the air. • The Kentucky Warbler's song may be confused with that of the Northern Cardinal and Carolina Wren. • Like the Worm-eating Warbler, the Kentucky is one of the most common breeding warblers in the Shawnee Hills of southern Illinois, where it prefers heavily shaded woods, especially wooded ravines with shade-loving plants, including ferns. • Once the young hatch, the male Kentucky Warbler sings less frequently to spend time feeding the young with the female. Unmated males may continue to sing throughout the summer. After fledging, young are often led to the protective cover of dense shrubs, thickets and briars.

ID: bright yellow "spectacles" and underparts; gray-and-black crown; black "sideburns" and "half mask"; uniform olive green upperparts.
Size: *L* 5–5½ in; *W* 8½ in.
Status: uncommon migrant; common breeder in the Shawnee Hills; uncommon to locally common in the rest of southern Illinois; rare to uncommon elsewhere; occurs from mid-April to mid-September.
Habitat: moist deciduous and mixed woodlands with dense shrubby cover and herbaceous plant growth, including wooded ravines, swamp edges and creek bottomlands.
Nesting: on or close to the ground; often at the base of a tree sapling or in dense foliage; pair builds a bulky cup nest of skeletonized leaves and other plant material; lined with rootlets and hair; female incubates 4–5 brown-spotted, cream-colored eggs for 12–13 days; often parasitized by Brown-headed Cowbird.
Feeding: gleans the ground and leaf litter for insects, including caterpillars and spiders; snatches prey from undersides of low foliage; also forages in forest canopy.
Similar Species: *Canada Warbler* (p. 300): migrant only; dark, streaky "necklace"; bluish gray upperparts; white undertail coverts. *Yellow-throated Warbler* (p. 280): blue gray upperparts; bold, white "eyebrow," ear patch and wing bars; white belly and undertail coverts; bold, black streaking on white flanks; jet black legs.
Best Sites: Mississippi Palisades SP; Forest Glen Preserve; Pere Marquette SP; Trail of Tears SF; Pine Hills–LaRue Ecological Area; Giant City SP; Atwood Ridge and Hamburg Hill; Pomona; Ferne Clyff SP; Pomona in Shawnee NF; Fox Ridge SP; Jubilee College SP.

CONNECTICUT WARBLER

Oporornis agilis

One of the most sought-after birds, the relatively rare Connecticut Warbler migrates through Illinois later than most other warblers on its way to breeding grounds in spruce-tamarack bogs, moist woodlands and pine barrens in northern Minnesota, Wisconsin, Michigan and Canada. During migration in Illinois, the Connecticut Warbler seeks soggy, impenetrable understory where it feeds and hides. • This warbler walks rather than hops, unlike the other *Oporornis* species in Illinois, the Mourning Warbler and the Kentucky Warbler. The Connecticut also sports duller yellow underparts compared with the Mourning Warbler. • Because of an elliptical migration route, the Connecticut Warbler can be seen statewide in spring, but only in northeastern and extreme east-central Illinois during fall.

ID: chunky shape; bold, white eye ring; pale yellow underparts; uniform olive green upperparts; long undertail coverts make tail look short; pink legs; longish bill; distinct gait. *Breeding male:* blue gray "hood." *Female* and *immature:* gray brown "hood"; light gray throat.
Size: *L* 5–6 in; *W* 9 in.
Status: rare to uncommon migrant in spring; very rare to rare migrant in fall in northeastern and east-central Illinois; occurs from mid-May to early June and from late August to late September.
Habitat: woodlands with dense ground and shrub layers; often wet woods that mimic its breeding grounds in spruce and tamarack bogs.
Nesting: does not nest in Illinois.
Feeding: gleans caterpillars, beetles, spiders, small snails and other invertebrates from ground leaf litter; occasionally forages among branches; may stretch or jump vertically to grab prey.
Voice: song is a loud, clear, explosive *chippi-tucka, chippi-tucka;* call is a brisk, metallic *cheep* or *peak.*
Similar Species: *Mourning Warbler* (p. 296): lacks eye ring; brighter yellow underparts; male has black breast patch and deeper gray "hood"; female and immature have pale gray to yellow "chin" and throats. *Nashville Warbler* (p. 270): more common; much smaller; often higher in understory and canopy; bright yellow throat; dark legs and bill. *Common Yellowthroat* (p. 297): much more common; more open habitat; female is slimmer, smaller, has longer tail, lacks white eye ring and has whitish belly.
Best Sites: Ryerson Woods; Water Tower and Seneca Parks in downtown Chicago; Montrose Point; Grant Park; Jackson Park (Chicago); Busey Woods, Champaign Co.

MOURNING WARBLER
Oporornis philadelphia

The Mourning Warbler sings his rather soft, gurgling song from within dense shrubs and tangles. A late migrant warbler, a few Mournings may remain to breed in northern Illinois, but most continue north to breed in wet, secondary growth or successional woodlands in Wisconsin, Michigan, Minnesota and Canada. Although essentially a bird of broadleaf shrubs, the Mourning Warbler sometimes breeds in boreal conifers, as long as there is some ground cover. • The Mourning is the eastern counterpart to the MacGillivray's Warbler. Except for the MacGillivray's bold, white eye arcs, these species look and sound similar. Most wood-warblers have primary and alternate songs, but the Mourning's song varies little throughout its breeding range. • This bird's dark "hood" and black breast patch reminded pioneering ornithologist Alexander Wilson of someone dressed in mourning. The one he collected was the only one he ever saw.

breeding

ID: blue gray "hood"; black upper breast patch; bright yellow underparts; olive green upperparts; short tail; pinkish legs. *Breeding male:* usually no eye ring, but may have broken eye ring. *Female:* gray "hood"; whitish "chin" and throat; may have partial eye ring.
Size: *L* 5–5½ in; *W* 7½ in.
Status: uncommon to fairly common migrant from early May to early June and from mid-August to early October; very rare breeder in northern Illinois.
Habitat: dense and shrubby thickets, tangles and brambles, often in moist areas of forest clearings and along the edges of ponds, lakes and streams.

Nesting: on the ground at the base of a shrub or plant tussock or in a small shrub; often in briars; bulky nest of leaves, weeds and grass is lined with fur and fine grass; female incubates 3–4 brown-blotched, creamy white eggs for about 12 days.
Feeding: forages in dense, low shrubs for caterpillars, beetles, spiders and other invertebrates.
Voice: husky, 2-part song is variable and lower-pitched at the end: *chirry, chirry, chirry, chorry;* call is a loud, low *check.*
Similar Species: *Connecticut Warbler* (p. 295): bold, complete, white eye ring; lacks black breast patch; long undertail coverts make tail look very short. *Nashville Warbler* (p. 270): more common; smaller; more active; bright yellow throat; white eye ring; dark legs and bill. *Common Yellowthroat* (p. 297): much more common; female has yellow throat; dark bill, uniform brown head and back.
Best Sites: *Summer:* Lowden-Miller SF. *In migration:* Chicago lakefront parks.

COMMON YELLOWTHROAT

Geothlypis trichas

One of North America's most widespread and common warbler species, the Common Yellowthroat prefers cattail marshes and wet, overgrown meadows. Observing a male yellowthroat in action will reveal the location of his favorite singing perches atop tall cattails and shrubs, which he visits in rotation. These strategic outposts mark the boundary of his territory, which he fiercely guards from intrusion by other males. The Common Yellowthroat also gives an energetic flight song during breeding season. • First collected in what is now Maryland in 1766, the Common Yellowthroat was one of the earliest species of birds from the New World to be described. The many subspecies of the Common Yellowthroat show a large variation in plumage across a wide geographical range.

ID: bright yellow throat, breast and undertail coverts; dark bill; dingy white belly; olive green to olive brown upperparts; orangy legs. *Breeding male:* broad, black "mask" with white upper border. *Female:* no "mask"; may show faint white eye ring.

Size: *L* 5 in; *W* 7 in.

Status: common to abundant migrant and common breeder from mid-April to late October, with some November stragglers; rare but regular on southern Illinois Christmas bird counts.

Habitat: wet, brushy habitats, weedy fields and marshes.

Nesting: on or near the ground, usually in tall grasses or among emergent aquatic vegetation; female builds a bulky open cup nest of vegetation and lines it with hair and soft plant fibers; female incubates 3–5 darkly spotted, creamy white eggs, for 12 days; parasitized by Brown-headed Cowbird.

Feeding: gleans vegetation and hovers for adult and larval insects, including dragonflies, spiders and beetles; occasionally eats seeds.

Voice: song is a clear, oscillating *witchety witchety witchety-witch;* call is a distinct *chup* or *check.*

Similar Species: male's black "mask" with white border is distinctive. *Kentucky Warbler* (p. 294): slightly larger; more robust; yellow "spectacles"; all-yellow underparts; "half mask." *Yellow-breasted Chat* (p. 301): much larger; more robust; large, black bill; black lores outlined above and below with white; black legs. *Connectictut Warbler* (p. 295): female has grayish "hood," all-yellow underparts, pinkish bill, longer wings and shorter tail. *Mourning Warbler* (p. 296): female has grayish "hood," all-yellow underparts, pinkish bill, longer wings and shorter tail. *Orange-crowned Warbler* (p. 269): dull olive yellow overall; faint breast streaks.

Best Sites: widespread in appropriate habitat.

HOODED WARBLER
Wilsonia citrina

Hooded Warblers are near the northern limit of their breeding range in Illinois. Birders here relish the clear, sweet song and striking appearance of the male. • Different species of wood-warblers can coexist in a limited environment because each species forages exclusively in certain areas. Male and female Hooded Warblers also partition their resources: males forage in treetops; females forage near the ground. Unlike other warbler species, they also partition on their wintering grounds—males use mature forests and females use shrubby and disturbed areas. • Both sexes frequently flash and spread their tails, a tactic which may help to flush prey. • As with some other warbler and songbird species, the male Hooded Warbler may return to the same nesting territory year after year, while the female often does not.

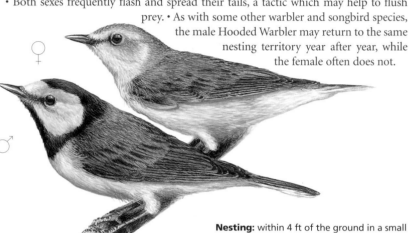

ID: bright yellow underparts; olive green upperparts; white undertail; pinkish legs. *Male:* black "hood"; bright yellow face. *Female:* yellow face; olive crown; some older females may show as much black "hood" as male.

Size: *L* 5½ in; *W* 7 in.

Status: rare migrant from early to mid-April through early to mid-September; fall migration largely goes unnoticed; uncommon breeder in the Shawnee Hills, decreasing northward; regular breeder in northeastern Illinois; rare or absent breeder elsewhere.

Habitat: clearings with dense, low shrubs and saplings in mature, upland deciduous and mixed forests; occasionally in moist ravines or mature pine plantations with deciduous shrubs and vines.

Nesting: within 4 ft of the ground in a small sapling or large forb; female builds an open cup nest of fine grass, grapevine bark strips, dead leaves and animal hair; female incubates 4 brown-spotted, creamy white eggs for about 12 days; parasitized by Brownheaded Cowbird and predated by snakes.

Feeding: gleans spiders, insects and larvae from the ground or from shrub branches; may scramble up tree trunks or flycatch, using rictal bristles to feel their prey.

Voice: clear, whistling song is some variation of *whitta-witta-wit-tee-yo;* call note is a metallic *tink, chink* or *chip.*

Similar Species: *Wilson's Warbler* (p. 299), *Yellow Warbler* (p. 272) and *Common Yellowthroat* (p. 297): females lack white outer tail feathers; Common Yellowthroat has some white on belly. *Kentucky Warbler* (p. 294): yellow "spectacles"; dark, triangular "half mask."

Best Sites: *Summer:* Palos Preserves; Deer Grove FP; Lowden-Miller SF; Pine Hills–LaRue Ecological Area; Trail of Tears SF; Atwood Ridge, Hamburg Hill and Pomona in Shawnee NF. *In migration:* Ryerson Woods; Jackson Park; Busey Woods, Champaign Co.

WILSON'S WARBLER
Wilsonia pusilla

Wilson's Warbler breeds throughout much of Canada and Alaska as well as the northern portions of the western United States. It also breeds and winters at a wide variety of altitudes. Long-term data show, however, that populations of this handsome yellow bird with a black "cap" are declining. Illinois birders observe small numbers of this species during migration, when it spends time foraging in shrubby areas and avoiding deep woods. • Three subspecies occur: breeders in eastern and central Canada, which are also found in Illinois, breeders from coastal Alaska south through the Rocky Mountains, and breeders in the Pacific coastal lowlands. Their plumages vary in brightness of yellow, with the western being the brightest, and the amount of dark olive behind the eye and on the forehead. Wilson's Warblers are only fairly common migrants in Illinois and are much more common in the western United States. • This bird is among a handful of wood-warblers with rictal bristles and flattened, flycatcher-like bills, which help them to catch their prey. This energetic warbler regularly darts after flying insects, jerking its tail.

ID: yellow underparts; yellow green upperparts; beady, black eyes; black bill; pink legs. *Male:* black "cap." *Female:* "cap" is very faint or absent.
Size: *L* 4½–5 in; *W* 7 in.
Status: uncommon to fairly common spring and fall migrant from early May to early June and from mid-August to early October, with some stragglers into November and December.
Habitat: shrubby areas and forest edges; willows and willow thickets.
Nesting: does not nest in Illinois.
Feeding: hovers, flycatches and gleans vegetation for caterpillars, spiders, bees, flies, mayflies and other insects.

Voice: song is a rapid chatter that drops in pitch at the end: *chi chi chi chi chet chet;* call is a flat, low *chet* or *chuck.*
Similar Species: male's black "cap" is distinctive. *Yellow Warbler* (p. 272): brighter yellow upperparts; male has red breast streaks; female has absent or faint streaks. *Common Yellowthroat* (p. 297): female has darker face, browner upperparts and shows white on belly. *Kentucky Warbler* (p. 294): yellow "spectacles"; dark, angular "half mask." *Orange-crowned Warbler* (p. 269): dull yellow olive overall; faint breast streaks. *Nashville Warbler* (p. 270): bold, complete eye ring; blue gray crown.
Best Sites: none.

CANADA WARBLER
Wilsonia canadensis

The inquisitive Canada Warbler, with its bold, white eye rings, will pop up from dense shrubs and tree tangles in response to "pishing." Along with the Wilson's, Mourning and Connecticut warblers, the Canada is the last of the migrant warblers to arrive in Illinois. A very few may remain to breed, but most nest in wet, tangled shrubbery in the northeastern United States, in boreal Canada and atop the ridges of the Allegheny Mountains. • The Canada Warbler is adept at catching flies and snapping its bill when prey touches its rictal bristles. It tilts its tail and flips its wings when eating. • The first confirmed breeding of this warbler in Illinois occurred in June 1980 on the ground in a forested park in Joliet.

ID: yellow "spectacles"; yellow underparts, except white undertail coverts; uniform blue gray upperparts and tail; yellow legs. *Male:* streaky, black "necklace"; dark, angular "half mask." *Female:* blue green back; faint "necklace."
Size: *L* 5–6 in; *W* 8 in.
Status: uncommon to fairly common migrant from early May to early June and from mid-August to early October; rare breeder in northern Illinois.
Habitat: wet, low-lying areas of mixed forest with a dense understory, especially riparian willow-alder thickets; also cedar woodlands and swamps.
Nesting: near shrubbery, bushes and vine tangles; among ferns, upturned roots or stumps; female builds a loose, bulky cup

nest of leaves, grass, ferns, weeds and bark; lines it with animal hair and soft plant fibers; female incubates 4 brown-spotted, creamy white eggs for 10–14 days.
Feeding: gleans the ground and vegetation for beetles, flies, hairless caterpillars, mosquitoes and other insects; occasionally hovers.
Voice: song begins with 1 sharp *chip* note and continues with a rich, variable warble; call is a loud, quick *chick* or *chip*.
Similar Species: *Kentucky Warbler* (p. 294): yellow undertail coverts; olive upperparts; half eye ring; lacks black "necklace." *Magnolia Warbler* (p. 274): black or olive back; yellow rump; white eye line; no white eye ring; extensive black streaking on throat and flanks; dark legs; white in tail feathers; adult male has large, white wing panel.
Best Sites: *Summer:* Lowden-Miller SF; Castle Rock SP.

YELLOW-BREASTED CHAT

Icteria virens

Despite DNA evidence connecting the chat with the wood-warbler family, its odd vocalizations suggest a closer relationship to the mimic thrushes, such as the Gray Catbird. • During courtship, the male chat advertises for a mate by hovering in the air, dangling his legs, clapping his wings over his back and giving his unusual array of squawks, clacks and chatters until he jerkily drops back to his perch. This noisy bird often sings on moonlit nights. One chat once sang all night, roughly every eight seconds. • In Illinois and elsewhere, chats often breed in association with Field Sparrows, Indigo Buntings, Common Yellowthroats, Prairie Warblers, White-eyed Vireos and Bell's Vireos. • The Yellow-breasted Chat is the only warbler in Illinois known to carry food and nesting material in its feet.

ID: white "spectacles"; white jaw line; heavy, black bill; yellow breast; white undertail coverts; olive green upperparts; long tail; gray black legs. *Male:* black lores. *Female:* dark lores.
Size: *L* 7½ in; *W* 9½ in.
Status: common migrant and breeder in southern Illinois, decreasing northward, from mid- to late April through mid- to late September.
Habitat: thickets, brambles and tangles in old fields, shrubby areas and forest edges; especially with thorny vegetation.
Nesting: in a shrub or deciduous sapling or in thorny vegetation, such as raspberry, multiflora rose, hawthorn or crab apple; well-concealed, bulky base of leaves and weeds holds an inner woven cup nest made of vine bark, grasses and plant fibers;

nest often has square appearance; female incubates 3–4 brown-spotted, creamy white eggs, for about 11 days; parasitized by Brown-headed Cowbird.
Feeding: gleans insects from low vegetation; eats berries, including honeysuckle, blackberry, mulberry and multiflora rose hips.
Voice: song is an assorted series of clear whistles, squeaks, grunts, rattles and mews; calls include a *whonk, chack* and *kook.*
Similar Species: *Common Yellowthroat* (p. 297): much smaller; black "mask"; much smaller tail; pink legs; petite, black bill; white above black "mask" extends from crown to neck.
Best Sites: Plum Creek FP; Kennekuk County Park; Eldon Hazlet SP; Kidd Lake NA; Pyramid SP; War Bluff Sanctuary; Cypress Creek NWR.

SUMMER TANAGER
Piranga rubra

The Summer Tanager is the only all-red bird in Illinois. More common in southern Illinois, this tanager is increasing its range northward in the state. • Summer Tanagers thrive on a wide variety of insects, including cicadas, but they especially like bees and wasps, raiding nests of both for adults and larvae. The tanager will beat a wasp or a bee until it dies, making sure the stinger is gone before eating the insect. Summer tanagers will also swallow berries whole or smash larger ones and drink the juice. • Like other red tanagers, the male and female Summer Tanagers differ in plumage so much that they can be mistaken for different species. Both tanager and oriole species seen in Illinois exhibit what is known as delayed plumage maturation; it takes birds more than one year to acquire full breeding plumage, explaining why you see some oddly colored males in spring.

♀

♂

ID: *Male:* rose red overall; pale bill; immature male has patchy red, orange and greenish plumage. *Female:* grayish to greenish yellow upperparts; dusky yellow underparts; may have orange or reddish wash overall.
Size: *L* 7–7½ in; *W* 7¾ in.
Status: common migrant and breeder in southern Illinois, decreasing northward; occurs from mid-April to early October.
Habitat: pine woodlands, open mixed savanna or parklike woodlands, especially those with oak or hickory; also riparian woodlands with oaks.
Nesting: well out on a horizontal limb, especially on an oak, 20–70 ft high; female builds a loose, shallow cup of plant stems and lines it with fine grasses; nest often has yellowish appearance; female incubates 4 variably marked, pale blue to pale

green eggs for 11–12 days; frequently parasitized by Brown-headed Cowbird.
Feeding: gleans insects from the tree canopy; may hover-glean or hawk insects in midair; eats click beetles, wood-borers, weevils, cicadas, dragonflies, sphinx moths and spiders; especially partial to bees and wasps; also eats berries and some fruits from feeders.
Voice: song is a series of 3–5 sweet, clear whistled phrases, like a faster version of the American Robin's song; call is *pit* or *pit-a-tuck* and *chippy-tucky-tuck.*
Similar Species: *Scarlet Tanager* (p. 303): smaller, darker bill; male has black tail and wings; female has darker wings, brighter underparts and uniformly olive upperparts. *Northern Cardinal* (p. 328): red bill; prominent head crest; male has black "mask" and "bib." *Orchard Oriole* (p. 342) and *Baltimore Oriole* (p. 343): females have sharper bills and wing bars.
Best Sites: Siloam Springs SP; Pere Marquette SP; Trail of Tears SF; Cache River Biosphere Reserve; Giant City SP; Garden of the Gods in Shawnee NF.

SCARLET TANAGER

Piranga olivacea

Each spring, birders eagerly await the robinlike song of the Scarlet Tanager. In spring, you may be lucky enough to view this high-canopy breeder at eye level. • More than 200 species of tanagers, of every imaginable color, occur in Central and South America. The Scarlet Tanager joins them in winter, migrating from as far north as Canada. • This bird builds nests similar to the Summer Tanager, but nests are often more hidden in clusters of leaves or vine tangles. Both species are heavily parasitized by the Brown-headed Cowbird; in some areas, tanagers may raise more cowbirds than tanagers. Though both the Scarlet Tanager and the Summer Tanager can be found in the same habitat, Scarlets prefer somewhat moister, interior forests. The Scarlet Tanager is more of a northerly breeder in the United States; the Summer's range is more southerly.

breeding

ID: *Breeding male:* bright red overall with pure black wings and tail; gray bill. *Spring male:* plumage is patchy red and greenish yellow. *Nonbreeding male:* bright yellow underparts; olive upperparts; black wings and tail. *Female:* uniformly olive upperparts; yellow underparts; grayish brown wings.

Size: *L* 6½–7½ in; *W* 11½ in.

Status: common migrant and breeder; occurs from mid-April to early October.

Habitat: fairly mature, upland deciduous and mixed forests and large woodlands.

Nesting: high in a deciduous tree, well away from the trunk; female builds a flimsy, shallow cup of grass, weeds and twigs and lines it with rootlets and fine grass; female incubates 2–5 brown-spotted, blue green eggs for 12–14 days; heavily parasitized by Brown-headed Cowbird.

Feeding: gleans insects from the tree canopy; may hover-glean or hawk insects in midair; may forage at lower levels during cold weather; eats aphids, weevils, wood-borers, leaf beetles, cicadas, ants, termites, dragonflies, wasps, bees, snails, slugs, worms and caterpillars; also eats berries; occasionally comes to feeders for peanut butter and suet.

Voice: song is a like a hoarse American Robin; call is a *chip-burrr* or *chip-churrr*.

Similar Species: *Summer Tanager* (p. 302): larger, lighter-colored bill; male has red tail and red wings; female has paler wings and is duskier overall, often with orange or reddish tinge. *Northern Cardinal* (p. 328): red bill, wings and tail; prominent head crest; male has black "mask" and "bib." *Orchard Oriole* (p. 342) and *Baltimore Oriole* (p. 343): females have sharper bills and wing bars.

Best Sites: in woodlands statewide.

SPOTTED TOWHEE

Pipilo maculatus

Towhees are large, long-tailed sparrows that hop forward and backward while searching for food. Like its cousin, the Eastern Towhee, the Spotted scratches at loose leaf litter, searching for food with both feet. • Until recently, the Spotted Towhee was grouped with the unspotted Eastern Towhee as a single species called the "Rufous-sided Towhee." In the Great Plains, these species interbreed regularly in a small zone. A third related species, the Collared Towhee, has interbred with the Spotted where their ranges overlap in Mexico. In Illinois, the Spotted was much less common than the Eastern, but more recently, since the change to full species status, sightings have increased. The Spotted Towhee is reported in Illinois more often in fall and winter than in spring. Many records of this species in northern and central Illinois occur in November, often after most Eastern Towhees have departed.

ID: *Male:* black "hood," back, wings and tail; rufous sides and flanks; dark, conical bill; red eyes; white spotting on wings and back; white outer tail corners; white breast and belly; buffy undertail. *Female:* paler overall.
Size: *L* 7–8½ in; *W* 10½ in.
Status: rare but regular migrant and winter visitor from mid-October to early May.

Habitat: brushy hedgerows and woods; overgrown fields; occasionally at feeders.
Nesting: does not nest in Illinois.
Feeding: scratches the ground vigorously for seeds and insects, including caterpillars, moths, beetles, ants and other common invertebrates; visits feeding stations periodically.
Voice: song is *here here here PLEASE;* distinctive call is a buzzy trill.
Similar Species: *Eastern Towhee* (p. 305): solid dark back; white patch at base of primaries.
Best Sites: none.

EASTERN TOWHEE

Pipilo erythrophthalmus

Birders often find Eastern Towhees by listening for their distinct *drink your tea* song or their equally distinct *chewink* call note. These noisy foragers hop rather than walk and rustle about in dense undergrowth, scraping back layers of dry leaves to expose the seeds, berries and insects hidden beneath. • This colorful bird belongs to the American Sparrow family—a group of birds that are usually dull in color. • Clearing of eastern deciduous forests in the 1800s helped this species to expand into New England, but as forests regenerate, their numbers may be declining. • The Eastern Towhee builds the first nest of the season on or near the ground in dense growth. If the nest and eggs are predated, the towhee will attempt a second nesting, this time higher in a shrub or tree. • Unlike most sparrows, towhees typically occur in singles or pairs and never in flocks. Eastern Towhees in Illinois have red eyes, but in the southeastern states white-eyed Eastern Towhees are more common.

ID: rufous sides and flanks; white outer tail corners; white spot at base of primaries; white lower breast and belly; buff undertail coverts; red eyes; dark, conical bill. *Male:* black "hood" and upperparts. *Female:* brown "hood" and upperparts.

Size: *L* 7–8½ in; *W* 10½ in.

Status: common migrant and breeder; arrives in early March and departs by mid-November; common winter resident in southern Illinois, decreasing northward.

Habitat: woodland edges; shrubby, abandoned fields; also forests with dense undergrowth and vine tangles, especially honeysuckle; pine plantations with dense understory in southern Illinois.

Nesting: first nest is on the ground or low in a dense shrub; second nest is up to 25 ft high, in shrubs or trees, especially those covered with vines; female builds a camouflaged cup nest of twigs, bark strips, grass, weeds, rootlets and animal hair; female incubates 3–4 brown-spotted, creamy white to pale gray eggs for 12–13 days; parasitized by Brown-headed Cowbird.

Feeding: scratches at leaf litter for insects, seeds and berries; sometimes forages in low shrubs and saplings.

Voice: song is 2 whistled notes followed by a trill: *drink your teeeee;* call is a slurred *cheweee* or *chewink.*

Similar Species: *Spotted Towhee* (p. 304): white spots on dark back and wings.

Best Sites: common in appropriate habitat in spring and summer.

AMERICAN TREE SPARROW

Spizella arborea

One bird always recorded on Illinois' Christmas bird counts is the rufous-capped, spot-breasted American Tree Sparrow. As the small flocks, numbering sometimes up to 100, flit about in shrubby fields, they give their bright, tinkling call notes that signal the arrival of winter. You can enjoy watching the interesting feeding habits of American Tree Sparrows in winter—they scratch among dried grasses, pop up at bent-over weeds, perch on grass stalks to extract seeds and beat weeds with their wings and then fly to the snowy ground to retrieve the seeds. • Despite its name, this sparrow does not live in woodlands, but rather in fields and semi-open, shrubby habitats. This hardy bird breeds in the Arctic right to the edge of the treeless zone and can survive temperatures as cold as −28° F. Come March, American Tree Sparrows start heading north. By the time the spring bird count begins in Illinois in early May, most tree sparrows have left.

ID: gray, unstreaked underparts; dark central breast spot; rufous "cap"; rufous stripe behind eye; gray face; streaked upperparts; notched tail; 2 white wing bars; dark legs; dark upper mandible; yellow lower mandible.

Size: *L* 6–6½ in; *W* 9½ in.

Status: very common migrant and winter resident; arrives in early to mid-October; most depart by mid-April; highest numbers occur in November and March when migrants mix with wintering birds.

Habitat: brushy thickets and weedy fields.

Nesting: does not nest in Illinois.

Feeding: catches flying insects; scratches exposed soil or snow for seeds; also, clings to grasses and forbs while extracting seeds; eats berries and catkins; prefers millet at feeders; eats mostly seeds in winter and insects during breeding season.

Voice: a high, whistled *tseet-tseet* is followed by a short, sweet, musical series of slurred whistles; song may be given in late winter and during spring migration; call is a 3-note *tsee-dle-eat*.

Similar Species: *Swamp Sparrow* (p. 320): white throat outlined in black; streaky, grayish breast; yellow base to bill; rufous rump; heavily streaked head and back; lacks dark breast spot and white wing bars. *Field Sparrow* (p. 309): white eye ring; pink bill; lacks dark breast spot.

Best Sites: none.

CHIPPING SPARROW
Spizella passerina

Just as the Dark-eyed Juncos are getting ready to leave Illinois to head north for spring, Chipping Sparrows are arriving from the south. Both species give similar, rapid trill songs that can confuse even a seasoned birder, but the Chipping Sparrow's trill is slightly faster, drier and less musical than the junco's. Other Illinois birds with songs like the Chipping Sparrow's include Worm-eating, Pine and Orange-crowned warblers. • Of North America's migrant sparrows, the Chipping Sparrow is the most common and widely distributed. It readily nests in suburban neighborhoods. • Populations of the Chipping Sparrow may be negatively affected by predation and competition with the nonnative House Sparrow and House Finch. The Chipping Sparrow migrates to the southern United States, Mexico and Central America for the winter.

breeding

ID: *Breeding:* prominent rufous "cap"; white "eyebrow"; black eye line; light gray, unstreaked underparts; streaked upperparts; all-dark bill; 2 faint wing bars; pale legs; gray rump. *Nonbreeding:* paler crown with dark streaks; buffy "eyebrow" and "cheek"; pinkish bill.
Size: *L* 5–6 in; *W* 8½ in.
Status: common migrant and breeder from late March through early November; rare winter resident.
Habitat: open conifers or mixed woodland edges with open, short grassy spaces; often in yards and gardens with evergreen trees and shrub borders.
Nesting: usually at midlevel in a conifer; female builds a compact cup nest of woven

grass and rootlets, often lined with hair; female incubates 4 pale blue eggs for 11–12 days; often has 2 broods; commonly parasitized by Brown-headed Cowbird.
Feeding: prefers seeds from grass, dandelions and clovers; also eats adult and larval invertebrates, including weevils, leafhoppers, grasshoppers, ants and spiders; occasionally visits feeders.
Voice: rapid, dry trill of *chip* notes; call is a high-pitched *chip*.
Similar Species: *Swamp Sparrow* (p. 320): rufous flanks; lacks white "eyebrow," black eye line and white wing bars. *Field Sparrow* (p. 309): white eye ring; gray throat; orange pink bill; lacks white "eyebrow." *Clay-colored Sparrow* (p. 308): much rarer during migration and breeding season; spring and breeding adults have darker crowns, brown "cheek" patches, pinkish bills and brown rumps.
Best Sites: widespread in appropriate habitat.

CLAY-COLORED SPARROW
Spizella pallida

In spring, the unmistakable loud, buzzy, insectlike call of the Clay-colored Sparrow elicits excitement from Illinois birders. Mostly a Great Plains species, the Clay-colored Sparrow is commonly found in the northeastern part of Illinois because of its migration pattern. It likely enters Illinois from the west-central region, moving eastward and northward. • Few Illinois summer records have been documented for this species, which has recently expanded its breeding range into Michigan and eastern Ontario. This sparrow winters in Texas and Mexico, often traveling with Chipping Sparrows. Fewer fall migrants have been reported in Illinois for this species. Distinguishing between first-winter Clay-colored Sparrows and Chipping Sparrows is extremely difficult. This could possibly explain why the number of migrant Clay-colored Sparrows reported in Illinois is low.

breeding

ID: unstreaked, white underparts; brown rump; buff breast wash; gray nape; light brown "cheek" edged with darker brown; brown crown with dark streak and pale central stripe; white "eyebrow"; white jaw stripe bordered by brown; white throat; mostly pale bill. *Juvenile:* sparsely streaked sides and belly with buffy undertones.
Size: *L* 5–6 in; *W* 7½ in.
Status: uncommon migrant in northeastern Illinois; rare migrant elsewhere; occurs from mid-April to mid-May and from early to mid-September through mid-October; very rare local breeder in northern Illinois.
Habitat: *Breeding:* abandoned fields, young conifer farms. *In migration:* shrubby edges, especially along L. Michigan.
Nesting: in a grassy tuft on the ground or in a small shrub at the base of small conifers; female builds an open cup nest of twigs, grass, weeds and rootlets and lines it with fine grass and fur; usually the female

incubates 4 brown-speckled, bluish green eggs for 10–12 days.
Feeding: feeds on the ground and in low vegetation; forages for mostly vegetable matter, including grass seeds and foxtail; also takes spiders and insects, including cankerworms, leafhoppers, ants, butterfly adults and larvae and grasshoppers; also eats catkins, berries and some cracked corn, millet and sunflower seeds at feeders.
Voice: song is a series of 2–5 slow, loud, low-pitched, insectlike buzzes; call is a soft *chip.*
Similar Species: *Chipping Sparrow* (p. 307): breeding adult has rufous rather than dark "cap," light grayish rather than dark "cheek," all-dark bill; juvenile more heavily streaked with gray rump; difficult to separate.
Best Sites: *Summer:* Christmas tree farm in Rockton, though not confirmed in recent years. *In migration:* L. Michigan shoreline parks, especially Gillson Park in Wilmette; old Northwestern University landfill in Evanston; Chicago lakefront parks.

FIELD SPARROW
Spizella pusilla

This pink-billed sparrow is a denizen of overgrown fields, pastures and forest clearings. The Field Sparrow nests in areas scattered with shrubs, tall, herbaceous plants and grasses. • Field Sparrows are not as heavily parasitized by Brown-headed Cowbirds as are other birds nesting in the same habitat because the female stays on the nest early in the morning at the time when Brown-headed Cowbirds lay most of their eggs. The Field Sparrow also may have learned to recognize when its nest has been parasitized, usually abandoning the nest and rebuilding elsewhere. • Field Sparrows gather in small foraging flocks, combing the ground for nourishing seeds. In winter, small numbers of Field Sparrows may often be found with larger flocks of American Tree Sparrows and other sparrows.

ID: pink bill; gray face and throat; rusty crown with gray central stripe; rusty streak behind eye; white eye ring; 2 white wing bars; unstreaked gray underparts with buffy red wash on breast, sides and flanks; pinkish legs. *Immature:* duller version of adult with streaked breast and faint buffy white wing bars.
Size: *L* 5–6 in; *W* 8 in.
Status: common migrant and breeder from mid-March to late November; fairly common winter resident, decreasing northward.
Habitat: abandoned or weedy and overgrown fields and pastures, woodland edges and clearings.
Nesting: on or near the ground; later nestings are higher above ground in large shrubs and saplings, especially raspberries, blackberries and red cedars; female weaves a frail, open cup nest of grass and lines it with animal hair and soft plant material; female incubates 3–5 brown-spotted, whitish to pale bluish eggs for 10–12 days.

Feeding: forages on the ground or on tips of grasses, bending over to catch seeds falling to the ground; mostly eats seeds of grass, chickweed and knotweed in winter; in summer eats more spiders and insects, such as weevils, beetles, grasshoppers, caterpillars, leafhoppers, ants, flies and wasps.
Voice: song is a series of musical, downslurred whistles accelerating into a trill, like a bouncing ping pong ball; call is a *chip* or *tsee*.
Similar Species: *American Tree Sparrow* (p. 306): dark central breast spot; dark upper mandible; lacks white eye ring. *Swamp Sparrow* (p. 320): white throat; dark upper mandible; lacks 2 white wing bars and white eye ring. *Chipping Sparrow* (p. 307): all-dark bill; white "eyebrow"; black eye line; lacks buffy red wash on underparts.
Best Sites: common in appropriate habitat.

VESPER SPARROW
Pooecetes gramineus

Though a ground nester, the Vesper Sparrow often chooses the highest singing perches available on its short-grass breeding grounds. • To attract a female, the male walks or runs with his tail spread and wings raised and expanded, occasionally rising into the air to give his flight-song. The song begins with two sets of double notes, followed by bubbling chatters and trills. • In Illinois, Vesper Sparrows often build nests in areas with short grass or in small depressions at the base of soybean, corn or weed plants or stubble. Changing agricultural practices are causing the decline of this sparrow's population. • "Vesper" is Latin for "evening," but other birds such as cuckoos, chats and Henslow's Sparrows sing more often at night than these sparrows. • Most sparrows gather in fairly large flocks, but Vespers are usually seen singly, in pairs or in very small flocks.

ID: chestnut brown shoulder patch; pale yellow lores; weak flank streaking; white eye ring; dark upper mandible; pink lower mandible; pink or light-colored legs. *In flight:* white outer tail feathers.
Size: *L* 5½–6½ in; *W* 10 in.
Status: common migrant and breeder from Effingham Co. northward; arrives in mid- to late March and departs by early November; very rare winter visitor in central and southern Illinois.
Habitat: open agricultural fields; usually with at least some grassy border strips; also pastures and hayfields.
Nesting: in a scrape on the ground, often under a canopy of grass or at the base of a plant stalk; loosely woven cup nest of grass is lined with rootlets, fine grass and hair; mostly the female incubates 3–5 brown-blotched, whitish to greenish white eggs for 11–13 days.
Feeding: walks and runs, picking up grasshoppers, beetles, cutworms and other pests such as weevils; also eats seeds, including ragweed and knotweed.
Voice: 4 characteristic, preliminary notes, with the 2nd higher in pitch, followed by a bubbly, flutelike trill.
Similar Species: *Savannah Sparrow* (p. 312): slimmer; shorter tail; white outer tail feathers either lacking or paler and less pronounced; lacks white eye ring and chestnut brown shoulder patch. *Lapland Longspur* (p. 325): nonbreeding has broad, pale "eyebrow," reddish edges on wing feathers and gives distinct rattling call; often seen in large flocks. *Bobolink* (p. 333): nonbreeding and immature are buffy overall and lack white in outer tail feathers and streaking on nape.
Best Sites: agricultural fields in central Illinois.

LARK SPARROW

Chondestes grammacus

The male Lark Sparrow engages in what is known as a "turkey-walk." Lifting his beak to the sky, the courting male spreads his rounded tail to expose white spots, droops his wings and struts back and forth in front of potential mates, singing all the while. The Lark Sparrow male also courts by passing a twig to the female. • In Illinois, Lark Sparrows nest on sandy or poor soils with low, sparse vegetation. During the breeding season, this bird is most numerous in Illinois in large sandy areas in Mason County along the Illinois River. In its main breeding range on the Great Plains, the Lark Sparrow has been documented using old nests of other birds such as the Western Kingbird and the Northern Mockingbird.

ID: distinctive "helmet" made up of white throat, "eyebrow" and crown stripe and black lines breaking up otherwise chestnut red head; grayish bill; unstreaked, pale breast with central spot; rounded black tail with extensive white corners; soft brown, mottled back and wings; light-colored legs.

Size: *L* 6½ in; *W* 11 in.

Status: rare to uncommon migrant; uncommon to locally common breeder; occurs from mid-April through mid- to late August, with records on Chicago lakefront in late October.

Habitat: sparsely vegetated areas with short grasses, showing exposed soil; often on sandy substrates in Illinois.

Nesting: on the ground, usually at the base of vegetation; mostly the female builds a bulky cup nest of grass and twigs and lines it with finer material; female incubates 4–5 blotched, glossy, white eggs for 11–12 days.

Feeding: gleans seeds and insects from the ground; eats more insects than seeds during breeding season; also eats mollusks.

Voice: melodious, variable song consists of short trills, buzzes, pauses and clear notes; often sings from exposed perches, usually trees along the edges of a field.

Similar Species: *Song Sparrow* (p. 318) and *Lincoln's Sparrow* (p. 319): difficult to separate juveniles, but both have reddish brown tones on wings and tail. *Vesper Sparrow* (p. 310): juvenile has chestnut on wings, white eye ring and lacks streaking on breast.

Best Sites: Iroquois County CA; Lost Mound NWR; Middlefork State Fish and Wildlife Area; Sand Ridge SF; Green River CA; Sand Prairie Scrub Oak Nature Preserve.

SAVANNAH SPARROW

Passerculus sandwichensis

From atop a low perch or on the ground, the male Savannah Sparrow sings his distinctive, buzzy tune to attract mates in spring and early summer. Once nesting begins, Savannah Sparrows become quieter. Like many grassland ground nesters, Savannah Sparrows react to intruders by running swiftly and inconspicuously through the grass, like feathered voles, rather than taking flight. • Scientists recognize 17 sub-species of the Savannah Sparrow, including two rare ones. Minor plumage differences include the extent of yellow behind the eye and overall color. • Savannah Sparrows winter in southern Illinois, sometimes in fairly large flocks. In Illinois, this sparrow's breeding range is very similar to that of the Vesper Sparrow, although the Savannah is more common in northern Illinois and the Vesper is more common in central Illinois.

ID: finely streaked breast, sides and flanks; white underparts; streaked and mottled brown upper-parts; yellow lores; pale jaw line; light-colored legs and bill; may show dark breast spot.
Size: *L* 4½–5½ in; *W* 6¾ in.
Status: common migrant; fairly common breeder in central and northern Illinois; arrives in mid- to late March and departs by early to mid-November; uncommon winter resident in southern Illinois, decreasing northward.
Habitat: *Breeding:* grassy strips in agricul-tural fields; moist sedge and grass areas; grazed pastures; prairies; sod farms and other short-grass situations. *In migration:* similar to breeding; also airports and golf courses. *Winter:* millet and sorghum plant-ings, grassy, weedy fields dominated by foxtail.
Nesting: on the ground; in a shallow scrape well concealed by grass or a shrub; female builds an open cup nest woven and lined with grass; mostly the female

incubates 3–6 brown-marked, whitish to greenish or pale tan eggs for 10–13 days; often has 2 broods.
Feeding: walks or runs on the ground to glean insects, including beetles, grasshop-pers, ants, spiders and snails; occasionally scratches; eats mostly insects in summer and seeds and fruits in fall and winter.
Voice: song is a high-pitched, clear, buzzy *tip tip tip teeeee say,* sometimes with a *slickit* on the end; call is a high, thin *tsit.*
Similar Species: *Vesper Sparrow* (p. 310): bulkier; longer tail; white eye ring; more prominent white outer tail feathers. *Lincoln's Sparrow* (p. 319): present only during migration; buff jaw line; buffy breast with more delicate black streaks; much more reddish brown in wings. *Henslow's Sparrow* (p. 314): flatter head; shorter tail; more reddish brown in wings; white scaling on back feathers. *Song Sparrow* (p. 318): larger; longer, rounded tail; larger bill; triangular "mustache" stripes; lacks yellow lores.
Best Sites: Momence Sod Farms; H & E Sod Farms in McHenry Co.

GRASSHOPPER SPARROW
Ammodramus savannarum

The Grasshopper Sparrow is named not for its diet, but for its buzzy, insectlike song. During courtship, males chase females through the air, buzzing. This species is one of few North American sparrows that sing two different courtship songs: one ends in a short trill and the other is a prolonged series of high trills that change in pitch and speed. • To deter predators, the female lands in the grass a distance from the nest and then walks concealed the rest of the way. • Mowing or harvesting grassy areas early in the nesting season may be detrimental to these birds. Convincing local landowners and state governments to delay cutting until mid-August or September would benefit this sparrow. In Illinois, loss of prairies, hayfields and pasture land has reduced breeding numbers of Grasshopper Sparrows.

ID: unstreaked, buff breast, sides and flanks; flattened head; dark crown with pale central stripe; buff "cheek"; mottled brown upperparts; beady, black eyes; sharp tail; pale legs; may show small yellow patch on edge of forewing.

Size: *L* 4½–5 in; *W* 7¾ in.

Status: uncommon to locally common migrant and breeder from mid-April to early October, with some November stragglers.

Habitat: grasslands and grassy fields, including pastures, hayfields and airports with minimal tree cover; fallow agricultural fields.

Nesting: in a shallow depression on the ground, usually concealed by grass; small domelike cup nest woven with grass is lined with rootlets, fine grass and hair; female incubates 4–5 creamy white eggs, spotted with gray and reddish brown, for 11–13 days.

Feeding: gleans insects and seeds from the ground and grass; eats many insects, including grasshoppers.

Voice: song is a long, insectlike buzz preceded by 1–3 high, thin whistled notes: *tea-tea-tea zeeeeeeeeee.*

Similar Species: *Le Conte's Sparrow* (p. 315): migrant only; prefers wetter habitat; fine streaking on breast and flanks. *Bobolink* (p. 333): nonbreeding and immature are larger and lack flattened head. *Henslow's Sparrow* (p. 314): greenish nape; more reddish brown in wings; lacks streaking on breast and flanks.

Best Sites: Plum Creek FP; Midewin National Tallgrass Prairie; Goose Lake Prairie SNA; Lost Mound NWR; Green River CA; Pyramid SP; Prairie Ridge SNA.

HENSLOW'S SPARROW

Ammodramus henslowii

Even if you hear a Henslow's Sparrow sing, don't expect to find it easily; these birds often sing from the ground. When disturbed, this ground-nesting grassland bird may fly a short distance before dropping back into cover, but more frequently it runs through dense vegetation. • Formerly one of the most abundant grassland species on Illinois' prairies, it is now state-endangered. The Crop Reserve Program (CRP) in Illinois gives farmers tax incentives to set aside grasslands for most of the year. This program has helped the Henslow's Sparrow find nesting spots. In addition, restoration research has shown that Henslow's Sparrows prefer grasses of a certain height and avoid grasslands that have just undergone prescribed burning or are becoming overgrown with shrubs and tree saplings.

ID: flattened head profile; olive green face, central crown stripe and nape; dark crown and whisker stripes; rusty tinge on back, wings and tail; white underparts with dark streaking on buff breast, sides and flanks; thick bill; deeply notched, sharp-edged tail.
Size: *L* 4½–5½ in; *W* 6½ in.
Status: state-endangered breeder; breeders have increased recently; occurs from mid-April to early to mid-October, with a few lingering later.
Habitat: large, fallow, grassy fields and meadows with a matted ground layer of dead vegetation; prefers low, damp situations.

Nesting: in a loose colony; on the ground at the base of a grass clump or herbaceous plant; in southern Illinois, prefers Kentucky bluegrass, orchard grass and broom sedge; mostly the female builds a well-concealed open cup nest of grass and weeds and lines it with fine grass and hair; female incubates 3–5 heavily speckled, whitish to pale green eggs for about 11 days.
Feeding: gleans insects, particularly crickets and katydids, as well as beetles, ants, parasitic wasps and caterpillars from the ground; also eats grass, sedge and weed seeds.
Voice: weak, liquidy, cricketlike *tslick-it* song is distinctive, often given during rain or at night.
Similar Species: *Savannah Sparrow* (p. 312): rounder head; yellow lores; lacks buffy breast. *Grasshopper Sparrow* (p. 313): unmarked, buffy breast; lacks greenish nape.
Best Sites: Goose Lake Prairie SNA; Midewin National Tallgrass Prairie; Des Plaines CA; Cypress Creek NWR; Pyramid SP; Prairie Ridge SNA.

LE CONTE'S SPARROW

Ammodramus leconteii

In the early 1900s, Le Conte's Sparrow nested along the Calumet River, in the wet edges of extensive marshlands. Because of habitat destruction and degradation, this species now only migrates through Illinois to reach its wet prairie breeding grounds in the upper Midwest and Canada. If patient Christmas bird counters in southern Illinois check many wet foxtail fields, they may flush one or two overwintering birds, getting a brief glimpse of this colorful sparrow. • Look for a small, yellowish bird with a short, sharply pointed tail. This sparrow will fly jerkily just above the vegetation for a short distance, land back in the grasses and then run into cover. • This bird's namesake, naturalist John Le Conte, was a distinguished 19th-century American entomologist.

ID: buff orange face; gray "cheek"; black line behind eye; light central crown stripe bordered by dark stripes; buff orange upper breast, sides and flanks; dark streaking on sides and flanks; white throat, lower breast and belly; mottled, straw-colored upperparts; buff streaks on back; purplish spots on nape; pale legs; sharply pointed tail. *Nonbreeding:* duller overall; appears yellowish or lighter-colored than other sparrows.
Size: *L* 5 in; *W* 6½ in.
Status: uncommon migrant; more numerous in fall than spring; occurs from mid-March to late April, with regular stragglers until mid-May along Chicago lakefront, and from mid-September to mid-November; uncommon winter resident in southern Illinois.
Habitat: open, grassy fields, especially those dominated by foxtail; prefers damp or wet fields; also borders of marshes and sedge meadows.
Nesting: does not nest in Illinois.
Feeding: gleans the ground and low vegetation for spiders, seeds and insects such as leafhoppers and stink bugs.
Voice: rarely sings while in Illinois; song is a weak, short, raspy, insectlike buzz: *t-t-t-zeeee zee* or *take-it ea-zeee;* alarm call is a high-pitched whistle.
Similar Species: *Grasshopper Sparrow* (p. 313): occurs in drier situations; darker appearance; flatter head; lacks buff orange face and streaking on underparts. *Nelson's Sharp-tailed Sparrow* (p. 316): white stripes on dark back; very dark rump; lacks purplish spots on nape.
Best Sites: *In migration:* Chicago lakefront parks. *Fall* and *winter:* L. Chautauqua; Rend L.; Horseshoe Lake CA, Alexander Co.; Crab Orchard NWR; Prairie Ridge SNA; Carlyle L.

NELSON'S SHARP-TAILED SPARROW

Ammodramus nelsoni

Nelson's Sharp-tailed Sparrow is another coveted sparrow for Illinois birders. Its habits and habitat resemble that of the Le Conte's Sparrow, although Nelson's Sharp-tailed prefers somewhat deeper water in cattail-dominated marshes rather than shallower areas dominated by sedges and foxtail. Nelson's Sharp-tailed also has a fairly narrow migration period and is later than Le Conte's in spring in Illinois. Both have sharply pointed tails, which help birders to distinguish them from other sparrow species. • Nelson's Sharp-tailed Sparrow and the Saltmarsh Sharp-tailed Sparrow were once classified as a single species, but are now separate. Nelson's is the interior species that breeds in Wisconsin, northeastern Minnesota and farther north. The Saltmarsh Sharp-tailed Sparrow is restricted to salt marshes along the East Coast. • Unlike many songbird species, male Nelson's Sharp-tailed Sparrows are not territorial, but rather promiscuous, roving around the marsh and mating with as many females as possible. • Famous Illinois ornithologist Edward William Nelson once served as chief of the U.S. Biological Survey and president of the American Ornithologists' Union. His greatest contribution to ornithology was the creation of the Migratory Bird Treaty, still in effect today.

ID: buff orange face, breast, sides and flanks; gray "cheek," central crown stripe and nape; dark line behind eye; light streaking on sides and flanks; white stripes on dark back; white to light buff throat; white belly; sharply pointed tail.

Size: *L* 5–6 in; *W* 7 in.

Status: rare to uncommon migrant from mid-May to the first few days of June and from early September to late October; more common in Chicagoland than southern Illinois in spring; more numerous in fall statewide.

Habitat: cattail marshes with standing water.

Nesting: does not nest in Illinois.

Feeding: gleans ants, beetles, grasshoppers and other insects, spiders and small snails from the ground, low vegetation and marshes; also eats seeds from grasses and weeds.

Voice: song is rarely heard in Illinois, a short, raspy buzz: *ts tse-sheeeee.*

Similar Species: *Grasshopper Sparrow* (p. 313): flatter head; lacks streaking on underparts. *Le Conte's Sparrow* (p. 315): lighter, straw-colored back; purplish spots on nape.

Best Sites: Chicago lakefront parks; Goose Lake Prairie SNA; Sangchris Lake SP; Prairie Ridge SNA. *In fall:* Illinois Beach SP, Clinton L. and Rice L.

FOX SPARROW

Passerella iliaca

Like the Eastern Towhee, the Fox Sparrow scratches out a living using both feet to stir up leaves and scrape organic matter along the forest floor. • An early spring migrant, the Fox Sparrow gives its beautiful song from brushy thickets. Four subspecies have been identified for the Fox Sparrow. Major differences include size, plumage and relative bill size. The Illinois subspecies is the *iliaca* or "red" species, called the "Red Fox Sparrow." • During the first few weeks in April, Fox Sparrows are seen with Hermit Thrushes, a species with which they can be confused because of their similar size and reddish brown color. • In migration, Fox Sparrows often roost in cedars, sometimes in groups of up to 50 birds.

ID: whitish underparts; heavy, reddish brown spotting and streaking on white breast and belly often converges into central breast spot; reddish brown wings, rump and tail; gray face and nape; brown-streaked gray back; stubby, conical, 2-tone bill; pale legs.
Size: *L* 7 in; *W* 10½ in.
Status: common migrant from late February to mid-April, with regular stragglers in the Chicago area until early May, and from late September to early December; fairly common winter resident in southern Illinois, decreasing northward.
Habitat: woodland edges, thickets, brushy and weedy areas.
Nesting: does not nest in Illinois.

Feeding: scratches the ground to uncover seeds, berries and invertebrates such as beetles and spiders; visits backyard feeders and feeds extensively on fruits of red cedar, pokeberry, multiflora rose and elderberry; also seeds from smartweed, ragweed and grasses in migration and winter.
Voice: song is a long series of melodic whistles, ending with *All I have is what's here dear, won't you won't you take it?;* sometimes ending in a very short buzz; calls include loud *chip* and *click* notes.
Similar Species: *Song Sparrow* (p. 318): smaller; darker bill; pale central crown stripe; less reddish overall; much less gray on head. *Hermit Thrush* (p. 256): thinner bill; light eye ring; black breast spots; unstreaked olive brown and reddish brown upperparts; lacks thin, white wing bars; often pumps its red tail; buffy streak on underwings in flight.
Best Sites: none.

SONG SPARROW

Melospiza melodia

The well-named Song Sparrow sings its complex, melodic, rhythmic rhapsodies very early in spring, and sometimes in the middle of winter. Males may have 5 to 13 different songs. • One of the most studied North American songbirds, the Song Sparrow has 31 different subspecies, from the pale desert birds to the larger and darker Alaskan forms. Illinois has at least two subspecies, the breeding *euphonia* and the central-western *juddi*. • A habitat generalist, the Song Sparrow is one of the most familiar songbirds across North America. Song Sparrows may raise two or three broods a season, sometimes even four as far north as Massachusetts. The young from the first brood may engage in some "nest-building," perhaps just for practice.

ID: whitish underparts with heavy brown streaking that converges into central breast spot; grayish face; dark line behind eye; white jaw line is bordered by dark "whisker" and "mustache" stripes; dark crown with pale central stripe; mottled brown upperparts; rounded tail tip; tail flops up and down during short flights.

Size: *L* 6 in; *W* 8¼ in.

Status: common migrant, arriving in late February and early March; fall migrants occur from mid-August to late November; common breeder, decreasing southward; common winter resident, decreasing northward.

Habitat: shrubby areas, including brushy fencerows and vegetation near agricultural fields; suburban backyards; often near water.

Nesting: on the ground or low in a shrub or small tree; female builds an open cup nest of grass, weeds, leaves and bark shreds and lines it with rootlets, fine grass

and hair; female incubates 3–5 brown-spotted, greenish white eggs for 12–14 days; may raise 2–3 broods each summer; frequently parasitized by Brown-headed Cowbird.

Feeding: gleans the ground, shrubs and trees for insects and seeds; also eats wild fruit such as blackberries, elderberries and grapes; prefers millet at feeders.

Voice: song is 2 or more bright, distinctive introductory notes, such as *sweet, sweet, sweet,* followed by a buzzy *towee,* then a short, descending trill; calls include a short *tsip* and a nasal *tchep.*

Similar Species: *Fox Sparrow* (p. 317): heavier breast spotting and streaking; reddish upperparts; lacks pale central crown stripe and dark "mustache." *Lincoln's Sparrow* (p. 319): lightly streaked breast with buff wash; buff jaw line. *Savannah Sparrow* (p. 312): smaller; shorter, notched tail; less breast streaking; yellow lores; lacks grayish face and triangular "mustache."

Best Sites: none.

LINCOLN'S SPARROW

Melospiza lincolnii

L incoln's Sparrows seem to be more timid than other sparrows seen in Illinois. When approached, they slip under the cover of nearby shrubs. A male is often only discovered when he sings his lovely, bubbly, wrenlike song. This species' remote breeding grounds and secretive, skulking behavior have kept the Lincoln's one of the least-known sparrows. It breeds right up to the treeline in northern Canada and winters in the southwestern U.S., Mexico and Guatemala. When migrating through Illinois, it often chooses wet, brushy areas that mimic its boggy summer home. • Two nesting records for the Lincoln's Sparrow come from Illinois. For an Illinois sparrow, the Lincoln's is a late migrant and is sometimes missed on early spring bird counts in the northern part of the state. • This sparrow bears the name of Thomas Lincoln, a young companion to John J. Audubon on his voyage to Labrador, Canada.

ID: buff breast band, sides and flanks with fine dark streaking; buff jaw stripe; gray "eyebrow," face and "collar"; dark line behind eye; dark reddish "cap" with gray central stripe; white throat and belly; mottled gray brown to reddish brown upperparts; very faint, buffy eye ring; raises crown to form crest.
Size: *L* 5½ in; *W* 7½ in.
Status: uncommon to fairly common migrant from mid-April to late May and from early September to early November; very rare winter resident in central and southern Illinois.
Habitat: shrubby edges of forests, bogs, swamps, beaver ponds and meadows; also in the shrubby growth of recent forest burns or clearings.
Nesting: does not nest in Illinois.
Feeding: scratches on the ground, exposing invertebrates and seeds; occasionally visits feeding stations.
Voice: wrenlike, musical mixture of buzzes, trills and warbled notes; calls include a buzzy *zeee* and *tsup.*
Similar Species: *Song Sparrow* (p. 318): heavier breast streaking; dark triangular "mustache"; lacks buff wash on breast, sides and flanks. *Savannah Sparrow* (p. 312): whiter breast; yellow lores. *Swamp Sparrow* (p. 320): reddish brown overall; rufous rump and tail; generally lacks fine streaking and buff on breast; immature has more chestnut in wings and grayer breast.
Best Sites: none.

SWAMP SPARROW
Melospiza georgiana

Swamp Sparrows skulk in the emergent vegetation of cattail marshes, foraging for a variety of invertebrates. They may even wade through shallow water to snatch insects off the surface. These sparrows have also been observed climbing up and down stems of reeds, grass and shrubs to take food from the water's surface. • Swamp Sparrow males sing their musical trills from atop cattails or shoreline shrubs. The Swamp Sparrow is tied to wetlands for nesting and is only found breeding in northern Illinois. This bird nests just above the ground or at the water's surface, and consequently, can easily lose its nest and eggs during flooding. Fledglings may also perish by falling into water and by being eaten by frogs, fish and turtles.

breeding

ID: gray face; reddish brown wings; brownish upperparts; dark streaking on back; dull gray breast; white throat and jaw line outlined by black stripes; dark line behind eye. *Breeding:* rusty "cap"; buff sides and flanks. *Nonbreeding:* streaked brown "cap" with gray central stripe; more brownish sides.
Size: *L* 5–6 in; *W* 7¼ in.
Status: common migrant; locally common breeder in northeastern Illinois; absent as breeder from rest of state; arrives in early to mid-March, departs by mid-November; common to locally abundant winter resident in southern Illinois, decreasing northward.
Habitat: *Breeding:* marshes with some permanent water. *In migration* and *winter:*

swamps, marshes, wet meadows, open woodlands, weedy fields and thickets.
Nesting: in aquatic vegetation or shoreline bushes; cup nest is woven with coarse grass and marsh vegetation and lined with fine grass; usually has partial canopy and a side entrance; female incubates 4–5 pale green eggs for 12–13 days; often has 2 broods.
Feeding: gleans spiders and insects, from the ground, vegetation and the water's surface; also takes seeds of sedges, grasses and weeds.
Voice: song is a sharp, metallic, slow trill: *weet-weet-weet-weet;* call is a harsh *chink.*
Similar Species: *Chipping Sparrow* (p. 307): clean white "eyebrow"; full black eye line; uniformly gray underparts; white wing bars. *American Tree Sparrow* (p. 306): winter resident; dark central breast spot; white wing bars; 2-tone bill. *Song Sparrow* (p. 318): heavily streaked underparts; lacks gray "collar." *Lincoln's Sparrow* (p. 319): less rufous rump, wings and tail.
Best Sites: none.

WHITE-THROATED SPARROW
Zonotrichia albicollis

This handsome sparrow can be easily identified by its bold white throat, striped crown and yellow lores. Two color morphs occur in Illinois; one has black and white stripes on the head, the other has brown and tan stripes. One morph almost always chooses the other for a breeding partner. • In spring and fall, White-throated Sparrows can appear anywhere in Illinois where there are brushy woodlands. • Urban backyards dressed with brushy fenceline tangles and a bird feeder brimming with seeds can attract these sparrows. • This hardy species breeds across much of Canada and the northeastern part of the United States and winters throughout eastern North America, including Illinois. The first confirmed nesting of the White-throated Sparrow in Illinois occurred in July 2001; a pair nested in a planted evergreen bed in downtown Chicago near the river. Summering birds and singing males have been recorded and suspected as nesters for the past 5 to 10 years.

white-striped morph

ID: black and white, or brown and tan, stripes on head; white throat; gray "cheek"; yellow lores; black eye line; gray, unstreaked to lightly streaked underparts; mottled, brown upperparts; grayish bill.
Size: *L* 6½–7½ in; *W* 9 in.
Status: common to abundant migrant from late March to early June and from early September to mid-November; extremely rare breeder in northern Illinois; common to abundant winter resident, decreasing northward.
Habitat: brushy fields and woodlands, hedgerows and suburban areas.
Nesting: on or near the ground, often concealed by low shrubs or a fallen log; often in a conifer; female builds an open cup nest

of grass, weeds, twigs and conifer needles lined with rootlets, fine grass and hair; female incubates 4–5 brown-marked, greenish blue to pale blue eggs for 12–14 days.
Feeding: scratches the ground to expose invertebrates; also gleans insects from vegetation and while in flight; eats fruit from dogwood, sumac, elderberry, cedar, spicebush and buds of oaks, maple and apple, weeds and seeds; also visits feeders.
Voice: variable song is a clear and distinct whistled: *oh, sweet Canada Canada Canada;* call is a sharp *chink.*
Similar Species: *White-crowned Sparrow* (p. 323): pinkish bill; gray "collar"; lacks bold, white throat and yellow lores.
Best Sites: widespread in appropriate habitat during migration.

321

HARRIS'S SPARROW

Zonotrichia querula

During spring and fall migration, the possibility exists that a birder might find the large and handsome Harris's Sparrow. This migrant passes through Illinois in small isolated trickles, frequently mixing with flocks of White-crowned Sparrows and, to a lesser extent, White-throated Sparrows. Strong north-westerly winds, especially in fall, may bring more Harris's Sparrows into Illinois and, occasionally, this species will visit backyard feeders. • Harris's Sparrows breed in the Far North where the treeline fades to tundra. It is the only songbird that breeds exclusively in Canada and was one of the last North American songbirds to have had its nest and eggs described. • Harris's Sparrows seen in fall in Illinois are usually immatures with buffy "cheeks" and a black "necklace." • The Harris's Sparrow spends winters in the central Great Plains. Increased backyard bird feeding as well as winter wheat plantings in Kansas may be helping this bird expand its winter range.

nonbreeding

Habitat: hedgerows, especially multiflora rose; brush piles and weedy areas; backyard feeders.

Nesting: does not nest in Illinois.

Feeding: gleans the ground and vegetation for seeds of ragweed and knotweed; eats fresh buds, berries and various insects, spiders and mites; occasionally visits feeders.

Voice: rarely heard singing in Illinois; song is a series of 2–4 long, quavering whistles; each series may be offered at the same or different pitch; call is a *jeenk* or *zheenk*.

Similar Species: *White-throated Sparrow* (p. 321): grayish bill; yellow lores; black-and-white-striped crown. *White-crowned Sparrow* (p. 323): black-and-white-striped crown; gray "collar"; immature has broad gray "eyebrow" bordered by brown eye line and crown. *House Sparrow* (p. 352): much more common; smaller; dark to yellowish bill; gray head; large, white wing patch.

Best Sites: Montrose Harbor; Jackson Park, Chicago; Clinton L.

ID: mottled brown-and-black upperparts; white underparts; pink orange bill. *Breeding:* black crown, ear patch, throat and "bib"; gray face; black streaks on sides and flanks; white wing bars. *Nonbreeding:* brown face; brownish sides and flanks; white flecks on black crown. *Immature:* white throat; mostly brownish crown with some black streaking.

Size: *L* 7–7½ in; *W* 10½ in.

Status: rare spring migrant from late April to mid-May; rare to uncommon fall migrant from late September to mid-November; rare winter resident.

WHITE-CROWNED SPARROW
Zonotrichia leucophrys

The boldly patterned White-crowned Sparrow brightens brushy expanses and suburban parks and gardens with its clear, whistled song. These birds with pink bills and clean gray breasts breed in far northern alpine environments as well as beach dunes in California. • The White-crowned Sparrow is one of North America's most studied sparrows. Research on this bird has given science tremendous insight into bird physiology, homing behavior and the geographic variability of song dialects. • Five subspecies of the White-crowned Sparrow have been identified, two of which are found in Illinois: the more common *leucophrys* and the *gambelii*, or "Gambel's," of the northwest. The "Gambel's" subspecies has white lores, the other has black, but this characteristic is difficult to see in the field. • In spring, White-crowned Sparrows feed on dandelion heads as well as young garden plants such as beets and peas. • In fall and winter, many more immatures are seen in Illinois than adults; the young birds have brown and buff rather than black and white head stripes.

ID: black and white head stripes; black eye line; pink orange bill; gray face; unstreaked, gray underparts; pale gray throat; mottled gray brown upperparts; 2 faint, white wing bars. *Immature:* brown and buff head stripes rather than bold black and white.
Size: *L* 7 in; *W* 9½ in.
Status: common migrant from late April to late May, with some stragglers in early June in Chicagoland, and from late September to early November; fairly common winter resident, decreasing northward.

Habitat: shrubby fencerows, tree rows and shrub lines in open areas and along roadsides; favors multiflora rose patches in Illinois.
Nesting: does not nest in Illinois.
Feeding: scratches the ground to expose spiders and insects such as flies and mosquitoes; also eats berries, willow catkins and buds; eats mostly seeds in winter; eats dandelion heads in spring; visits bird feeders.
Voice: song is 1–3 clear whistled notes on the same pitch, ending with 3 buzzy notes, the last lower in pitch; call is a high, thin *seet* or sharp *pink*.
Similar Species: *White-throated Sparrow* (p. 321): bold, chalky white throat; grayish bill; yellow lores; browner upperparts.
Best Sites: L. Michigan parks.

DARK-EYED JUNCO

Junco hyemalis

The Dark-eyed Junco inhabits nearly the entire North American continent from Alaska south to Mexico. • This species, often called "Snow Bird," arrives in Illinois for winter vacation, congregating in backyards with bird feeders and sheltering shrubs, and along brushy roadsides. • Juncos spend most of their time feeding on the ground, and prefer to snatch up seeds that are knocked to the ground by other bird feeder visitors such as chickadees, sparrows, nuthatches and jays. Small flocks of juncos feed in a hierarchy, with males dominating females and young. • Juncos roost in cedars and other evergreens in Illinois. When flushed from wooded trails, they display their distinctive white outer tail feathers. • The junco complex of subspecies is somewhat complicated and includes the Oregon, Gray-headed and White-winged juncos. Illinois mostly hosts the "Slate-colored Junco" and occasionally the Oregon subspecies.

"Slate-colored Junco"

ID: white outer tail feathers; pink bill. *Male:* dark slate gray overall, except for white lower breast, belly and undertail coverts. *Female:* brown tones on gray.
Size: *L* 6¼ in; *W* 9¼ in.
Status: abundant migrant and winter resident; occurs from mid-September to late April, with some stragglers into late May.
Habitat: open, shrubby and weedy areas including hedgerows, edges of fields and forests; grasslands, lawns and corn fields.

Nesting: does not nest in Illinois.
Feeding: scratches the ground for seeds of ragweed, smartweed, pigweed, thistles, grasses and sedges; in summer, eats spiders and insects, including beetles, weevils, ants and wasps; also eats berries.
Voice: song is a long, dry trill, very similar to the call of the Chipping Sparrow, but more musical; call is a smacking *chip* note, often given in series.
Similar Species: none.
Best Sites: none.

LAPLAND LONGSPUR
Calcarius lapponicus

In migration and winter in Illinois, Lapland Longspurs travel with Horned Larks and, to a lesser extent, Snow Buntings. Lapland Longspurs can be seen over fields and farmlands, feeding on seeds and waste grain. • In fall, these birds arrive from their breeding grounds looking like mottled, brownish sparrows. They retain their dull plumage throughout the winter. By the time farmers work their fields in spring, Lapland Longspurs have molted into their bold breeding plumage. • This bird breeds in arctic tundra regions, including the region of northern Europe known as Lapland. • The Lapland Longspur has a greatly extended back toenail; hence the name "longspur." • These birds are frequent victims of late winter storms during migration. About 750,000 Lapland Longspurs fell to their deaths on two Minnesota lakes in 1904 when a sudden storm interrupted their migration.

nonbreeding

ID: whitish outer tail feathers; pale yellowish bill. *Breeding male:* black crown, face and "bib"; chestnut nape; broad, white stripe curves down to shoulder from eye (may be tinged with buff behind eye). *Breeding female:* often has rufous in wings; mottled brown-and-black upperparts; lightly streaked flanks. *Nonbreeding:* male has faint chestnut on nape and diffuse black breast; female has narrow, lightly streaked buff breast band.
Size: *L* 6½ in; *W* 11½ in.
Status: common to abundant migrant in spring and fall with numbers peaking in March and November; common to locally abundant winter resident, with smaller numbers in northeastern Illinois.
Habitat: corn and soybean stubble fields (especially wet), other short-grass fields; mudflats; rural roads after snowstorms.

Nesting: does not nest in Illinois.
Feeding: gleans the ground and snow for seeds of grasses, weeds, sedges and waste grain, including corn in winter; eats beetles, weevils, craneflies, caterpillars and spiders in spring.
Voice: flight song is a rapid slurred warble; common flight call is a sharp rattle, *pit-tic-tic* interspersed with a descending *teew*.
Similar Species: *Horned Lark* (p. 230): sandy-colored upperparts; distinctive yellow-and-black head pattern; shallower flight pattern. *Smith's Longspur* (p. 326): all-buff to buff orange underparts; white shoulder patch; breeding male has bold, black-and-white face. *American Pipit* (p. 264): lightly streaked, buff breast; lacks rufous on wings; bobs tail while walking.
Best Sites: corn and soybean stubble fields; L. Michigan shoreline with sparse vegetation in fall and spring.

SMITH'S LONGSPUR
Calcarius pictus

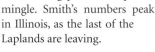

The uncommon and secretive Smith's Longspur is one of the more sought-after birds in North America—Illinois offers birders one of the best chances to see breeding-plumaged males. Some of the first specimens of Smith's Longspurs were obtained from Illinois. • The Smith's Longspur is one of the least-studied passerines because of its restricted United States range and its mostly inaccessible breeding territory. • These birds spend their summers far from Illinois, along the Hudson Bay coast in Canada and west into Alaska. • This bird's winter range is limited to a few south-central states, mainly Texas and Oklahoma, where it prefers short-grass prairie and pastureland. • Smith's Longspurs have an unusual breeding system. Referred to as polygynandrous, both males and females breed with two or three partners. • Both Smith's Longspurs and Lapland Longspurs may feed in the same field, but they do not mingle. Smith's numbers peak in Illinois, as the last of the Laplands are leaving.

breeding

ID: 2 mainly white outer tail feathers; white shoulder patch; mottled brown-and-black upperparts. *Breeding male:* black crown; black triangle on white face; buff orange underparts and "collar"; faint streaking on sides and flanks. *Nonbreeding* and *immature:* streaked crown and nape; buff underparts with faint streaking on breast.
Size: *L* 6 in; *W* 11¼ in.
Status: uncommon to locally common spring migrant; rare fall migrant; very rare winter visitor; occurs from March to early May and from mid-October to late November.
Habitat: wet corn stubble fields with foxtail; other short-grass areas, including emerging clover and alfalfa fields; occasionally airports and golf courses.

Nesting: does not nest in Illinois.
Feeding: gleans seeds, mostly foxtail in Illinois, from the ground; also eats beetles and grass seeds; occasionally eats cracked corn.
Voice: mostly sings on calm, sunny days in spring; song is a warbling *switoo-whideedeedew, whee-tew;* alarm call is a rapid clicking, like the winding of an old-fashioned watch.
Similar Species: *Lapland Longspur* (p. 325): whitish belly and undertail coverts; black on neck, throat or breast; lacks white shoulder patch; breeding male has black throat and "bib," and chestnut brown nape. *Vesper Sparrow* (p. 310): chestnut brown shoulder patch; white underparts. *American Pipit* (p. 264): thinner bill; streaking on breast; lacks white shoulder patch; bobs tail.
Best Sites: Prairie Ridge SNA; corn stubble fields with foxtail in Champaign, McLean, Sangamon and Mason Counties.

SNOW BUNTING
Plectrophenax nivalis

In early winter, when flocks of Snow Buntings descend on rural fields, their startling black-and-white wings and tail flash in contrast with the snow-covered backdrop. It may seem strange that Snow Buntings are whiter in summer than in winter, but the darker winter plumage may help these birds absorb heat cold, on clear winter days. • Snow Buntings venture farther north than any other songbird in the world. • In winter, Snow Buntings prefer expansive soybean and corn fields, and occasionally pastures and other short-grass areas, where they scratch and peck at exposed seeds and grains. They will also ingest small grains of sand or gravel from roadsides as a source of minerals and to help digestion. • Snow Buntings are definitely cold-weather songbirds: they often bathe in snow in early spring and burrow into it during bitter cold snaps to stay warm.

♂

nonbreeding

♀

ID: black-and-white wings and tail; white underparts. *Breeding male:* black back; all-white head and rump; black bill. *Breeding female:* streaky, brown-and-whitish crown and back; dark bill. *Nonbreeding:* yellowish bill; golden brown "cheek," crown, back and rump; female has dark forecrown and golden back with dark streaks.
Size: *L* 6¾ in; *W* 14 in.
Status: uncommon to locally common migrant and winter resident in northern Illinois; rare to uncommon migrant and winter resident in central Illinois; rare in southern Illinois; occurs from mid-October to early April.

Habitat: agricultural fields, feedlots, pastures, grassy meadows, lakeshores and roadsides.
Nesting: does not nest in Illinois.
Feeding: gleans the ground and snow for seeds and waste grain; also takes insects when available.
Voice: spring song is a musical, high-pitched *chi-chi-churee;* call is a whistled *tew* and a soft rattle.
Similar Species: *Lapland Longspur* (p. 325): overall brownish upperparts; lacks black-and-white wing pattern.
Best Sites: Illinois Beach SP; Waukegan Beach; Chicago lakefront, especially Montrose; LaSalle Nuclear Power Plant; rural roadsides in winter.

NORTHERN CARDINAL

Cardinalis cardinalis

In the early 1900s, the Northern Cardinal was rare in Chicagoland; today it is common there year-round. In southern Illinois, flocks of 50 to 100 cardinals gather in winter. Winter feed, climate and habitat changes probably helped to extend the northern range of this once more southerly bird. • Some cardinals maintain their pair bonds throughout the winter; others join loose flocks. To reestablish or create pair bonds, this species engages in "courtship feeding." A male offers a seed to the female, and she accepts and eats it. You can often observe this behavior at backyard feeders. • Scientists believe that when the female sings on the nest, she is informing her partner whether she and the young need food. • Males vigorously defend their territories and will even attack their reflections in a window or the hubcap of a car. • The cardinal's habit of being one of the last species to go to roost at night makes it particularly vulnerable to predators, especially Cooper's Hawk and Long-eared Owl in winter.

ID: *Male:* red overall; pointed crest; black "mask" and throat; red, conical bill. *Female:* brown buff overall; red bill, crest, wings and tail. *Juvenile male:* similar to female but has dark bill and crest.
Size: *L* 7½–9 in; *W* 12 in.
Status: common year-round resident.
Habitat: brushy thickets and shrubby tangles along forest and woodland edges, in backyards and in suburban and urban parks.
Nesting: in a dense shrub, thicket, vine tangle or low in a conifer; female builds an open cup nest of twigs, bark shreds, weeds, grass, leaves and rootlets and lines it with hair and fine grass; female incubates 3–4 heavily marked, whitish to bluish or green-

ish white eggs, for 12–13 days; often has 2 broods; often parasitized by Brown-headed Cowbird.
Feeding: feeds on the ground or in low shrubs; eats insects, including beetles, cicadas, dragonflies and leafhoppers; eats wild fruits and weed seeds; also eats corn and rice; drinks maple sap from sapsucker holes; readily takes sunflower and safflower seeds and cracked corn from feeders.
Voice: song is a variable series of clear, bubbly whistled notes: *what cheer! what cheer! birdie-birdie-birdie what cheer!;* call is a metallic *chip.*
Similar Species: *Summer Tanager* (p. 302) and *Scarlet Tanager* (p. 303): lack head crest, black "mask" and throat and red, conical bill; Scarlet Tanager has black wings and tail.
Best Sites: widespread.

ROSE-BREASTED GROSBEAK
Pheucticus ludovicianus

If you hear a melancholy, melodic, robinlike song in deciduous woodlands in Illinois, you are probably listening to the Rose-breasted Grosbeak. Although the female lacks the magnificent colors of the male, she shares his talent for beautiful song. • The grosbeak usually builds its nest fairly low in a tree, but typically forages high in the canopy. Luckily for birders, an abundance of berries, especially mulberries, often draws these birds to eye level. • The Rose-breasted Grosbeak hybridizes with the Black-headed Grosbeak where their ranges overlap in the Great Plains. In fall, separating the common female Rose-breasted Grosbeak from the rare, vagrant, Black-headed Grosbeak female can be extremely challenging. • Within the last two decades, this species has been extending its breeding range southward in Illinois.

breeding

ID: pale, conical bill; dark wings with small white patches; dark tail. *Male:* black "hood," wings and back; red triangle on white breast; rose inner underwings; white underparts and rump. *Female:* bold, whitish "eyebrow"; thin crown stripe; brown upperparts; buff underparts with dark brown streaking; yellowish to orangy inner underwings in flight.

Size: *L* 7–8½ in; *W* 12½ in.

Status: common migrant; fairly common breeder, decreasing southward; occurs from mid- to late April through early to mid-October; occasional at feeders in winter.

Habitat: secondary growth in deciduous forests; often in parklike habitat and forest edges.

Nesting: fairly low in a tree or tall shrub, often near water; mostly the female builds a flimsy cup nest with various vegetation and lines it with rootlets and hair; pair incubates 3–5 brown-spotted, pale greenish blue eggs for 13–14 days; often parasitized by Brown-headed Cowbird; sometimes has 2 broods.

Feeding: gleans vegetation for insects; occasionally hover-gleans or catches insects on the wing; eats grasshoppers, beetles and gypsy moths; eats seeds of elm, catalpa and foxtail; also eats blossoms, buds, various fruits; visits feeders for sunflower and safflower seeds and peanuts.

Voice: song is a long, melodious series of whistled notes, much like a fast version of a robin's song; call is a distinctive squeak, resembling someone scraping their shoe against a gym floor.

Similar Species: male is distinctive. *Purple Finch* (p. 344): female is much smaller and has heavier streaking on underparts. *Sparrows* (pp. 304–27): smaller; all lack large, conical bill.

Best Sites: widespread.

BLUE GROSBEAK
Passerina caerulea

While Blue Grosbeaks are wintering in Mexico and Central America, their brown feather tips slowly wear away, leaving the deep blue plumage seen when they arrive on their breeding grounds. Look carefully for the rusty wing bars that help distinguish this bird from the similar, and much more common, Indigo Bunting. • The Blue Grosbeak often sings atop utility lines or fences. It has become more common as a breeder in central Illinois in the last five years, preferring sandy soils found in certain areas of the state. Illinois is the northernmost part of its breeding range in the Midwest. • Common associates in the grosbeak's southern Illinois breeding habitat include the Northern Mockingbird, Yellow-breasted Chat, Prairie Warbler, Indigo Bunting and White-eyed Vireo.

ID: large, pale grayish, conical bill. *Male:* blue overall; 2 rusty wing bars; black around base of bill. *Female:* soft brown plumage overall; whitish throat; buffy brown to rusty wing bars; rump and shoulders faintly washed with blue.

Size: *L* 6¾ in; *W* 11 in.

Status: uncommon migrant; uncommon breeder, decreasing northward; fairly common breeder in the Shawnee Hills; occurs from mid- to late April through early to mid-September; very rare winter resident at feeders.

Habitat: fields overgrown with saplings and brambles; thickets along streams, woods or roadsides; hedgerows; sandy areas in central and northern Illinois.

Nesting: low to the ground in a bush or tree sapling; female builds a cup nest lined with roots and fine material; female incubates 3–4 pale blue eggs for 11–12 days; sometimes has 2 broods; parasitized by Brown-headed Cowbird.

Feeding: gleans insects, especially grasshoppers and crickets, from the ground while hopping; also takes seeds and some fruit; rarely visits feeders.

Voice: sweet, melodious, warbling song with phrases that rise and fall; call is a loud *chink*.

Similar Species: *Indigo Bunting* (p. 331): smaller body and bill; male lacks rusty wing bars; female has dark brown breast streaks. *Brown-headed Cowbird* (p 341): female has thin, sharp bill and lacks wing bars.

Best Sites: Pembroke Township near Kankakee; Sand Ridge SF; Cypress Creek NWR; successional areas of Shawnee NF.

INDIGO BUNTING
Passerina cyanea

I n the shadow of a tree, a male Indigo Bunting appears black. In bright sunlight, it reveals its incomparable indigo color. • In an interesting feeding strategy, the Indigo Bunting lands midway on a stem and then shuffles slowly toward the seed head, which eventually bends under the bird's weight, giving it easier access to the seeds. • Males don't learn their couplet songs from their parents, but from neighboring males during their first year on their own. • One of the most abundant southern Illinois nesting species, the Indigo Bunting often abandons a nest in which a female Brown-headed Cowbird has laid eggs. • During spring migration, one of the most common call notes heard at night over Illinois comes from the Indigo Bunting.

breeding

ID: stout, gray, conical bill; black eyes; black legs; no wing bars. *Male:* blue overall; black lores; mostly black wings and tail. *Female:* soft brown overall; brown streaks on breast; whitish throat; some blue in tail. *Fall male:* similar to female, but usually with some blue in wings and tail.
Size: *L* 5½ in; *W* 8 in.
Status: common to abundant migrant and breeder, decreasing northward, from mid-April through mid- to late October; rare winter resident in southern Illinois.
Habitat: deciduous upland and bottom-land forest and woodland edges, regenerating forest clearings, shrubby fields, abandoned pastures and hedgerows, open woodlands and clear-cuts.

Nesting: usually low in the fork of a small tree or shrub, in a vine tangle or dense, tall forb; female builds a cup nest made of grass, leaves and bark strips and lines it with rootlets, hair and feathers; female incubates 3–4 white to pale bluish eggs for 12–13 days; frequently parasitized by Brown-headed Cowbird.
Feeding: gleans low vegetation and the ground for insects, especially grasshoppers, beetles, weevils, flies and larvae; also, eats the seeds of thistles and goldenrods; feeds on dandelions during spring migration.
Voice: song consists of paired whistles: *fire-fire, where-where, here-here, see-it see-it;* call is a quick *spit.*
Similar Species: *Blue Grosbeak* (p. 330): larger overall; larger, more robust bill; 2 rusty wing bars; female lacks streaking on breast.
Best Sites: widespread in appropriate habitat.

DICKCISSEL

Spiza americana

Illinois is at the heart of the Dickcissel's breeding range and this species is quite common along country roads in central and southern parts of the state. It may be somewhat nomadic in northern Illinois, found in one area during the breeding season one year, then completely absent the next. • The male Dickcissel announces his presence with trilled renditions of his name, often singing all day, even in the heat of summer. One male may mate with up to six females in a single breeding season. • This "miniature meadowlark" prefers grasslands with dense forb growth, as well as alfalfa and clover fields. In winter, one Dickcissel may occasionally be found with flocks of House Sparrows, but identification can be tricky. • Most Dickcissels winter in South America, where many farmers kill this species to protect crops. Because of this practice and other situations such as habitat alteration on breeding grounds, Dickcissel numbers are declining.

breeding

ID: yellow "eyebrow" and jaw line; gray head, nape and sides; yellow breast; gray-and-brown upperparts and underparts; rufous shoulder patch; conical bill. *Male:* white "chin"; black "bib"; duller colors in nonbreeding plumage. *Female:* duller version of male; white throat; lacks black "bib." *Immature:* similar to female; very faint "eyebrow"; dark streaking on crown, breast, sides and flanks.

Size: *L* 6¼ in; *W* 9¾ in.

Status: common migrant and breeder from late April to early October, with regular stragglers into November.

Habitat: abandoned fields, weedy meadows, cropland edges, grasslands, grassy roadsides and levees, hayfields.

Nesting: on or near the ground, in tall, dense vegetation; female builds a bulky open cup nest of forbs, grass and leaves and lines it with rootlets, fine grass or hair; female incubates 4 pale blue eggs for 12–13 days; often has 2 broods.

Feeding: eats spiders and insects, especially grasshoppers; gleans seeds from the ground and low vegetation.

Voice: song consists of 2–3 single notes followed by a trill, often paraphrased as *dick dick dick-cissel;* flight call is a buzzer-like *bzrrrrt.*

Similar Species: *Eastern Meadowlark* (p. 335) and *Western Meadowlark* (p. 336): larger; plumper; long, pointed bill. *House Sparrow* (p. 352): female has yellowish bill, dull crown, dingy grayish overall, unstreaked throat and breast.

Best Sites: country roads in central and southern Illinois.

BOBOLINK
Dolichonyx oryzivorus

A long-distance migrant, the Bobolink regularly flies south 5000 miles for winter. It travels from its breeding grounds in Canada and the northern United States to the pampas of Argentina. • Male Bobolinks perform aerial displays and sing their bubbly, effervescent songs while females tend to the nests. Occasionally, several males will mob potential predators, creating quite a ruckus. Once the young have hatched, males spend most of the time foraging and the females care for the young. • The Bobolink is one of the fastest declining North American songbirds. Modern agricultural practices often thwart their reproductive efforts. • Known as "Rice Bird," the Bobolink eats rice on its wintering grounds in South America. Bobolinks also feed in rice fields during migration through the southern United States. To protect crops, farmers used to shoot and sell Bobolinks for food.

breeding

ID: stiff, pointed tail. *Breeding male:* black bill, head, wings, tail and underparts; buff nape; white rump and wing patch. *Breeding female:* pinkish bill; buff brown overall; streaked back, sides, flanks and rump; pale "eyebrow"; dark eye line; light central crown stripe; whitish throat. *Nonbreeding male:* similar to breeding female, but darker above and rich golden buff below.
Size: *L* 7 in; *W* 11½ in.
Status: common migrant; fairly common breeder in northern Illinois, decreasing southward; occurs from late April to late September and early October.
Habitat: *In spring* and *breeding season:* tall, grassy meadows and ditches, hayfields and lightly grazed pastures. *In fall:* marshy areas.
Nesting: usually in hayfields and sometimes clover; cup nest of grass and forb stems sits in a shallow depression and is lined with fine grass; female incubates 5–6 heavily blotched, grayish to light reddish brown eggs for 13 days.
Feeding: gleans the ground and low vegetation for invertebrates; also eats seeds of barnyard grass, panic grass, ragweed, smartweed and some grains, especially rice.
Voice: song is a series of bubbly, musical notes: *bobolink bobolink spink spank spink;* call is a metallic *pink.*
Similar Species: male is distinctive. *Grasshopper Sparrow* (p. 313): smaller; white belly; unstreaked sides and flanks. *Vesper Sparrow* (p. 310): white outer tail feathers; reddish in wings; streaked nape; lacks overall buffy coloration.
Best Sites: Glacial Park; Bartel and Orland Grasslands; Midewin National Tallgrass Prairie; Lost Mound NWR; Bussey Woods (Cook Co).

333

RED-WINGED BLACKBIRD
Agelaius phoeniceus

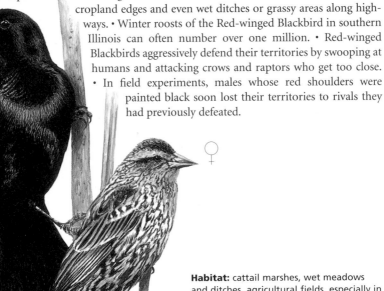

These blackbirds are the first songbirds to arrive in spring, appearing in their wetland habitats when snow is still on the ground. • Though most Red-winged Blackbirds nested in marshes in Illinois in the early 20th century, they have expanded to breed in grasslands and fields with scattered shrubs, cultivated cropland edges and even wet ditches or grassy areas along highways. • Winter roosts of the Red-winged Blackbird in southern Illinois can often number over one million. • Red-winged Blackbirds aggressively defend their territories by swooping at humans and attacking crows and raptors who get too close. • In field experiments, males whose red shoulders were painted black soon lost their territories to rivals they had previously defeated.

Habitat: cattail marshes, wet meadows and ditches, agricultural fields, especially in migration and winter; shoreline shrubs; dry upland fallow and hayfields.
Nesting: colonial and sometimes polygynous; female weaves an open cup nest of dried cattail leaves and grass blades and lines it with fine grass; female incubates 3–4 darkly marked, pale bluish green eggs for 10–12 days.
Feeding: gleans the ground and vegetation for seeds, waste grain, berries and invertebrates, including grasshoppers, mayflies and caddisflies; occasionally catches insects in flight; may visit feeders.
Voice: song is a loud, raspy *onka-reeeee;* call is a harsh *check* or a high *tseert;* female may give a loud *che-che-che chee chee chee.*
Similar Species: male is distinctive. *Brewer's Blackbird* (p. 339) and *Rusty Blackbird* (p. 338): females lack streaked underparts. *Common Grackle* (p. 340): longer, wider tail; larger, longer, heavier bill; metallic, bluish green sheen to head.
Best Sites: *Summer* and *in migration:* widespread in appropriate habitat. *Winter:* LaSalle Nuclear Power Plant; Rend L.; Carlyle L.; Horseshoe Lake CA.

ID: *Male:* all black, except for large, red shoulder patch edged in yellow (sometimes concealed). *Female:* heavily streaked underparts; mottled brown upperparts; faint red shoulder patch; light "eyebrow."
Size: *L* 7–9½ in; *W* 13 in.
Status: abundant migrant and breeder statewide from late January to mid-February through April and departs by early to mid-December; abundant winter resident in the south; rare to uncommon winter resident in central and northern Illinois.

EASTERN MEADOWLARK
Sturnella magna

L isten for the Eastern Meadowlark as it sings its lively *spring-of-the-year* across the grasslands. • Both the male and female have colorful yellow underparts and white outer tail feathers; the male to attract mates and the female to deter predators. At the approach of a predator, the incubating female explodes from the grass in a burst of flashing color. She leads the predator away from the nest, then folds away her white tail flags, exposes her camouflaged back and disappears into the grass. • As grasslands have been converted to croplands, Eastern Meadowlark numbers have declined. In Illinois, predation and mowing take a great toll on nest success. • Once thought to be a single species, today scientists recognize the Eastern Meadowlark and Western Meadowlark as two distinct species. • Look for Eastern Meadowlarks along roadsides after a winter storm.

breeding

ID: yellow underparts; broad, black breast band; mottled brown upperparts; short, wide tail with white outer tail feathers; long, pinkish legs; yellow lores; long, sharp bill; blackish crown stripes and eye line border pale "eyebrow" and median crown stripe; dark streaking on white sides and flanks; choppy, flap-and-glide flight.
Size: *L* 9–9½ in; *W* 14 in.
Status: common migrant and breeder from early to mid-February through early to mid-November; common winter resident in southern Illinois, decreasing northward.
Habitat: grassy meadows and pastures; also in some croplands, weedy fields, grassy roadsides, hayfields and airports.
Nesting: in a depression or scrape on the ground; domed grass nest is woven into surrounding vegetation; female incubates 3–6 heavily spotted, white eggs for 13–15 days; commonly parasitized by Brownheaded Cowbird.

Feeding: gleans grasshoppers, crickets, beetles and spiders from the ground and vegetation; probes the soil for grubs and worms; also eats seeds.
Voice: song is a rich series of 2–8 melodic, clear, slurred whistles: *spring-of-the-year;* gives a rattling flight call and a high, buzzy *dzeart.*
Similar Species: *Western Meadowlark* (p. 336): paler overall; more yellow on face; less white in outer tail; more whitish on flanks; distinctive song. *Dickcissel* (p. 332): grayer overall; smaller; shorter, less pointed bill; dark crown; white throat; reddish brown shoulder patch; lacks brown streaking on sides and flanks.
Best Sites: widespread in appropriate habitat.

335

WESTERN MEADOWLARK
Sturnella neglecta

The two meadowlark species are so similar in appearance that birders must often listen for their songs and distinct calls to distinguish them. • Be careful when walking through meadowlark and other grassland birds' nesting habitats. The meadowlark's grassy, domed nests are so well concealed that they can be crushed before being seen. • Eastern and Western Meadowlarks may occasionally interbreed where their ranges overlap, producing infertile offspring. • Compared with the Eastern, the Western Meadowlark will use sparser, more barren fields, including sandy areas in Illinois. Both meadowlark species sing atop fence posts, utility lines or a lone tree in a field. • Some scientists think the Western Meadowlark was overlooked by Lewis and Clark, who mistakenly thought it was the same species as the Eastern Meadowlark; thus the scientific name *neglecta.*

breeding

ID: yellow underparts; broad, black breast band; mottled brown upperparts; short, wide tail with white outer tail feathers; long, pinkish legs; yellow lores; brown crown stripes and eye line border pale "eyebrow" and median crown stripe; dark streaking on white sides and flanks; long, sharp bill; yellow on throat extends onto lower "cheek."
Size: *L* 9–9½ in; *W* 14½ in.
Status: common migrant; common breeder in northwestern Illinois, decreasing eastward and southward; arrives in mid-February to early March, departs by mid- to late November; a few overwinter, especially in southern Illinois.
Habitat: grassy meadows, pastures, some croplands, weedy fields and grassy roadsides.

Nesting: in a depression or scrape on the ground; domed grass nest, with a side entrance, is woven into the surrounding vegetation; female incubates 3–6 heavily spotted, white eggs for about 13–15 days.
Feeding: gleans grasshoppers, crickets and their eggs, beetles, alfalfa weevils, cutworms, sow bugs and spiders from the ground and vegetation; extracts grubs and worms from the soil; also eats grain and seeds.
Voice: song is a melodic series of bubbly, flutelike notes; call is a low, loud *chuck* or *chupp.*
Similar Species: *Eastern Meadowlark* (p. 335): darker upperparts; less yellow on face; more white in outer tail and on flanks. *Dickcissel* (p. 332): smaller; shorter, less pointed bill; dark crown; white throat; reddish brown shoulder patch; lacks brown streaking on sides and flanks.
Best Sites: Lost Mound NWR; Momence Sod Farms.

YELLOW-HEADED BLACKBIRD
Xanthocephalus xanthocephalus

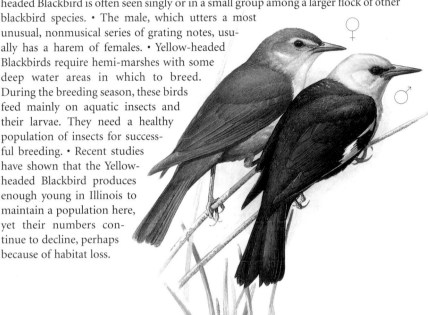

The Yellow-headed Blackbird was formerly much more common and wide-spread, breeding in the marshes of the Grand Prairie region of Illinois, much of which has been drained for agricultural use. In migration, the Yellow-headed Blackbird is often seen singly or in a small group among a larger flock of other blackbird species. • The male, which utters a most unusual, nonmusical series of grating notes, usu-ally has a harem of females. • Yellow-headed Blackbirds require hemi-marshes with some deep water areas in which to breed. During the breeding season, these birds feed mainly on aquatic insects and their larvae. They need a healthy population of insects for success-ful breeding. • Recent studies have shown that the Yellow-headed Blackbird produces enough young in Illinois to maintain a population here, yet their numbers con-tinue to decline, perhaps because of habitat loss.

ID: *Male:* distinctive; yellow head and breast on black body; white wing patches; black lores; long tail; black bill. *Female:* dusky brown overall; yellow breast, throat and "eyebrow"; hints of yellow in face. *Immature:* similar to female.

Size: *L* 8–11 in; *W* 15 in.

Status: state-endangered; rare migrant and breeder in northern Illinois; rare migrant elsewhere; arrives in early to mid-April; most breeders depart by late August; migrants depart by mid-September, with stragglers into early October; rare winter resident.

Habitat: *Breeding:* deep, permanent hemi-marshes with cattails, bulrushes and reeds. *Postbreeding* and *fall migration:* agricul-tural fields.

Nesting: loosely colonial; female builds a bulky, deep basket of aquatic plants lined with dry grass and other vegetation; nest is woven into emergent vegetation over water; female incubates 4 darkly marked, pale green to pale gray eggs for 11–13 days.

Feeding: gleans the water's surface and vegetation for seeds and aquatic insects; probes cattail heads for larval inverte-brates; visits feeders and agricultural fields for seeds and grains.

Voice: song is a nonmusical series of grat-ing notes; call is a deep *krrt* or *ktuk;* low quacks and liquidy *clucks* given during breeding season.

Similar Species: *Rusty Blackbird* (p. 338) and *Brewer's Blackbird* (p. 339): females lack yellow throat and face. *Red-winged Blackbird* (p. 334): female has fine streak-ing on sides and belly.

Best Sites: Broberg Marsh and Rollins Savanna FP, Lake Co., Black Tern Marsh at Moraine Hills SP; Eggers Woods FP, Cook Co.; Fulton Marsh, Whiteside Co.

RUSTY BLACKBIRD
Euphagus carolinus

The Rusty Blackbird owes its name to the color of its fall plumage, but its name could just as well reflect this bird's grating, squeaky song, which sounds very much like a rusty hinge. • Rusty Blackbirds travel either in segregated groups, usually in spring, or in large flocks with other blackbirds and grackles, usually in fall and winter. • In southern Illinois during the annual Christmas bird counts, birders often find small flocks of Rusty Blackbirds in swampy bottomland woods, especially during mild winters. • These boreal forest breeders feed along the water's edge, sometimes even wading in shallow water. Rusty Blackbirds nest singly rather than in colonies like other blackbird species; they also eat more animal matter than other blackbirds with about 50 percent of their diet consisting of insects.

nonbreeding

ID: yellow eyes; dark legs; sharp, downcurved bill. *Breeding:* male is darker, with subtle green gloss on body and subtle purplish or greenish gloss on head; female is gray brown overall. *Nonbreeding male:* rusty wings, back and crown; grayish rump. *Nonbreeding female:* much more buffy or rusty overall; grayish rump.
Size: *L* 9 in; *W* 14 in.
Status: common migrant; uncommon to locally common winter resident, decreasing northward; occurs from mid- to late February through mid- to late April and from late September to late November, with some lingering into early December.
Habitat: swamps, wet woodland edges and wet agricultural fields.
Nesting: does not nest in Illinois.
Feeding: gleans waterbugs, beetles, dragonflies, snails, grasshoppers, crustaceans and salamanders from shorelines or swamps; also eats waste grain, seeds and berries from dogwood and hackberry trees.
Voice: song is a squeaky, creaking *kush-leeeh ksh-lay;* call is a harsh *chack.*
Similar Species: *Brewer's Blackbird* (p. 339): prefers open fields and pastures; shorter, thicker bill; male has glossier plumage, more purple on head and greener body; female has dark eyes; fall birds lack conspicuous rusty highlights. *Common Grackle* (p. 340): longer, keeled tail; larger body and bill; more iridescent. *European Starling* (p. 263): shorter tail; plumper body; dark eyes; pinkish to orange legs.
Best Sites: *Winter:* Rend L.; Cypress Creek NWR; Horseshoe Lake CA; Union County CA; Mermet L.

BREWER'S BLACKBIRD
Euphagus cyanocephalus

Scattered populations of Brewer's Blackbirds breed throughout the Great Plains, and some come as far east as Illinois. Some August records imply a few regular breeding sites in northeastern Illinois. • The Brewer's feathers show an iridescent quality, reflecting rainbows of sunlight along the feather shafts. As the bird walks, it jerks its head back and forth like a chicken, enhancing the glossy effect and distinguishing it from other blackbirds. • The male Brewer's Blackbird may take one mate or several. To court, a male holds his bill nearly horizontal, puffs up his head, neck and breast feathers, spreads his wings, depresses his tail and utters a short, gurgling call. • John J. Audubon named this bird after his friend and prominent oologist, a student of eggs, Thomas Mayo Brewer.

breeding

ID: *Male:* iridescent, green body and purplish head often looks black; yellow eyes; some fall and winter males may show faint, rusty feather edgings. *Female:* flat brown plumage; dark eyes.
Size: *L* 9 in; *W* 15½ in.
Status: uncommon and erratic migrant from late February through early to mid- April and from early October to mid-November; very rare breeder in northeastern Illinois; rare winter resident.
Habitat: grassy meadows; open shrublands; sod farms; pastures and cattle feedlots, especially in winter.
Nesting: in small colonies; on the ground or in a shrub or small tree; female builds an open cup nest with vegetation, mud or dried cow dung and lines it with rootlets, fine grass and horse hair; female incubates 4–6 brown-spotted, pale gray to greenish gray eggs for 12–14 days; parasitized by Brown-headed Cowbird.

Feeding: gleans invertebrates such as grasshoppers, crickets, tent caterpillars and cankerworms; also eats waste grain, seeds and some fruit.
Voice: song is a creaking, 2-note *k-shee;* call is a short, hoarse *ket.*
Similar Species: *Rusty Blackbird* (p. 338): longer, more slender bill; subtler green gloss on body and subtle bluish or greenish gloss on head; female has yellow eyes. *Common Grackle* (p. 340): much longer, keeled tail; larger body and bill. *Brown-headed Cowbird* (p. 341): shorter tail; stubbier, thicker bill; male has dark eyes and brown head; female has paler streaked underparts and very pale throat. *European Starling* (p. 263): shorter tail; plumper body; bill is yellow in summer; speckled appearance in winter; pinkish to orange legs; dark eyes.
Best Sites: *Summer:* Illinois Beach SP; Fremont Township in Lake Co. *Late summer* and *early fall:* H & E Sod Farms in McHenry Co. *In migration:* Carlyle L.

COMMON GRACKLE

Quiscalus quiscula

Common Grackles arrive and breed early in Illinois; by midsummer, they are already forming flocks and foraging for waste grain in open fields and at backyard feeders. • In winter, grackles commonly roost in flocks numbering in the tens to hundreds of thousands with European Starlings, Red-winged Blackbirds and Brown-headed Cowbirds. Sometimes, a flock of more than one million of these birds can be found in southern Illinois. Watching these huge flocks pass by in clouds can give you a glimpse of what it must have been like to watch the Passenger Pigeons in Illinois before they became extinct. • Common Grackles can be found in nearly every habitat and they thrive in altered habitats. Their diet changes with the seasons. They will eat corn in fields, wade belly deep in streams or ponds to catch fish and crayfish, kill small birds and even snatch earthworms out of the mouths of robins. Grackles also chase mice and catch bats.

bronze morph

ID: iridescent plumage; purple blue head and breast; bronze back and sides; purple wings and tail; often looks blackish; long, keeled tail; yellow eyes; long, heavy, sharply pointed bill; female is smaller, duller and browner than male.

Size: *L* 11–13½ in; *W* 17 in.

Status: common to abundant year-round resident in the south; common to abundant migrant and breeder and rare winter resident in central and northern Illinois; arrives in mid- to late February and departs by mid- to late November.

Habitat: wetlands, hedgerows, agricultural fields, wet meadows, riparian woodlands, woodland edges, gardens, urban and suburban parks with shrubs.

Nesting: singly or in small colonies; often in a conifer, buttonbush or other woody vegetation; often near water; female builds a bulky open cup nest made of twigs, grass, forbs and mud and lines it with fine grass or feathers; female incubates 4–5 brown-blotched, pale blue eggs for 12–14 days.

Feeding: gleans and probes on the ground or in water for insects, grubs, earthworms, seeds, waste grain and fruit; catches insects in flight; also eats crayfish, snakes, lizards, salamanders and small vertebrates, such as small fish; occasional bird nest predator.

Voice: song is a series of harsh, strained notes ending with a metallic squeak: *tssh-schleek* or *gri-de-leeek;* call is a quick, loud *swaaaack* or *chaack.*

Similar Species: *Rusty Blackbird* (p. 338) and *Brewer's Blackbird* (p. 339): smaller overall; shorter, rounder tails, lack heavy bill. *Red-winged Blackbird* (p. 334): shorter tail; male has red shoulder patch and dark eyes. *European Starling* (p. 263): shorter tail; plumper; long, thin bill (yellow in summer); speckled appearance in winter; dark eyes.

Best Sites: widespread.

BROWN-HEADED COWBIRD

Molothrus ater

Historically, Brown-headed Cowbirds followed bison herds across the plains and prairies of Illinois—they now follow cattle—feeding on insects kicked up by the animals. The cowbirds' formerly nomadic lifestyle made it impossible for them to construct and tend a nest. Instead, cowbirds engage in "nest parasitism," laying their eggs in the nests of other songbirds. Some songbirds have evolved to recognize the eggs; for example, Yellow Warblers sometimes build new nests atop parasitized ones. Other songbirds do not recognize the cowbird eggs, incubating them and raising the young as their own. Cowbird chicks typically hatch first and nestmates are often pushed out of the nest or outcompeted for food. • Forest fragmentation and more numerous short grassy areas in the state have left Illinois with one of the highest rates of cowbird parasitism in the nation.

ID: thick, conical bill; short, squared tail; dark eyes. *Male:* iridescent, green blue body plumage usually looks glossy black; dark brown head. *Female:* brown plumage overall; faint streaking on light brown underparts; pale throat.

Size: *L* 6–8 in; *W* 12 in.

Status: common to locally abundant migrant; common breeder; occurs from late February or early March to mid- to late November; common winter resident in southern Illinois, decreasing northward.

Habitat: agricultural and residential areas, including fields, pastures, woodland edges, roadsides, landfills, campgrounds and areas near livestock.

Nesting: does not build a nest; each female may lay up to 40 or more eggs annually in the nests of other birds; average 3–4 eggs per nest for many Illinois species; whitish eggs, marked with gray and brown, hatch after 10–13 days.

Feeding: gleans short grassy areas and lawns for seeds, waste grain and invertebrates; also eats fruit; feeds with tail tilted upward.

Voice: song is a high, liquidy gurgle *glug-glug-glug;* call is a squeaky, high-pitched *seep, psee* or *wee-tse-tse,* often given in flight; also a fast, chipping *ch-ch-ch-ch-ch-ch,* or rattle given mostly by female.

Similar Species: *Rusty Blackbird* (p. 338) and *Brewer's Blackbird* (p. 339): slimmer, longer bills; longer tails; lack contrasting brown head and darker body; all have yellow eyes except for female Brewer's Blackbird. *Common Grackle* (p. 340): much larger; longer, heavier bill; longer, keeled tail. *Blue Grosbeak* (p. 330): 1st-year and female have thicker, conical bills and rusty to brownish wing bars.

Best Sites: widespread.

ORCHARD ORIOLE
Icterus spurius

In Illinois, the Orchard Oriole often nests very close to or in the same tree as the Eastern Kingbird, perhaps taking advantage of the kingbird's aggressive protection of its nest. • Like other orioles, the Orchard exhibits delayed plumage maturation; first-year males sing very well and also breed, but show an entirely different plumage than second-year males. • Although females of other bird species do sing, this characteristic is especially well developed in the Orchard Oriole. • The Orchard is the smallest oriole in North America and sometimes returns to its wintering grounds in Mexico and Central America as early as mid-July.

♂

adult

♀

ID: *Male:* black "hood," back and tail; chestnut brown underparts, shoulder and rump; dark wings with white wing bar and feather edgings. *Female* and *immature:* olive upperparts; yellow to olive yellow underparts; faint, white wing bars on dusky gray wings.
Size: *L* 7 in; *W* 9½ in.
Status: common migrant and breeder in southern Illinois, decreasing northward; occurs from mid- to late April to late August or early September.
Habitat: open second-growth woodlands, suburban parklands, forest edges, hedgerows and groves of shade trees; orchards, especially near water.
Nesting: in a deciduous or coniferous tree or shrub, 10–40 ft above ground; female builds a bright yellow hanging pouch nest woven from grass and other fine plant fibers; female incubates 4–5 pale bluish

white eggs, blotched with gray, brown and purple, for 12–14 days; often parasitized by Brown-headed Cowbird.
Feeding: eats wasps, ants, caterpillars, mayflies, spiders and berries; forages for grasshoppers and crickets; probes flowers for fruit nectar and insects; useful bird in destroying the cotton boll weevil.
Voice: song is a loud, rapid, varied series of whistled notes; call is a quick *chuck.*
Similar Species: *Baltimore Oriole* (p. 343): male has bright orange plumage with orange in tail; female has orange overtones. *Summer Tanager* (p. 302) and *Scarlet Tanager* (p. 303): females have thicker, pale bills and lack wing bars.
Best Sites: Lost Mound NWR; Mississippi R. levee in Union Co.; Crab Orchard NWR; Cypress Creek NWR.

BALTIMORE ORIOLE
Icterus galbula

Developing an ear for their whistled *tea dear dear dear here dear* tune and frequently scanning local deciduous trees may grant birders a glimpse of the beloved Baltimore Oriole with its black-and-orange attire. • Like the Orchard Oriole, the Baltimore males exhibit different first-year and second-year plumages. • This Illinois species sometimes hybridizes with its western counterpart, the Bullock's Oriole, which is rarely found in the state; they were once considered the same species. • The Baltimore Oriole builds one of the most well-constructed nests of all North American bird species; the hanging, pouchlike nests often remain intact even through the harshest of Illinois winters. These birds will often use yarn that has been left out at bird feeders to build their nests.

ID: *Male:* black "hood," back, wings and central tail feathers; bright orange underparts, shoulder, rump and outer tail feathers; white wing patch and feather edgings. *Female:* darkish upperparts; mottled, dusky head; dull, yellow orange underparts, tail and rump; white wing bar.
Size: *L* 8¾ in; *W* 11½ in.
Status: common migrant and breeder; arrives in mid- to late April and departs by mid-September; rare in winter at bird feeders.
Habitat: deciduous and mixed forests, particularly riparian woodlands, natural openings, roadsides, orchards, gardens and parklands.
Nesting: in a deciduous tree, especially a cottonwood, 25–90 ft above ground; female builds a deep, hanging pouch nest and lines it with fine grass, rootlets and fur;

occasionally adds string and fishing line; nest often has a silver gray appearance; female incubates 4–5 darkly marked, pale gray to bluish white eggs for 12–14 days.
Feeding: gleans canopy vegetation and shrubs for insects and larvae, especially caterpillars; also eats some fruit such as mulberries and garden peas; probes flowers for nectar; may visit feeders that offer orange halves and suet.
Voice: song consists of slow, loud, clear, flutelike whistles: *tea dear dear dear hear dear;* calls include a 2-note *tea-too* and a rapid chatter: *ch-ch-ch-ch-ch.*
Similar Species: *Orchard Oriole* (p. 342): male has chestnut plumage; female is olive yellow overall and lacks orange tones. *Summer Tanager* (p. 302) and *Scarlet Tanager* (p. 303): females have thicker, pale bills and lack wing bars.
Best Sites: widespread in appropriate habitat.

PURPLE FINCH

Carpodacus purpureus

Mild winters, competition with House Finches and increased feeding on their northerly breeding grounds have made the Purple Finch less common in Illinois. Still, during years when food is scarce in the north, the Purple Finch continues to vie with the Pine Siskin as Illinois' most common, irruptive winter finch. • Illinois birders may confuse the Purple Finch with the introduced House Finch, a bird with more orange tones, rather than raspberry red. • Purple Finches have a strong liking for box elder, ash and sycamore seeds in Illinois. • Purple *(purpureus)* is an inaccurate description of this bird's coloration. Roger Tory Peterson said it best when he described the Purple Finch as "a sparrow dipped in raspberry juice." • Illinois birders will have to travel north to observe the fascinating courtship display of the male Purple Finch, who beats his wings so fast they appear as a blur as he chips and "dances" for his intended mate.

ID: *Male:* light bill; raspberry red head, throat, breast and nape; brown and red streaks on back and flanks; reddish brown "cheek"; red rump; notched tail; light, unstreaked belly and undertail coverts. *Female:* bold, brown-and-white head pattern; white "eyebrow" and lower "cheek" stripe; white underparts, heavily streaked with brown; unstreaked undertail coverts.
Size: *L* 6 in; *W* 10 in.
Status: uncommon to fairly common migrant and winter resident; migrants occur from late March or early April to early May and from early to mid-September through late November.

Habitat: *In migration* and *winter:* deciduous upland and especially bottomland forests, pine plantations, shrubby open areas and feeding stations with nearby tree cover.
Nesting: does not nest in Illinois.
Feeding: gleans the ground and box elder, sycamore, elm and other trees for seeds; also eats buds of apple, aspen, maple and birch; eats fruits and insects such as beetles and caterpillars; visits feeders for sunflower seeds.
Voice: song is a bubbly, continuous warble; call is a sharp, metallic *tick*.
Similar Species: *House Finch* (p. 345): tail only slightly notched; male lacks reddish flanks and wings and has brownish back and bold streaks on flanks; female has plain brown head, lacking bold, brown-and-white head pattern, and has blurry streaks on flanks and belly. *Pine Siskin* (p. 349): smaller; thinner, pointier bill; bold wing bars.
Best Sites: Sand Ridge SF; Klehm Arboretum in Rockford.

344

HOUSE FINCH
Carpodacus mexicanus

A native to western North America, House Finches were released in the early 1940s in New York by pet shop owners to avoid prosecution and fines. The descendants of those birds have since colonized the eastern United States. • The House Finch was first recorded in Illinois in November 1971, with a first nest record in June 1982. By the mid-1980s, the species was documented in all Illinois counties. This species since has developed a north-south migration pattern in parts of its eastern range. • House Finches will nest in planters and ornamental conifers in backyards. • Because of their affinity for bird feeders, House Finches are readily observed by humans. A serious eye disease in this species called "conjunctivitis" has been documented and may be limiting population growth. Symptoms include the formation of a crusty substance around the eye, which can render the bird unable to see or find food.

ID: streaked undertail coverts; brown-streaked back; square tail. *Male:* brown "cap"; bright red "eyebrow," forecrown, throat and breast; heavily streaked flanks and breast. *Female:* indistinct facial patterning; heavily streaked underparts.
Size: *L* 5–6 in; *W* 9½ in.
Status: common permanent resident with regular fall and spring migration, sometimes in flocks of 50–100.
Habitat: cities, towns, agricultural areas; overgrown shrubby fields.
Nesting: usually well-hidden in dense foliage, in an abandoned bird nest, in a vent, on a ledge, in evergreens, native red cedars or ornamental shrubs near buildings; female builds an open cup nest of grass, twigs, forbs, leaves, hair and feathers, often adding string and other debris;

female incubates 4–5 sparsely marked, pale blue eggs for 12–14 days.
Feeding: gleans vegetation and the ground for seeds; also takes berries, buds and some flower parts; insects comprise a small portion of diet; often visits feeders.
Voice: song is a bright, disjointed warble lasting about 3 seconds, often ending with a harsh *jeeer* or *wheer;* flight call is a sharp *cheep,* given singly or in series.
Similar Species: *Purple Finch* (p. 344): distinctly notched tail; male has more red overall; little or no streaking on flanks and breast; female has bold, brown-and-white head pattern. *Red Crossbill* (p. 346): bill has crossed mandibles; dark wings; no wing bars. *Pine Siskin* (p. 349): more slender body; thinner, pointier bill; bold wing bars; mostly seen in winter.
Best Sites: widespread, especially in towns.

RED CROSSBILL

Loxia curvirostra

Crossbills are among the most nomadic of birds, moving to where food can be found. Illinoisans most often see Red Crossbills in winter, when they wander from their northerly breeding grounds searching for food. Red Crossbills breed any time of year if they discover bumper crops of conifer seeds. They also breed in the mountains of Mexico. • Eight variations of this species exist, each with different call notes, body size and bill size and shape, depending on which type of conifer cones they eat. Three of the eight subspecies of this bird have been documented in Illinois. • The Red Crossbill uses its feet to hold down a conifer cone while cracking it open with its oddly shaped bill. Even if the Red Crossbill is not calling, a birder can locate this bird by listening for falling pine cone pieces.

twigs, grass, bark shreds and rootlets and lines it with moss, rootlets, feathers and hair; female incubates 3–4 sparsely marked, pale bluish white to greenish white eggs for 12–14 days.

ID: bill has crossed tips. *Male:* dull orange red to brick red plumage; dark wings and tail; always has color on throat. *Female:* olive gray to dusky yellow plumage; plain, dark wings. *Juvenile:* streaky brown overall.

Size: *L* 6½ in; *W* 11 in.

Status: rare, irregular migrant and winter resident; arrives in mid- to late March and departs by early to late May; arrives in mid- or late October (September or August arrivals not uncommon); very rare and local breeder.

Habitat: pine plantations; arboretums, gardens and parks with conifer collections.

Nesting: high on the outer branch of a conifer; female builds an open cup nest of

Feeding: primarily conifer seeds, especially pines, spruce, Douglas-fir and hemlock; also eats buds and seeds from birch, alder and box elder; occasionally eats insects and larvae; often eats grit, road salt and snow; rarely visits feeders.

Voice: distinctive *jip-jip* call note, often given in flight; song is a varied series of warbles, trills and chips that are similar to other finches.

Similar Species: *White-winged Crossbill* (p. 347): usually smaller, thinner bill; 2 broad, white wing bars; pinkish red plumage. *House Finch* (p. 345): conical bill; male lacks red on back and belly.

Best Sites: *Winter:* Morton Arboretum where it is a potential breeder; Crab Orchard NWR; Big River SF. *Summer, in migration and winter:* Illinois Beach SP; Sand Ridge SF.

WHITE-WINGED CROSSBILL
Loxia leucoptera

Like a parrot, a crossbill hangs upside down from a limb or pine cone while feeding, often using its strong bill as a third foot. White-winged Crossbills primarily eat spruce, fir and tamarack seeds, and like Red Crossbills, they have crossed mandibles adapted for prying open cones. • A foraging group of White-winged Crossbills can be noisy as they chatter and drop pieces of conifer cones. Like Red Crossbills, after feeding silently, a flock of White-winged Crossbills begins calling as they leave, their notes reaching a crescendo until they are all gone. Like many finches, White-winged Crossbills can be abundant one year, then absent the next. • Three subspecies of White-winged Crossbills exist; only one occurs in North America. The other two subspecies live on Hispaniola and in northern Eurasia and have larger bills. • White-winged Crossbills, which are somewhat less common in Illinois than Red Crossbills, ingest grit from winter roads to help digest food. Mainly a daytime migrant, the White-winged Crossbill relies heavily on black spruce cones on its northern breeding grounds.

ID: bill has crossed tips; 2 bold, white wing bars. *Male:* pinkish red overall; black wings and tail. *Female:* streaked brown upperparts; dusky yellow underparts slightly streaked with brown; dark wings and tail.
Size: *L* 6½ in; *W* 10½ in.
Status: rare to uncommon, irregular migrant and winter resident, decreasing southward; occurs from early March to early April, with occasional May records, and in early to mid-November, with most remaining through the winter.
Habitat: coniferous plantations, primarily spruce and fir.

Nesting: does not nest in Illinois.
Feeding: prefers conifer seeds (mostly spruce, fir and tamarack); also eats seeds of red cedar, alder, birch, cottonwood, sunflower, foxtail and various grasses; occasionally eats insects; often eats grit and road salt; visits feeders.
Voice: song is a high-pitched series of warbles, trills and chips; call is a series of *cheat* notes, often given in flight; weaker, but more metallic than Red Crossbill's.
Similar Species: *Red Crossbill* (p. 346): usually larger, thicker bill; lacks white wing bars; male is red. *House Finch* (p. 345) and *Purple Finch* (p. 344): conical bills; less red overall; lighter brownish wings.
Best Sites: *Winter:* Lyons Woods Lake Co.; Morton Arboretum; Sand Ridge SF.

347

COMMON REDPOLL

Carduelis flammea

The Common Redpoll visits Illinois in winter, appearing in flocks of a few or dozens, sometimes even hundreds. • These birds breed in all the boreal regions of the world as well as on the edge of the tundra. • The redpoll gives calls similar to those of the closely related Pine Siskin, but careful listeners can separate these two with practice. • Three subspecies of the Common Redpoll are found in North America, two of which have been documented in Illinois. *C. f. flammea* is most common in the state. • Redpolls must feed constantly in winter to retain their body heat, and appear tame at feeders, oblivious to anything else but eating. Still, these birds can survive colder temperatures than any other songbird. • A redpoll has a special storage pouch in its esophagus, which it often fills with food just before dark, enabling the bird to digest the food overnight. Redpolls prefer birch and alder seeds because of their high calorie content.

nonbreeding

ID: red forecrown; black lores and "chin"; yellowish bill; streaked upperparts, including rump; notched tail. *Male:* pink rump; pinkish red breast is brightest in breeding plumage. *Female:* whitish to pale gray breast.
Size: *L* 5 in; *W* 9 in.

Status: rare to uncommon winter resident; regular in northern Illinois, occasional in central Illinois and very rare in southern Illinois; arrives in late October or early November and departs by late March or early April.
Habitat: open fields, meadows, alder plantings, forest edges and feeders.

Nesting: does not nest in Illinois.
Feeding: gleans the ground, snow and vegetation for seeds of pine, hemlock, sweetgum and other trees and grasses; eats buds of larch, lilac and other trees and shrubs; often visits feeders.
Voice: song is a twittering series of dry trills; calls are a soft *chit-chit-chit-chit* and a faint *swe-eet;* many calls resemble those of a Pine Siskin.
Similar Species: *Hoary Redpoll:* extremely rare; generally paler and plumper; bill may look stubbier. *Pine Siskin* (p. 349): longer, more, pointed, less conical, black bill; heavily streaked overall; yellow highlights in wings and tail; lacks black throat and lores.
Best Sites: Chicago Botanic Garden; Lincoln Park in Chicago; LaSalle Nuclear Power Plant; Clinton L.

PINE SISKIN
Carduelis pinus

Small flocks of these gregarious finches alert you to their presence with their rising *zzzreeeee* calls on a winter day. Food availability plays the most important role in determining if a northerly breeding species will move south in the winter. Pine Siskins and other winter finches are considered irruptive species in Illinois—their presence in the state each winter is irregular. Flocks of 25 to 100 or more Pine Siskins are common in irruptive years. This species also makes easterly and westerly movements. • The Pine Siskin is like a sparrow with its drab colors and streaked flanks, breast and belly, but yellow in the wings and tail help separate it from other similar species. • The Pine Siskin often flocks with redpolls and goldfinches. • This species occasionally remains in Illinois to nest, especially in irruptive years. Some Illinois nests are started but never finished.

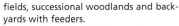

ID: heavily streaked underparts; yellow highlights in tail feathers; slightly forked tail; indistinct facial pattern; male has yellow-colored wing bars, which appear as yellow stripe in flight. *Female* and *immature:* similar to male, but often lack yellow in tail and wings.
Size: *L* 5 in; *W* 9 in.
Status: common but irruptive migrant and winter resident; rare breeder in central and northern Illinois; arrives in early to mid-October and departs by early to mid-May, with some stragglers into June.
Habitat: *Breeding:* conifer plantations, especially in suburban areas with ornamental conifers. *Winter:* conifer, alder and birch plantations, sunflower seed patches, weedy

fields, successional woodlands and backyards with feeders.
Nesting: loosely colonial, usually seen singly in Illinois; 15–30 ft above ground in a conifer; female builds a loose cup nest of twigs, grass and rootlets and lines it with feathers, hair and fine plant fibers; female incubates 3–5 sparsely spotted, pale blue eggs for about 13 days.
Feeding: gleans the ground and vegetation for seeds, especially thistle; also eats buds of elm; attracted to sap, road salts and ashes; visits feeders.
Voice: call is a buzzy, rising *zzzreeeee.*
Similar Species: *Common Redpoll* (p. 348): conical, yellowish bill; red forecrown; black throat and lores; lacks yellow in wings and tail. *Purple Finch* (p. 344) and *House Finch* (p. 345): larger; thicker, conical bills; lack yellow in wings and tail. *Sparrows* (pp. 304–27): all lack yellow in wings and tail.
Best Sites: *In migration* and *winter:* Clinton L. *Summer, in migration* and *winter:* Morton Arboretum.

AMERICAN GOLDFINCH
Carduelis tristis

American Goldfinches wait until late summer, when thistles have bloomed and gone to seed, to begin nesting. They use thistledown to build their nests and the seeds to feed their young. The genus name *Carduelis*, in fact, comes from a Latin word meaning "thistle." Young are commonly still in the nest in September, sometimes even into early October. • Goldfinches feed on burdock plants, and as with hummingbirds, kinglets and warblers, may get caught on the sticky seeds and perish. • In spring migration, flocks of goldfinches may join small flocks of Indigo Buntings and White-crowned Sparrows to eat dandelion seeds. In spring, migrant flocks of male goldfinches sit in a tree and begin singing one after the other, creating a loud, melodic chorus. • Banding studies have shown that even though you may see only 15–20 goldfinches at your feeder, between 100 and 200 different goldfinches may be visiting at various times throughout the day.

breeding

edges, meadows, parks, gardens and backyard feeders.

Nesting: in late summer and fall; 3–20 ft above ground in a deciduous shrub or tree; female builds a compact cup nest of thistle, grass and spider silk, lined with plant down and hair; female incubates 4–6 bluish white eggs for about 12–14 days.

Feeding: gleans vegetation for seeds, primarily thistle; also eats some insects and berries; commonly visits feeders.

Voice: song is a long and varied series of trills, twitters, warbles and sibilant notes; calls include *po-ta-to-chip* or *per-chick-or-ee*, often delivered in flight, and a whistled *dear-me, see-me*.

Similar Species: *Evening Grosbeak* (p. 351): much larger; enormous bill; lacks black forehead. *Pine Siskin* (p. 349): extensive brown streaking; dark feet and bill. *Wilson's Warbler* (p. 299): olive upperparts; olive wings without wing bars; thin, dark bill; black "cap" does not extend onto forehead.

Best Sites: widespread in appropriate habitat.

ID: *Breeding male:* black "cap" extends onto forehead; black wings and tail; bright yellow body; bright white wing bars, undertail coverts and tail base; orange bill and legs. *Female:* yellow green upperparts and belly; yellow throat and breast; buffy white wing bars. *Nonbreeding male:* olive brown back; yellow-tinged head; gray underparts.

Size: *L* 5 in; *W* 9 in.

Status: very common migrant and year-round resident; migration peaks occur from mid-April to mid-May and from early October to mid-November.

Habitat: weedy fields, especially those with thistles; also shrublands, woodland

EVENING GROSBEAK
Coccothraustes vespertinus

First sightings of this bird at a backyard feeder in winter often elicit this statement: "There's a huge goldfinch at my feeder." Indeed, Evening Grosbeak plumage is black and yellow like that of a male goldfinch, but the bill on this bird is much more enormous and powerful, and the bird itself is much larger. As any bird bander will tell you, the Evening Grosbeak's bill can exert an incredible force per unit area—it may be the most powerful of any North American bird. • The Evening Grosbeak is an irruptive species in Illinois and sightings have become much rarer in the last decade. • Flocks roost in pines and spruces at night, then visit backyard feeders, maple woods and other places with ample seeds during the day. • The Evening Grosbeak may visit your feeder singly or in a small flock, either remaining throughout the winter or for only a few hours.

ID: massive, ivory to greenish, conical bill; black wings and tail; broad, white wing patches; deep pink legs and feet. *Male:* black crown; bright yellow "eyebrow" and forehead band; dark brown to blackish head; golden yellow belly and lower back. *Female:* gray head and upper back; gray underparts tinged with yellow; white undertail coverts; smaller areas of white on wings.
Size: *L* 7–8½ in; *W* 14 in.
Status: very rare to rare migrant and winter resident from late October or early November through early May, with some June stragglers.

Habitat: open, successional deciduous woodlands, parks and gardens; suburban areas with feeders.
Nesting: does not nest in Illinois.
Feeding: gleans the ground and vegetation for buds and seeds; eats insects such as beetles and spruce budworms in summer; licks mineral-rich soil; often visits feeders for sunflower seeds.
Voice: call is a loud, sharp *clee-ip* or a ringing *kleeer*, reminiscent of a loud House Sparrow.
Similar Species: *American Goldfinch* (p. 350): much smaller; small bill; narrower wing bars; male has black "cap" and forehead; lacks large, white wing patches.
Best Sites: backyard bird feeders.

351

HOUSE SPARROW

Passer domesticus

House Sparrows were introduced to North America in the 1850s around Brooklyn, New York, as part of a plan to control insects that were damaging grain and cereal crops at the time. This bird's diet is largely vegetarian, so its impact on crop pests was minimal. • This Eurasian sparrow has managed to colonize most human-altered environments on the continent. Unfortunately, its aggressive behavior has helped it to usurp territory from many beloved native bird species, especially cavity nesters, including bluebirds and woodpeckers. In Illinois and other midwestern states, this species is responsible for the virtual disappearance of breeding Cliff Swallows. • House Sparrows are not closely related to other North American sparrows; they belong to the family of "Weaver Finches." This bird's native Eurasian populations are declining substantially.

breeding

ID: *Breeding male:* large head; gray crown; black "mask" and "bib"; heavy bill; chestnut brown nape begins behind eye; light gray "cheek"; white wing patch; brown, mottled upperparts; gray underparts, rump and tail. *Nonbreeding male:* duller overall; smaller black "bib"; light-colored bill. *Female:* plain gray brown overall; buffy "eyebrow"; streaked upperparts; indistinct facial patterns; grayish, unstreaked underparts.
Size: *L* 6 in; *W* 9½ in.
Status: abundant permanent resident.
Habitat: townsites, urban and suburban areas; farmyards and agricultural areas, especially with livestock and railroad yards.
Nesting: often communal; uses a bluebird box, Purple Martin house, old Cliff Swallow nest, rafter, ornamental shrub or natural cavity; pair builds a large, dome-shaped nest lined with feathers; pair incubates 4–6 whitish to greenish white eggs, dotted with gray and brown, for 12–13 days; 2–3 broods per year.
Feeding: gleans the ground and vegetation for seeds, spiders and insects; also eats small fruits and crabgrass seeds; frequently feeds at feeders and garbage dumps.
Voice: noisy chirps and chatters; a familiar, plain *cheep-cheep-cheep-cheep;* call is a short *chill-up.*
Similar Species: *Harris's Sparrow* (p. 322): much larger and rarer; gray face; black "cap"; pink orange bill; lacks white wing patch. *Eurasian Tree Sparrow* (p. 353): rufous crown; black spot on ear patch; white "collar"; rufous flanks.
Best Sites: widespread.

EURASIAN TREE SPARROW
Passer montanus

In 1870, 20 Eurasian Tree Sparrows were gathered from Germany and liberated into farmlands near St. Louis, Missouri. The bird is now common in Illinois and has slowly spread eastward and northward, following major river valleys, including the Mississippi, Illinois and Sangamon Rivers. Birds can now be found all the way to Henderson County in the north, Pekin along the Illinois River and Springfield to the east. • A close relative of the similar House Sparrow, the Eurasian Tree Sparrow is a "roller-feeder." Birds at the back of the flock hopscotch over the others to keep the flock moving in one direction. • In winter, Eurasian Tree Sparrows may form flocks of 100 or more. • The Eurasian Tree Sparrow prefers rural locations and may move from a nesting site if the area becomes too developed. Little is known about this species' basic life history and even the types of foods it eats.

ID: reddish brown crown, black spot on ear patch; white "collar"; black lores and throat; rufous wash on flanks.
Size: *L* 6 in; *W* 9 in.
Status: locally common permanent resident in west-central Illinois.
Habitat: farms, especially with livestock; agricultural fields, bottomland areas with numerous snags; suburban and rural areas.
Nesting: in a woodpecker hole, snag, building or nest box; pair builds a nest from grass, straw and other materials; pair incubates 4–6 heavily marked, whitish eggs for 11–14 days; 2–3 broods per year.
Feeding: eats on the ground and occasionally in trees; eats waste grain and native seeds.
Voice: similar to House Sparrow but with clear, more distinct notes; flight call is *pick, pick, pick*.
Similar Species: *House Sparrow* (p. 352): black "chin" extends down onto breast; gray crown; rusty patch behind eye; white "cheek" patch.
Best Sites: Spring Lake State Fish and Wildlife Area, Tazewell Co.; rural areas around Springfield; L. Chautauqua south levee road; Meredosia NWR; Mark Twain NWR; Mississippi levee roads; Horseshoe Lake SP.

OCCASIONAL BIRD SPECIES

BRANT
Branta bernicla

Brant

In Illinois, a birder may find a Brant feeding in a field among a large flock of Canada Geese. A Brant is about the size of the smallest subspecies of Canada Geese. The light-bellied form is most often seen in Illinois with most records occurring October through early January. Flocks of Brants are occasionally seen along Lake Michigan in Illinois. This bird breeds in the Arctic and winters along coasts in North America, Asia and Europe.

ID: deep brown overall; black head, neck and breast; dark wings and bill; broken white "collar" is variable; gray-and-white barred sides; extensive white uppertail coverts.
Size: *L* 25 in; *W* 3½ ft.

KING EIDER
Somateria spectabilis

King Eider

Two eider species have been recorded in Illinois. The King Eider is more common than the Common Eider, and birders usually find it in late fall and winter on large lakes and occasionally rivers. Immatures or females are more commonly seen. An Arctic breeder, the King Eider migrates along both North American coasts, rarely venturing inland.

ID: *Male:* large; blue crown; green "cheek"; orange nasal disc; red bill; black wings; white neck, breast, back, upperwing patches and flank patches. *Female:* mottled rich rufous brown overall; black bill extends into a nasal shield; sides have V-shaped markings. *Immature male:* dark overall; whitish breast; pale orange bill, pale circle around eye; pale line extends behind eye onto neck.
Size: *L* 22 in; *W* 3 ft.

BARROW'S GOLDENEYE
Bucephala islandica

Illinois birders typically find a single Barrow's, usually a male, on Lake Michigan or other large body of water, with large flocks of the regularly occurring Common Goldeneye. At least 30 Illinois records exist for this bird. Look for yellow on the female Barrow's bill to compare it with the Common.

Barrow's Goldeneye

ID: medium-sized; yellow eyes; short bill; steep forehead. *Male:* glossy, green black head; white crescent between eye and bill; extensive white on underparts; black and white spots on back and shoulders. *Female:* chocolate brown head with peaked forehead; short, orange yellow bill; gray brown body.
Size: *L* 16–20 in; *W* 28 in.

NEOTROPIC CORMORANT
Phalacrocorax brasilianus

Neotropic Cormorant

Formerly called the Olivaceous Cormorant, the Neotropic Cormorant was once a very rare vagrant in Illinois, this species is now being found singly or in pairs nearly every year. A pair and a subadult, stayed at Carlyle Lake from mid-summer until early October 2002. Two different records came from Crabtree Nature Center within the past 15 years.

ID: slender black body; thick, hooked bill; yellow throat patch coming to a point behind mouth. *Breeding:* white outline on throat patch, white plume on back of head.
Size: *L* 23–27 in; *W* 40 in.

ANHINGA
Anhinga anhinga

Like hawks, Anhingas can soar on thermals, and occasionally one will fly north beyond its typical southeastern United States range into Illinois. Records of Anhingas in extreme southern Illinois were somewhat common in the mid-1800s. One of the most recent records is from Jersey County.

Anhinga

ID: black body with silver and white streaking on upperparts; long curved neck; fanlike tail; red eyes; yellow bill. *Breeding:* blue green eye rims; heavier streaking (not attained until 3rd year). *Female* and *Immature:* buffy from neck up; less streaking.
Size: *L* 35 ft; *W* 4 ft.

TRICOLORED HERON
Egretta tricolor

A southern heron, the Tricolored is found in spring as a vagrant and in late summer as a post-breeding wanderer, in Illinois. This bird has been found singly in various spots throughout the state, including Hennepin Lake and Vermilion County and may soon gain the status of a regularly occurring species in Illinois.

Tricolored Heron

ID: *Breeding:* long, slender bill, neck and legs; purplish to grayish blue plumage with white underparts and foreneck; pale rump; long plumes appear on head and back during breeding season. *Immature:* chestnut on hindneck and wing coverts.
Size: *L* 26 in; *W* 3 ft.

WHITE IBIS
Eudocimus albus

White Ibis

The rarest of the three ibis species found in Illinois, the White Ibis is typically found as a vagrant immature with very few adult records. It normally breeds in the southern U.S. and has about 20 Illinois records, mostly from the central-southern part of the state.

ID: white body; red face and legs; long, red, decurved bill. *Breeding:* tip of bill becomes dark. *Immature:* brown gray head, neck and uppersides; white rump and belly. *In flight:* underside of wing has restricted dark wing tips; outstretched neck.
Size: *L* 25 in; *W* 3 ft.

GLOSSY IBIS
Plegadis falcinellus

Glossy Ibis

At least 50 Glossy Ibises have been documented in Illinois with most occurring in May and many of them in south-western Illinois. There are several summer and fall records also. When in nonbreeding plumage this species can be easily confused with the White-faced Ibis.

ID: long, downcurved, brownish olive bill; long legs; dark skin in front of brown eye is bordered by 2 pale stripes. *Breeding:* chestnut head, neck and sides; green and purple sheen on wings, tail, crown and face. *Nonbreeding* and *immature:* dark grayish brown head and neck streaked with white; gray facial skin and sometimes pale blue line from eye to bill.
Size: *L* 23 in; *W* 3 ft.

WHITE-FACED IBIS
Plegadis chihi

White-faced Ibis

Late April to late May is the best time to search for the White-faced Ibis at Lake Chautauqua and marshes in the East St. Louis area. More than 20 have been seen in Illinois in spring with most in breeding plumage; many have been noted in fall and are usually seen singly or occasionally in groups of three to eight birds. In nonbreeding plumage the White-faced Ibis can look very much like its eastern counterpart, the Glossy Ibis.

ID: slender; dark chestnut overall; long, downcurved, grayish bill; long, dark legs; white feathers border naked facial patch; irridescent, greenish lower back and wing coverts. *Breeding:* red legs and facial patch bordered by white "semi-circle." *Nonbreeding* and *immature:* similar to nonbreeding Glossy; pale pink facial skin; reddish eye. *In flight:* gangly-looking but graceful; rapid wing-beats with brief periods of gliding.
Size: *L* 23 in; *W* 3 ft.

GYRFALCON
Falco rusticolus

This arctic breeder occasionally wanders into Illinois for the winter if food is scarce farther north. Twenty-three of these spectacular raptors have been seen in central or northern Illinois between October and March, since the first one was noted in 1953. Look for this species where large numbers of waterfowl and other open-country bird species gather in late fall and winter.

Gyrfalcon

ID: long, barred tail. *Gray morph:* dark grey upperparts and streaking on the white underparts; weak "mustache" mark. *Brown morph:* dark brown upperparts; dark brown streaking on the white underparts. *White morph:* pure white head and breast; white back, tail and wings have dark flecking and barring. *Immature:* darker and more heavily streaked than the adult; gray feet and cere.
Size: *L* 22 in; *W* 4 ft.

PURPLE GALLINULE
Porphyrio martinica

Purple Gallinule

This extraordinarily colored wetland species has bred at Lake Mermet in southern Illinois many times since 1963, though not every year. In 1999, 13 Purple Gallinules, which winter from southern Florida to Argentina, migrated into Illinois, as far north as Chicagoland. Most records of this bird in the state have occurred in April and May.

ID: all-white undertail coverts; glossy, purplish blue head and underparts; greenish upper-parts; light blue forehead shield; red bill with yellow tip; bright yellow legs and feet. *Immature:* tawny brown overall with greenish tinge in wings; darkish bill and crown. **Size:** *L* 12–14 in; *W* 22 in.

MEW GULL
Larus canus

Mew Gull

If you can spot and identify a Mew Gull out on Lake Michigan on a cold winter day, you've proven what a great gull-watcher you are. This bird looks extremely similar to the abundant Ring-billed Gull in all plumages. Though the Mew Gull stays only a day or two, sightings in Illinois increased in the 1990s. This small gull lives along the Pacific Coast and northwestern North America.

ID: dainty; small, thin bill; darkish eye. *Breeding:* large white spot on tips of outer primaries, all yellow bill. *Nonbreeding:* greenish yellow bill; dark smudge on lower mandible; medium gray back; dusky streaking on head, neck and upper breast; pale green yellow legs and feet. **Size:** *L* 15–16 in; *W* 3½ ft.

ARCTIC TERN
Sterna paradisaea

Arctic Tern

Between 1992 and 2002, the Arctic Tern has been recorded seven times in Illinois—and in 2001, this species even attempted to breed with a Common Tern at the Great Lakes Naval Training Center in northeastern Illinois. The regularly occurring Common Tern has relatively longer legs, a larger bill and a different flight style.

ID: *Breeding:* blood-red bill and legs; short neck; black "cap" on rounded head; white "cheeks"; gray wash on underparts. *Nonbreeding* and *immature:* black bill; white shoulders; white underparts and forehead; shorter tail. **Size:** *L* 12 in; *W* 29–33 in.

WHITE-WINGED DOVE
Zenaida asiatica

The White-winged Dove first appeared in Illinois in July 1998. As of July 2003, seven others have been documented in the state. This species was introduced in southern Florida and eats sorghum and other crop grains. It's range appears to be spreading northward.

White-winged Dove

ID: light, brownish gray plumage; bold blue patch around red eye; black streak on lower "cheek"; large white patch across center of wing; bulkier body than Mourning Dove; blunt, rounded tail with white corners in flight. **Size:** *L* 11–12 in; *W* 19 in.

TOWNSEND'S SOLITAIRE
Myadestes townsendi

Townsend's Solitaire

Townsend's Solitaires sometimes visit Illinois' arboretums for the winter, where there are junipers and other berry-producing trees. Lucky birders may even hear it sing on a sunny, winter day. At least 19 Townsend's Solitaires have been documented in Illinois; a bird that appeared at the Klehm Arboretum in Rockford in 1995 was the first seen in ten years.

ID: gray overall; darker wings and tail; buff-colored wing patches; white eye ring; white outer feathers on long, thin, square-ended tail.
Size: L 8½ in; W 14½ in.

BOHEMIAN WAXWING
Bombycilla garrulus

Bohemian Waxwing

A bird of the northern coniferous forests, the Bohemian Waxwing sometimes flies south to northern Illinois for the winter. Careful examination of flocks of Cedar Waxwings in winter may produce a Bohemian or two intermixed, but don't count on it every year. The Bohemian Waxwing's more colorful wings and larger, grayer body easily separate it from the smaller Cedar Waxwing.

ID: golden crest; cinnamon forehead; black "mask" and throat; gray brown body; yellow terminal tail band; rufous undertail coverts; white, red and yellow spots on wings.
Size: L 8¼ in; W 14½ in.

SWAINSON'S WARBLER
Limnothlypis swainsonii

In the late 20th and early 21st century, some have heard the bird singing and even caught a glimpse of this species, especially in its historic stronghold at Cave and Cedar Creeks near Pomona. Habitat destruction has caused the decline, perhaps even the extirpation of this bird as an Illinois breeder.

Swainson's Warbler

ID: reddish brown crown, pale "eyebrow" and thin black eyeline; olive brown above; buffy gray underparts; long, sharp bill.
Size: L 5½ in; W 9 in.

WESTERN TANAGER
Piranga ludoviciana

The Western Tanager winters in Costa Rica and once every few years, wanders into Illinois. Birders usually spot the brightly colored, unmistakable male in April or early May. A female Western Tanager, which can be confused with the female Scarlet Tanager, was found in downtown Chicago. Of the 19 Illinois records, 15 occurred in spring and 12 come from the northeastern region of the state.

Western Tanager

ID: *Breeding male:* yellow underparts and rump; one yellow and one white wing bar; black back, wings and tail; often has red on the forehead or the entire head (variable); orangish bill. *Breeding female:* olive green overall with gray or dusky back; distinct whitish or yellow wing bars on darkish wings.
Size: L 7 in; W 11½ in.

LARK BUNTING
Calamospiza melanocorys

Lark Bunting

A bird of the open country in the Great Plains, the 22 Illinois Lark Bunting records have occurred mostly in spring, with a few in fall and winter. Most of this species' population winters in the southwestern part of the United States and Mexico. The male in his black plumage with large white wing patches is unmistakable, but the female is similar to the Song Sparrow and other sparrow species.

ID: dark, conical, blue black bill; large, sparrowlike species. *Breeding male:* all-black plumage; large, white shoulder patch and white tail tip. *Female:* mottled brown upperparts; streaked underparts; pale "eyebrow"; white tail tip and upperwing feathers.
Size: *L* 7 in; *W* 10½ in.

BLACK-HEADED GROSBEAK
Pheucticus melanocephalus

Reports of the Black-headed Grosbeak in Illinois require documentation; the breeding and nonbreeding females can be tricky to separate from the female Rose-breasted Grosbeak, its eastern counterpart. Illinois records of this species have occurred mostly at feeders in winter, spring and fall.

Black-headed Grosbeak

ID: large; dark, conical bill. *Male:* burnt orange underparts and rump; black head, back, wings and tail; bold white wing bars and undertail coverts. *Female:* dark brown upperparts; buffy underparts; lightly streaked flanks; pale "eyebrow," wide, dark crown stripe and dark brown "cheek" with white patch below it; lemon yellow wing linings in flight.
Size: *L* 8 in; *W* 12 in.

PAINTED BUNTING
Passerina ciris

Painted Bunting

The Painted Bunting recently became part of Illinois' breeding avifauna when a pair built a nest at East St. Louis in the year 2000. Since then, one to two males and/or a pair have been seen there annually. Illinois has had five other records of this bird between 1993 and 2003, found in northern, central and southern Illinois.

ID: *Male:* blue head; bright red eye ring, underparts and rump; bright green back; dark wings and tail. *Female:* light green upperparts and yellow green underparts. *Immature:* drab plumage with green highlights on upperparts and yellow highlights on underparts.
Size: *L* 5½ in; *W* 8¾ in.

PINE GROSBEAK
Pinicola enucleator

Pine Grosbeak

The Pine Grosbeak is an irruptive bird species of the northern coniferous forests. Single birds or small flocks sometimes fly as far south as northern Illinois in winter to find food. Look for this rarity from late October to the end of March in pine plantations, in fruiting trees and occasionally at backyard feeders. Only four records in Illinois exist for this bird in the 1990s.

ID: stout, conical, dark bill; white wing bars; black wings; darkish tail. *Male:* bright pink head, underparts, rump and back. *Female* and *immature:* yellowish or orangish crown, face and rump; ashy gray back and underparts.
Size: *L* 8–10 in; *W* 14½ in.

SELECT REFERENCES

American Ornithologists' Union. 1998. *Check-list of North American Birds.* 7th ed. (and its supplements). American Ornithologists' Union, Washington, D.C.

Bohlen, H.D. *The birds of Illinois.* 1989. Indiana University Press, Bloomington, Indiana.

Choate, E.A. 1985. *The Dictionary of American Bird Names.* Rev. ed. Harvard Common Press, Cambridge, MA.

Cox, R.T. 1996. *Birder's Dictionary.* Falcon Publishing Inc., Helena, Montana.

DeVore, S. 2000. *Birding Illinois.* Falcon Publishing, Inc., Helena, Montana.

DeVore, S., ed. 1992–2003. *Meadowlark: A Journal of Illinois Birds.* Illinois Ornithological Society, Lake Forest, Illinois.

Erlich, P.R., D.S. Dobkin and D. Wheye. 1988. *The Birder's Handbook.* Simon & Schuster Inc., New York.

Elphick, C., J. B. Dunning, Jr., and D.A. Sibley, eds. 2001. *National Audubon Society The Sibley Guide to Bird Life & Behavior.* Alfred A. Knopf, New York.

Jones, J.O. 1990. *Where The Birds Are.* William Morrow and Company, Inc., New York.

Kaufman, K. 1990. *Peterson Field Guides, Advanced Birding.* Houghton Mifflin Co., Boston.

Kaufman, K. 1996. *Lives of North American Birds.* Houghton Mifflin Co., Boston.

Kaufman, K. 2000. *Birds of North America.* Houghton Mifflin Co., New York.

National Geographic Society. 2002. *Field Guide to the Birds of North America.* 4th ed. National Geographic Society, Washington, D.C.

Sibley, D.A. 2000. *National Audubon Society The Sibley Guide to Birds.* Alfred A. Knopf, New York.

Sibley, D.A. 2002. *Sibley's Birding Basics.* Alfred A. Knopf, New York.

Terres, J.K. 1980. *The Audubon Society Encyclopedia of North American Birds.* Alfred A. Knopf, New York.

White-Winged Scoter

GLOSSARY

accipiter: a forest hawk (genus *Accipiter*), characterized by a long tail and short, rounded wings; feeds mostly on birds.

brood: *n.* a family of young from one hatching; *v.* to incubate the eggs.

brood parasite: a bird that lays its eggs in other birds' nests.

buteo: a high-soaring hawk (genus *Buteo*), characterized by broad wings and a short, wide tail; feeds mostly on small mammals and other land animals.

cere: found on birds of prey, a fleshy area at the base of the bill that contains the nostrils.

clutch: the number of eggs laid by the female at one time.

dabbling: a foraging technique used by some ducks, in which the head and neck are submerged but the body and tail remain on the water's surface; dabbling ducks can usually walk easily on land, can take off without running and have brightly colored speculums.

diurnal: most active during the day.

"eclipse" plumage: a cryptic plumage, similar to that of females, worn by some male ducks in fall when they molt their flight feathers and consequently are unable to fly.

endangered: a species that is facing extirpation or extinction in all or part of its range.

extinct: a species that no longer exists.

extirpated: a species that no longer exists in the wild in a particular region but occurs elsewhere.

flushing: a behavior in which frightened birds explode into flight in response to a disturbance.

flycatching: a feeding behavior in which the bird leaves a perch, snatches an insect in midair and returns to the same perch; also known as "hawking" or "sallying."

forbs: an herb other than grass.

gallinaceous: heavy-bodied, terrestrial birds, including pheasants, turkeys, grouse and domestic fowl.

hawking: attempting to capture insects through aerial pursuit.

hemi-marsh: a marsh with a 50:50 ratio of emergent vegetation and open water.

irruption: a sporadic mass migration of birds into an unusual range.

kettle: a large concentration of hawks, usually seen during migration.

lek: a place where males gather to display for females in the spring.

mantle: the area of a bird that includes the back and uppersides of the wings.

molt: the periodic shedding and regrowth of worn feathers (often twice a year).

Neotropical: biogeographic region that includes southern Mexico, Central and South America and the West Indies.

nocturnal: most active at night.

peep: certain sandpipers of the *Calidris* genus.

"pishing": a repeated sibilant sound made especially to attract birds.

polyandry: a mating strategy in which one female breeds with many males.

polygyny: a mating strategy in which one male breeds with many females.

precocial: a bird that is relatively well developed at hatching; precocial birds usually have open eyes, extensive down and are fairly mobile.

primaries: the outermost flight feathers of a bird's wing.

raft: a gathering of birds resting on the water.

raptor: a carnivorous (meat-eating) bird; includes eagles, hawks, falcons and owls.

riparian: habitat along rivers or streams.

sexual dimorphism: a difference in plumage, size, or other characteristic between males and females of the same species.

special concern: a species that has characteristics that make it particularly sensitive to human activities or disturbance, requires a very specific or unique habitat or whose status is such that it requires careful monitoring.

speculum: a brightly colored patch on the wings of many dabbling ducks. .

stage: to gather in one place during migration, usually when birds are flightless or partly flightless during molting.

stoop: a steep dive through the air, usually performed by birds of prey during courtship displays or while foraging .

syrinx: a bird's voice organ.

thistle feeder: a feeder that dispenses thistle (niger) seed; especially attractive to finches.

threatened: a species likely to become endangered in the near future in all or part of its range.

understory: the shrub or thicket layer beneath a canopy of trees.

vagrant: a bird that has wandered outside of its normal migration range.

vent: the single opening for excretion of uric acid and other wastes and for sexual reproduction; also known as the "cloaca."

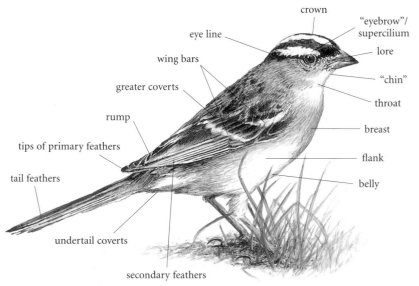

CHECKLIST

The following list of 430 regular and casual bird species is based on the Illinois State Checklist published in 1999 by the Illinois Ornithological Society and the Illinois Ornithological Records Committee. The checklist was updated in early 2003 to reflect recent recorded sightings. Species are grouped by family and listed in taxonomic order in accordance with the A.O.U. *Checklist of North American Birds* (7th ed.).

Regular species listed are those for which records exist in at least eight of the past ten years. Species recorded in fewer than 8 of the last 10 years are casual and listed in *italics*. In addition, the following risk categories are noted: extinct or extirpated (ex), endangered (en) and threatened (th).

Waterfowl (Anatidae)
❑ *Fulvous Whistling-Duck*
❑ Greater White-fronted Goose
❑ Snow Goose
❑ Ross's Goose
❑ Canada Goose
❑ *Brant*
❑ Mute Swan
❑ Trumpeter Swan
❑ Tundra Swan
❑ Wood Duck
❑ Gadwall
❑ *Eurasian Wigeon*
❑ American Wigeon
❑ American Black Duck
❑ Mallard
❑ Blue-winged Teal
❑ Cinnamon Teal
❑ Northern Shoveler
❑ Northern Pintail
❑ *Garganey*
❑ Green-winged Teal
❑ Canvasback
❑ Redhead
❑ Ring-necked Duck
❑ *Tufted Duck*
❑ Greater Scaup
❑ Lesser Scaup
❑ *King Eider*
❑ Harlequin Duck
❑ Surf Scoter
❑ White-winged Scoter
❑ Black Scoter
❑ Long-tailed Duck
❑ Bufflehead
❑ Common Goldeneye
❑ *Barrow's Goldeneye*

❑ Hooded Merganser
❑ Common Merganser
❑ Red-breasted Merganser
❑ Ruddy Duck

Grouse & Allies (Phasianid ae)
❑ Gray Partridge
❑ Ring-necked Pheasant
❑ *Ruffed Grouse*
❑ Sharp-tailed Grouse (ex)
❑ Greater Prairie-Chicken (en)
❑ Wild Turkey

New World Quails (Odontophoridae)
❑ Northern Bobwhite

Loons (Gaviidae)
❑ Red-throated Loon
❑ Pacific Loon
❑ Common Loon
❑ *Yellow-billed Loon*

Grebes (Podicipedidae)
❑ Pied-billed Grebe (th)
❑ Horned Grebe
❑ Red-necked Grebe
❑ Eared Grebe
❑ Western Grebe
❑ *Clark's Grebe*

Gannets (Sulidae)
❑ *Northern Gannet*

Pelicans (Pelecanidae)
❑ American White Pelican

❑ *Brown Pelican*

Cormorants (Phalacrocoracidae)
❑ *Neotropic Cormorant*
❑ Double-crested Cormorant

Darters (Anhingidae)
❑ *Anhinga*

Frigatebirds (Fregatidae)
❑ *Magnificent Frigatebird*

Herons (Ardeidae)
❑ American Bittern (en)
❑ Least Bittern (en)
❑ Great Blue Heron
❑ Great Egret
❑ Snowy Egret (th)
❑ Little Blue Heron (en)
❑ *Tricolored Heron*
❑ *Reddish Egret*
❑ Cattle Egret
❑ Green Heron
❑ Black-crowned Night-Heron (en)
❑ Yellow-crowned Night-Heron (th)

Ibises (Threskiornithidae)
❑ *White Ibis*
❑ *Glossy Ibis*
❑ *White-faced Ibis*

Storks (Ciconiidae)
❑ *Wood Stork*

363

Vultures (Cathartidae)
- ❏ Black Vulture
- ❏ Turkey Vulture

Kites, Hawks & Eagles (Accipitridae)
- ❏ Osprey (en)
- ❏ *Swallow-tailed Kite*
- ❏ *White-tailed Kite*
- ❏ Mississippi Kite (en)
- ❏ Bald Eagle (en)
- ❏ Northern Harrier (en)
- ❏ Sharp-shinned Hawk
- ❏ Cooper's Hawk
- ❏ Northern Goshawk
- ❏ Red-shouldered Hawk (en)
- ❏ Broad-winged Hawk
- ❏ Swainson's Hawk (en)
- ❏ Red-tailed Hawk
- ❏ *Ferruginous Hawk*
- ❏ Rough-legged Hawk
- ❏ Golden Eagle

Falcons (Falconidae)
- ❏ American Kestrel
- ❏ Merlin
- ❏ *Gyrfalcon*
- ❏ Peregrine Falcon (en)
- ❏ Prairie Falcon

Rails & Coots (Rallidae)
- ❏ Yellow Rail
- ❏ Black Rail (en)
- ❏ King Rail (th)
- ❏ Virginia Rail
- ❏ Sora
- ❏ *Purple Gallinule*
- ❏ Common Moorhen (th)
- ❏ American Coot

Cranes (Gruidae)
- ❏ Sandhill Crane
- ❏ *Whooping Crane*

Plovers (Charadriidae)
- ❏ Black-bellied Plover
- ❏ American Golden-Plover
- ❏ *Snowy Plover*
- ❏ Semipalmated Plover
- ❏ Piping Plover (en)
- ❏ Killdeer

Stilts and Avocets (Recurvirostridae)
- ❏ Black-necked Stilt
- ❏ American Avocet

Sandpipers & Allies (Scolopacidae)
- ❏ Greater Yellowlegs
- ❏ Lesser Yellowlegs
- ❏ Solitary Sandpiper
- ❏ Willet
- ❏ Spotted Sandpiper
- ❏ Upland Sandpiper
- ❏ Eskimo Curlew (ex)
- ❏ Whimbrel
- ❏ *Long-billed Curlew*
- ❏ Hudsonian Godwit
- ❏ Marbled Godwit
- ❏ Ruddy Turnstone
- ❏ Red Knot
- ❏ Sanderling
- ❏ Semipalmated Sandpiper
- ❏ Western Sandpiper
- ❏ Least Sandpiper
- ❏ White-rumped Sandpiper
- ❏ Baird's Sandpiper
- ❏ Pectoral Sandpiper
- ❏ *Sharp-tailed Sandpiper*
- ❏ Purple Sandpiper
- ❏ Dunlin
- ❏ *Curlew Sandpiper*
- ❏ Stilt Sandpiper
- ❏ Buff-breasted Sandpiper
- ❏ Ruff
- ❏ Short-billed Dowitcher
- ❏ Long-billed Dowitcher
- ❏ Wilson's Snipe
- ❏ American Woodcock
- ❏ Wilson's Phalarope (en)
- ❏ Red-necked Phalarope
- ❏ Red Phalarope

Gulls & Allies (Laridae)
- ❏ Long-tailed Jaeger
- ❏ Pomarine Jaeger
- ❏ Parasitic Jaeger
- ❏ Laughing Gull
- ❏ Franklin's Gull
- ❏ Little Gull
- ❏ *Black-headed Gull*
- ❏ Bonaparte's Gull
- ❏ *Mew Gull*
- ❏ Ring-billed Gull
- ❏ California Gull
- ❏ Herring Gull
- ❏ Thayer's Gull
- ❏ Iceland Gull
- ❏ Lesser Black-backed Gull
- ❏ *Slaty-backed Gull*
- ❏ *Western Gull*
- ❏ *Glaucous-winged Gull*
- ❏ Glaucous Gull
- ❏ Great Black-backed Gull
- ❏ Sabine's Gull
- ❏ Black-legged Kittiwake
- ❏ *Ross's Gull*
- ❏ *Ivory Gull*
- ❏ *Gull-billed Tern*
- ❏ Caspian Tern
- ❏ *Royal Tern*
- ❏ *Sandwich Tern*
- ❏ Common Tern
- ❏ *Arctic Tern*
- ❏ Forster's Tern (en)
- ❏ Least Tern (en)
- ❏ *Large-billed Tern*
- ❏ Black Tern (en)
- ❏ *Black Skimmer*

Alcids (Alcidae)
- ❏ *Dovekie*
- ❏ *Ancient Murrelet*

Pigeons and Doves (Columbidae)
- ❏ Rock Dove
- ❏ *Band-tailed Pigeon*
- ❏ Eurasian Collared-Dove
- ❏ *White-winged Dove*
- ❏ Mourning Dove
- ❏ *Passenger Pigeon* (ex)
- ❏ *Common Ground-Dove*

Parakeets (Psittacidae)
- ❏ *Carolina Parakeet* (ex)
- ❏ Monk Parakeet

Cuckoos (Cuculidae)
❏ Black-billed Cuckoo
❏ Yellow-billed Cuckoo
❏ *Groove-billed Ani*

Barn Owls (Tytonidae)
❏ Barn Owl (en)

Owls (Strigidae)
❏ Eastern Screech-Owl
❏ Great Horned Owl
❏ Snowy Owl
❏ *Northern Hawk-Owl*
❏ *Burrowing Owl*
❏ Barred Owl
❏ Long-eared Owl
❏ Short-eared Owl (en)
❏ *Boreal Owl*
❏ Northern Saw-whet Owl

Nightjars (Caprimulgidae)
❏ Common Nighthawk
❏ Chuck-will's-widow
❏ Whip-poor-will

Swifts (Apodidae)
❏ Chimney Swift

Hummingbirds (Trochilidae)
❏ *Broad-billed Hummingbird*
❏ Ruby-throated Hummingbird
❏ Rufous Hummingbird
❏ *Allen's Hummingbird*

Kingfishers (Alcedinidae)
❏ Belted Kingfisher

Woodpeckers (Picidae)
❏ Red-headed Woodpecker
❏ Red-bellied Woodpecker
❏ *Williamson's Sapsucker*
❏ Yellow-bellied Sapsucker
❏ Downy Woodpecker
❏ Hairy Woodpecker

❏ *Red-cockaded Woodpecker*
❏ *Black-backed Woodpecker*
❏ Northern Flicker
❏ Pileated Woodpecker

Flycatchers (Tyrannidae)
❏ Olive-sided Flycatcher
❏ Eastern Wood-Pewee
❏ Yellow-bellied Flycatcher
❏ Acadian Flycatcher
❏ Alder Flycatcher
❏ Willow Flycatcher
❏ Least Flycatcher
❏ Eastern Phoebe
❏ *Say's Phoebe*
❏ *Vermilion Flycatcher*
❏ *Ash-throated Flycatcher*
❏ Great Crested Flycatcher
❏ Western Kingbird
❏ Eastern Kingbird
❏ *Gray Kingbird*
❏ Scissor-tailed Flycatcher

Shrikes (Laniidae)
❏ Loggerhead Shrike (th)
❏ Northern Shrike

Vireos (Vireonidae)
❏ White-eyed Vireo
❏ Bell's Vireo
❏ Yellow-throated Vireo
❏ *Cassin's Vireo*
❏ Blue-headed Vireo
❏ Warbling Vireo
❏ Philadelphia Vireo
❏ Red-eyed Vireo

Crows, Jays & Magpies (Corvidae)
❏ Blue Jay
❏ *Western Scrub-Jay*
❏ *Clark's Nutcracker*
❏ *Black-billed Magpie*
❏ American Crow
❏ Fish Crow
❏ *Common Raven* (ex)

Larks (Alaudidae)
❏ Horned Lark

Swallows (Hirundinidae)
❏ Purple Martin
❏ Tree Swallow
❏ *Violet-green Swallow*
❏ Northern Rough-winged Swallow
❏ Bank Swallow
❏ Cliff Swallow
❏ *Cave Swallow*
❏ Barn Swallow

Chickadees & Titmice (Paridae)
❏ Carolina Chickadee
❏ Black-capped Chickadee
❏ *Boreal Chickadee*
❏ Tufted Titmouse

Nuthatches (Sittidae)
❏ Red-breasted Nuthatch
❏ White-breasted Nuthatch
❏ *Brown-headed Nuthatch*

Creepers (Certhiidae)
❏ Brown Creeper (th)

Wrens (Troglodytidae)
❏ *Rock Wren*
❏ Carolina Wren
❏ Bewick's Wren (en)
❏ House Wren
❏ Winter Wren
❏ Sedge Wren
❏ Marsh Wren

Kinglets (Regulidae)
❏ Golden-crowned Kinglet
❏ Ruby-crowned Kinglet

Gnatcatchers (Sylviidae)
❏ Blue-gray Gnatcatcher

Thrushes (Turdidae)
❏ *Northern Wheatear*
❏ Eastern Bluebird

- Mountain Bluebird
- Townsend's Solitaire
- Veery
- Gray-cheeked Thrush
- Swainson's Thrush
- Hermit Thrush
- Wood Thrush
- American Robin
- Varied Thrush

Mockingbirds & Thrashers (Mimidae)
- Gray Catbird
- Northern Mockingbird
- Sage Thrasher
- Brown Thrasher
- Curve-billed Thrasher

Starlings (Sturnidae)
- European Starling

Pipits (Motacillidae)
- American Pipit
- Sprague's Pipit

Waxwings (Bombycillidae)
- Bohemian Waxwing
- Cedar Waxwing

Wood Warblers (Parulidae)
- Blue-winged Warbler
- Golden-winged Warbler
- Tennessee Warbler
- Orange-crowned Warbler
- Nashville Warbler
- Northern Parula
- Yellow Warbler
- Chestnut-sided Warbler
- Magnolia Warbler
- Cape May Warbler
- Black-throated Blue Warbler
- Yellow-rumped Warbler
- Black-throated Gray Warbler
- Black-throated Green Warbler
- Townsend's Warbler

- Hermit Warbler
- Blackburnian Warbler
- Yellow-throated Warbler
- Pine Warbler
- Kirtland's Warbler
- Prairie Warbler
- Palm Warbler
- Bay-breasted Warbler
- Blackpoll Warbler
- Cerulean Warbler
- Black-and-white Warbler
- American Redstart
- Prothonotary Warbler
- Worm-eating Warbler
- Swainson's Warbler
- Ovenbird
- Northern Waterthrush
- Louisiana Waterthrush
- Kentucky Warbler
- Connecticut Warbler
- Mourning Warbler
- MacGillivray's Warbler
- Common Yellowthroat
- Hooded Warbler
- Wilson's Warbler
- Canada Warbler
- Yellow-breasted Chat

Tanagers (Thraupidae)
- Hepatic Tanager
- Summer Tanager
- Scarlet Tanager
- Western Tanager

Sparrows & Allies (Emberizidae)
- Green-tailed Towhee
- Spotted Towhee
- Eastern Towhee
- Cassin's Sparrow
- Bachman's Sparrow
- American Tree Sparrow
- Chipping Sparrow
- Clay-colored Sparrow
- Brewer's Sparrow
- Field Sparrow
- Vesper Sparrow
- Lark Sparrow
- Black-throated Sparrow

- Lark Bunting
- Savannah Sparrow
- Grasshopper Sparrow
- Henslow's Sparrow (en)
- Le Conte's Sparrow
- Nelson's Sharp-tailed Sparrow
- Fox Sparrow
- Song Sparrow
- Lincoln's Sparrow
- Swamp Sparrow
- White-throated Sparrow
- Harris's Sparrow
- White-crowned Sparrow
- Golden-crowned Sparrow
- Dark-eyed Junco
- Lapland Longspur
- McCown's Longspur
- Smith's Longspur
- Chestnut-collared Longspur
- Snow Bunting

Grosbeaks & Buntings (Cardinalidae)
- Northern Cardinal
- Rose-breasted Grosbeak
- Black-headed Grosbeak
- Blue Grosbeak
- Lazuli Bunting
- Indigo Bunting
- Painted Bunting
- Dickcissel

Blackbirds & Allies (Icteridae)
- Bobolink
- Red-winged Blackbird
- Eastern Meadowlark
- Western Meadowlark
- Yellow-headed Blackbird (en)
- Rusty Blackbird
- Brewer's Blackbird
- Common Grackle
- Great-tailed Grackle
- Brown-headed Cowbird
- Orchard Oriole

❏ Baltimore Oriole
❏ *Scott's Oriole*

Finches (Fringillidae)
❏ *Gray-crowned Rosy-Finch*
❏ *Pine Grosbeak*
❏ Purple Finch
❏ House Finch
❏ Red Crossbill
❏ White-winged Crossbill

❏ Common Redpoll
❏ *Hoary Redpoll*
❏ Pine Siskin
❏ American Goldfinch
❏ Evening Grosbeak

Old World Sparrows (Passeridae)
❏ House Sparrow
❏ Eurasian Tree Sparrow

Yellow-crowned Night Heron

INDEX OF SCIENTIFIC NAMES

This index references only the primary species accounts.

INDEX OF COMMON NAMES

Page numbers in boldface type refer to the primary, illustrated species accounts.

COMMON INDEX

S

Sanderling, 136, **137,** 138, 139, 142, 145
Sandpiper. *See also* Dowitcher; Dunlin;
   Godwit; Sanderling; Snipe;
   Turnstone; Willet; Yellowlegs
   Baird's, 141, **142**
   Buff-breasted, 131, **147,** 148
   Least, 138, 139, **140,** 142, 143
   Pectoral, 131, 142, **143**
   Purple, 136, **144,** 145
   Semipalmated, 137, **138,** 139, 140, 142
   Solitary, 127, **128,** 130
   Spotted, 128, **130**
   Stilt, 145, **146,** 149, 150
   Upland, **131,** 147
   Western, 137, 138, **139,** 140, 142
   White-rumped, **141,** 142
Sapsucker, Yellow-bellied, **200,** 201, 202
Sawbill. *See* Merganser, Red-breasted
Scaup
   Greater, 52, 53, **54,** 55
   Lesser, 52, 53, 54 **55**
Scoter
   Black, 57, 58, **59,** 66
   Surf, 56, **57,** 58, 59
   White-winged, 56, 57, **58,** 59
Screech-Owl, Eastern, **184,** 190
Sea-Robin. *See* Merganser, Red-
   breasted
Shoveler, Northern, 45, 46, **48**
Shrike
   Loggerhead, **218,** 219, 261
   Northern, 218, **219,** 261
Siskin, Pine, 344, 345, 348, **349,** 350
Snipe
   Grass. *See* Sandpiper, Pectoral
   Wilson's, **151,** 152
Snow Bird. See Junco, Dark-eyed
Solitaire, Townsend's, **357**
Sora, 111, 112, 114, **115**
Sparrow. *See also* Bunting, Lark;
   Bunting, Snow; Junco; Longspur;
   Towhee
   American Tree, **306,** 309, 320
   Chipping, **307,** 308, 309, 320
   Clay-colored, 307, **308**
   Eurasian Tree, 352, **353**
   Field, 306, 307, **309**
   Fox, 256, 257, **317,** 318
   Gambel's. *See* White-Crowned S.
   Grasshopper, **313,** 314, 315, 316, 333
   Harris's, **322,** 352
   Henslow's, 312, 313, **314**
   House, 322, 332, **352,** 353

   Lark, **310**
   Le Conte's, 313, **315,** 316
   Lincoln's, 311, 312, 318, **319,** 320
   Nelson's Sharp-tailed, 315, **316**
   Red Fox. *See* Fox S.
   Saltmarsh Sharp-tailed, 316
   Savannah, 310, **312,** 314, 318, 319
   Song, 311, 312, 317, **318,** 319, 320
   Swamp, 306, 307, 309, 319, **320**
   Vesper, **310,** 311, 312, 326, 333
   White-crowned, 321, 322, **323**
   White-throated, 320, **321,** 323
Speckle Belly. *See* Goose, Greater
   White-fronted
Starling, European, **263,** 338, 339, 340
Stilt, Black-necked, **124,** 125
Swallow. *See also* Martin
   Bank, 232, 233, **234**
   Barn, 231, 232, 235, **236**
   Cliff, 231, 233, 234, **235,** 236
   Northern Rough-winged, 232, **233,** 234
   Tree, 231, **232,** 233, 234, 236
Swan
   Mute, 35, 36, **38,** 39, 40
   Trumpeter, 35, 36, 38, **39,** 40
   Tundra, 35, 36, 38, 39, **40**
Swift, Chimney, **194**

T

Tanager
   Scarlet, 302, **303,** 328, 342, 343
   Summer, **302,** 303, 328, 342, 343
   Western, **358**
Teal
   Blue-winged, **46,** 47, 48, 49, 50
   Cinnamon, 46, **47,** 50
   Green-winged, 46, 47, **50**
Tern
   Arctic, **357**
   Black, 175, **176**
   Caspian, **172,** 173, 174
   Common, 172, **173,** 174, 175
   Forster's, 172, 173, **174,** 175
   Least, **175**
Thrasher, Brown, **262**
Thrush. *See also* Robin; Veery
   Gray-cheeked, 253, **254,** 255, 256
   Hermit, 253, 254, 255, **256,** 317
   Olive-backed. *See* Swainson's T.
   Swainson's, 253, 254, **255,** 256
   Varied, 258, **259**
   Wood, **257,** 262

374

ABOUT THE AUTHORS

Sheryl DeVore

Sheryl DeVore is an award-winning environmental journalist and editor. She works as an editor for Pioneer Press Newspapers, where she has been honored as Journalist of the Year and Best Feature Writer. DeVore is also department editor for the American Birding Association's *Birding* magazine and serves as the founding and Chief Editor of *Meadowlark: A Journal of Illinois Birds*. She was recently named Environmental Writer of the Year by the Chicago Audubon Society. DeVore also consults on breeding bird surveys, teaches journalism and nature classes and writes for many publications.

Steven D. Bailey

Steven D. Bailey, an ornithologist with the Illinois Natural History Survey, works with the Critical Trends Assessment Program, a long-term project documenting breeding bird and plant communities in randomly selected forests, prairies and wetlands statewide. With more than 30 years in the field, Bailey is an associate editor for the Illinois Ornithological Society and is considered one of the top experts on the breeding birds of Illinois. He is a past member of the Illinois Ornithological Records Committee and has writtten articles for various state and national publications.

Gregory Kennedy

Gregory Kennedy has been an active naturalist since he was very young. He is the author of many books on natural history and has produced film and television shows on environmental and indigenous concerns in Southeast Asia, New Guinea, South and Central America, the High Arctic and elsewhere. He has also been involved in countless research projects around the world ranging from studies in the upper-canopy of tropical and temperate rainforests to deepwater marine investigations.